对话杨宪益、霍克斯

《红楼梦》英译赏析(第一至四十回)

张文锦 张锦萍 主编
杨浩楠 赵青 彭雪妮 薛雯 编著

北京大学出版社
PEKING UNIVERSITY PRESS

图书在版编目(CIP)数据

对话杨宪益、霍克斯:《红楼梦》英译赏析:第一至四十回 / 张文锦,张锦萍主编.—北京:北京大学出版社,2022.6
ISBN 978-7-301-32989-4

Ⅰ.①对… Ⅱ.①张…②张… Ⅲ.①《红楼梦》—英语—文学翻译—研究 Ⅳ.① H315.9 ② I207.411

中国版本图书馆 CIP 数据核字(2022)第 071208 号

书 名	对话杨宪益、霍克斯——《红楼梦》英译赏析(第一至四十回) DUIHUA YANG XIANYI、HUOKESI——《HONGLOUMENG》YINGYI SHANGXI (DI-YI ZHI SISHI HUI)
著作责任者	张文锦 张锦萍 主编
责任编辑	严 悦
标准书号	ISBN 978-7-301-32989-4
出版发行	北京大学出版社
地 址	北京市海淀区成府路 205 号 100871
网 址	http://www.pup.cn 新浪微博:@北京大学出版社
电子信箱	pkupress_yan@qq.com
电 话	邮购部 010-62752015 发行部 010-62750672 编辑部 010-62754382
印 刷 者	北京鑫海金澳胶印有限公司
经 销 者	新华书店
	720 毫米 ×1020 毫米 16 开本 25.5 印张 550 千字 2022 年 6 月第 1 版 2023 年 2 月第 2 次印刷
定 价	88.00 元

未经许可,不得以任何方式复制或抄袭本书之部分或全部内容。
版权所有,侵权必究
举报电话:010-62752024 电子信箱:fd@pup.pku.edu.cn
图书如有印装质量问题,请与出版部联系,电话:010-62756370

益、霍克斯 ——《红楼梦》英译赏析（第一至四十回）

接和句际连接现象；还会利用文本为学生讲解汉译英的策略和技
学生在语料中反复识别这些翻译策略及技巧。经过多年的教学实
，学生们非常喜欢这门课程，多渠道地给我反馈了这门课程对他们
来，机缘成熟，我决定编写这本教材。

编写重点是"注释评点"部分。在该部分的编写过程中，编者会强
是如何翻译的，它对应的英语句子的结构是什么，与汉语原句结构
等，目的在于帮助学生看清楚英语复杂句的脉络。除此之外，"注
会强调汉译英的翻译策略及技巧，让学习者反复地、大量地观察两
异，进而掌握双语转化的方法。总之，编者会从双语结构差异、双
、二位译者不同的翻译策略和风格，以及用词的准确性等方面进行
从而帮助学习者找到门径，掌握规律，熟知技巧，加强基本功，为
实践打下坚实的基础。

主要特色在于：

优秀传统文化：《红楼梦》是中国古典小说的最高峰，也是中华传
范之作。读者在阅读经典文本的过程中，接受古典美学的洗礼；接
文化思想的熏陶，从而帮助自身提高人文修养，增强民族文化自信

性长：因为《红楼梦》原著以及所选的两个英文全译本都是经过时
典著作和译作精品，所以本书中所选的语料不存在过时问题，它的
较长。

归纳讲解法：传统教授翻译的方法是演绎法，即为了讲清楚翻译
，专门找适配的例证加以说明，容易出现前面提到的学生上课听得
下课仍感茫然、无从下手的局面。本书则是反其道行之，使用归纳
中带领学生发现、识别翻译技巧和策略，并在全书四十回的学习过
证所学，巩固所学。

多门课程："注释评点"中既分析长、难句，也讲授中英双语、中
差异及转化策略和手法。所以，本书的讲解内容实际上将精读、英
以及翻译三门课程融为一体。

群体广泛：考虑到程度不同的学习者的差异化需求，本教材体例设

我在西安外国语大学英文学院教书已近3〔〕选修课也有近20年的历史。我发现，无论是〔〕习者，可能为了提高翻译水平花费了很大的〔〕感觉很难入门，更不用说登堂入室了。老师〔〕自为营，单兵作战，自主选材，自主授课，〔〕的兴趣和侧重，学习成果的好坏主要依赖学〔〕翻译课下来，学生可能会感觉收获不太明显，〔〕滔滔不绝，学生实际操作时仍感心下茫然、〔〕是教材不给力，授课时理论脱离实践，无法〔〕无法帮助学生内化翻译技巧，缺乏定量练习〔〕续存在，成为一个久悬未解的问题。

多年的教学实践使我体会到，学生要想〔〕第一关：语法；第二关：句内、句际连接；〔〕不是我们的母语，作为外语学习者，我们一〔〕法这把尺子，来判断我们所说所写是否正确。〔〕习写长句。英语句子经常有叠床架屋式的长〔〕学习这种句式，尤其要注意学习英语句式的〔〕关后，就进入最后一关的学习，这一关要求〔〕式丰富多样，长、短句并用，不断接近母语〔〕

为了帮助学生突破这三关，近年来，我〔〕梦》的两个著名的英文全译本中选取经典段〔〕层面上分析长、难句，从而提高学生的语法〔〕生分析中英语言差异和中英文化差异，尤其〔〕

1

置灵活，使用方法也具有多样性。学习者既可以选取某些章节学习，也可以贯穿全书，逐章学习。本书既可以为广大英语学习者自学所用，又可以作为高校英语专业翻译课教材使用。

  为了编好这本书，主编和编者都投入了极大的热情和精力。我们希望为读者呈现一本真正实用的好书，从而帮助大家提高英语水平。在编写过程中，我们不放过任何一个细节，努力做到语言准确凝练，充分达意。但是，由于编者水平有限，书中难免有疏漏之处，还望各位专家、读者不吝赐教，帮助我们更好地完善本书，全体编者不胜感激。

主　编

2022年晚春

关于版本的说明

《红楼梦》的版本特别多，可以分为两大系统：脂本和程本。脂本一般包括八十回，自出现以后，以抄本的形式在社会上流传，因为上面有脂砚斋的批注，故称为脂本。流传至今的脂本系统的《红楼梦》有十多个版本：甲戌本、己卯本、庚辰本、有正本、蒙府本、甲辰本等。程本指的是程伟元、高鹗整理的版本。他们整理了《红楼梦》并以印本的形式发行，从而结束了抄本的历史，并极大地推动了该书的流传。程本也有十几个版本，其中最重要的是程甲本和程乙本，这两个版本出版的时间相隔很近，只有70天，但内容却有两万多字的差异。

面对版本如此复杂的《红楼梦》，我们在选择版本编写本书的过程中，一度感到很迷惑，不知道从何下手。后来，在本书责任编辑严悦老师的建议下，我们决定使用人民文学出版社出版的第3版《红楼梦》作为原文的来源。从该书的"序言"中可以看出，它是以庚辰本为底本，第1版于1982年面世，第2版于1994年，第3版于2008年，前后历经26年，不断修订，不断吸收红学研究的新成果，拥有数量庞大的研究者和读者群。

《红楼梦》的两个英文全译本（杨宪益译本和霍克斯译本）所依据的底本情况也十分复杂。目前，在学界关于这个问题有一些讨论，但重视度不够，仍然缺乏一致认可的结论性成果。学者大都通过回目的翻译、片段的译文来探究英译的底本，但要看到庐山的全面目，恐怕只有深入全文本的比对中去，才能得出最终结论。

在此，我们只从两个英译本卷首的出版介绍文字中，一窥两位译者在翻译时所依据的底本。杨宪益的译本（首次出版于1978年）在"介绍"中提到："本译文前八十回依据的是戚蓼生作序的有正大字本，后四十回依据的是1974年人民文学出版社出版的'程乙本'。"戚蓼生作序的版本又叫戚序本，该版包括

| 对话杨宪益、霍克斯 |——《红楼梦》英译赏析（第一至四十回）

四个本子，其中两个是上海有正书局出的"大字本"和"小字本"。霍克斯的译本（首次出版于1973年）在"介绍"中提到："关于本书的翻译，虽然我偶尔会在前八十回的抄本中遵循一个或另一个版本，但本书仍然是以高鹗版的一百二十回本翻译的。"在后文中，他还提到："在极少数的情况下，我自己也会做些小的修改。"所以，粗略地说，杨宪益的译本依据脂本多些，霍克斯的译本依据程本多些。

我们从每回中选材时，遵循两点原则：一是尽量体现本回的核心内容，二是尽量体现两位翻译大师的风采。

本书主要侧重于讲解翻译技巧、欣赏双语之美，版本不是我们重点考虑的问题，但版本的确给我们带来了困扰，主要体现在回目的翻译上。在前四十回中，涉及版本问题的章回回目有：第三、五、七、八、九、十四、十八回。在这些章回回目的翻译上，两位译者的译文有时出入较大，那是因为他们参照的底本不同，具体内容详见书内的相关注解。

第一回	1
第二回	9
第三回	23
第四回	35
第五回	44
第六回	54
第七回	64
第八回	75
第九回	83
第十回	94
第十一回	102
第十二回	113
第十三回	124
第十四回	132
第十五回	141
第十六回	150
第十七回	161
第十八回	172
第十九回	181
第二十回	190
第二十一回	199

第二十二回	208
第二十三回	218
第二十四回	228
第二十五回	236
第二十六回	246
第二十七回	254
第二十八回	263
第二十九回	271
第三十回	281
第三十一回	290
第三十二回	298
第三十三回	310
第三十四回	321
第三十五回	330
第三十六回	341
第三十七回	351
第三十八回	363
第三十九回	373
第四十回	385
后　记	395
参考文献	397

甄士隐梦幻识通灵　贾雨村风尘怀闺秀

Chen Shih-yin in a Dream Sees the Jade of Spiritual Understanding
Chia Yu-tsun in His Obscurity Is Charmed by a Maid (Yang)

Zhen Shi-yin makes the Stone's acquaintance in a dream
And Jia Yu-cun finds that poverty is not incompatible with romantic feelings (Hawkes)

一、本回概述

　　此开卷第一回，开篇交代《石头记》（又名《红楼梦》）一书的来由：一僧一道携女娲所弃的一块补天石（通灵宝玉），下凡历练，空空道人将其历尽离合悲欢、炎凉世态的故事抄录下来，问世传奇。后来，曹雪芹于悼红轩中将此故事批阅增删，纂成目录，分出章回。书云：姑苏乡宦甄士隐结交了寄居于葫芦庙的贾雨村。某日，贾雨村造访甄士隐，无意中瞧见甄家丫鬟娇杏，以为娇杏对其有意。恰逢中秋，士隐于家中宴请雨村，得知其抱负后，资助银两衣物，随后，雨村不辞而别，上路赴考。元宵之夜，甄家仆人霍启在看社火花灯时，丢失了甄士隐唯一的女儿英莲。三月十五日，葫芦庙失火，殃及甄家，狼狈落魄的士隐带家人投奔岳丈封肃，颇受冷遇，后经跛足道人点化出家。

二、篇章节选

原文

好了歌[1]

世人都晓神仙好，[2]惟有功名忘不了！[3]古今将相在何方？荒冢一堆草没了。[4]

世人都晓神仙好，只有金银忘不了！终朝只恨聚无多，及到多时眼闭了。[5]

世人都晓神仙好，只有姣妻忘不了！[6]君生日日说恩情，君死又随人去了。

世人都晓神仙好，只有儿孙忘不了！[7]痴心父母古来多，孝顺儿孙谁见了？[8]

士隐听了，便迎上来道："你满口说些什么？只听见'好''了''好''了'。"[9]那道人笑道："你若果听见'好''了'二字，还算你明白。可知世上万般，好便是了，了便是好。若不了，便不好；若要好，须是了。我这歌儿，便名《好了歌》。"

杨译

All Good Things Must End[1]

"All men long to be immortals[2]
Yet to riches and rank each aspires;[3]
The great ones of old, where are they now?
Their graves are a mass of briars.[4]

All men long to be immortals,
Yet silver and gold they prize
And grub for money all their lives
Till death seals up their eyes.[5]

All men long to be immortals

Yet dote on the wives they've wed, [6]

Who swear to love their husband evermore

But remarry as soon as he's dead.

All men long to be immortals

Yet with getting sons won't have done. [7]

Although fond parents are legion,

Who ever saw a really filial son?" [8]

At the close of this song Shih-yin stepped forward.

"What was that you just chanted?" he asked. "I had the impression that it was about the vanity of all things." [9]

"If you gathered that, you have some understanding," the Taoist remarked. "You should know that all good things in this world must end, and to make an end is good, for there is nothing good which does not end. My song is called *All Good Things Must End*."

霍译

Won-Done Song [1]

'Men all know that salvation [2] should be won,

But with ambition won't have done, have done. [3]

Where are the famous ones of days gone by?

In grassy graves they lie now, every one. [4]

Men all know that salvation should be won,

But with their riches won't have done, have done.

Each day they grumble they've not made enough.

When they've enough, it's goodnight everyone! [5]

Men all know that salvation should be won,
But with their loving wives they won't have done.[6]
The darlings every day protest their love:
But once you're dead, they're off with another one.

Men all know that salvation should be won,
But with their children won't have done, have done.[7]
Yet though of parents fond there is no lack,
Of grateful children saw I ne'er a one.'[8]

Shi-yin approached the Taoist and questioned him. 'What is all this you are saying? All I can make out is a lot of "won" and "done".'[9]

'If you can make out "won" and "done",' replied the Taoist with a smile, 'you may be said to have understood; for in all the affairs of this world what is won is done, and what is done is won; for whoever has not yet done has not yet won, and in order to have won, one must first have done. I shall call my song the "Won-Done Song".'

三、注释评点

【1】《好了歌》是《红楼梦》开篇中跛足道人点化甄士隐时唱念的歌谣。歌谣分为四小节，分别说人们忘不了功名、金银、娇妻、儿孙。跛足道人通过这首歌，提醒芸芸众生人生如梦，每个人难逃一死，我们忙碌一生汲汲追求的功名利禄、娇妻儿孙一样也带不走，所以要及时觉悟，看淡身外之物。《好了歌》分为四小节，每小节的最后一个字分别是："好、了、方、了；好、了、多、了；好、了、情、了；好、了、多、了"。可以看出，汉语十分工整，每小节的第一、第二、第四的尾词是一样的：好、了、了。杨宪益译文（以下简称"杨译"）形式上也是四小节，每小节也是四句，每小节的第一、第二、第四的尾词分别是：immortals, aspires, briars; immortals, prize, eyes; immortals, wed, dead; immortals, done, son。对比原文可以发现，杨译只能做到每小节的第二句和第四句的尾词押韵，但是没法像原文那样保持每小

节的第二、第四句的尾词不变的形式。也就是说，原文的韵尾形式是：abcb，abdb，abeb，abdb；杨译的韵尾形式是：abcb，aded，afgf，ahih。译文的韵脚与原文中的"好、了、了"无法完全对应，不能一贯到底，增加了下文中翻译跛足道人关于"好、了"二字所发议论的困难。

霍克斯译文（以下简称"霍译"）把"好了歌"这个题目翻译为"Won-Done Song"，这是一个绝妙的字对字翻译："Won"有"好"的意思；"Done"有"了"的意思；"Song"是"歌"的意思。原文题目是"好了歌"，每小节第一、第二、第四句的尾词和题目呼应，分别是"好、了、了"。霍译题目是"Won-Done Song"，译文每小节第一、第二、第四句的尾词也基本上做到了与题目呼应，分别是"won，done，one"。译文的尾韵形式是：abca，abda，abea，abfa，虽然和原文的韵脚稍显不同：原文第一、二、四句的韵脚是abb；译文第一、二、四句的韵脚是aba，但是基本保留了"好、了、了"的韵脚和意义，也为下文中翻译跛足道人关于"好、了"二字的议论扫除了障碍。

【2】"世人都晓神仙好"一句，杨译使用了异化策略将"神仙"一词译成"immortals"；霍译使用了归化策略将该词译成宗教色彩浓厚的"salvation"，salvation是"解救、拯救"的意思。

【3】"惟有功名忘不了！"一句，"功名"一词与下文的"金银""姣妻""儿孙"为并列而非包含关系。杨译"Yet to riches and rank each aspires"将"功名"译为"riches and rank"，其中的"riches"是"财富"的意思，显然与下文"silver and gold"语义重复，不符合作者原意。霍译"But with ambition won't have done, have done"则将"功名"译为"ambition"，"ambition"有"抱负、志向"之意，虽与"功名"不完全对应，但可达意。

【4】"古今将相在何方？荒冢一堆草没了。"一句，杨译"The great ones of old, where are they now? Their graves are a mass of briars."采用了直译手法，和原文形式对应，其中第二句的主语是"Their graves"，对应原文的"荒冢"。霍译"Where are the famous ones of days gone by? In grassy graves they lie now, every one."中第二句的主语用的是"they"，指代前一句中的"the famous ones of days"，对应的是原文中的"古今将相"，更直接、更连贯地回答了"古今

将相在何方？"的问题。

【5】"终朝只恨聚无多，及到多时眼闭了。"一句，杨译是"And grub for money all their lives Till death seals up their eyes"，前半句使用"grub for"这个短语，中文意思为"翻找、搜寻"，来描述人们终其一生汲汲搜寻财富的样子，十分形象生动，但没有译出"只恨聚无多"的贪婪心理。后半句使用了短语"seal up their eyes"来翻译"眼闭了"，准确形象。相比之下，霍译"Each day they grumble they've not made enough. When they've enough, it's goodnight everyone!"的第一句"Each day they grumble they've not made enough" 较为贴切地传达了人们对财富的贪婪心理；第二句则使用了委婉语"it's goodnight"来表达人死眼闭时。

【6】"只有姣妻忘不了！"一句，杨译"Yet dote on the wives they've wed"使用动词短语"dote on"，"dote on"有"溺爱、宠爱"之义。霍译"But with their loving wives they won't have done."则将"姣妻"直接译为"loving wives"，其中的"loving"一词对应原文中的"姣"字，二者都是形容词。

【7】"只有儿孙忘不了！"一句，杨译"Yet with getting sons won't have done."使用"sons"翻译原文的"儿孙"，符合中国封建社会重男轻女的思想。霍译"But with their children won't have done, have done"用的是"children"一词，更符合西方读者的思维习惯。

【8】"痴心父母古来多，孝顺儿孙谁见了？"一句，杨译"Although fond parents are legion, Who ever saw a really filial son?"整体句式清晰、流畅；霍译"Yet though of parents fond there is no lack, of grateful children saw I ne'er a one."为了音节和押韵，调整了语序；正常的语序应该是：Yet though there is no lack of fond parents, I ne'er saw a one of grateful children。

【9】"只听见'好''了''好''了'"一句，杨译"I had the impression that it was about the vanity of all things."采用了意译法，因为杨译在前文的处理上没有完全照应每一小节中出现的"好"和"了"，所以此处只能笼统地译为"the vanity of all things"，另外，在翻译关于"好""了"的论述时，和前文的关联较弱。霍译"All I can make out is a lot of "won" and "done"."

中的"won"和"done"分别含有"好"和"了"之义，歌谣名是"好了歌"，歌谣中反复出现"好""了"二字，其后又有关于"好""了"的论述，霍译用的"won"和"done"也同样出现在歌名、歌中以及后文"好""了"的论述中，而且，译者做到了兼顾语义和韵脚，前后照应，一气呵成，实为神来之笔。

四、词汇表

1. immortal [ɪˈmɔːtl]　　　　　*n.*　　a god or other being who is believed to live for ever 神；永生不灭者

2. aspire [əˈspaɪə]　　　　　　*v.*　　to have a strong desire to achieve or to become sth 渴望（成就）；有志（成为）

3. briar [ˈbraɪə]　　　　　　　*n.*　　any prickly wild bush, especially a wild rose bush 多刺野灌木；（尤指）野蔷薇丛

4. prize [praɪz]　　　　　　　 *v.*　　to value sth highly 珍视；高度重视

5. grub [grʌb]　　　　　　　　*v.*　　to look for sth, especially by digging or by looking through or under other things 翻找；搜寻；挖掘寻找

6. seal [siːl]　　　　　　　　　*v.*　　to close an envelope, etc. by sticking the edges of the opening together 封上（信封）

7. dote [dəʊt]　　　　　　　　*v.*　　to feel and show great love for sb, ignoring their faults 溺爱；宠爱；过分喜爱

8. legion [ˈliːdʒən]　　　　　　*adj.*　very many 很多；极多

9. filial [ˈfɪliəl]　　　　　　　　*adj.*　connected with the way children behave towards their parents 子女（对父母）的

10. salvation [sælˈveɪʃn]　　　　*n.*　　(in Christianity) the state of being saved from the power of evil 得救；救恩；救世

11. grumble [ˈgrʌmbl]　　　　 *v.*　　to complain about sb/sth in a bad-tempered way 咕哝；嘟囔；发牢骚

12. protest [prəˈtest;ˈprəʊtest]　　v.　　to say firmly that sth is true, especially when you have been accused of sth or when other people do not believe you 坚决地表示；申辩

第二回

贾夫人仙逝扬州城　　冷子兴演说荣国府[1]

Lady Chia Dies in the City of Yangchow
Leng Tzu-hsing Describes the Jung Mansion[1] (Yang)

A daughter of the Jias ends her days in Yangchow city
And Leng Zi-xing discourses on the Jias of Rong-guo House[1] (Hawkes)

一、本回概述

贾雨村上京赴考，高中进士，官封大如州知府。上任之际，偶从封肃家门前经过，认出了甄士隐的丫头娇杏，念及当年回头频顾之情，纳娇杏为妾，后扶为正室。不上一年，雨村因恃才侮上，被参革职。安顿家小后，游历四海，至淮扬病倒，盘缠不继，相托友力，谋入巡盐御史林如海之府任西宾，教其幼女黛玉念书。一年后，黛玉之母贾敏病逝，黛玉哀痛过伤，无法上学，雨村闲居。一日，偶至郭外，在村肆吃酒，巧遇旧识冷子兴，冷子兴向雨村演说金陵贾府的情况。

二、篇章节选

原文

原来,雨村因那年士隐赠银之后,他于十六日便起身入都,[2]至大比之期,不料他十分得意,已会了进士,选入外班,今已升了本府知府。虽才干优长,未免有些贪酷之弊;且又恃才侮上,那些官员皆侧目而视。不上一年,便被上司寻了个空隙,作成一本,参他"生情狡猾,擅纂礼仪,且沽清正之名,而暗结虎狼之属,致使地方多事,民命不堪"等语。[3]龙颜大怒,即批革职。该部文书一到,本府官员无不喜悦。[4]那雨村心中虽十分惭恨,却面上全无一点怨色,仍是嘻笑自若;交代过公事,将历年做官积的些资本并家小人属送至原籍,安排妥协,却是自己担风袖月,游览天下胜迹。[5]

那日,偶又游至维扬①地面,因闻得今岁鹾政点的是林如海。[6]这林如海姓林名海,字表如海,乃是前科的探花,今已升至兰台寺大夫,本贯姑苏人氏,今钦点出为巡盐御史,到任方一月有馀。原来这林如海之祖,曾袭过列侯,今到如海,业经五世。起初时,只封袭三世,因当今隆恩盛德,远迈前代,额外加恩,至如海之父,又袭了一代;至如海,便从科第出身。虽系钟鼎之家,却亦是书香之族。[7]只可惜这林家支庶不盛,子孙有限,[8]虽有几门,却与如海俱是堂族而已,没甚亲支嫡派的。今如海年已四十,只有一个三岁之子,偏又于去岁死了。虽有几房姬妾,奈他命中无子,亦无可如何之事。[9]今只有嫡妻贾氏生得一女,乳名黛玉,年方五岁。夫妻无子,故爱如珍宝,且又见他聪明清秀,便也欲使他读书识得几个字,不过假充养子之意,聊解膝下荒凉之叹。[10]

杨译

Yu-tsun, after receiving Shih-yin's gift of silver that year, had left on the

---

① 维扬:即扬州,今江苏省扬州市。转引自曹雪芹著,无名氏续:《红楼梦》,人民文学出版社,2008年,第23页。

sixteenth for the capital.[2] He did so well in the examinations that he became a Palace Graduate and was given a provincial appointment. He had now been promoted to this prefectship.

But although a capable administrator Yu-tsun was grasping and ruthless, while his arrogance and insolence to his superiors made them view him with disfavour. In less than two years they found a chance to impeach him. He was accused of "ingrained duplicity, tampering with the rites and, under a show of probity, conspiring with his ferocious underlings to foment trouble in his district and make life intolerable for the local people."[3a]

The Emperor, much incensed, sanctioned his dismissal. The arrival of this edict rejoiced the hearts of all officials in the Prefecture.[4] But Yu-tsun, although mortified and enraged, betrayed no indignation and went about looking as cheerful as before. After handing over his affairs he gathered together the capital accumulated during his years in office and moved his household back to his native place. Having settled them there he set off, "the wind on his back, moonlight in his sleeves," to see the famous sights of the empire.[5]

One day his travels again took him to Yangchow, where he learned that the Salt Commissioner that year was Lin Hai—his courtesy name was Lin Ju-hai[6]—who had come third in a previous Imperial examination and recently been promoted to the Censorate. A native of Kusu, he had now been selected by the Emperor as a Commissioner of the Salt Inspectorate. He had been little more than a month in this present post.

One of Lin Ju-hai's ancestors five generations earlier had been ennobled as a marquis. The rank had been conferred for three generations; then, as the benevolence of the present gracious Emperor far exceeded that of his noble predecessors, he had as a special favour extended it for one more generation, so that Lin Ju-hai's father had inherited the title as well. He himself, however, had made his career through the examinations, for his family was cultured as well as noble.[7] Unfortunately it was not prolific,[8] although several branches existed, and Lin Ju-hai had cousins but no brothers or sisters. Now he was in his forties and his only son had died at the age of three the previous year. He had several concubines but fate had not granted him another son, and he could not remedy this. [9] By his wife, nee' Chia, he had a daughter Tai-yu just five years old. Both parents loved her dearly. And because she was as intelligent as she was pretty, they decided to give her a good education to make up for their lack of a son and help them forget their loss. [10a]

霍译

When Yu-cun received the gift of money from Zhen Shi-yin he had left for the capital on the day after the festival. [2] He had done well in the Triennial examination, passing out as a Palace Graduate, and had been selected for external service. And now he had been promoted to the magistracy of this district.

But although his intelligence and ability were outstanding, these qualities were unfortunately offset by a certain cupidity and harshness and a tendency to use his intelligence in order to outwit his superiors; all of which caused his fellow-officials to cast envious glances in his direction, with the result that in less than a year an unfavourable report was sent in by a senior official stating that his 'seeming ability was no more than a mask for cunning and duplicity' and citing one or two instances in which he had aided and abetted the peculations of his underlings or allied himself with powerful local interests in order to frustrate the course of justice. [3b]

The imperial eye, lighting on this report, kindled with wrath. Yu-cun's instant dismissal was commanded. The officials at the Prefecture, when notice that he was to be cashiered arrived from the Ministry, rejoiced to a man. [4] But Yu-cun, in spite of all the shame and chagrin that he felt, allowed no glimmer of resentment to appear on his face. Indeed, he joked and smiled as before, and when the business of handing over was completed, he took his wife and family and the loot he had accumulated during his years of office and having settled them all safely in his native Hu-zhou, set off, free as the air, on an extended tour of some of the more celebrated places of scenic interest in our mighty empire. [5]

One day Yu-cun chanced to be staying in the Yangchow area when he heard that the Salt Commissioner for that year was a certain Lin Ru-hai.[6] This Lin Ru-hai had passed out Florilege, or third in the whole list of successful candidates, in a previous Triennial, and had lately been promoted to the Censorate. He was a Soochow man and had not long taken up his duties in Yangchow following his nomination by the emperor as Visiting Inspector in that area.

Lin Ru-hai came of an aristocratic family and was himself fifth in line since his ancestor's ennoblement. The original patent had been inheritable only up to the third generation, and it was only through the magnanimity of the reigning sovereign that an exceptional act of grace had extended it for a further generation in the case of Lin Ru-hai's father. Lin Ru-hai himself had therefore been obliged to make his way up through the examination system. It was fortunate for him that, though the family had up to his time enjoyed hereditary emoluments, it had nevertheless enjoined a high standard of education on all of its members.[7]

Lin Ru-hai was less fortunate, however, in belonging to a family whose numbers were dwindling.[8] He could still point to several related households, but they were all on the distaff side. There was not a single relation in the direct line who bore his name. Already he was fifty, and his only son had died the year before at the age of three. And although he kept several concubines, he seemed fated to have no son, and had all but resigned himself to this melancholy fact.[9]

His chief wife, who had been a Miss Jia, had given him a daughter called Dai-yu. Both parents doted on her, and because she showed exceptional intelligence, conceived the idea of giving her a rudimentary education as a substitute for bringing up a son, hoping in this way somewhat to alleviate the sense of desolation left by the death of their only heir.[10b]

三、注释评点

【1】本回回目"贾夫人仙逝扬州城　冷子兴演说荣国府",杨译是"Lady Chia Dies in the City of Yangchow　Leng Tzu-hsing Describes the Jung Mansion",霍译是"A daughter of the Jias ends her days in Yangchow city　And Leng Zi-xing discourses on the Jias of Rong-guo House"。对于上句中的"贾夫人",杨宪益将其直译为"Lady Jia",而霍克斯可能担心译为"Lady Jia"会让人误解成贾母,所以意译为"a daughter of the Jias"。"冷子兴演说荣国府"一句,杨译给人的感觉是冷子兴在讲述荣国府的建筑,霍译增加了"the Jias",说明冷子兴评论的是荣国府中的贾氏族人。

【2】"原来,雨村因那年士隐赠银之后,他于十六日便起身入都"一句,杨译"Yu-tsun, after receiving Shih-yin's gift of silver that year, had left on the sixteenth for the capital."和霍译"When Yu-cun received the gift of money from Zhen Shi-yin he had left for the capital on the day after the festival."都将动词短语"赠银"处理为名词短语:"gift of silver"和"gift of money"。另外,杨译用介词短语"after receiving…"作时间状语;霍译用"when"引导的从句做时间状语,两者的效果相同。

【3a】"虽才干优长,未免有些贪酷之弊;且又恃才侮上,那些官员皆侧目而视。不上一年,便被上司寻了个空隙,作成一本,参他'生性狡猾,擅纂礼仪,且沽清正之名,而暗结虎狼之属,致使地方多事,民命不堪'等语。"杨译以脂本为底本,霍译以程本为底本。脂本和程本在本句的表述上虽有些差异,但整体意思基本一致。这句话的特点是主语比较多,从雨村到官员到上司又到雨村,主语变化很快,杨译和霍译的处理各具特色。杨译是"But although a capable administrator Yu-tsun was grasping and ruthless, while his arrogance and insolence to his superiors made them view him with disfavour. In less than two years they found a chance to impeach him. He was accused of 'ingrained duplicity, tampering with the rites and, under a show of probity, conspiring with his ferocious underlings to foment trouble in his district and make life intolerable for the local people.'"。原文第一句的第二部分是"且又恃才侮上，那些官员皆侧目而视"，其主语分别是"雨村"和"那些官员"。译者在此处没有拘泥于原文，而是把其中的动词短语"恃才侮上"翻译为名词短语"his arrogance and insolence to his superiors"，在译文"while his arrogance and insolence to his superiors made them view him with disfavour"中充当主语，这样的处理方式不仅符合英语是静态语言、喜用名词这一特征，而且把"（雨村）恃才侮上"和"那些官员皆侧目而视"这两个小句自然地衔接起来。原句中的"不上一年"，杨译为"In less than two years"，似为误译。

【3b】程本这句的表述为："虽才干优长，未免贪酷，且恃才侮上，那同寅皆侧目而视。不上一年，便被上司参了一本，说他貌似有才，性实狡猾，又题了一两件徇庇蠹役、交结乡绅之事……"霍译是"But although his intelligence and ability were outstanding, these qualities were unfortunately offset by a certain cupidity and harshness and a tendency to use his intelligence in order to outwit his superiors; all of which caused his fellow-officials to cast envious glances in his direction, with the result that in less than a year an unfavourable report was sent in by a senior official stating that his 'seeming ability was no more than a mask for cunning and duplicity' and citing one or two instances in which he had aided and abetted the peculations of his underlings or allied himself with powerful local interests in order to frustrate the course of justice."译者将整段文字翻译成一句英文，结构较为复杂。该句开头用了"But although"，其中But用于承上，although用于启下。该句主要使用了But although，all of which，with the result that和in which将整个句子连接起来。值得注意的是，霍译基本没有选用人称主语，而是用了物化主语，如：his intelligence and ability，these qualities，an unfavourable report，his seeming ability。另外，霍译将"侧目"一词译为"envious glances"，"侧目"虽然也有嫉妒的意思，但更多强调的是不满，杨译中的"disfavour"更好一些。

【4】"该部文书一到，本府官员无不喜悦"一句，杨译"The arrival of this edict rejoiced the hearts of all officials in the Prefecture."使用了句子化词（组）法将小句"该部文书一到"处理为名词短语"the arrival of this edict"，在译

文中充当主语，连句手法十分巧妙。霍译"The officials at the Prefecture, when notice that he was to be cashiered arrived from the Ministry, rejoiced to a man."是一个主从复合句：主句是"The officials at the Prefecture rejoiced to a man"，其中，"… rejoiced to a man"的意思是"Every single one of them rejoiced. None didn't rejoice.（每个人都很高兴，没有人不高兴）"；主句中间插入了一个"when"引导的时间状语从句，这个时间状语从句中又包含一个"that"引导的同位语从句，用来解释说明"notice"的具体内容。

【5】"交代过公事，将历年做官积的些资本并家小人属，送至原籍安排妥协，却又自己担风袖月，游览天下胜迹。"句中，被省略的主语"雨村"发出了好几个动作：交代、送至、安排妥协、担风袖月、游览。杨译是"After handing over his affairs he gathered together the capital accumulated during his years in office and moved his household back to his native place. Having settled them there he set off, "the wind on his back, moonlight in his sleeves," to see the famous sights of the empire."。此译文由两个句子构成：第一句中，"After handing over…"是介词短语做时间状语，"gathered"和"moved"并列做谓语。第二句中，"Having settled them there"是现在分词短语做时间状语，句子的主干部分是"he set off to see the famous sights of the empire"，译者在谓语"set off"和目的状语"to see the famous sights of the empire"之间插入了"担风袖月"的译文"the wind on his back, moonlight in his sleeves"，该部分是独立主格结构；为了保留中国文化的特点，译者对"担风袖月"采用了异化手法。霍译"… and when the business of handing over was completed, he took his wife and family and the loot he had accumulated during his years of office and having settled them all safely in his native Hu-zhou, set off, free as the air, on an extended tour of some of the more celebrated places of scenic interest in our mighty empire."是一个结构复杂的长句。首先是"when"引导的时间状语从句，然后是主句"he took his wife and family and the loot..."，其中，"he had accumulated during his years of office"是"loot"的定语从句；"and"之后，现在分词短语"having settled them all safely in his native Hu-zhou"在句中作时间状语，此处，现在分词短语用的是完成式，体现出它与谓语"set off"发生的先后顺序。另外，从霍译中可以看出，英语

的定语很有特点：当英语中的定语由短语构成的时候，总是放在所修饰的名词之后。例如："of scenic interest"是"places"的定语，"of the more celebrated places"是"some"的定语，"of some"是"an extended tour"的定语。对于"担风袖月"一词，霍译"free as the air"采用的是归化法，没有出现喻体，意为"自由自在地"。

【6】"那日，偶又游至维扬地面，因闻得今岁鹾政点的是林如海。"一句中，被省略的主语"雨村"发出了两个动作：游至、闻得。杨译是"One day his travels again took him to Yangchow, where he learned that the Salt Commissioner that year was Lin Ju-hai"，译者没有选择人称主语，而是把原文中的动词"游"译为名词"travels"，在译文中充当主语，句内用"where"连接，即"在那里（淮扬地面）他得知……"。霍译是"One day Yu-cun chanced to be staying in the Yangchow area when he heard that the Salt Commissioner for that year was a certain Lin Ru-hai"，译者用"when"进行句内连接，"chance to do sth"是"碰巧做某事"的意思，"to be staying"是不定式的进行式，表示一种持续状态。该译文所用的句型是：sb was doing sth when sb else did sth else，主句中的动作要用过去进行时，表示一种持续状态，"when"引导的时间状语从句中用一般过去时，表示在主句动作持续过程中突然发生的动作。

【7】"至如海，便从科第出身。虽系钟鼎之家，却亦是书香之族。"杨译是"He himself however, had made his career through the examinations, for his family was cultured as well as noble."译者在句中增加了表示原因的连词"for"，点明了上下文的逻辑关系。汉语是意合语言，英语是形合语言，连词"for"使该句上下文的逻辑关系在汉语向英语转换时，从隐性变成显性。另外，杨译巧妙地将原文中的两个名词短语"钟鼎之家"和"书香之族"处理为两个形容词"noble"和"cultured"。汉语的重心偏后，"虽系钟鼎之家，却亦是书香之族"，着重强调"书香之族"；而英语的重心偏前，所以先说"cultured"，然后才是"as well as noble"。此句的程高本为"到了如海便从科第出身。虽系世禄之家，却是书香之族"，霍译是"Lin Ru-hai himself had therefore been obliged to make his way up through the examination system. It was fortunate for him that, though the family had up to his time enjoyed hereditary emoluments, it had nevertheless enjoined a high standard of education on all of its members." 该译文依据的是程高本，故内容与杨译有所不同。但是，第二句中that引导的主语从句里用"though"引导的让步状语从句翻译原文的"虽系世禄之家"，用主句翻译原文的"却是书香之族"，也是在强调后者，这一点和杨译是异曲同工。

【8】"只可惜这林家支庶不盛，子孙有限"一句中，两个并列短语"支庶不盛"和"子孙有限"表达的意思一致。杨译"Unfortunately it was not prolific..."将其译为形容词"(not) prolific"；霍译"Lin Ru-hai was less fortunate, however, in belonging to a family whose numbers were dwindling"则使用了定语从句"whose numbers were dwindling"来翻译。

【9】"虽有几房姬妾，奈他命中无子，亦无可如何之事。"杨译是"He had several concubines but fate had not granted him another son, and he could not remedy this."，其中的第二个分句使用了物化主语"fate"。霍译是"And although he kept several concubines, he seemed fated to have no son, and had all but resigned himself to this melancholy fact."，其中，"all but"是"几乎、差不多"的意思，"resign oneself to sth"是"听任、只好接受；顺从"的意思，因此，"(he) had all but resigned himself to this melancholy fact"充分表达出林如海对于自己命中无子的事实的无可奈何。

【10a】"且又见他聪明清秀，便也欲使他读书识得几个字，不过假充养子之意，聊解膝下荒凉之叹。"杨译是"And because she was as intelligent as she was pretty, they decided to give her a good education to make up for their lack of a son and help them forget their loss." 其中的"as... as..."结构用于表示同一个人或物不同性质的比较，意为"既……又……"；另外，译者使用句子化短语法将小句"不过假充养子之意"和"聊解膝下荒凉之叹"分别处理为两个并列的不定式短语"to make up for their lack of a son"和"help them forget their loss"，由"and"连接，在译文中充当目的状语。

【10b】"故爱如珍宝，且又见他聪明清秀，便也欲使他读书识得几个字，不过假充养子之意，聊解膝下荒凉之叹。"霍译是"Both parents doted on her, and because she showed exceptional intelligence, conceived the idea of giving her a rudimentary education as a substitute for bringing up a son, hoping in this way somewhat to alleviate the sense of desolation left by the death of their only heir." 其

中，"and"连接两个并列的谓语"doted on"和"conceived"；小句"不过假充养子之意"被处理为介词短语"as a substitute for bringing up a son"；小句"聊解膝下荒凉之叹"被处理为现在分词短语"hoping in this way somewhat to alleviate the sense of desolation left by the death of their only heir"，在译文中充当目的状语。

四、词汇表

1. grasping [ˈgrɑːspɪŋ]	*adj.*	always trying to get money, possessions, power, etc. for yourself 一味攫取的；贪婪的；贪心的
2. ruthless [ˈruːθləs]	*adj.*	(of people or their behavior) hard and cruel; determined to get what you want and not caring if you hurt other people 残忍的；残酷无情的
3. insolent [ˈɪnsələnt]	*adj.*	extremely rude and showing a lack of respect 粗野的；无礼的；侮慢的
	n.	insolence
4. impeach [ɪmˈpiːtʃ]	*v.*	(of a court or other official body, especially in the US) to charge an important public figure with a serious crime 控告（显要公职人员）犯有重大罪行；弹劾
5. ingrained [ɪnˈgreɪnd]	*adj.*	(of a habit, an attitude, etc.) that has existed for a long time and is therefore difficult to change 根深蒂固的；日久难改的
6. duplicity [djuˈplɪsəti]	*n.*	dishonest behaviour that is intended to make sb believe sth which is not true 欺骗；奸诈（行为）

7. tamper [ˈtæmpə]	v.	to make changes to sth without permission, especially in order to damage it 篡改，擅自改动，胡乱摆弄（尤指有意破坏）
8. probity [ˈprəʊbɪti]	n.	the quality of being completely honest 正直；诚实
9. conspire [kənˈspaɪə]	v.	to secretly plan with other people to do sth illegal or harmful 密谋；图谋；阴谋
10. underling [ˈʌndəlɪŋ]	n.	a person with a lower rank or status 走卒；喽啰；手下
11. foment [ˈfəʊment]	v.	to create trouble or violence or make it worse 挑起；激起；煽动（事端或暴力）
12. incensed [ɪnˈsenst]	adj.	very angry 非常愤怒的；大怒的
13. sanction [ˈsæŋkʃən]	v.	to give permission for sth to take place 许可；准许；准予
14. edict [ˈiːdɪkt]	n.	an official order or statement given by sb in authority 法令；命令；敕令
15. mortify [ˈmɔːtɪfaɪ]	v.	to make sb feel very ashamed or embarrassed 使难堪；使羞惭
16. inspectorate [ɪnˈspektərət]	n.	an official group of inspectors who work together on the same subject or at the same kind of institution 视察团；检查团
17. marquis [ˈmɑːkwɪs]	n.	a nobleman of high rank 侯爵
18. confer [kənˈfɜː]	v.	to give sb an award, a university degree or a particular honour or right 授予（奖项、学位、荣誉或权利）
19. predecessor [ˈpriːdɪsesə]	n.	a person who did a job before sb else 前任
20. prolific [prəʊˈlɪfɪk]	adj.	(of plants, animals, etc.) producing a lot of fruit, flowers, young, etc. 丰硕的；多产的；多育的

21. concubine [ˈkɒnkjʊbaɪn]	n.	(especially in some societies in the past) a woman who lives with a man, often in addition to his wife or wives, but who is less important than they are（尤指旧时某些社会里的）妾；姨太太；小老婆
22. remedy [ˈremɪdi]	v.	to correct or improve sth 改正；纠正；改进
23. triennial [traɪˈeniəl]	adj.	happening every three years 每三年一次的；每三年的
24. magistracy [ˈmædʒɪstrəsi]	n.	**the magistracy:** magistrates as a group（统称）地方行政官；地方法官；治安官
25. offset [ɒfˈset]	v.	to use one cost, payment or situation in order to cancel or reduce the effect of another 抵消；弥补；补偿
26. outwit [aʊtˈwɪt]	v.	to defeat sb/sth or gain an advantage over them by doing sth clever（智力上）超过；胜过
27. cunning [ˈkʌnɪŋ]	adj.	able to get what you want in a clever way, especially by tricking or deceiving sb 狡猾的；奸诈的；诡诈的
28. abet [əˈbet]	v.	to help or encourage sb to do sth wrong 教唆；唆使；煽动；怂恿
29. ally [ˈælaɪ]	v.	to give your support to another group or country 与……结盟
30. kindle [ˈkɪndl]	v.	to start burning 开始燃烧；点燃；激起
31. wrath [rɒθ]	n.	extreme anger 盛怒；震怒；怒火
32. loot [luːt]	n.	money and valuable objects taken by soldiers from the enemy after winning a battle 战利品；掠夺品

33. patent [ˈpeɪtənt]	n.	an official right to be the only person to make, use or sell a product or an invention; a document that proves this 专利权；专利证书
34. magnanimous [mægˈnænɪməs]	adj.	kind, generous and forgiving, especially towards an enemy or a rival 宽宏的，大度的（尤指对敌人或对手）
	n.	magnanimity
35. emolument [ɪˈmɒljʊmənt]	n.	money paid to sb for work they have done, especially to sb who earns a lot of money（尤指付给高收入者的）酬金，薪水，工资
36. dwindle [ˈdwɪndl]	v.	to become gradually less or smaller（逐渐）减少，变小，缩小
37. melancholy [ˈmelənkəli]	adj.	very sad or making you feel sadness（令人）悲哀的；（令人）沮丧的
38. rudimentary [ˌruːdɪˈmentəri]	adj.	dealing with only the most basic matters or ideas 基础的；基本的
39. alleviate [əˈliːvieɪt]	v.	to make sth less severe 减轻；缓和；缓解
40. desolation [ˌdesəˈleɪʃən]	n.	the feeling of being very lonely and unhappy 孤寂；悲哀；忧伤

贾雨村夤缘复旧职　林黛玉抛父进京都[1]

托内兄如海荐西宾　接外孙贾母惜孤女[1]
Lin Ju-hai Recommends a Tutor to His Brother-in-Law
The Lady Dowager Sends for Her Motherless Grand-Daughter[1] (Yang)

托内兄如海荐西宾　接外孙贾母惜孤女[1]
Lin Ru-hai recommends a private tutor to his brother-in-law
And old Lady Jia extends a compassionate welcome to the motherless child[1] (Hawkes)

一、本回概述

　　贾雨村昔日一案参革的同僚张如圭前来报喜，告知起复旧员之事，雨村遂请林如海转托其妻兄贾政推荐自己复职，如海慨然应允，为雨村写荐信，以报教女之恩，并托雨村护送黛玉入都，投靠其外祖母。黛玉初入荣府，相继与贾母、熙凤、宝玉等见面，宝、黛二人一见如故，似曾相识，宝玉因黛玉无玉而发狂砸玉。第二天，黛玉早起请安，见王夫人正查看其兄来信，信中告知薛蟠倚财仗势杀人一案。

对话杨宪益、霍克斯——《红楼梦》英译赏析(第一至四十回)

二、篇章节选

原文

贾母因笑道:"外客未见,就脱了衣裳,还不去见你妹妹!"[2]宝玉早已看见多了一个姊妹,便料定是林姑妈之女,忙来作揖。厮见毕归坐,细看形容,与众各别:[3]

两弯似蹙非蹙罥烟眉,一双似泣非泣含露目,[4]态生两靥之愁,娇袭一身之病。泪光点点,娇喘微微。闲静时如姣花照水,行动处似弱柳扶风。心较比干多一窍,病如西子胜三分。[5]

……

又问黛玉:"可也有玉没有?"众人不解其语,黛玉便忖度着因他有玉,故问我有也无,[6]因答道:"我没有那个。想来那玉是一件罕物,岂能人人有的。"

宝玉听了,登时发作起痴狂病来,摘下那玉,就狠命摔去,骂道:"什么罕物,连人之高低不择,还说'通灵'不'通灵'呢!我也不要这劳什子了,"[7]吓的众人一拥争去拾玉。贾母急的搂了宝玉道:"孽障!你生气,要打骂人容易,何苦摔那命根子!"[8]宝玉满面泪痕泣道:"家里姐姐妹妹都没有,单我有,我说没趣。如今来了这们一个神仙似的妹妹也没有,[9]可知这不是个好东西。"贾母忙哄他道:"你这妹妹原有这个来的,因你姑妈去世时,舍不得你妹妹,无法处,遂将他的玉带了去了:一则全殉葬之礼,尽你妹妹之孝心;二则你姑妈之灵,亦可权作见了女儿之意。因此,他只说没有这个,不便自己夸张之意。你如今怎比得他?还不好生慎重带上,仔细你娘知道了。"说着,便向丫鬟手中接来,亲与他带上。宝玉听如此说,想一想大有情理,也就不生别论了。[10]

杨译

With a smile at Pao-yu, the Lady Dowager scolded, "Fancy changing your clothes before greeting our visitor. Hurry up now and pay your respects to your cousin." [2]

Of course, Pao-yu had seen this new cousin earlier on and guessed that she was the daughter of his Aunt Lin. He made haste to bow and, having greeted her, took a seat. Looking at Tai-yu closely, he found her different from other girls. [3]

Her dusky arched eyebrows were knitted and yet not frowning, her speaking eyes held both merriment and sorrow; [4] her very frailty had charm. Her eyes sparkled with tears, her breath was soft and faint. In repose she was like a lovely flower mirrored in the water; in motion, a pliant willow swaying in the wind. She looked more sensitive than Pi Kan[1], more delicate than Hsi Shih[2]. [5]

……

Then, to the mystification of them all, he asked Tai-yu if she had any jade.

Imagining that he had his own jade in mind, she answered, [6] "No, I haven't. I suppose it's too rare for everybody to have."

This instantly threw Pao-yu into one of his frenzies. Tearing off the jade he flung it on the ground.

"What's rare about it?" he stormed. "It can't even tell good people from bad. What spiritual understanding has it got? I don't want this nuisance either." [7]

In consternation all the maids rushed forward to pick up the jade while the Lady Dowager in desperation took Pao-yu in her arms.

"You wicked monster!" she scolded. "Storm at people if you're in a passion. But why should you throw away that precious thing your life depends on?" [8]

His face stained with tears, Pao-yu sobbed, "None of the girls here has one, only me. What's the fun of that? Even this newly arrived cousin who's lovely as a fairy hasn't got one either. [9] That shows it's no good."

"She did have one once," said the old lady to soothe him. "But when your aunt was dying and was unwilling to leave her, the best she could do was to take the jade with her instead. That was like burying the living with the dead and showed your cousin's filial piety. It meant, too, that now your aunt's spirit can still see your cousin.

That's why she said she had none, not wanting to boast about it. How can you compare with her? Now put it carefully on again lest your mother hears about this."

She took the jade from one of the maids and put it on him herself. And Pao-yu, convinced by her tale, let the matter drop. [10]

霍译

'Fancy changing your clothes before you have welcomed the visitor!' Grandmother Jia chided indulgently on seeing Bao-yu back again. 'Aren't you going to pay your respects to your cousin?' [2]

Bao-yu had already caught sight of a slender, delicate girl whom he surmised to be his Aunt Lin's daughter and quickly went over to greet her. Then, returning to his place and taking a seat, he studied her attentively. How different she seemed from the other girls he knew! [3]

Her mist-wreathed brows at first seemed to frown, yet were not frowning;
Her passionate eyes at first seemed to smile, yet were not merry. [4]
Habit had given a melancholy cast to her tender face;
Nature had bestowed a sickly constitution on her delicate frame.
Often the eyes swam with glistening tears;
Often the breath came in gentle gasps.
In stillness she made one think of a graceful flower reflected in the water;
In motion she called to mind tender willow shoots caressed by the wind.
She had more chambers in her heart than the martyred Bi Gan;
And suffered a tithe more pain in it than the beautiful Xi Shi. [5]

……

He returned to his interrogation of Dai-yu.

'Have you got a jade?'

The rest of the company were puzzled, but Dai-yu at once divined that he was asking her if she too had a jade like the one he was born with. [6]

'No,' said Dai-yu. 'That jade of yours is a very rare object. You can't expect everybody to have one.'

This sent Bao-yu off instantly into one of his mad fits. Snatching the jade from his neck he hurled it violently on the floor as if to smash it and began abusing it passionately.

'Rare object! Rare object! What's so lucky about a stone that can't even tell which people are better than others? Beastly thing! I don't want it!' [7]

The maids all seemed terrified and rushed forward to pick it up, while Grandmother Jia clung to Bao-yu in alarm.

'Naughty, naughty boy! Shout at someone or strike them if you like when you are in a nasty temper, but why go smashing that precious thing that your very life depends on?' [8]

'None of the girls has got one,' said Bao-yu, his face streaming with tears and sobbing hysterically. 'Only I have got one. It always upsets me. And now this new cousin comes here who is as beautiful as an angel and she hasn't got one either; [9] so I *know* it can't be any good.'

'Your cousin did have a jade once,' said Grandmother Jia, coaxing him like a little child, 'but because when Auntie died she couldn't bear to leave her little girl behind, they had to let her take the jade with her instead. In that way your cousin could show her mamma how much she loved her by letting the jade be buried with her; and at the same time, whenever Auntie's spirit looked at the jade, it would be just like looking at her own little girl again.

'So when your cousin said she hadn't got one, it was only because she didn't want to boast about the good, kind thing she did when she gave it to her mamma. Now you put yours on again like a good boy, and mind your mother doesn't find out how naughty you have been.'

So saying, she took the jade from the hands of one of the maids and hung it round his neck for him. And Bao-yu, after reflecting for a moment or two on what she had said, offered no further resistance. [10]

三、注释评点

【1】人民文学出版社的《红楼梦》版本中，本回回目是"贾雨村夤缘复旧职　林黛玉抛父进京都"，程本本回的回目是"托内兄如海荐西宾　接外孙贾母惜孤女"，从两个英译本中都可以看出，杨译和霍译对第三回回目的翻译依据的是程本。在这个回目中，"内兄"指贾政，即林如海亡妻贾敏的哥哥；"西宾"是家庭老师，此处指林黛玉的家教贾雨村。该回目中一共有四个动词，分别为"托、荐、接、惜"。杨译是"Lin Ju-hai Recommends a Tutor to His Brother-in-Law　The Lady Dowager Sends for Her Motherless Grand-Daughter"；霍译是"Lin Ru-hai recommends a private tutor to his brother-in-law　And old Lady Jia extends a compassionate welcome to the motherless child"。两个译文的上句都只翻译了动词"荐"，即"recommend"，没有翻译"托"字。对于下句的翻译，两位译者的侧重点不同：杨译侧重于"接"，即"send for"，而霍译侧重于"惜"，即"extend a compassionate welcome"。

【2】"外客未见，就脱了衣裳，还不去见你妹妹！"一句，杨译是"Fancy changing your clothes before greeting our visitor. Hurry up now and pay your respects to your cousin."霍译是"Fancy changing your clothes before you have welcomed the visitor!... Aren't you going to pay your respects to your cousin?"两位译者都将"脱了衣裳"译为"changing your clothes"，将"见你妹妹"译为"pay your respects to your cousin"，该句中的"脱"和"见"不能直接译为"take off"和"see"，两位译者在此处的处理手法相同。

【3】"宝玉早已看见多了一个姊妹，便料定是林姑妈之女，忙来作揖，厮见毕归坐，细看形容，与众各别。"句中，主语"宝玉"发出了一连串的动作：看见、料定、忙来、作揖、厮见、归坐、细看。杨译"Of course, Pao-yu had seen this new cousin earlier on and guessed that she was the daughter of his Aunt Lin. He made haste to bow and, having greeted her, took a seat. Looking at Tai-yu closely, he found her different from other girls."由三个句子构成：第一句中将"看见"和"料定"两个动词处理为并列谓语"had seen"和"guessed"，

两个动词分别是过去完成时和一般过去时,表示这两个动作是先后发生的;第二句将"忙来作揖"和"归座"处理为并列谓语"made haste to bow"和"took a seat","厮见毕"处理成现在分词短语"having greeted her",而且用了完成式,表明"先厮见,后归座";第三句"Looking at Tai-yu closely, he found..."用了现在分词短语做伴随状语,表示looking和found是两个几乎同时发生的动作。霍译"Bao-yu had already caught sight of a slender, delicate girl whom he surmised to be his Aunt Lin's daughter and quickly went over to greet her. Then, returning to his place and taking a seat, he studied her attentively. How different she seemed from the other girls he knew!"也是由三个句子构成:第一句中的"whom"一词用得很好:原文"便料定是林姑妈之女"中有两个隐性主语,即"(宝玉)料定(黛玉)是林姑妈之女",译者没有用"黛玉"做主语,而直接用"whom he surmised to be"将前后两部分连接起来,十分巧妙。第二句中也同样使用了现在分词短语做伴随状语:"Then, returning to his place and taking a seat, he studied her attentively.(宝玉先回到原处,然后坐下,再仔细打量黛玉。)"表示这一连串动作先后发生。第三句选用了感叹句式,强调出黛玉不同寻常的美貌和气质。

【4】"两弯似蹙非蹙罥烟眉,一双似泣非泣含露目"一句,在甲辰本中是"两弯似蹙非蹙笼烟眉,一双似喜非喜含情目",杨译和霍译对此句的翻译所用的底本应该更接近于甲辰本。杨译是"Her dusky arched eyebrows were knitted and yet not frowning, her speaking eyes held both merriment and sorrow;";霍译是"Her mist-wreathed brows at first seemed to frown, yet were not frowning; Her passionate eyes at first seemed to smile, yet were not merry."。霍译前半句中的"seemed to frown(似蹙)"是动作,"yet were not frowning(非蹙)"表示状态;紧接着的"seemed to smile(似喜)"也是动作,"yet were not merry(非喜)"是状态——句式上都是先动作后状态的结构,表示猛一看是蹙是喜,仔细一看又是非蹙非喜的状态。杨译将"含情目"译为"her speaking eyes",即"会说话的眼睛",比较含蓄委婉,颇有东方情调;霍译将"含情目"译为"her passionate eyes",比较大胆直接,颇具西方色彩,可谓各具特色。

【5】"心较比干多一窍,病如西子胜三分"一句中包含了两个极具中国文化意涵的人名"比干"和"西子"。杨译"She looked more sensitive than Pi

Kan[1], more delicate than Hsi Shih[2]"在当页页脚给出了这两个历史人物的注释：[1]A prince noted for his great intelligence at the end of the Shang Dynasty；[2]A famous beauty of the ancient kingdom of Yueh，属于文外补偿的翻译手法。霍译"She had more chambers in her heart than the martyred Bi Gan; And suffered a tithe more pain in it than the beautiful Xi Shi."采用了直译手法，容易引起读者的误解，以为黛玉天生有心脏病，心室长得比别人多。同时，霍译采用了文内补偿的手法，在"比干"和"西施"这两个文化词汇前分别增加了做定语的形容词"martyred（殉难的、受到折磨的）"和"beautiful（美丽的）"，这样更方便读者，不打扰阅读的连贯性。而杨译用脚注的优点是给出的信息更加具体，方便外国读者了解这两个历史人物。

【6】"又问黛玉：'可也有玉没有？'众人不解其语。黛玉便忖度着因他有玉，故问我有也无。"杨译"Then, to the mystification of them all, he asked Tai-yu if she had any jade. Imagining that he had his own jade in mind, she answered…"使用了句子化短语法，将原文中的小句"众人不解其语"译为介词短语"to the mystification of them all"。霍译是"He returned to his interrogation of Dai-yu. 'Have you got a jade?' The rest of the company were puzzled, but Dai-yu at once divined that he was asking her if she too had a jade like the one he was born with."。其中，在"又问黛玉"的译文"He returned to his interrogation of Dai-yu."中，汉语中的动词"问"被转化为英语中的名词"interrogation"，体现出汉语是喜用动词的动态语言，英语是喜用名词、形容词的静态语言。同时，"returned"一词的运用显示出和上文的连接关系。该译文增译了"like the one he was born with"，点明了宝玉是问黛玉有没有一块"像他出生时所衔的玉一样"的玉，意思更为清楚。

【7】"宝玉听了，登时发作起痴狂病来，摘下那玉，就狠命摔去，骂道：'什么罕物，连人之高低不择，还说"通灵"不"通灵"呢！我也不要这劳什子了！'"主语"宝玉"发出了一连串的动作：听了、发作、摘下、摔去、骂道。杨译是"This instantly threw Pao-yu into one of his frenzies. Tearing off the jade he flung it on the ground. "What's rare about it?" he stormed. "It can't even tell good people from bad. What spiritual understanding has it got? I don't want this nuisance either."译者用句子化词法把"宝玉听了"这个小短句译为代词

"This（指代上文中黛玉说的那番话）"，并让它充当主语，和后文"threw Pao-yu into one of his frenzies"自然衔接成一句；接着，"摘下"和"摔去"两个动词分别被处理成现在分词短语充当的伴随状语"Tearing off..."和谓语"flung"，表明这两个动作先后发生。霍译是"This sent Bao-yu off instantly into one of his mad fits. Snatching the jade from his neck he hurled it violently on the floor as if to smash it and began abusing it passionately. 'Rare object! Rare object! What's so lucky about a stone that can't even tell which people are better than others? Beastly thing! I don't want it!'"，第一句的处理方法和杨译的完全相同：将"宝玉听了"译为代词"this"；接着，在翻译"宝玉"发出的一连串动作时，译者用了现在分词"snatching"翻译原文中的"摘下"，snatch一词非常生动，有"迅速拿走、夺走"的意思，比"tear off"表达的动作更快、更猛烈；"摔去"被译为"hurled it... on the floor"，为强化"狠命"的效果，译者增加了表达程度的副词"violently"和表达方式的"as if to smash it"，来描写他发疯要把玉砸碎的状态；最后，译者将"辱骂"译为"began abusing"，并增加副词"passionately"，这些动词、副词以及现在分词的使用增加了译文的画面感和生动性。

【8】"吓的地下众人一拥争去拾玉。贾母急的搂了宝玉道：'孽障！你生气，要打骂人容易，何苦摔那命根子！'"杨译是"In consternation all the maids rushed forward to pick up the jade while the Lady Dowager in desperation took Pao-yu in her arms. 'You wicked monster!' she scolded. 'Storm at people if you're in a passion. But why should you throw away that precious thing your life depends on?'"第一句的句式结构很平衡，用"while"连接了两个主语不同的分句，第一个分句中"all the maids"的状态是"in consternation（在惊恐中）"，第二个分句中"the Lady Dowager"的状态是"in desperation（在绝望中）"。下文中将"打骂人"译为"storm at people"，显然只强调了"骂人"。"你生气"被译为"if you're in a passion"，译者在此处增加了连词"if"，将上下文的逻辑关系明确地表达了出来。霍译是"The maids all seemed terrified and rushed forward to pick it up, while Grandmother Jia clung to Bao-yu in alarm. 'Naughty, naughty boy! Shout at someone or strike them if you like when you are in a nasty temper, but why go smashing that precious thing that your very life depends on?'"第一句中也使用了"while"连句,同时将"贾母急的"译为"Grandmother Jia... in alarm",更准确地表达出贾母担心焦急的状态。"打骂人"译为"shout at someone or strike them",分别译出了"打"和"骂"的意思。"你生气"被译为"when you are in a nasty temper",增加了表示逻辑关系的连词"when"。动词"摔"分别被两位译者处理为"throw away"和"smashing","smash"表达的程度更强烈一些。"命根子"一词在英语中没有对应词汇,两位译者都采用了解释性的翻译手法:杨译是"that precious thing your life depends on",霍译是"that precious thing that your very life depends on"。

【9】"如今来了这们一个神仙似的妹妹也没有,"一句中,"神仙似的妹妹"具有中国文化意涵,杨译"Even this newly arrived cousin who's lovely as a fairy hasn't got one either."采用了异化法,将"神仙"一词译为"fairy";霍译"And now this new cousin comes here who is as beautiful as an angel and she hasn't got one either."采用了归化法,将其译为"angel"。

【10】"宝玉听如此说,想一想大有情理,也就不生别论了。"主语"宝玉"发出一连串的动作:听、想、不生别论。杨译是"And Pao-yu, convinced by her tale, let the matter drop."其中,"听如此说""想一想大有情理"被处理为过去分词短语"convinced by her tale",在句中充当原因状语。霍译是"And Bao-yu, after reflecting for a moment or two on what she had said, offered no further resistance.""听如此说""想一想大有情理"被处理为介词短语"after reflecting",在句中充当时间状语。

四、词汇表

1. dusky [ˈdʌski]	adj.	not very bright; dark or soft in colour 昏暗的;暗淡的;(颜色)暗的,柔和的
2. arch [ɑːtʃ]	v.	to be in a curved line or shape across or over sth 呈拱形覆盖;呈弧形横跨
	adj.	arched

3. frailty [ˈfreɪlti]		n.	weakness and poor health 虚弱；衰弱
4. sparkle [ˈspɑːk(ə)l]		v.	to shine brightly with small flashes of light 闪烁；闪耀
5. repose [rɪˈpəʊz]		n.	a state of rest, sleep or feeling calm 休息；睡眠；平静；镇静
6. pliant [ˈplaɪənt]		adj.	(of sth) that can be bent easily without breaking it 易弯的；柔韧的
7. mystify [ˈmɪstɪfaɪ]		v.	to make sb confused because they do not understand sth 迷惑；使迷惑不解；使糊涂
		n.	mystification
8. frenzy [ˈfrenzi]		n.	a state of great activity and strong emotion that is often violent or frightening and not under control 疯狂；狂乱；狂暴
9. consternation [ˌkɒnstəˈneɪʃ(ə)n]		n.	a feeling of great surprise, shock or anxiety （极度的）惊愕；震惊；惊惶
10. piety [ˈpaɪəti]		n.	the state of having or showing a deep respect for sb/sth, especially for God and religion 虔诚
11. chide [tʃaɪd]		v.	to criticize or blame sb because they have done sth wrong 批评；指责；责备
12. indulgent [ɪnˈdʌldʒ(ə)nt]		adj.	tending to allow sb to have or do whatever they want 放纵的；纵容的
		adv.	indulgently
13. surmise [səˈmaɪz]		v.	to guess or suppose sth using the evidence you have, without definitely knowing 推测；猜测
14. wreathe [riːð]		v.	to surround or cover sth 环绕；覆盖；笼罩
15. bestow [bɪˈstəʊ]		v.	to give sth to sb, especially to show how much they are respected 给予；授予；献给

16. glisten ['glɪs(ə)n]	v.	(of sth wet) to shine 闪光；闪亮
17. gasp [gɑːsp]	n.	a quick deep breath, usually caused by a strong emotion（常指由强烈情感引起的）深吸气；喘气；倒抽气
18. caress [kəˈres]	v.	to touch sb/sth gently, especially in a sexual way or in a way that shows affection 抚摩；爱抚
19. tithe [taɪð]	n.	(especially in the past) a tenth or other fixed part of the goods that sb produces or the money that they earn, that they give regularly to help support the Church（尤指旧时按固定比例缴纳给教会的）什一税；捐税；捐款
20. interrogate [ɪnˈterəgeɪt]	v.	to ask sb a lot of questions over a long period of time, especially in an aggressive way 讯问；审问；盘问
	n.	interrogation
21. divine [dɪˈvaɪn]	v.	to find out sth by guessing 猜到；领悟
22. fit [fɪt]	n.	a short period of very strong feeling（强烈感情）发作；冲动
23. hurl [hɜːl]	v.	to throw sth/sb violently in a particular direction 猛扔；猛投；猛摔
24. hysterical [hɪˈsterɪk(ə)l]	adj.	in a state of extreme excitement, and crying, laughing, etc. in an uncontrolled way 歇斯底里的；情绪狂暴不可抑止的
	adv.	hysterically
25. coax [kəʊks]	v.	to persuade sb to do sth by talking to them in a kind and gentle way 哄劝；劝诱

薄命女偏逢薄命郎　　葫芦僧乱判葫芦案[1]

An Ill-Fated Girl Meets an Ill-Fated Man
A Confounded Monk Ends a Confounded Case [1] (Yang)

The Bottle-gourd girl meets an unfortunate young man
And the Bottle-gourd monk settles a protracted lawsuit [1] (Hawkes)

一、本回概述

遭薛蟠家奴打死之人名叫冯渊。冯渊年十九，本好男风，遇被拐后长大的英莲，愿结良缘，遂于拐贩处买下英莲，择定三日后过门。谁知拐贩又将英莲卖于薛蟠。冯渊与薛蟠争夺英莲，互不相让，冯渊遇害。由贾政举荐，时任应天府府尹的贾雨村恰巧受理此案。雨村本想秉公明断，却被府中门子（昔日葫芦庙沙弥）劝阻。门子把薛蟠及本省贾、史、王、薛四大家族之间的利害关系相告后，雨村徇私枉法，依从门子之计，草草结案。随后，薛夫人带领薛蟠、薛宝钗上京投靠贾府，借住梨香院。

二、篇章节选

原文

雨村听了，亦叹道："这也是他们的孽障遭遇，亦非偶然。[2]不然冯渊如何偏只看准了这英莲？这英莲受了拐子这几年折磨，才得了个头路，且又是个多情的，若能聚合了，倒是件美事，[3]偏又生出这段事来。这薛家纵比冯家富贵，想其为人，自然姬妾众多，淫佚无度，未必及冯渊定情于一人者。[4]这正是梦幻情缘，恰遇一对薄命儿女。[5]且不要议论他，只目今这官司，如何剖断才好？"门子笑道："老爷当年何其明决，[6]今日何反成了个没主意的人了！小的闻得老爷补升此任，亦系贾府王府之力，此薛蟠即贾府之亲，[7]老爷何不顺水行舟，作个整人情，将此案了结，日后也好去见贾府王府。[8]"雨村道："你说的何尝不是。但事关人命，蒙皇上隆恩，起复委用，实是重生再造，正当殚心竭力图报之时，岂可因私而废法？是我实不能忍为者。"门子听了，冷笑道："老爷说的何尝不是大道理，但只是如今世上是行不去的。[9]岂不闻古人有云：'大丈夫相时而动'，又曰：'趋吉避凶者为君子'。[10]依老爷这一说，不但不能报效朝廷，亦且自身不保，还要三思为妥。"

杨译

"This was retribution, no accident," replied Yu-tsun with a sigh. [2] "Otherwise, why should Feng Yuan have taken a fancy to Ying-lien and no one else? As for her, after being knocked about all those years by the kidnapper she at last saw a way out with a man who loved her, and if she'd married him all would have been well; [3] but then this had to happen! Of course, Hsueh's family is richer than Feng's, but a profligate like Hsueh Pan is sure to have troops of maids and concubines and to be thoroughly debauched—he could never be as true to one girl as Feng Yuan. [4] So this romance was an empty dream, a chance encounter between an ill-fated young couple. [5] Well, enough of that. What's the best way to settle this case?"

"Your Honour used to be shrewd enough in the past,"[6] said the attendant with a smile. "What's made you so short of ideas today? I heard that your appointment was due to the good offices of the Chias and Wangs, and this Hsueh is related to the Chias by marriage.[7] So why not sail with the stream and do them a good turn, settling this case in such a way that you can face them in future?"[8]

"There's much in what you say. But a man's life is involved. Moreover, I've been re-instated by the Emperor's favour and am in fact beginning a new life. I should be doing my utmost to show my gratitude. How can I flout the law for private considerations? I really can't bring myself to do such a thing."

The attendant sneered: "Your Honour is right, of course. But that won't get you anywhere in the world today.[9] Remember the old sayings: 'A gentleman adapts himself to circumstances' and 'The superior man is one who pursues good fortune and avoids disaster.'[10] If you do as you just said, not only will you be unable to repay the Emperor's trust, you may endanger your own life into the bargain. Better think it over carefully."

霍译

Yu-cun sighed sympathetically. 'Their meeting cannot have been coincidental. It must have been the working out of some destiny. An atonement.[2] Otherwise, how is one to account for Feng Yuan's sudden affection for that particular girl?

'And Ying-lian, after all those years of ill-treatment at the hands of her kidnapper, suddenly seeing a road to freedom opening in front of her—for she was a girl of feeling, and there is no doubt that they would have made a fine couple if they had succeeded in coming together[3]—and then for this to have happened!

'And even though Xue may be far wealthier and better-placed than Feng was, a man like that is sure to have numbers of concubines and paramours and to be licentious and debauched in his habits—quite incapable of concentrating all his affections on one girl as Feng Yuan would have done.[4]

'A real case of an ideal romance on the one hand and a pair of unlucky young things on the other adding up to make a tragedy!'[5]

'But a truce to this discussion of other people's affairs! Let us rather consider how this case is to be settled!'

'Your Honour used to be decisive enough in the old days,'[6] said the usher with a smile. 'What has become of your old resolution today? Now, I was told that your promotion to this post was due to the combined influence of the Jias and the Wangs; and this Xue Pan is related to the Jias by marriage.[7] Why not trim your sails to the wind in your handling of this case? Why not make a virtue of necessity by doing them a favour which will stand you in good stead next time you see them?'[8]

'What you say is, of course, entirely correct,' said Yu-cun. 'But there is, after all, a human life involved in this case; and you have to remember that I have only just been restored to office by an act of Imperial clemency. I really cannot bring myself to pervert justice for private ends at the very moment when I ought to be doing my utmost to show my gratitude.'

The usher smiled coldly. 'What Your Honour says is no doubt very right and proper, but it won't wash.'[9] Not the way things are in the world today! Haven't you heard the old saying "The man of spirit shapes his actions to the passing moment"? And there's another old saying: "It is the mark of a gentleman to avoid what is inauspicious".[10] If you were to act in accordance with what you have just said, not only would you *not* be able to show your gratitude to the Emperor, but also you would probably put your own life in danger. If I were you, I should think very carefully before you do anything.'

三、注释评点

【1】本回回目"薄命女偏逢薄命郎 葫芦僧乱判葫芦案"中出现了两组重复词语："薄命"和"葫芦"，杨译是："An Ill-Fated Girl Meets an Ill-Fated Man A Confounded Monk Ends a Confounded Case"。可以看出，杨译想尽量保留原文的形式和内容，所以，"ill-fated"和"confounded"在译文中出现了两

次，但美中不足之处在于，"confounded"只能传达"葫芦"的内涵意义（葫芦的谐音是"糊涂"），而无法保留其外在形式。霍译是"The Bottle-gourd girl meets an unfortunate young man And the Bottle-gourd monk settles a protracted lawsuit"，译文与原文出入较大，译者自己创造的成分较多。

【2】"雨村听了，亦叹道：'这也是他们的孽障遭遇，亦非偶然。'"一句，杨译"'This was retribution, no accident,' replied Yu-tsun with a sigh."将"孽障"一词译为"retribution"，即"报应"的意思，语意有些重，有道德审判的口气，因为本句只是表达贾雨村对英莲和冯渊遭遇的同情。霍译是"Yu-cun sighed sympathetically. 'Their meeting cannot have been coincidental. It must have been the working out of some destiny. An atonement.'"。译者首先用"sighed sympathetically"点明了贾雨村的同情之意，然后将"孽障"译为"the working out of some destiny"，即此事是命运的安排，不由人力做主，接着又补充了一句"An atonement."，"atonement"意为"赎罪"，即过去做了不好的事，现在是补赎。对比两个译文，霍译将贾雨村同情的语气翻译得更准确一些。

【3】"若能聚合了，倒是件美事，"是假设句，杨译"... if she'd married him all would have been well"和霍译"... they would have made a fine couple if they had succeeded in coming together"都使用了与过去事实相反的虚拟语气。

【4】"自然姬妾众多，淫佚无度，未必及冯渊定情于一人者。"一句，杨译"... but a profligate like Hsueh Pan is sure to have troops of maids and concubines and to be thoroughly debauched—he could never be as true to one girl as Feng Yuan."将"姬妾众多"处理为"have troops of maids and concubines"，其中，量词"troops（成群的）"用得很好；但"maids"是"女仆"的意思，显然不是原文中"姬妾"要表达的意思。霍译"... a man like that is sure to have numbers of concubines and paramours and to be licentious and debauched in his habits—quite incapable of concentrating all his affections on one girl as Feng Yuan would have done."将句子"未必及冯渊定情于一人者"处理为形容词短语"quite incapable of concentrating all his affections on one girl as Feng Yuan would have done"，并用破折号与前文连接，用以解释说明前文。另外，"concentrating all his affections on..."把"定情"中的专注之意表达了出来。

【5】"这正是梦幻情缘,恰遇一对薄命儿女。"是贾雨村对这个案子的一句断语,杨译"So this romance was an empty dream, a chance encounter between an ill-fated young couple."用"an empty dream"翻译"梦幻情缘",用"a chance encounter(偶然邂逅)"做"an empty dream"的同位语,对其进行补充说明。霍译"A real case of an ideal romance on the one hand and a pair of unlucky young things on the other adding up to make a tragedy!"中增译了一些内容,译者首先用"a real case"作为统领,带出下文两件事:一是"an ideal romance on the one hand";二是"a pair of unlucky young things on the other",然后增加了"adding up to make a tragedy"。原文中的"恰遇"强调的是梦幻情缘,加上薄命儿女,造成了这场悲剧,霍译把原文中隐含的语义全部表达出来了。

【6】"老爷当年何其明决,"一句中,"明决"是"聪明决断"的意思,杨译"Your Honour used to be shrewd enough in the past"将"明决"译为"shrewd(精明的)",强调的是聪明。霍译"Your Honour used to be decisive enough in the old days"使用的是"decisive(果断的)"一词,意思更准确一些,因为"果断"暗含"聪明"之意。

【7】"此薛蟠即贾府之亲,"一句,王夫人与薛姨妈是一母所生的同胞姐妹,因王夫人嫁入贾府,所以王夫人之妹与其子女俱是贾府之亲。此处杨、霍二位译者都将本句译为"... is related to the Chias / Jias by marriage",是非常准确的,强调通过联姻,薛蟠与贾府结为亲戚。

【8】"老爷何不顺水行舟,作个整人情,将此案了结,日后也好去见贾府王府。"是一句反说,来表示委婉建议,二位译者都使用了"why not"省略结构。另外,本句汉语是流水递进结构,共有三层意思:一、何不顺水行舟做个人情;二、将此案了结;三、也好去见贾、王二公。杨译文是"So why not sail with the stream and do them a good turn, settling this case in such a way that you can face them in future?",整个句子由主干加上现在分词短语构成,整体上呈现偏正态势,译者先用句子主干"why not sail with the stream and do them a good turn"给出建议,然后用现在分词短语"settling this case"做结果状语,即"顺水行舟做个人情"的结果就会是"settling this case",接着又是"such... that..."结构引导的结果状语从句。杨译的连句手段十分巧妙,将汉语的三段信

息译成了一个长句，体现了英语的层次感。霍译"Why not trim your sails to the wind in your handling of this case? Why not make a virtue of necessity by doing them a favour which will stand you in good stead next time you see them?"连用了两个"why not"省略结构，表达出强烈建议的语气，并在第二句中使用"which"进行句内连接。

【9】"老爷说的何尝不是大道理，但只是如今世上是行不去的。"句中，"行不去"的意思是"行不通的"。霍译文"What Your Honour says is no doubt very right and proper, but it won't wash."在翻译"行不去的"时，使用了句型"sth won't/doesn't wash with sb"，意思是：（解释、借口等）站不住脚，令某人不能接受（used to say that sb's explanation, excuse, etc. is not valid or that you/sb. else will not accept it）。

【10】"'大丈夫相时而动'，又曰：'趋吉避凶者为君子'。"两位译者的处理各不相同。杨译"'A gentleman adapts himself to circumstances' and 'The superior man is one who pursues good fortune and avoids disaster.'"将"大丈夫"译为"gentleman"，下文中的"who pursues good fortune and avoids disaster"将"趋吉避凶"的意涵都表达了出来。霍译"Haven't you heard the old saying 'The man of spirit shapes his actions to the passing moment'? And there's another old saying:'It is the mark of a gentleman to avoid what is inauspicious'."将"大丈夫"译为"the man of spirit"，处理得很有特色，"spirit"在此处是"勇气、志气"的意思，"the man of spirit"即"志勇兼备之人"。另外，霍译"to avoid what is inauspicious"省译了"趋吉"，只译出了"避凶"的意思。

四、词汇表

1. retribution [ˌretrɪˈbjuːʃən]   n.   severe punishment for sth seriously wrong that sb has done 严惩；惩罚；报应

2. profligate [ˈprɒflɪɡət]   n.   a person who uses money, time, materials, etc. in a careless way 放荡者；享乐者

3. debauched [dɪˈbɔːtʃt]   adj.   a debauched person is immoral in their

		sexual behavior, drinks a lot of alcohol, takes drugs, etc. 道德败坏的；淫荡的；沉湎酒色的；嗜毒的
4. chance [tʃɑːns]	*adj.*	not planned 意外的；偶然的；碰巧的
5. shrewd [ʃruːd]	*adj.*	clever at understanding and making judgments about a situation 精明的；敏锐的；有眼光的；精于盘算的
6. flout [flaʊt]	*v.*	to show that you have no respect for a law, etc. by openly not obeying it 公然藐视；无视（法律等）
7. atone [əˈtəʊn]	*v.*	to act in a way that shows you are sorry for doing sth wrong in the past 赎（罪）；弥补（过错）
	n.	atonement
8. paramour [ˈpærəmʊə]	*n.*	a person that sb is having a romantic or sexual relationship with 情人；情妇；情夫
9. licentious [laɪˈsenʃəs]	*adj.*	behaving in a way that is considered sexually immoral 放荡的；淫荡的；淫乱的
10. truce [truːs]	*n.*	an agreement between enemies or opponents to stop fighting for an agreed period of time; the period of time that this lasts 停战协定；休战；停战期
11. decisive [dɪˈsaɪsɪv]	*adj.*	able to decide sth quickly and with confidence 坚决的；果断的；决断的
12. trim your sails		to arrange the sails of a boat to suit the wind so that the boat moves faster 随风扬帆；见风使舵
13. stand sb in good stead		to be useful or helpful to sb when needed

			（需要时）对某人有用；对某人有利
14. clemency [ˈklemənsi]		*n.*	kindness shown to sb when they are being punished; willingness not to punish sb so severely（对受惩罚的人表现出的）仁慈，慈悲；宽恕；宽容
15. pervert [pəˈvɜːt]		*v.*	to change a system, process, etc. in a bad way so that it is not what it used to be or what it should be 败坏；使走样；误导；误用
16. inauspicious [ˌɪnɔːˈspɪʃəs]		*adj.*	showing signs that the future will not be good or successful 预示前景黯淡的；不祥的；不吉利的

第五回

游幻境指迷十二钗　饮仙醪曲演红楼梦[1]

灵石迷性难解仙机　警幻多情秘垂淫训[1]
The Spiritual Stone Is too Bemused to Grasp the Fairy's Riddles
The Goddess of Disenchantment in Her Kindness Secretly Expounds on Love[1] (Yang)

贾宝玉神游太虚境　警幻仙曲演红楼梦[1]
Jia Bao-yu visits the Land of Illusion
And the fairy Disenchantment performs the 'Dream of Golden Days'[1] (Hawkes)

一、本回概述

　　黛玉入贾府后，与宝玉一起于贾母处抚养。一日，贾母一行人到宁府赏花，宝玉倦怠，入秦可卿内室歇息，于梦中遇警幻仙子指引，游太虚幻境，获阅《金陵十二钗正册》《金陵十二钗副册》等判词，又听《红楼梦》曲。之后，警幻仙子授宝玉云雨之事，并许其妹可卿于宝玉。后宝玉与可卿同游至"迷津"，被夜叉、海鬼拖拉，受惊，唤可卿相救。袭人等忙上前安慰。室外，秦氏听见十分诧异，因其乳名正是"可卿"。

二、篇章节选

原文

如今且说林黛玉自在荣府以来,贾母万般怜爱,寝食起居,一如宝玉,迎春、探春、惜春三个亲孙女倒且靠后;便是宝玉和黛玉二人之亲密友爱处,亦自较别个不同,[2]日则同行同坐,夜则同息同止,真是言和意顺,略无参商。[3]不想如今忽然来了一个薛宝钗,年岁虽大不多,然品格端方,容貌丰美,人多谓黛玉所不及。[4]而且宝钗行为豁达,随分从时,不比黛玉孤高自许,目无下尘,故比黛玉大得下人之心。便是那些小丫头子们,亦多喜与宝钗去顽。[5]因此黛玉心中便有些悒郁不忿之意,宝钗却浑然不觉。那宝玉亦在孩提之间,况自天性所禀来的一片愚拙偏僻,[6]视姊妹弟兄皆出一意,并无亲疏远近之别。其中因与黛玉同随贾母一处坐卧,故略比别个姊妹熟惯些。既熟惯,便更觉亲密;既亲密,则不免一时有求全之毁,不虞之隙。这日不知为何,他二人言语有些不合起来,黛玉又气的独在房中垂泪,宝玉又自悔言语冒撞,前去俯就,那黛玉方渐渐的回转来。[7]

杨译

Since her coming to the Jung Mansion, the Lady Dowager had been lavishing affection on her, treating her in every respect just like Pao-yu so that Ying-chun, Tan-chun and Hsi-chun, the Chia girls, all had to take a back seat. And Pao-yu and Tai-yu had drawn closer to each other than all the others.[2] By day they strolled or sat together; at night they went to bed in the same apartment. On all matters, indeed, they were in complete accord.[3]

But now Pao-chai had suddenly appeared on the scene. Although only slightly older, she was such a proper young lady and so charming that most people considered Tai-yu inferior to her.[4]

Besides, Pao-chai's generous, tactful, and accommodating ways contrasted strongly with Tai-yu's stand-offish reserve and won the hearts of her subordinates, so that nearly all the maids liked to chat with her. [5] Because of this, Tai-yu began to feel some twinges of jealousy. But of this Pao-chai was completely unaware.

Pao-yu was still only a boy and a very absurd and wilful one at that, [6] who treated his brothers, sisters and cousins alike, making no difference between close and distant kinsmen. Because he and Tai-yu both lived in the Lady Dowager's quarters, he was closer to her than to the other girls, and being closer had grown more intimate; but precisely because of this he sometimes offended her by being too demanding and thoughtless.

Today the two of them had fallen out for some reason and Tai-yu, alone in her room, was again shedding tears. Sorry for his tactlessness, Pao-yu went in to make it up and little by little contrived to comfort her. [7a]

霍译

From the moment Lin Dai-yu entered the Rong mansion, Grandmother Jia's solicitude for her had manifested itself in a hundred different ways. The arrangements made for her meals and accommodation were exactly the same as for Bao-yu. The other three granddaughters, Ying-chun, Tan-chun and Xi-chun, were relegated to a secondary place in the old lady's affections, and the objects of her partiality themselves began to feel an affection for each other which far exceeded what they felt for any of the rest. [2] Sharing each other's company every minute of the day and sleeping in the same room at night, they developed an understanding so intense that it was almost as if they had grown into a single person. [3]

And now suddenly this Xue Bao-chai had appeared on the scene—a young lady who, though very little older than Dai-yu, possessed a grown-up beauty and aplomb in which all agreed Dai-yu was her inferior. [4] Moreover, in contrast to Dai-yu with her air of lofty self-sufficiency and total obliviousness to all who did not move on the same exalted level as herself, Bao-chai had a generous, accommodating disposition which greatly endeared her to subordinates, so that even the tiniest maid looked on Miss Bao-chai as a familiar friend. [5] Dai-yu could not but feel somewhat put out by this—a fact of which Bao-chai herself, however, was totally unaware.

As for Bao-yu, he was still only a child—a child, moreover, whom nature had endowed with the eccentric obtuseness of a simpleton.[6] Brothers, sisters, cousins, were all one to him. In his relationships with people he made no distinction between one person and another. If his relationship with Dai-yu was exceptional, it was because greater proximity—since she was living with him in his grandmother's quarters—made her more familiar to him than the rest; and greater familiarity bred greater intimacy.

And of course, with greater intimacy came the occasional tiffs and misunderstandings that are usual with people who have a great deal to do with each other.

One day the two of them had fallen out over something or other and the argument had ended with Dai-yu crying alone in her room and Bao-yu feeling remorsefully that perhaps he had spoken too roughly. Presently he went in to make his peace with her and gradually, very gradually, Dai-yu's equanimity was restored.[7b]

三、注释评点

【1】人民文学出版社的《红楼梦》版本中,该回回目是"游幻境指迷十二钗 饮仙醪曲演红楼梦"。有正本此回回目是"灵石迷性难解仙机 警幻多情秘垂淫训"。程本此回回目是"贾宝玉神游太虚境 警幻仙曲演红楼梦"。杨译和霍译因为采用的底本不同,所以,在第五回回目的翻译上,呈现出不同的译文。此处,杨译依据的是有正本,霍译依据的是程本。

【2】"如今且说林黛玉自在荣府以来,贾母万般怜爱,寝食起居,一如宝玉,迎春、探春、惜春三个亲孙女倒且靠后;便是宝玉和黛玉二人之亲密友爱处,亦自较别个不同,"一句中,为了体现贾母的万般怜爱和黛玉的与众不同,作者列举了三件事:一是黛玉的饮食起居和宝玉一样;二是三个孙女靠后;三是宝、黛二人的亲密程度也较别人不同。杨译"Since her coming to the Jung Mansion, the Lady Dowager had been lavishing affection on her, treating her in every respect just like Pao-yu so that Ying-chun, Tan-chun and Hsi-chun, the Chia girls, all had to take a back seat. And Pao-yu and Tai-yu had drawn closer to each other than all the others." 包含两句话，第一句的连句手段使用了现在分词短语 "treating her in every respect just like Pao-yu" 作方式状语，后接 "so that" 引导的结果状语从句。第一句和第二句译文之间使用了 "And"，将三件事说到了一起。另外，译者使用了句子化短语法将句子 "如今且说林黛玉，自在荣府以来，" 译为介词短语 "Since her coming to the Jung Mansion"。霍译 "From the moment Lin Dai-yu entered the Rong mansion, Grandmother Jia's solicitude for her had manifested itself in a hundred different ways. The arrangements made for her meals and accommodation were exactly the same as for Bao-yu. The other three granddaughters, Ying-chun, Tan-chun and Xi-chun, were relegated to a secondary place in the old lady's affections, and the objects of her partiality themselves began to feel an affection for each other which far exceeded what they felt for any of the rest." 是由三个句子构成：首先在第一句译文中用 "in a hundred different ways" 总领概括，然后在接下来的两句译文中将三件事情一一罗列出来。"the objects of her partiality" 指的是贾母偏爱的两个对象，即宝玉和黛玉。

【3】"日则同行同坐，夜则同息同止，真是言和意顺，略无参商。"一句中，"略无参商"一词指两人感情非常和睦，参商指二十八星宿中的参星和商星。两星不同时在天空出现，因此 "参商" 被用来比喻亲友分隔两地不得相见，也比喻人与人感情不和睦。杨译 "By day they strolled or sat together; at night they went to bed in the same apartment. On all matters, indeed, they were in complete accord." 使用了短语 "in accord with sth/sb" 来翻译 "言和意顺，略无参商"，意为 "与……一致或相符合"。霍译 "Sharing each other's company every minute of the day and sleeping in the same room at night, they developed an understanding so intense that it was almost as if they had grown into a single person." 使用了 "sharing..." 和 "sleeping..." 两个现在分词短语做原因状语。另外，"developed an understanding" 表达出两人因相处日久而逐渐情投意合的意思。霍译又用了 "as if they had grown into a single person" 这一生动的比喻表达出两人略无参商、如胶似漆的亲密关系。

【4】"不想如今忽然来了一个薛宝钗，年岁虽大不多，然品格端方，容貌丰美，人多谓黛玉所不及。"一句，杨译"But now Pao-chai had suddenly appeared on the scene. Although only slightly older, she was such a proper young lady and so charming that most people considered Tai-yu inferior to her." 首先用"But now"承上启下，第二句句内使用了"Although"和"such/so... that..."进行连句。霍译是一个长句："And now suddenly this Xue Bao-chai had appeared on the scene—a young lady who, though very little older than Dai-yu, possessed a grown-up beauty and aplomb in which all agreed Dai-yu was her inferior."，译者使用了"And, who, though, in which"进行连接：开句使用"and now"承上启下，接着用一个破折号引出下文，进一步描述薛宝钗。"a young lady"是主语"this Xue Bao-chai"的同位语，对其进行补充说明，后面带了一个"who"引导的定语从句，这个定语从句中又包含一个"though"引导的让步状语从句的省略式和一个"in which"引导的定语从句。"inferior"既可当形容词也可当名词使用：杨译中是形容词，霍译中是名词。

【5】"而且宝钗行为豁达，随分从时，不比黛玉孤高自许，目无下尘，故比黛玉大得下人之心。便是那些小丫头子们，亦多喜与宝钗去顽。"一句，两位译者都是用长句翻译的。杨译是"Besides, Pao-chai's generous, tactful, and accommodating ways contrasted strongly with Tai-yu's stand-offish reserve and won the hearts of her subordinates, so that nearly all the maids liked to chat with her."本句没有用"Pao-chai"做主语，而是用"Pao-chai's generous, tactful, and accommodating ways"做主语，接着是并列谓语"contrasted"和"won"，句尾是"so that"引导的结果状语从句。霍译是"Moreover, in contrast to Dai-yu with her air of lofty self-sufficiency and total obliviousness to all who did not move on the same exalted level as herself, Bao-chai had a generous, accommodating disposition which greatly endeared her to subordinates, so that even the tiniest maid looked on Miss Bao-chai as a familiar friend." 译者在句首用"in contrast to"这个介词短语将宝钗和黛玉作对比，接着，全句通过"who"，"which"和"so that"进行句内连接。另外，"小丫头子"一词的翻译，杨译用的是"nearly all the maids"，霍译用的是"even the tiniest maid"，显然后者更加符合原文的语气。

【6】"那宝玉亦在孩提之间,况自天性所禀来的一片愚拙偏僻"一句,杨译是"Pao-yu was still only a boy and a very absurd and wilful one...";霍译是"As for Bao-yu, he was still only a child—a child, moreover, whom nature had endowed with the eccentric obtuseness of a simpleton."相较之下,霍译通过使用"nature had endowed with"把"天性所禀"的意思表达了出来。

【7a】"宝玉又自悔言语冒撞,前去俯就,那黛玉方渐渐的回转来。"句中有两个主语:宝玉和黛玉。杨译是"Sorry for his tactlessness, Pao-yu went in to make it up and little by little contrived to comfort her."译者使用了句子化短语法将小句"宝玉又自悔言语冒撞"译为形容词短语"Sorry for his tactlessness",在译文中充当原因状语,接着,译者使用"Pao-yu"做主语,紧跟一连串的动作"went in","make it up","contrived"和"comfort",放弃了原文中的"黛玉"这一主语,翻译得很有技巧。

【7b】"这日不知为何,他二人言语有些不合起来,黛玉又气的独在房中垂泪,宝玉又自悔言语冒撞,前去俯就,那黛玉方渐渐的回转来。"霍译是"One day the two of them had fallen out over something or other and the argument had ended with Dai-yu crying alone in her room and Bao-yu feeling remorsefully that perhaps he had spoken too roughly. Presently he went in to make his peace with her and gradually, very gradually, Dai-yu's equanimity was restored."其中,"with Dai-yu crying alone in her room and Bao-yu feeling remorsefully that…"是独立主格结构,现在分词 feeling 具有动词的特性:后面带了宾语从句"that perhaps he had spoken too roughly"。"黛玉方渐渐的回转来"中的"渐渐"一词,霍译是"gradually, very gradually",生动地体现出黛玉爱使小性子,很难平复情绪的性格特征。

四、词汇表

| 1. lavish [ˈlævɪʃ] | v. | to give a lot of sth, often too much, to sb/sth 过分给予;滥施 |
| 2. stroll [strəʊl] | v. | to walk somewhere in a slow relaxed way 散步;溜达;闲逛 |

3. tactful [ˈtæktfʊl]	adj.	careful not to say or do anything that will annoy or upset other people 圆通的；得体的；不得罪人的
4. accommodating [əˈkɒmədeɪtɪŋ]	adj.	willing to help and do things for other people 乐于助人的；与人方便的
5. stand-offish [stændˈɔːfɪʃ]	adj.	not friendly towards other people 冷淡的；冷漠的
6. reserve [rɪˈzɜːv]	n.	the quality that sb has when they do not talk easily to other people about their ideas, feelings, etc. 内向；寡言少语；矜持
7. subordinate [səˈbɔːdɪnət]	n.	a person who has a position with less authority and power than sb else in an organization 下级；部属
8. twinge [twɪn(d)ʒ]	n.	a sudden short feeling of an unpleasant emotion （一阵）不快；难过；痛苦
9. absurd [əbˈsɜːd]	adj.	completely ridiculous; not logical and sensible 荒谬的；荒唐的；怪诞不经的
10. wilful [ˈwɪlfʊl]	adj.	determined to do what you want; not caring about what other people want 任性的；固执的；倔强的
11. fall out (with sb)		to quarrel with sb so that you are no longer friendly with them （与某人）争吵，吵架
12. contrive [kənˈtraɪv]	v.	to manage to do sth in spite of difficulties （不顾困难而）设法做到
13. solicitude [səˈlɪsɪtjuːd]	n.	anxious care for sb's comfort, health or happiness 牵挂；关怀；关切
14. partiality [ˌpɑːʃɪˈæləti]	n.	the unfair support of one person, team,

		idea, etc. 偏袒
15. aplomb [əˈplɒm]	n.	if sb does sth with aplomb, they do it in a confident and successful way, often in a difficult situation 镇定；沉着；泰然自若
16. lofty [ˈlɒfti]	adj.	showing a belief that you are worth more than other people 傲慢的；高傲的
17. oblivious [əˈblɪviəs]	adj.	not aware of sth 不知道；未注意；未察觉
	n.	obliviousness
18. exalted [ɪgˈzɔːltɪd]	adj.	of high rank, position or great importance 地位高的；高贵的；显赫的
19. put sb out		to make sb upset or offended 使烦恼；使生气
20. eccentric [ɪkˈsentrɪk]	adj.	considered by other people to be strange or unusual 古怪的；异乎寻常的
21. obtuse [əbˈtjuːs]	adj.	slow or unwilling to understand sth 迟钝的；愚蠢的；态度勉强的
	n.	obtuseness
22. simpleton [ˈsɪmp(ə)lt(ə)n]	n.	a person who is not very intelligent and can be tricked easily 傻瓜；易上当受骗的人
23. proximity [prɒkˈsɪmɪti]	n.	the state of being near sb/sth in distance or time （时间或空间）接近；邻近；靠近
24. tiff [tɪf]	n.	a slight argument between close friends or lovers （朋友或情人之间的）争执；拌嘴，口角，吵嘴
25. remorse [rɪˈmɔːs]	n.	the feeling of being extremely sorry for sth wrong or bad that you have done 懊悔；自责
	adj.	remorseful

	adv.	remorsefully
26. equanimity [ˌekwəˈnɪmɪti]	*n.*	a calm state of mind which means that you do not become angry or upset, especially in difficult situations（尤指处于困境时的）镇静；沉着；冷静

贾宝玉初试云雨情　刘姥姥一进荣国府[1]

Pao-yu Has His First Taste of Love
Granny Liu Pays Her First Visit to the Jung Mansion[1] (Yang)

Jia Bao-yu conducts his first experiment in the Art of Love
And Grannie Liu makes her first entry into the Rong-guo mansion[1] (Hawkes)

一、本回概述

袭人发现宝玉梦遗，宝玉把梦中之事说与袭人，并与袭人同领警幻所训云雨之事，自此宝玉与袭人更加亲密。一日，昔年曾与王夫人之父连宗的一户王姓人家之孙，小名狗儿，因家业萧条、难以为继，与岳母刘姥姥商议，计划去贾府走动，得些周济。次日，刘姥姥带着孙子板儿，依靠王夫人的陪房周瑞家的引见，见到了熙凤，熙凤给了刘姥姥二十两银子，邀她改日来逛，刘姥姥感激不尽。

第六回

二、篇章节选

原文

刘姥姥道:"这倒不然。谋事在人,成事在天。咱们谋到了,看菩萨的保佑,有些机会,也未可知。[2]我倒替你们想出一个机会来。当日你们原是和金陵王家连过宗的,二十年前,他们看承你们还好;如今自然是你们拉硬屎,不肯去亲近他,故疏远起来。[3]想当初我和女儿还去过一遭。他们家的二小姐着实响快,会待人,倒不拿大。如今现是荣国府贾二老爷的夫人。听得说,如今上了年纪,越发怜贫恤老,最爱斋僧敬道,舍米舍钱的。[4]如今王府虽升了边任,只怕这二姑太太还认得咱们。你何不去走动走动,或者他念旧,有些好处,也未可知。要是他发一点好心,拔一根寒毛比咱们的腰还粗呢。"[5]刘氏一旁接口道:"你老虽说的是,但只你我这样个嘴脸,怎么好到他门上去的。[6]先不先,他们那些门上的人也未必肯去通信。没的去打嘴现世。"[7]

谁知狗儿利名心最重,听如此一说,心下便有些活动起来。又听他妻子这话,便笑接道:"姥姥既如此说,况且当年你又见过这姑太太一次,何不你老人家明日就走一遭,先试试风头再说。"[8]刘姥姥道:"嗳哟哟!可是说的'侯门深似海',[9]我是个什么东西,他家人又不认得我,我去了也是白去的。"狗儿笑道:"不妨,我教你老人家一个法子:你竟带了外孙子板儿,先去找陪房周瑞,若见了他,就有些意思了。[10]这周瑞先时曾和我父亲交过一件事,我们极好的。"刘姥姥道:"我也知道他的。只是许多时不走动,知道他如今是怎样。这也说不得了,你又是个男人,又这样个嘴脸,自然去不得;我们姑娘年轻媳妇子,也难卖头卖脚的,倒还是舍着我这付老脸去碰一碰。[11]果然有些好处,大家都有益;便是没银子来,我也到那公府侯门见一见世面,也不枉我一生。"说毕,大家笑了一回。当晚计议已定。

杨译

"Don't be so sure," said Granny Liu. "Man proposes, Heaven disposes. Work out a plan, trust to Buddha, and something may come of it for all you know. [2]

"As a matter of fact, I've thought of a chance for you. In the old days you joined families with the Wangs of Chinling, and twenty years back they treated you not badly. Since then of course you've been too pig-headed to go near them, so that now you've drifted apart. [3]

"I recollect calling on them once with my daughter. Their second young lady was really open-handed, so pleasant and free from airs. She's now the wife of the second Lord Chia of the Jung Mansion. I hear she's grown even more charitable and is always setting aside rice and money to give alms to Buddhists and Taoists. [4] Her brother has been promoted to some post at the frontier, but I'm sure this Lady Wang would remember us. Why not go and try your luck? She may do something for us for old times' sake. If she's at all willing to help, one hair from her body would be thicker than our waist." [5]

"Mother's right," put in her daughter. "But how could frights like us go to their gate? [6] Most likely their gatekeepers would refuse to announce us. Why ask for a slap on the face?" [7]

But Kou-erh had an eye to the main chance. Attracted by this suggestion, he laughed at his wife's objection and proposed:

"Since this is your idea, mother, and you've called on the lady before, why not go there tomorrow and see how the wind blows?" [8]

"Aiya! 'The threshold of a noble house is deeper than the sea.' [9] And who am I? The servants there don't know me, it's no use my going."

"That's no problem. I'll tell you what to do. Take young Pan-erh with you and ask for their steward Chou Jui. If you see him, we stand a chance. [10] This Chou Jui had dealings with my old man and used to be on the best of terms with us."

"I know him too. But how will they receive me after all this time? Still, you're a man and too much of a fright to go, and my daughter's too young to make a show of herself. I'm old enough not to mind risking a snub. [11] If I have any luck we'll all share it. And even if I don't bring back any silver the trip won't be wasted—I'll have seen a little high life."

They all laughed at that, and that same evening the matter was settled.

霍译

'I wouldn't say that,' said Grannie Liu. 'Man proposes, God disposes. It's up to us to think of something. We must leave it to the good Lord to decide whether He'll help us or not. Who knows, He might give us the opportunity we are looking for.[2]

'Now I can think of a chance you might try. Your family used to be connected with the Wang clan of Nanking. Twenty years ago the Nanking Wangs used to be very good to you folk. It's only because of late years you have been too stiff-necked to approach them that they have become more distant with you.[3]

'I can remember going to their house once with my daughter. The elder Miss Wang was a very straightforward young lady, very easy to get on with, and not at all high and mighty. She's now the wife of the younger of the two Sir Jias in the Rong mansion. They say that now she's getting on in years she's grown even more charitable and given to good works than she was as a girl.[4] Her brother has been promoted; but I shouldn't be surprised if she at least didn't still remember us. Why don't you try your luck with *her?* You never know, she might do something for you for the sake of old times. She only has to feel well disposed and a hair off her arm would be thicker than a man's waist to poor folks like us!'[5]

'That's all very well, Mother,' put in Gou-er's wife, 'but just take a look at us! What sort of state are we in to go calling on great folks like them?[6] I doubt the people at the door would bother to tell them we were there. Who's going to all that trouble just to make a fool of themselves?'[7]

Gou-er's cupidity, however, had been aroused by the words of his mother-in-law, and his reaction to them was less discouraging than his wife's.

'Well, if it's as you say, Grannie, and being as you've already seen this lady, why not go there yourself and spy out the land for us?'[8]

'Bless us and save us!' said Grannie Liu. 'You know what they say: "A prince's door is like the deep sea."[9] What sort of creature do you take me for? The servants there don't know me; it would be a journey wasted.'

'That's no problem,' said Gou-er. 'I'll tell you what to do. You take young Ban-er with you and ask for Old Zhou that stayed in service with your lady after she married. If you tell them you've come to see him, it will give you an excuse for the visit.[10] Old Zhou once entrusted a bit of business to my father. He used to be very friendly with us at one time.'

'I knew all about that,' said Grannie Liu. 'But it's a long time since you had anything to do with him and hard to say how he may prove after all these years. Howsomever. Being a man, you naturally can't go in your present pickle; and a young married woman like my daughter can't go gallivanting around the countryside showing herself to everybody. But as my old face is tough enough to stand a slap or two, it's up to me to go.[11] So be it, then. If any good does come of the visit, we shall all of us benefit.'

And so, that very evening, the matter was settled.

三、注释评点

【1】本回回目为"贾宝玉初试云雨情 刘姥姥一进荣国府",杨译是"Pao-yu Has His First Taste of Love Granny Liu Pays Her First Visit to the Jung Mansion",霍译是"Jia Bao-yu conducts his first experiment in the Art of Love And Grannie Liu makes her first entry into the Rong-guo mansion",两个译文都完整地译出了原文的意思。相比之下,霍译更加工整,其中,"Jia Bao-yu"对应"Grannie Liu","conducts his first experiment"对应"makes her first entry","in the Art of Love"对应"into the Rong-guo mansion",上下句字数相当,句式对仗工整。

【2】"谋事在人,成事在天。咱们谋到了,看菩萨的保佑,有些机会,也未可知。"句中,"谋事在人,成事在天"和"菩萨"都带有宗教色彩。杨译"Man proposes, Heaven disposes. Work out a plan, trust to Buddha, and something may come of it for all you know."使用了异化策略，将"天"译为"Heaven"；"菩萨"是佛教的专有名词，杨译为"Buddha"，即"佛"，虽然意思不一样，但都属于佛教名词。霍译"Man proposes, God disposes. It's up to us to think of something. We must leave it to the good Lord to decide whether He'll help us or not. Who knows, He might give us the opportunity we are looking for."使用了归化策略，将"天"译为"God"，"菩萨"译为"the good Lord"，宗教色彩浓厚。

【3】"如今自然是你们拉硬屎，不肯去亲近他，故疏远起来。"一句，杨译是"Since then of course you've been too pig-headed to go near them, so that now you've drifted apart."；霍译是"It's only because of late years you have been too stiff-necked to approach them that they have become more distant with you."，两位译者都采用了归化的翻译手法，将"拉硬屎"分别译为"pig-headed（顽固的；固执的）"和"stiff-necked（固执的；倔强的）"。两个译文的句内连接手段略有不同。原文的上下文是因果关系，杨译的句内连接是用"too... to"和"so that..."完成的；霍译用的是强调句型"It's... that..."，强调原因状语"only because of late years you have been too stiff-necked to approach them"，原因状语中又包含了一个"too... to..."句型。

【4】"听得说，如今上了年纪，越发怜贫恤老，最爱斋僧敬道，舍米舍钱的。"一句，杨译是"I hear she's grown even more charitable and is always setting aside rice and money to give alms to Buddhists and Taoists."汉语是意合语言，句子的主语经常被省略，译者在翻译原句时，增加了两个主语"I"和"she"；另外，杨译将"怜贫恤老"笼统地译为"charitable"，"斋僧敬道"译为"give alms to Buddhists and Taoists"，其中"Buddhist"一词和佛教中"僧"的概念并不完全对等，"Buddhist"即佛教徒，是信仰佛、法、僧三宝的在家、出家四众的通称，比"僧"的概念大。霍译"They say that now she's getting on in years she's grown even more charitable and given to good works than she was as a girl."则将西方文化中没有的"僧、道"概念舍弃，直接将"斋僧敬道，舍米舍钱"译为"given to good works"。

【5】"拔一根寒毛比咱们的腰还粗呢。"是一句俗语，杨译是"one

hair from her body would be thicker than our waist."；霍译是"a hair off her arm would be thicker than a man's waist to poor folks like us!"，两位译者都采用了异化的翻译策略，保留了原文的喻体。两者的一点区别是，杨译将"寒毛"译为"one hair from her body"；霍译是"a hair off her arm"，相比之下，霍译更强调寒毛的细小，以突出两者经济地位的悬殊，意为"最细小的寒毛都比我们的腰粗"。

【6】"你老虽说的是，但只你我这样个嘴脸，怎么好到他门上去的。"一句中的"嘴脸"一词语带双关，具有隐含意义，是说他们现在很落魄贫困，不好意思拜访贾府这样的公侯富贵之家，所以不能直译为"嘴巴和脸"。杨译"Mother's right... But how could frights like us go to their gate?"用显性手段处理隐含意义，即"frights like us（像我们这样丑陋奇怪的人）"。霍译"That's all very well, Mother... but just take a look at us! What sort of state are we in to go calling on great folks like them?"也是将隐含的信息显化，先用"What sort of state are we in（我们处于何种境地！）"来暗示"我们现在地位很低，境况很窘迫"，接着"to go calling on great folks like them?"增译了"great folks（大人物）"，意为"怎好去拜访他们这样的大人物？"，表明了两家身份、地位差距悬殊。

【7】"没的去打嘴现世。"一句中，"打嘴现世"是"丢人现眼"的意思。杨译"Why ask for a slap on the face?"主要翻译了原文中的"打嘴"，即"为什么请人扇我们的脸？"，这个译文容易造成读者的误解：为什么请人通报一下，就会让人打脸？霍译"Who's going to all that trouble just to make a fool of themselves?"主要翻译了原文中的"现世"，即"我们现在去人家府上，不是去出丑吗？"，更加符合原文本意。

【8】"何不你老人家明日就走一趟，先试试风头再说。"一句，杨译"why not go there tomorrow and see how the wind blows?"采用了直译法，"see how the wind blows"和中文的"试试风头"不仅字面对应，实际含义也对应，即"打探消息"的意思。霍译"why not go there yourself and spy out the land for us?"使用了意译法："spy out the land"的字面意思是"查探地形"，实际含义也是"（事先）摸清情况，窥探虚实"。

【9】"嗳哟哟！可是说的'侯门深似海'"一句，杨译是"Aiya! 'The

threshold of a noble house is deeper than the sea.'" "侯门深似海"的"侯"被译为"a noble（贵族）"；霍译是"'Bless us and save us!' said Grannie Liu. 'You know what they say: "A prince's door is like the deep sea.'"，译者将"嗳哟哟"译为"'Bless us and save us!'"，宗教色彩浓厚；将"侯"译为"a prince（王爷）"。如何翻译"侯"字的确有点困难，"noble"一词显得宽泛，"prince"又太具体，能封侯的不一定是皇亲国戚，外姓大臣功勋卓著也可以封侯。

【10】"若见了他，就有些意思了。"一句中的"意思"不能直译，杨译是"If you see him, we stand a chance."；霍译是"If you tell them you've come to see him, it will give you an excuse for the visit."，两位译者手法相同，都是将"意思"中的隐性信息做了显化处理。

【11】"你又是个男人，又这样个嘴脸，自然去不得；我们姑娘年轻媳妇子，也难卖头卖脚的，倒还是舍着我这付老脸去碰一碰。"一句，杨译是"Still, you're a man and too much of a fright to go, and my daughter's too young to make a show of herself. I'm old enough not to mind risking a snub."，这句译文的句内连接是通过"and too... to..., and, too... to..."完成的，"自然去不得"这个小句用"to go"就解决了，这种连句的技巧值得学习。霍译是"Howsomever. Being a man, you naturally can't go in your present pickle; and a young married woman like my daughter can't go gallivanting around the countryside showing herself to everybody. But as my old face is tough enough to stand a slap or two, it's up to me to go."，译者用了句子化短语法将小句"又这样个嘴脸"译为介词短语"in your present pickle"。pickle本意是"泡菜"，此处是"困境"的意思。接着，将"我们姑娘年轻媳妇子"译为"a young married woman like my daughter"，信息较杨译更为全面，体现了已婚年轻媳妇的意思；"卖头卖脚"译为"go gallivanting around the countryside showing herself to everybody（在村中游荡，在别人跟前现眼）"，和原文"抛头露面去贾府走一趟"的意思不太吻合。将"舍着我这付老脸去碰一碰"译为"as my old face is tough enough to stand a slap or two, it's up to me to go"，容易引起误解，原文只是说，刘姥姥年纪大了，不怕遭遇碰壁的难堪，还没有到要受人一两个巴掌羞辱的程度，所以此处霍译有点翻译过度。

四、词汇表

1. dispose [dɪˈspəʊz]　　　v.　　to arrange things or people in a particular way or position 排列；布置；安排

2. for all you know　　　used to emphasize that you do not know sth and that it is not important to you（强调不知道对自己无关紧要的事）不知道；说不定；亦未可知

3. open-handed [ˌəʊpənˈhændɪd]　adj.　generous and giving willingly 慷慨的；大方的

4. set sth aside　　　to save or keep money or time for a particular purpose 省出；留出（钱或时间）

5. alms [ɑːmz]　　　n.　　[pl.] money, clothes and food that are given to poor people 施舍物（或金）；救济金（或物）

6. threshold [ˈθreʃəʊld; ˈθreʃˌhəʊld]　　　n.　　the floor or ground at the bottom of a doorway, considered as the entrance to a building or room 门槛；门口

7. steward [ˈstjuːəd]　　　n.　　a person employed to manage another person's property, especially a large house or land （私人家中的）管家

8. snub [snʌb]　　　n.　　an action or a comment that is deliberately rude in order to show sb that you do not like or respect them 冷落；怠慢的言辞（或行为）

9. good works　　　kind acts to help others 善行；善举

10. cupidity [kjuːˈpɪdɪti] *n.* a strong desire for more wealth, possessions, power, etc. than a person needs 贪心；贪婪

11. spy out the land to collect information before deciding what to do （事先）摸清情况；窥探虚实

12. entrust [ɪnˈtrʌst] *v.* to make sb responsible for doing sth or taking care of sb 委托；交托；托付

13. gallivant [ˈgælɪvænt; ˌgælɪˈvænt] *v.* to go from place to place enjoying yourself 游玩；游览；闲游

第七回

送宫花贾琏戏熙凤　宴宁府宝玉会秦钟[1]

尤氏女独请王熙凤　贾宝玉初会秦鲸卿[1]
Madam Yu Invites Hsi-feng Alone
At a Feast in the Ning Mansion Pao-yu First Meets Chin Chung [1] (Yang)

Zhou Rui's wife delivers palace flowers and finds Jia Lian pursuing night sports by day Jia Bao-yu visits the Ning-guo mansion and has an agreeable colloquy with Qin-shi's brother [1] (Hawkes)

一、本回概述

　　刘姥姥走后，周瑞家的来薛姨妈住处梨香院回王夫人话，随后，应薛姨妈之命，把宫里头做的堆纱花分送给熙凤、黛玉等人。周瑞家的到熙凤处时，正值熙凤与贾琏在房中嬉戏，宫花由平儿代为收下。最后于宝玉房中寻得黛玉，黛玉得知最后给她送花，认为是别人挑剩下的，心中不满。次日，宝玉在宁国府初识秦钟，二人惺惺相惜，相约同上贾府家塾念书。回程时，听到宁府老仆焦大酒后醉骂。

二、篇章节选

原文

尤氏叹道:"你难道不知这焦大的?连老爷都不理他的,你珍大哥哥也不理他。只因他从小儿跟着太爷们出过三四回兵,从死人堆里把太爷背了出来,[2] 得了命;自己挨着饿,却偷了东西来给主子吃;两日没得水,得了半碗水给主子喝,他自己喝马溺。不过仗着这些功劳情分,有祖宗时都另眼相待,如今谁肯难为他去。他自己又老了,又不顾体面,[3] 一味吃酒,吃醉了,无人不骂。我常说给管事的,不要派他差事,全当一个死的就完了。今儿又派了他。"

……

那焦大又恃贾珍不在家,即在家亦不好怎样他,更可以任意洒落洒落。因趁着酒兴,先骂大总管赖二,说他不公道,欺软怕硬,"有了好差事就派别人,像这等黑更半夜送人的事,就派我。没良心的王八羔子![4] 瞎充管家!你也不想想,焦大太爷跷跷脚,比你的头还高呢。二十年头里的焦大太爷眼里有谁?[5] 别说你们这一起杂种王八羔子们!"

正骂的兴头上,贾蓉送凤姐的车出去,众人喝他不听,贾蓉忍不得,便骂了他两句,使人捆起来,"等明日酒醒了,问他还寻死不寻死了!"那焦大那里把贾蓉放在眼里,反大叫起来,赶着贾蓉叫:"蓉哥儿,你别在焦大跟前使主子性儿。别说你这样儿的,就是你爹、你爷爷,也不敢和焦大挺腰子!不是焦大一个人,你们就做官儿享荣华受富贵?你祖宗九死一生挣下这家业,到如今了,不报我的恩,反和我充起主子来了。[6] 不和我说别的还可,若再说别的,咱们红刀子进去白刀子出来!"凤姐在车上说与贾蓉道:"以后还不早打发了这个没王法的东西!留在这里岂不是祸害?倘或亲友知道了,岂不笑话咱们,这样的人家连个王法规矩都没有。"贾蓉答应"是"。

众小厮见他太撒野了,只得上来几个,揪翻捆倒,拖往马圈里去。焦大越发连贾珍都说出来,乱嚷乱叫说:"我要往祠堂里哭太爷去。那里承望到如今生下这些畜生来!每日家偷狗戏鸡,[7] 爬灰的爬灰,养小叔子的养小叔子,[8] 我什么不知道?咱们'胳膊折了往袖子里藏'!"众小厮听他说出这些没天日

对话杨宪益、霍克斯——《红楼梦》英译赏析(第一至四十回)

的话来,唬的魂飞魄散,也不顾别的了,便把他捆起来,用土和马粪满满的填了他一嘴。

杨译

"You know Chiao Ta, surely?" Madam Yu sighed. "Not even the master can control him, let alone your Cousin Chen. He went out with our great-grandfather on three or four expeditions when he was young, and saved his master's life by carrying him off a battlefield heaped with corpses.[2] He went hungry himself but stole food for his master; and after two days without water, when he got half a bowl he gave it to his master and drank horse urine himself. Because of these services, he was treated with special consideration in our great-grandfather's time and nobody likes to interfere with him now. But since growing old he has no regard for appearances.[3] He does nothing but drink and when he's drunk he abuses everyone. Time and again I've told the stewards to write him off and not give him any jobs. Yet he's being sent again today."

……

Because Chia Chen was out—though he could have done nothing even if at home—Chiao Ta was fairly letting himself go. Roaring drunk, he lashed out at the head steward Lai Erh's injustice, calling him a cowardly bully.

"You give all the soft jobs to others, but when it comes to seeing someone home late at night in the dark you send me. Black-hearted son of a turtle![4] A fine steward you are! I can lift my leg up higher than your head. Twenty years ago I'd nothing but contempt for this household,[5] not to mention you bastards, you crew of turtle-eggs."

He was cursing away full blast as Chia Jung saw Hsi-feng in her carriage out, and ignored all the servants' shouts to him to be quiet. Chia Jung could hardly let this pass. He swore at Chiao Ta and told men to tie him up.

"We'll ask him tomorrow, when he's sobered up, what he means by this disgraceful behaviour," he blustered.

Chiao Ta had a low opinion, of course, of Chia Jung. He bore down on him bellowing still more angrily:

"Don't try to lord it over Chiao Ta, young Brother Jung! Not to speak of the likes of you, not even your dad or granddad dare stand up to Chiao Ta. If not for me, and me alone, you'd have no official posts, fancy titles or riches. It was your great-granddad who built up this estate, and nine times I snatched him back from the jaws of death. Now instead of showing yourselves properly grateful, you try to lord it over me.[6] Shut up, and I'll overlook it. Say one word more, and I'll bury a white blade in you and pull it out red!"

"Why don't you get rid of this lawless wretch?" asked Hsi-feng from her carriage. "He's nothing but a source of trouble. If this came to the ears of our relatives and friends, how they'd laugh at the lack of rules and order here."

As Chia Jung agreed to this, some servants overpowered Chiao Ta and dragged him off towards the stables, for this time he had really gone too far. Then he let loose a flood of abuse in which even Chia Chen was included.

"Let me go to the Ancestral Temple and weep for my old master," he fumed. "Little did he expect to beget such degenerates, a houseful of rutting dogs and bitches in heat,[7] day in and day out scratching in the ashes and carrying on with younger brothers-in-law.[8] Don't think you can fool me. I only tried to hide the broken arm in your sleeve...."

These obscenities frightened the servants half out of their wits. Hurriedly trussing him up, they stuffed his mouth with mud and horse-dung.

霍译

'You don't know Big Jiao,' said You-shi. 'Even Father couldn't do anything with him, let alone Zhen. When he was young he went with Grandfather on three or four of his campaigns and once saved his life by pulling him from under a heap of corpses and carrying him to safety on his back.[2] He went hungry himself and stole things for his master to eat; and once when he had managed to get half a cupful of water, he gave it to his master and drank horse's urine himself. Because of these one or two acts of heroism he was always given special treatment during Grandfather's lifetime; so naturally we don't like to upset him now. But since he's grown old he has let himself go completely. [3] He drinks all the time, and when he's drunk he starts abusing everybody—literally *everybody*. I've repeatedly told the steward not to give him jobs to do—to behave exactly as though he were dead and ignore him completely. Why on earth should he have chosen him today?'

……

In the flickering light of many lanterns the pages stood stiffly to attention on the pavement below, while Big Jiao, encouraged by Cousin Zhen's absence to indulge his talent for drunken abuse, was getting to work on the Chief Steward, Lai Sheng, accusing him of being unfair, of always dropping on the weakest, and so on and so forth.

'If there's a cushy job going you give it to someone else, but when it's a question of seeing someone home in pitch bloody darkness, you pick on me. Mean, rotten bugger! [4] Call yourself a steward? Some steward! Don't you know who Old Jiao is? I can lift my *foot* up higher than your head! Twenty years ago I didn't give a damn for *anybody*, [5] never mind a pack of little misbegotten abortions like you!'

He was just getting into his stride when Jia Rong came out to see Xi-feng off in her carriage. The servants shouted to Big Jiao to stop, but without success. Impatient of the old man's insolence, Jia Rong cursed him angrily.

'Tie him up,' he said to the servants. 'We shall see if he is still so eager for death tomorrow morning, when he has sobered up a bit.'

But Big Jiao was not to be intimidated by such as Jia Rong. On the contrary, he staggered up to him and bellowed even louder.

'Oh ho! Little Rong, is it? Don't you come the Big Master stuff with me, sonny boy! Never mind a little bit of a kid like you, even your daddy and your granddaddy don't dare to try any funny stuff with Old Jiao. If it wasn't for Old Jiao, where would you lot all be today, with your rank and your fancy titles and your money and all the other things you enjoy? It was your great-granddad, whose life I saved when he was given up for dead, that won all this for you, by the sweat of his brow. And what reward do I get for saving him? Nothing. Instead you come to me and you put on your Big Master act. [6] Well, I'll tell you something. You'd better watch out. Because if you don't, you're going to get a shiny white knife inside you, and it's going to come out red!'

'You'd better hurry up and send this unspeakable creature about his business,' said Xi-feng to Jia Rong from her carriage. 'It's positively dangerous to keep a man like this on the premises. If any of our acquaintance get to know that a family like ours can't keep even a semblance of discipline about the place, we shall become a laughing-stock.'

Jia Rong assented meekly.

Several of the servants, seeing that Big Jiao had got quite out of hand and that something had to be done at all costs, rushed up and overpowered him, and throwing him face downward on the ground, frog-marched him off to the stables. By now even Cousin Zhen was being included in his maledictions, which became wilder and noisier as he shouted to his captors that he wanted to go to the ancestral temple and weep before the tablet of his old Master.

'Who would ever have believed the Old Master could spawn this filthy lot of animals?' he bawled. 'Up to their dirty little tricks every day. [7] I know. Father-in-law pokes in the ashes. Auntie has it off with nevvy. [8] Do you think I don't know what you're all up to? Oh, we "hide our broken arm in our sleeve"; but you don't fool me.'

Terrified out of their wits at hearing a fellow-servant utter such enormities, the grooms and pages tied him up and stuffed his mouth with mud and horse-dung.

三、注释评点

【1】本回回目有不同的版本，杨译"Madam Yu Invites Hsi-feng Alone At a Feast in the Ning Mansion Pao-yu First Meets Chin Chung"依据的是有正本（尤氏女独请王熙凤　贾宝玉初会秦鲸卿），可以看出，杨译上、下

句句式不太工整，上句很短，下句较长。霍译"Zhou Rui's wife delivers palace flowers and finds Jia Lian pursuing night sports by day Jia Bao-yu visits the Ning-guo mansion and has an agrccablc colloquy with Qin-shi's brother"上、下句句式较为工整，都采用了主谓宾的结构，且使用了并列谓语。

【2】"从死人堆里把太爷背了出来"一句中的"死人堆"指的是战场，杨译"(He) saved his master's life by carrying him off a battlefield heaped with corpses."是符合原文含义的；霍译"(He) once saved his life by pulling him from under a heap of corpses and carrying him to safety on his back."有再创作的意味，把场景细节化，把"死人堆"直译处理了。

【3】"他自己又老了，又不顾体面"一句，杨译是"But since growing old he has no regard for appearances."，意为"他年纪大了，不太注意形象"；霍译是"But since he's grown old he has let himself go completely."，意为"他任由自己的性子行事"，结合上下文可以看出，霍译更贴近作者的原意。

【4】"没良心的王八羔子……别说你们这一起杂种王八羔子们！"一句中，多次出现骂人的习语。杨译"Black-hearted son of a turtle! ... not to mention you bastards, you crew of turtle-eggs."基本上采用了异化策略，直译这些习语。霍译"Mean, rotten bugger!... never mind a pack of little misbegotten abortions like you!"采用了归化策略，将"王八羔子"和"杂种王八羔子们"分别译为"bugger"和"misbegotten abortions"。

【5】"二十年头里的焦大太爷眼里有谁？"一句，杨译是"Twenty years ago I'd nothing but contempt for this household"，其中的"household"指的是这个家里的人；霍译"Twenty years ago I didn't give a damn for *anybody*"用"*anybody*"翻译原文中的"谁"，而且用斜体的方式加强语气，表示"我焦大谁也瞧不起"，更充分地展示了原文的含义。

【6】"你祖宗九死一生挣下这家业，到如今了，不报我的恩，反和我充起主子来了。"一句，杨译是"It was your great-granddad who built up this estate, and nine times I snatched him back from the jaws of death. Now instead of showing yourselves properly grateful, you try to lord it over me."其中，"nine times I snatched him back from the jaws of death"指出了焦大和宁国公的关系：因为我救了他，而他给你们打下了家业；"nine times"不是实指"九次"，而是指"多次"。霍译是"It was your great-granddad, whose life I saved when he was given up for dead, that won all this for you, by the sweat of his brow. And what reward do I get for saving him? Nothing. Instead you come to me and you put on your Big Master act.",其中的定语从句"whose life I saved when he was given up for dead"表明了焦大认为自己应该在贾家享受地位的原因。两位译者都把原文中没有的焦大救主的信息在译文中补充完整了。另外，两位译者都使用了强调句型，强调"祖宗"，无非是提醒贾家子孙不要忘本，尤其是不能忘记他这个恩人，霍译中"whose"引导的非限定性定语从句更充分地传达出这层意思。

【7】"那里承望到如今生下这些畜生来！每日家偷狗戏鸡"一句，杨译是"Little did he expect to beget such degenerates, a houseful of rutting dogs and bitches in heat",译者将"畜生"一词译为"degenerates（堕落之人）"；将"偷狗戏鸡"译为"a houseful of rutting dogs and bitches in heat（一屋子发情难耐的公狗和母狗）"，译得很妙，为下文的"爬灰""养小叔子"做了铺垫。霍译是"Who would ever have believed the Old Master could spawn this filthy lot of animals'? ... Up to their dirty little tricks every day.",译者将"畜生"译为"filthy lot of animals（一群肮脏的动物）"；"偷狗戏鸡"译为"dirty little tricks（下流卑劣的小把戏）","filthy""dirty"表达出贾府子孙干的都是肮脏下流之事。

【8】"爬灰的爬灰，养小叔子的养小叔子"一句，杨译"... day in and day out scratching in the ashes and carrying on with younger brothers-in-law."用直译手法将"爬灰"译为"scratching in the ashes",然后在本页尾注中，译者只是说这是"A slang",所以译文读者是无法知晓"爬灰"的真实含义的。霍译"Father-in-law pokes in the ashes. Auntie has it off with nevvy."采用的也是直译手法，"pokes in the ashes"意为"在灰中戳、捅",显然也没有译出"爬灰"的真正含义。

四、词汇表

1. lash out (at sb/sth)		to criticize sb in an angry way 怒斥；严厉斥责
2. (at) full blast		with the greatest possible volume or power 最大音量地；最大马力地
3. bluster [ˈblʌstə]	v.	to talk in an aggressive or threatening way, but with little effect 气势汹汹地说；咄咄逼人；威吓（但效果不大）
4. bear down on sb/sth		to move quickly towards sb/sth in a determined or threatening way 冲向；咄咄逼近
5. lord it over sb		to act as if you are better or more important than sb 对某人举止霸道（或逞威风）
6. wretch [retʃ]	n.	an evil, unpleasant or annoying person 恶棍；坏蛋；无赖
7. fume [fju:m]	v.	to be very angry about sth （对……）大为生气；十分恼火
8. beget [bɪˈget]	v.	to become the father of a child 成为……之父
9. rutting [ˈrʌtɪŋ]	adj.	(of male animals, especially deer) in a time of sexual activity 处于发情期的
10. in heat		(of a female mammal) to be in a sexual condition ready for mating 在发情期
11. obscenity [əbˈsenɪti]	n.	an obscene word or act 下流话（或动作）
12. truss [trʌs]	v.	to tie up sb's arms and legs so that they cannot move 把（人的双臂和双腿）捆紧；缚牢

13. flicker [ˈflɪkə]	v.		(of a light or a flame) to keep going on and off as it shines or burns 闪烁；闪现；忽隐忽现
14. cushy [ˈkʊʃɪ]	adj.		very easy and pleasant; needing little or no effort 轻松愉快的；安逸的；不费劲的
15. pitch [pɪtʃ]	n.		a black sticky substance made from oil or coal, used on roofs or the wooden boards of a ship to stop water from coming through 沥青；柏油
16. bugger [ˈbʌgə]	n.		an offensive word used to insult sb, especially a man, and to show anger or dislike（侮辱性称呼，尤用于男子）家伙；浑蛋；坏蛋
17. misbegotten [ˌmɪsbɪˈgɒt(ə)n]	adj.		badly designed or planned 设计（或规划）拙劣的
18. get into one's stride			to begin to do sth with confidence and at a good speed after a slow, uncertain start 进入状态；开始顺利地做某事
19. stagger [ˈstægə]	v.		to walk with weak unsteady steps, as if you are about to fall 摇摇晃晃地走；踉跄；跟跄
20. sweat of his brow	n.		额头上的汗水
21. premises [ˈpremɪsɪz]	n.		the building and land near to it that a business owns or uses（企业的）房屋建筑及附属场地；营业场所
22. semblance [ˈsembləns]	n.		a situation in which sth seems to exist although this may not, in fact, be the case 假象；外观；外貌
23. frog-march [frɒgˈmɑːtʃ]	v.		to force sb to go somewhere by holding their arms tightly so they have to walk

		along with you 紧抓双臂押送；挟持而行
24. bawl [bɔːl]	*v.*	to shout loudly, especially in an unpleasant or angry way 大喊；怒吼
25. enormity [ɪˈnɔːməti]	*n.*	a very serious crime 滔天罪行；罪大恶极

比通灵金莺微露意　探宝钗黛玉半含酸[1]

拦酒兴李奶母讨厌　掷茶杯贾公子生嗔[1]
Nanny Li Makes a Nuisance of Herself by Warning Against Drinking
Pao-yu Breaks a Teacup and Flies into a Temper[1] (Yang)

贾宝玉奇缘识金锁　薛宝钗巧合认通灵[1]
Jia Bao-yu is allowed to see the strangely corresponding golden locket
And Xue Bao-chai has a predestined encounter with the Magic Jade[1] (Hawkes)

一、本回概述

宝玉到宝钗处探病，宝钗看到宝玉项上戴着通灵宝玉，不由地仔细观赏，发现玉上刻着八个字：莫失莫忘，仙寿恒昌。莺儿顺口感慨宝钗所戴的金项圈上刻的字与这玉上刻的字十分配对，宝玉观看项圈，发现也有八个字：不离不弃，芳龄永继。宝玉闻到宝钗身上有丝丝幽香，宝钗解释这乃是自己服用"冷香丸"所致。正说着，黛玉也来探病，撞见宝玉，心中不喜，便借雪雁送手炉一事奚落宝、钗，宝玉嘻笑不语。薛姨妈留宝、黛吃饭，宝玉喝醉而归，趁酒意大骂李嬷嬷。

二、篇章节选

原文

　　说话时，宝玉已是三杯过去。李嬷嬷又上来拦阻。[2]宝玉正在心甜意洽之时，和宝黛姊妹说说笑笑的，那肯不吃。宝玉只得屈意央告：“好妈妈，我再吃两钟就不吃了。”李嬷嬷道：“你可仔细老爷今儿在家，隄防问你的书！”宝玉听了这话，便心中大不自在，慢慢的放下酒，垂了头。[3]黛玉先忙的说："别扫大家的兴！舅舅若叫你，只说姨妈留着呢。这个妈妈，他吃了酒，又拿我们来醒脾了！"一面悄推宝玉，使他赌气；一面悄悄的咕哝说："别理那老货，咱们只管乐咱们的。"那李嬷嬷不知黛玉的意思，因说道："林姐儿，你不要助着他。你倒劝劝他，只怕他还听些。"[4]林黛玉冷笑道："我为什么助他？我也不犯着劝他。你这妈妈太小心了，往常老太太又给他酒吃，如今在姨妈这里多吃一口，料也不妨事。必定姨妈这里是外人，不当在这里的也未可定。"李嬷嬷听了，又是急，又是笑，说道："真真这林姐儿，说出一句话来，比刀子还尖。你——这算了什么。"宝钗也忍不住笑着，把黛玉腮上一拧，说道："真真这个颦丫头的一张嘴，叫人恨又不是，喜欢又不是。"薛姨妈一面又说："别怕，别怕，我的儿！来这里没好的你吃，别把这点子东西唬的存在心里，[5]倒叫我不安。只管放心吃，都有我呢。越发吃了晚饭去，[6]便醉了，便跟着我睡罢。"因命："再烫热酒来！姨妈陪你吃两杯，可就吃饭罢。"宝玉听了，方又鼓起兴来。[7]

杨译

　　By now Pao-yu had already drunk three cups, and Nanny Li came in again to **remonstrate**.[2] But he was enjoying himself so much talking and laughing with his cousins, he refused to stop. "Dear nanny," he coaxed, "just two more cups—that's all."

　　"You'd better look out," she warned. "Lord Cheng's at home today, and he may want to examine you on your lessons."

　　With a sinking heart, Pao-yu slowly put his cup down and hung his head.[3]

"Don't be such a spoil-sport," protested Tai-yu. "If Uncle sends for you, cousin, we can say Aunt Hsuen is keeping you. This nanny of yours has been drinking and is working off the effects of the wine on us." She nudged Pao-yu to embolden him and whispered, "Never mind the old thing. Why shouldn't we enjoy ourselves?"

"Now, Miss Lin, don't egg him on," cried Nanny Li. "You're the only one whose advice he might listen to."[4]

"Why should I egg him on?" Tai-yu gave a little snort. "I can't be bothered with offering him advice either. You're too pernickety, nanny. The old lady often gives him wine, so why shouldn't he have a drop more here with his aunt? Are you suggesting that auntie's an outsider and he shouldn't behave like that here?"

Amused yet vexed, Nanny Li expostulated, "Really, every word Miss Lin says cuts sharper than a knife. How can you suggest such a thing?"

Even Pao-chai couldn't suppress a smile. She pinched Tai-yu's cheek and cried, "What a tongue the girl has! One doesn't know whether to be cross or laugh."

"Don't be afraid, my child," said Aunt Hsueh. "I've nothing good to offer you, but I'll feel bad if you get a fright which gives you indigestion.[5] Just drink as much as you want, I'll answer for it. You needn't leave till after supper.[6] And if you do get tipsy you can sleep here." She ordered more wine to be heated, saying, "I'll drink a few cups with you and then we'll have our rice."

Pao-yu's spirits rose again at this.[7]

> 霍译

Bao-yu had soon finished his third cup of wine and Nannie Li once more came forward to restrain him.[2] But Bao-yu, who was now warm and happy and in the midst of a hilarious conversation with his cousins, was naturally unwilling to stop, and pleaded humbly with the old lady for a reprieve.

'Nannie darling, just two more cups and then I'll stop!'

'You'd better look out,' said Nannie Li. 'Your father's at home today. He'll be asking you about your lessons before you know where you are.'

At these words all Bao-yu's happiness drained away. Slowly he set down his cup and bowed his head in dejection. [3]

'Don't spoil everyone's enjoyment,' said Dai-yu. 'Even if Uncle *does* call for you, you can always say that Aunt Xue is keeping you. I think that old Nannie of yours has had a cup too many and is looking for a bit of excitement at our expense.' She gave him a gentle nudge to encourage a more valiant spirit in him, muttering, as she did so, 'Take no notice of the old fool! Let's go on enjoying ourselves and not mind about her!'

Nannie Li knew only too well what Dai-yu was capable of.

'Now Miss Lin,' she said, 'don't you go taking his part! If *you* encourage him he's only too likely to do what you say!' [4]

Dai-yu smiled dangerously. 'Take his part? Why should I want to encourage him? You are over-cautious, my dear Nannie. After all, Lady Jia often lets him drink; why should it matter if Mrs Xue lets him have a cup or two? I suppose you think he can't be trusted to drink here because Mrs Xue is not one of us?'

Nannie Li did not know whether to feel upset or amused.

'Really, Miss Lin. Some of the things you say cut sharper than a knife!'

Bao-chai could not suppress a giggle. She pinched Dai-yu's cheek playfully.

'Really, Miss Frowner, the things you say! One doesn't know whether to grind one's teeth or laugh!'

Aunt Xue laughed too.

'Don't be afraid, my boy! Heaven knows I've got little enough to offer you when you come to see me. You mustn't get upset over a small thing like this, [5] or I shall feel quite uncomfortable. Drink as much as you like; I'll look after you! You may as well stay to supper, [6] in any case; and even if you *do* get drunk, you can always spend the night here.' She told a maid to heat some more wine. 'There! Auntie will drink a cup or two with you, and then we shall have some supper.'

Bao-yu's spirits began to revive a bit under his aunt's encouragement. [7]

三、注释评点

【1】本回回目有不同的版本，本书所用的人民文学出版社的版本中，本回回目是"比通灵金莺微露意　探宝钗黛玉半含酸"，有正本为"拦酒兴李奶母讨厌　掷茶杯贾公子生嗔"，程本为"贾宝玉奇缘识金锁　薛宝钗巧合认通灵"。杨译和霍译分别依据有正本和程本。

【2】"说话时，宝玉已是三杯过去。李嬷嬷又上来拦阻。"一句，杨译是"By now Pao-yu had already drunk three cups, and Nanny Li came in again to remonstrate."；霍译是"Bao-yu had soon finished his third cup of wine and Nannie Li once more came forward to restrain him."，两个译文都使用了过去完成时和一般过去时，同时，两位译者都使用了"and"连句，将事情发生的先后顺序表述得非常清楚。

【3】"宝玉听了这话，便心中大不自在，慢慢的放下酒，垂了头。"一句，杨译"With a sinking heart, Pao-yu slowly put his cup down and hung his head."使用了句子化短语法将小句"心中大不自在"译为介词短语"with a sinking heart"；在翻译"放下酒，垂了头"时，译者很自然地增加了连接词"and"，体现出意合语言（汉语）转化为形合语言（英语）时，要增加表示逻辑关系的连接词。霍译"At these words all Bao-yu's happiness drained away. Slowly he set down his cup and bowed his head in dejection."也使用了句子化短语法，将小句"宝玉听了这话"译为介词短语"at these words"。另外，译者将"Slowly"置于第二句译文的句首，有强调作用，使得译文的画面感更强；句尾处还加译了"in dejection"，一方面表达出宝玉当时的心情，另一方面增加了句子尾重，使句子更符合英语的表达习惯，读起来也更上口。

【4】"你倒劝劝他，只怕他还听些。"一句中，前半句的主语是"你"，后半句的主语是"他"。杨译"You're the only one whose advice he might listen to."选择了"你"（you）做主语，并通过"whose"将原文的两个短句非常巧妙地连接起来。霍译"If *you* encourage him he's only too likely to do what you say!"增加了表示逻辑关系的连接词"if"，体现出意合语言（汉语）转化为形合语言（英语）时做出的结构调整。另外，霍译对于"听"字的处理非常准

确，它显然不仅是表面的"listen to"，更指行动上控制自己不再喝酒，"he's only too likely to do what you say!"充分表达出这两层含义。

【5】"别把这点子东西唬的存在心里"一句，"这点了东西"指的是食物。薛姨妈的意思是宽慰宝玉不要因为情绪低落而影响消化。杨译"I'll feel bad if you get a fright which gives you indigestion."直接将中文隐含的内容翻译了出来：如果你因为受到惊吓引起积食，身体不适，我就要感到愧疚了。霍译"You mustn't get upset over a small thing like this,"的意思是：不要因为这么一点小事感到不安。"upset"一词主要强调内心不安而非身体不适。

【6】"越发吃了晚饭去"一句，杨译是"You needn't leave till after supper."；霍译是"You may as well stay to supper,"，"may as well"常用于委婉地给出建议，此处，比"needn't leave"更加自然。

【7】"宝玉听了，方又鼓起兴来。"一句，杨译"Pao-yu's spirits rose again at this."和霍译"Bao-yu's spirits began to revive a bit under his aunt's encouragement."都使用了句子化短语法，将小句"宝玉听了"分别译为介词短语"at this"和"under his aunt's encouragement"。

四、词汇表

1. remonstrate [ˈremənstreɪt]	v.	to protest or complain about sth/sb 抗议；抱怨；埋怨
2. spoil-sport [ˈspɔɪlspɔːt]	n.	a person who spoils other people's enjoyment, for example by not taking part in an activity or by trying to stop other people from doing it 扫兴的人
3. work sth off		to get rid of sth, especially a strong feeling, by using physical effort（通过消耗体力）宣泄感情
4. nudge [nʌdʒ]	v.	to push sb gently, especially with your elbow, in order to get their attention（用

肘）轻推；轻触

5. embolden [ɪmˈbəʊld(ə)n]	v.	to make sb feel braver or more confident 使增加勇气；使更有胆量；使更有信心
6. egg sb on		to encourage sb to do sth, especially sth that they should not do 鼓动；怂恿；煽动
7. snort [snɔːt]	n.	a loud sound that you make by breathing air out noisily through your nose, especially to show that you are angry or amused（尤指表示气愤或被逗乐）喷鼻息；哼
8. pernickety [pəˈnɪkɪti]	adj.	worrying too much about unimportant details 爱挑剔的；吹毛求疵的
9. vexed [vekst]	adj.	upset or annoyed（指人）恼火；烦恼；伤脑筋
10. expostulate [ɪkˈspɒstjʊleɪt]	v.	to argue, disagree or protest about sth 争论；争执；抗议
11. indigestion [ˌɪndɪˈdʒestʃ(ə)n]	n.	pain caused by difficulty in digesting food 消化不良
12. tipsy [ˈtɪpsi]	adj.	slightly drunk 微醉的；略有醉意的
13. restrain [rɪˈstreɪn]	v.	to stop sb/sth from doing sth, especially by using physical force（尤指用武力）制止；阻止；管制
14. hilarious [hɪˈleərɪəs]	adj.	extremely funny 极其滑稽的
15. reprieve [rɪˈpriːv]	n.	a delay before sth bad happens 延缓；缓解
16. dejection [dɪˈdʒekʃ(ə)n]	n.	a feeling of unhappiness and disappointment 沮丧；情绪低落；垂头丧气

17. valiant [ˈvæliənt]　　　*adj.*　　very brave or determined 勇敢的；果敢的；坚定的

18. grind [graɪnd]　　　*v.*　　to rub together, or to make hard objects rub together, often producing an unpleasant noise 摩擦（发出刺耳声）

第九回

恋风流情友入家塾　起嫌疑顽童闹学堂[1]

Devoted Friends Join the Clan School
Mud-Slinging Boys Brawl in the Classroom [1] (Yang)

训劣子李贵承申饬　嗔顽童茗烟闹书房[1]

A son is admonished and Li Gui receives an alarming warning
a pupil is abused and Tealeaf throws the classroom in an uproar [1] (Hawkes)

一、本回概述

宝玉急于和秦钟相见，择定后日上学。是日一早，袭人为他收拾妥当，叮嘱宝玉功课不必过于操劳。宝玉向家中长辈辞行之后，又独去向黛玉作辞。上学期间，宝玉与秦钟形影不离，引发不少风言风语。秦钟又因与"香怜"交好，引发贾家远亲金荣（贾璜之妻的侄儿）争风吃醋，适逢代儒外出，其孙儿贾瑞处理不公，引发学堂内一场大混战，最后，金荣被迫磕头道歉，风波暂时平息。

二、篇章节选

原文

　　原来这学中虽都是本族人丁与些亲戚的子弟，俗语说的好："一龙生九种，九种各别。"未免人多了，就有龙蛇混杂，下流人物在内。[2] 自宝、秦二人来了，都生的花朵儿一般的模样，又见秦钟腼腆温柔，未语面先红，怯怯羞羞，有女儿之风；[3] 宝玉又是天生成惯能作小服低，赔身下气，情性体贴，话语缠绵，因此二人更加亲厚，也怨不得那起同窗人起了疑，背地里你言我语，诟谇谣诼，满书房内外。

　　原来薛蟠自来王夫人处住后，便知有一家学，学中广有青年子弟，不免偶动了龙阳之兴，[4] 因此也假来上学读书，不过是三日打鱼，两日晒网，[5] 白送些束脩礼物与贾代儒，却不曾有一些儿进益，只图结交些契弟。[6] 谁想这学内就有好几个小学生，图了薛蟠的银钱吃穿，被他哄上手的，也不消多记。更又有两个多情的小学生，亦不知是那一房的亲眷，亦未考真名姓，只因生得妩媚风流，满学中都送了他两个外号，一号"香怜"，一号"玉爱"。[7] 虽都有窃慕之意，将不利于孺子之心，只是都惧薛蟠的威势，不敢来沾惹。如今宝、秦二人一来，见了他两个，也不免缱绻羡慕，亦因知系薛蟠相知，故未敢轻举妄动。[8] 香、玉二人心中，也一般的留情与宝、秦。因此四人心中虽有情意，只未发迹。每日一入学中，四处各坐，却八目勾留，或设言托意，或咏桑寓柳，遥以心照，却外面自为避人眼目。不意偏又有几个滑贼看出形景来，都背后挤眉弄眼，或咳嗽扬声，这也非止一日。

杨译

　　Now although all the pupils in this school were members of the Chia clan or relations by marriage, as the proverb so aptly says, "A dragon begets nine offspring, each one different." And inevitably among so many boys there were low types too, snakes mixed up with dragons.[2]

　　These two new arrivals were both remarkably handsome. Chin Chung was bashful and gentle, so shy that he blushed like a girl before he spoke,[3] while Pao-yu was naturally self-effacing and modest, considerate to others and pleasant in his speech. And they were on such intimate terms, it was no wonder that their schoolmates suspected the worst. They began to talk about the pair behind their backs, spreading ugly rumours inside the school and out.

Now Hsueh Pan had not been long in the Jung Mansion before he learned of this school, and the thought of all the boys there appealed to his baser instincts.[4] So he enrolled as a student. But he was like the fisherman who fishes for three days and then suns his net for two[5]. The fee he paid Chia Tai-ju was thrown away, for he had no intention of really studying, his sole aim being to find some 'sweet-hearts' there.[6] In fact, tempted by his money and other gifts several boys did fall into his clutches, but we need not dwell on this.

Chief among these were two amorous youths whose real names have not been ascertained, nor the branches of the family to which they belonged. But on account of their good looks and charm they were nicknamed Sweetie and Lovely.[7] Although the object of general admiration, so that others also had designs on them, they were left unmolested for fear of Hsueh Pan.

Pao-yu and Chin Chung were naturally attracted by these boys too, but knowing them to be Hsueh Pan's friends they did not venture to make any overtures.[8] Sweetie and Lovely were equally drawn to them. But not one of the four spoke of what was in his heart. Every day from four different seats four pairs of eyes kept meeting, and while trying to escape detection they contrived by hints and allusions to reveal their thoughts. However, some sly rascals discovered their secret and began to raise their eyebrows, wink, and cough or clear their throats behind their backs.

霍译

All the pupils at the clan school were either members of the Jia clan or relations by marriage; but as the proverb rightly says, 'there are nine kinds of dragon and no two kinds are alike'. Where many are gathered together the wheat is sure to contain a certain amount of chaff; and this school was no exception in numbering some very ill-bred persons among its pupils.[2]

The two new boys, Qin Zhong and Bao-yu, were both as beautiful as flowers; the other scholars observed how shrinking and gentle Qin Zhong was, blushing almost before you spoke to him and timid and bashful as a girl;[3] they saw in Bao-yu one whom nature and habit had made humble and accommodating in spite of his social position, always willing to defer to others in the interest of harmony; they observed his affectionate disposition and familiar manner of speech; and they could see that the two friends were devoted to each other. Perhaps it is not to be wondered at that these observations should have given rise to certain suspicions in the minds of those ill-bred persons, and that both in school and out of it all kinds of ugly rumours should have circulated behind their backs.

When Xue Pan learned, some time after moving into his aunt's place in the capital, that the establishment included a clan school plentifully stocked with young males of a certain age, his old enthusiasm for 'Lord Long-yang's vice' was re-awakened,[4] and he had hastened to register himself as a pupil. His school-going was, needless to say, a pretence—'one day fishing and two days to dry the nets'[5] as they say—and had nothing to do with the advancement of learning. Having paid a generous fee to Jia Dai-ru, he used his membership of the school merely as a means of picking up 'soul-mates' from among his fellow-students.[6] It must with regret be recorded that a surprisingly large number of the latter were deluded into becoming his willing victims by the prospect of receiving those ample advances of money and goods which he was in a position to offer.

Among them were two amorous young creatures whose names and parentage escape us but who, because of their glamorous looks and affected manners, were universally known by the nicknames of 'Darling' and 'Precious'.[7] Although their fellow-students much admired them and entertained towards them feelings not at all conducive to that health of mind which the Young Person should at all times endeavour to cultivate, they were deterred from meddling with them for fear of what

Xue Pan might do.

When Qin Zhong and Bao-yu joined the school it was only to be expected that they too should fall under the spell of this charming pair; but like the rest they were inhibited from overt declaration of their feelings by the knowledge that Xue Pan was their 'friend'.[8] Their feelings were reciprocated by Darling and Precious, and a bond of mutual attraction grew up between the four, which nevertheless remained unexpressed, except for the significant looks that every day passed between them across the classroom, or the occasional rather too loud utterance to a neighbour of some remark really intended for the ears of the opposite pair.

They were persuaded that these cryptic communications had escaped the notice of their fellows; but they were wrong. Certain young hooligans among their classmates had long since discerned the true nature of what was going on, and while the two handsome couples were engaged in their silent and (as they thought) secret communion, these others would be winking and leering behind their backs or becoming suddenly convulsed with paroxysms of artificial coughing.

三、注释评点

【1】本回回目有不同版本，脂本为"恋风流情友入家塾 起嫌疑顽童闹学堂"；程本为"训劣子李贵承申饬 嗔顽童茗烟闹书房"。杨译和霍译分别依据了脂本和程本。

【2】"未免人多了，就有龙蛇混杂，下流人物在内。"一句，杨译是"And inevitably among so many boys there were low types too, snakes mixed up with dragons.", 译者采用了异化策略，用独立主格结构将"龙蛇混杂"译为"snakes mixed up with dragons"。霍译是"Where many are gathered together the wheat is sure to contain a certain amount of chaff; and this school was no exception in numbering some very ill-bred persons among its pupils.", 译者舍弃了"龙""蛇"这两个喻体，将"龙蛇混杂"译为"the wheat is sure to contain a certain amount of chaff（小麦中不可避免混有麦麸）"，采用了归化的策略。

【3】"又见秦钟腼腆温柔，未语面先红，怯怯羞羞，有女儿之风"一句，杨译是"Chin Chung was bashful and gentle, so shy that he blushed like a girl before he spoke"，译者采用了"so... that"引导的结果状语从句和表示时间关系的连词"before"将"未语面先红""怯怯羞羞""有女儿之风"三个小句自然地连接了起来。霍译是"the other scholars observed how shrinking and gentle Qin Zhong was, blushing almost before you spoke to him and timid and bashful as a girl"，在连句手段上，霍译使用了"how"引导的宾语从句，在宾语从句的后半部分，使用了现在分词短语"blushing almost before..."做伴随状语，进一步说明秦钟的腼腆温柔。另外，"未语面先红"的主语是"秦钟"，霍译处理为"blushing almost before you spoke to him"，译者可能想更深入地刻画秦钟的腼腆之态：别人同他说话，他都会害羞得脸红。

【4】"原来薛蟠自来王夫人处住后，便知有一家学，学中广有青年子弟，不免偶动了龙阳之兴，"一句中，"龙阳之兴"典出《战国策·魏策》，原指战国时龙阳君以男色事魏王而得宠，后来代指喜好男色。杨译"Now Hsueh Pan had not been long in the Jung Mansion before he learned of this school, and the thought of all the boys there appealed to his baser instincts."用归化法将"龙阳之兴"译为"baser instincts（不道德的本能）"。霍译"When Xue Pan learned, some time after moving into his aunt's place in the capital, that the establishment included a clan school plentifully stocked with young males of a certain age, his old enthusiasm for 'Lord Long-yang's vice' was reawakened,"采取了异化法，将"龙阳之兴"译为"Lord Long-yang's vice"。关于句子结构，杨译使用了"before... and..."进行连句；"had not been long"和"learned"分别是过去完成时和一般过去时，显示出动作发生的先后顺序。霍译使用了"when... that..."进行连句，译者在"when"引导的时间状语从句中套了"that"引导的宾语从句，英语中这种从句套从句的结构和汉语流水铺排的句式结构非常不同。另外，两位译者都用了句子化短语法把小句"学中广有青年子弟"译为介词短语"of all the boys there"和过去分词短语"plentifully stocked with young males of a certain age"。

【5】"三日打鱼，两日晒网"是句俗语，杨译"who fishes for three days

and then suns his net for two"完全对应原文;霍译"one day fishing and two days to dry the nets"则对原文做了改动,变成了"一天打鱼,两天晒网"。

【6】"白送些束脩礼物与贾代儒,却不曾有一些儿进益,只图结交些契弟。"此句由三个小句构成,主语都是"薛蟠",他发出了一连串动作:"白送、不曾有、只图结交"。杨译"The fee he paid Chia Tai-ju was thrown away, for he had no intention of really studying, his sole aim being to find some 'sweet-hearts' there."处理得很有技巧:译者给原文的三小句分别加上了对应的主语,依次是"the fee""he"和"his sole aim",并且采用了"for"引导的原因状语从句和从句中的独立主格(his sole aim being to find some 'sweet-hearts' there)进行连句。霍译"Having paid a generous fee to Jia Dai-ru, he used his membership of the school merely as a means of picking up 'soul-mates' from among his fellow-students."中只使用了一个主语:"he";句首使用了现在分词短语的完成式(having paid a generous fee to Jia Dai-ru)做时间状语,表示状语中的动作(pay)和谓语的动作(use)先后发生。

【7】"更又有两个多情的小学生,亦不知是那一房的亲眷,亦未考真名姓,只因生得妩媚风流,满学中都送了他两个外号,一号'香怜',一号'玉爱'。"杨译是"Chief among these were two amorous youths whose real names have not been ascertained, nor the branches of the family to which they belonged. But on account of their good looks and charm they were nicknamed Sweetie and Lovely."译者使用"whose""nor""to which""But"等词进行连句。开句是倒装句,主语"two amorous youths"因为后跟定语从句显得头重而被后置;"nor..."一句是省略句,完整的句式是:nor have the branches of the family to which they belonged been ascertained。霍译是"Among them were two amorous young creatures whose names and parentage escape us but who, because of their glamorous looks and affected manners, were universally known by the nicknames of 'Darling' and 'Precious'."译者是通过"whose""but""who""because of"进行连句的。开句因为同上原因也采用了倒装语序,主语"two amorous young creatures"带了两个定语从句,分别由"whose"和"who"引导,两个定语从句由"but"连接。两位译者都使用了句子化短语法,将小句"只因生得妩媚

风流"译为介词短语"on account of their good looks and charm"或"because of their glamorous looks and affected manners"。

【8】"如今宝、秦二人一来，见了他两个，也不免缱绻羡慕，亦因知系薛蟠相知，故未敢轻举妄动。"主语"宝、秦二人"发出了一连串的动作："一来""见了""缱绻羡慕""亦知""未敢""轻举妄动"，体现出汉语连动句式的特点。杨译是"Pao-yu and Chin Chung were naturally attracted by these boys too, but knowing them to be Hsueh Pan's friends they did not venture to make any overtures."，译者用转折连词"but"连接两个分句，在第二个分句中，因为是同一个主语（Pao-yu and Chin Chung）发出的连串动作，译者使用了现在分词短语"knowing them to be Hsueh Pan's friends"作原因状语。霍译是"When Qin Zhong and Bao-yu joined the school it was only to be expected that they too should fall under the spell of this charming pair; but like the rest they were inhibited from overt declaration of their feelings by the knowledge that Xue Pan was their 'friend'."译者用分号以及转折连词"but"连接两个分句；在第一句中用"when"引导时间状语从句，主句中"it"是形式主语，真正的主语"that they too should fall under the spell of this charming pair"后置句尾；在第二句的句尾有一个"that"引导的同位语从句，用来解释说明"knowledge"的具体内容。另外，译者将原文中的动词"知"译为名词"knowledge"，使用了汉译英中常见的词性转化法。

四、词汇表

1. apt [æpt]	adj.	suitable or appropriate in the circumstances 恰当的；适当的
	adv.	aptly
2. bashful [ˈbæʃfʊl]	adj.	shy and easily embarrassed 羞怯的；忸怩的
3. self-effacing [ˌselfɪˈfeɪsɪŋ]	adj.	not wanting to attract attention to yourself or your abilities 谦逊的；不求闻达的

4. base [beɪs]	*adj.*	not having moral principles or rules 卑鄙的；不道德的
5. amorous [ˈæm(ə)rəs]	*adj.*	showing sexual desire and love towards sb 表示性爱的；含情脉脉的
6. have designs on sb		to want to start a sexual relationship with sb 企图占有某人；存心与某人发生性关系；对某人存心不良
7. unmolested [ˌʌnməˈlestɪd]	*adj.*	not disturbed or attacked by sb 不受打搅（或攻击）
8. overture [ˈəʊvətj(ʊ)ə]	*n.*	a suggestion or an action by which sb tries to make friends, start a business relationship, have discussions, etc. with sb else（向某人作出的）友好姿态；建议
9. chaff [tʃɑːf; tʃæf]	*n.*	the outer covering of the seeds of grain such as wheat, which is separated from the grain before it is eaten 谷壳；糠
10. defer to sb/sth		to agree to accept what sb has decided or what they think about sb/sth because you respect him or her 遵从；听从；顺从
11. pretence [prɪˈtens]	*n.*	the act of behaving in a particular way, in order to make other people believe sth that is not true 假象；伪装；虚伪的表现
12. delude [dɪˈl(j)uːd]	*v.*	to make sb believe sth that is not true 欺骗；哄骗
13. glamorous [ˈglæmərəs]	*adj.*	especially attractive and exciting, and different from ordinary things or people 特别富有魅力的；富于刺激的；独特的
14. conducive [kənˈdjuːsɪv]	*adj.*	**be conducive to sth**: if a situation is conducive to sth such as work, rest, etc., it provides conditions that make it easy for

			you to work, etc. 有助于某事；有益于某事
15. deter [dɪˈtɜ:]		v.	**~ sb from sth/from doing sth**: to make sb decide not to do sth or continue doing sth, especially by making them understand the difficulties and unpleasant results of their actions 制止；阻止；威慑；使不敢
16. meddle [ˈmedl]		v.	to become involved in sth that does not concern you 管闲事
17. spell [spel]		n.	a quality that a person or thing has that makes them so attractive or interesting that they have a strong influence on you 魅力；魔力
18. overt [əʊˈvɜ:t]		adj.	done in an open way and not secretly 公开的；明显的；不隐瞒的
19. reciprocate [rɪˈsɪprəkeɪt]		v.	to behave or feel towards sb in the same way as they behave or feel towards you 回报；回应
20. cryptic [ˈkrɪptɪk]		adj.	with a meaning that is hidden or not easily understood 含义隐晦的；晦涩难懂的
21. discern [dɪˈsɜ:n]		v.	to know, recognize or understand sth, especially sth that is not obvious 觉察出；识别；了解
22. communion [kəˈmju:njən]		n.	the state of sharing or exchanging thoughts and feelings（思想感情的）交流；交融
23. leer [lɪə]		v.	to look or smile at sb in an unpleasant way that shows an evil or a sexual interest in them（邪恶地或色迷迷地）看；发笑
24. convulse [kənˈvʌls]		v.	to be laughing so much, so angry, etc. that

you cannot control your movements （因笑、生气等）全身抖动

25. paroxysm [ˈpærəksɪzəm]   *n.*   a sudden strong feeling or expression of an emotion that cannot be controlled 突然发作

第十回

金寡妇贪利权受辱　张太医论病细穷源

Widow Chin Pockets Her Pride Because of Self-Interest
Dr. Chang Diagnoses Ko-ching's Illness (Yang)

Widow Jin's self-interest gets the better of her righteous indignation
And Doctor Zhang's diagnosis reveals the origin of a puzzling disease (Hawkes)

一、本回概述

　　金荣迫于压力，向秦钟道歉，心里始终不服，回家后向母亲抱怨，被其母劝住。金荣的母亲与金荣姑姑即贾璜之妻金氏谈及此事，金氏闻言大怒，欲前去宁府，找秦可卿理论，却只见到尤氏。闲谈中，尤氏提起秦可卿的病势迁延不愈，自己颇感忧虑烦心，又说及秦钟在学堂里被人欺侮，金氏遂不敢多言，自去不提。贾珍之友冯紫英推荐的大夫张友士为可卿看病，他把脉极准，指出病源，并开出药方，让秦氏服用。

第十回

二、篇章节选

原文

话说金荣因人多势众，又兼贾瑞勒令，赔了不是，给秦钟磕了头，宝玉方才不吵闹了。[1] 大家散了学，金荣回到家中，越想越气，[2] 说："秦钟不过是贾蓉的小舅子，又不是贾家的子孙，附学读书，也不过和我一样。他因仗着宝玉和他好，他就目中无人。[3] 他既是这样，就该做些正经事，人也没的说。他素日又和宝玉鬼鬼祟祟的，只当人都是瞎子，看不见。[4] 今日他又去勾搭人，偏偏的撞在我眼睛里。就是闹出事来，我还怕什么不成？"

他母亲胡氏听见他咕咕哝哝的说，因问道："你又要争什么闲气？好容易我望你姑妈说了，你姑妈千方百计的才向他们西府里的琏二奶奶跟前说了，你才得了这个念书的地方。[5] 若不是仗着人家，咱们家里还有力量请的起先生？况且人家学里，茶也是现成的，饭也是现成的。你这二年在那里念书，家里也省好大的嚼用呢。省出来的，你又爱穿件鲜明衣服。再者，不是因你在那里念书，你就认得什么薛大爷了？那薛大爷一年不给不给，这二年也帮了咱们有七八十两银子。[6] 你如今要闹出了这个学房，再要找这么个地方，我告诉你说罢，比登天还难呢！[7] 你给我老老实实的顽一会子睡你的觉去，好多着呢。"于是金荣忍气吞声，不多一时他自去睡了。次日仍旧上学去了。不在话下。

杨译

With heavy pressure on him and orders from Chia Jui to apologize, Chin Jung had to appease Pao-yu by kowtowing to Chin Chung.[1] Then school was dismissed and he went home, where the more he brooded the angrier he grew.[2]

"That flunkey Chin Chung is only Chia Jung's brother-in-law, not a son or grandson of the Chia family," he fumed. "He's only in the school on sufferance, just as I am. But on the strength of his friendship with Pao-yu he looks down on everyone else.[3] If he at least behaved decently no one would mind; but the two of them must think the rest of us are blind, the way they carry on.[4] Well, I caught him today making up to someone else, so I needn't be afraid even if the whole thing comes out."

"What scrape are you in now?" asked his mother, née Hu, when she heard this muttering. "I had to rope in your aunt and put her to no end of trouble to beg Madam Hsi-feng in the West Mansion to get you this place in the family school.[5] Where would we be if not for their help? We couldn't afford a tutor. Besides, you get free meals there, don't you? That's meant a great saving on your board these last two years. It's fitted you out in all those smart clothes you're so fond of. It was through the school, too, that you met Mr. Hsueh who's helped us this last year or so to the tune of seventy or eighty taels of silver at least.[6] If you're expelled because of this row, don't expect me to find another school like this. I can tell you, that would be harder than climbing up to heaven.[7] Just amuse yourself quietly now before going to bed. That would be much better."

Chin Jung had to swallow his anger and hold his tongue, and very soon he turned in. The next day he went back to school as if nothing had happened.

霍译

Outnumbered, and hard pressed by Jia Rui to apologize, Jokey Jin made a kotow to Qin Zhong, whereupon Bao-yu agreed to let the matter drop.[1] Back in his own home, when school was over, he brooded with mounting anger on his humiliation.[2]

'Qin Zhong is Jia Rong's brother-in-law: it's not as if he were one of the Jia clan. He's only an external scholar, the same as me; and it's only because he is friends with Bao-yu that he can afford to be so high and mighty.[3] Well, in that case he ought to behave himself, then no one would have any cause to complain. But he's always carrying on in such a sneaky, underhand way with Bao-yu, as though he thought the rest of us were all blind and couldn't see what he was up to.[4] And now today he's started making up to someone else and I happen to have found him out. So what if there *were* a row about this? I've got nothing to be afraid of.'

His mother, Widow Jin, overheard his muttering.

'What have you been getting up to this time?' she asked. 'Look at the job we had getting you into that school. All the talks I had with your aunt and the trouble she went to to see Mrs Lian about it.[5] Suppose we hadn't had their help in getting you in there, we could never have afforded a tutor. What's more, you get free tea and free dinners there, don't you? That has meant a big saving for us during the two years you have been going there. And you're glad enough to have something decent to wear out of the money saved, aren't you? And another thing. If you hadn't been going to that school, how would you ever have met that Mr Xue of yours? Between seventy and eighty taels of silver we've had out of him during this past year.[6] I can tell you this, my boy. If you get yourself thrown out of there, you needn't think you can get in anywhere else, because you could easier fly to the moon than find another place like that.[7] Now you just play quietly for a bit and then go to bed like a good boy!'

Thus admonished, Jokey Jin swallowed his anger and fell silent. Before long he went to bed and to sleep, and next day was back at the school again as usual. Of him no more.

三、注释评点

【1】"话说金荣因人多势众，又兼贾瑞勒令，赔了不是，给秦钟磕了头，宝玉方才不吵闹了。"杨译是"With heavy pressure on him and orders from Chia Jui to apologize, Chin Jung had to appease Pao-yu by kowtowing to Chin Chung." 霍译是"Outnumbered, and hard pressed by Jia Rui to apologize, Jokey Jin made a kotow to Qin Zhong, whereupon Bao-yu agreed to let the matter drop." 原文的句内逻辑关系是：人多势众、贾瑞勒令是原因，结果是金荣给秦钟赔不是磕了头；磕头赔不是的结果是宝玉不再吵闹了。可以看出，此句前前为因，后后为果，因果关系层层递进。相较之下，霍译更清楚地表达了原文的逻辑关系：译者先是用过去分词"outnumbered"和过去分词短语"hard pressed by Jia Rui to apologize"做原因状语，说明金荣屈服的两个原因，导致的结果用主句来表达："Jokey Jin made a kotow to Qin Zhong"，接着用"whereupon"引导出连锁结果："Bao-yu agreed to let the matter drop"。两位译者都使用了句子化短语法：将小

句"金荣因人多势众，又兼贾瑞勒令"分别译为介词短语（With heavy pressure on him and orders from Chia Jui to apologize）和过去分词短语（Outnumbered, and hard pressed by Jia Rui to apologize），在译文中充当原因状语。

【2】"大家散了学，金荣回到家中，越想越气"一句，杨译是"Then school was dismissed and he went home, where the more he brooded the angrier he grew."，此处译者用"then"承接前句，用"and"和"where"进行句内连接，这些词汇的使用充分体现出意合语言转化为形合语言时，要增加表示逻辑关系的连接词。霍译"Back in his own home, when school was over, he brooded with mounting anger on his humiliation."则在主句之前放置两个状语，分别是表示地点的状语"back in his own home"和表示时间的状语从句"when school was over"，句尾的"with mounting anger"是方式状语。在英语中，状语使用得非常频繁，且位置灵活，可置于句首、句中或句尾。另外，霍克斯把"越想越气"翻译为"he brooded with mounting anger on his humiliation"，他增加了短语"on his humiliation"，指出他想的内容以及生气的原因，这样的表达不仅内容上很准确，而且符合英语行文注重结构完整性的语言习惯。

【3】"他因仗着宝玉和他好，他就目中无人。"一句，杨译是"But on the strength of his friendship with Pao-yu he looks down on everyone else."，译者用句子化短语法将小句"他因仗着宝玉和他好"转化为介词短语"on the strength of his friendship with Pao-yu"。霍译"... and it's only because he is friends with Bao-yu that he can afford to be so high and mighty."使用了强调句型，强调他目中无人的原因：only because he is friends with Bao-yu。

【4】"他素日又和宝玉鬼鬼祟祟的，只当人都是瞎子，看不见。"一句，杨译是"… but the two of them must think the rest of us are blind, the way they carry on"，译者没有直接翻译"他素日又和宝玉鬼鬼祟祟的"，而是含糊地译为"the way they carry on"。霍译是"But he's always carrying on in such a sneaky, underhand way with Bao-yu, as though he thought the rest of us were all blind and couldn't see what he was up to."在内容上，译者充分表达出原文的所有信息；在句子结构上，他使用了"as though"和"and"进行句内连接；在翻译"看不见"时，他增译了"what he was up to"，不仅增加了句子尾重，而且更加符合英语句

式结构注重完整性的行文习惯。

【5】"好容易我望你姑妈说了，你姑妈千方百计的才向他们西府里的琏二奶奶跟前说了，你才得了这个念书的地方。"一句中包含三个主语：我、你姑妈、你。杨译是"I had to rope in your aunt and put her to no end of trouble to beg Madam Hsi-feng in the West Mansion to get you this place in the family school."其连句方法很有特点，全句只保留了一个主语"I（我）"，将"你姑妈"和"你"分别译为"put"和"get"的宾语。霍译"Look at the job we had getting you into that school. All the talks I had with your aunt and the trouble she went to see Mrs Lian about it."则调换了原文的句序，先翻译结果（the job we had getting you into that school），后翻译达到结果的手段和方法（all the talks… 和 the trouble…）。而且，"Look at the job..."是祈使句，主语是被省略的"you"，"the job"的内容是后文的"all the talks..."和"the trouble..."。祈使句的运用生动地再现了原文的场景：母亲罗列儿子上学的难处，责备儿子太不懂事。

【6】"再者，不是因你在那里念书，你就认得什么薛大爷了？那薛大爷一年不给不给，这二年也帮了咱们有七八十两银子。"，杨译是"It was through the school, too, that you met Mr. Hsueh who's helped us this last year or so to the tune of seventy or eighty taels of silver at least."译者将原文第一句的反问结构译为陈述句，并且使用了强调结构，同时用定语从句的引导词"who"代替了原文中第二句的主语"那薛大爷"，避免了表述上的重复。霍译是"If you hadn't been going to that school, how would you ever have met that Mr Xue of yours? Between seventy and eighty taels of silver we've had out of him during this past year."该译文的第一句使用了虚拟语气，同时保留了原文的反问语气；第二句把宾语"Between seventy and eighty taels of silver"置于句首，有强调的作用。

【7】"比登天还难呢！"是一句俗语，杨译"... that would be harder than climbing up to heaven."采用了异化策略；霍译"... you could easier fly to the moon than find another place like that."则创造性地将原文译为"再寻找一个这样的学校比登月还难呢"。

四、词汇表

1. appease [əˈpiːz] v. to make sb calmer or less angry by giving them what they want 安抚；抚慰

2. brood [bruːd] v. to think a lot about sth that makes you annoyed, anxious or upset 焦虑；忧思（使人厌烦、担忧或不安的事）

3. flunkey [ˈflʌŋki] n. a person who tries to please sb who is important and powerful by doing small jobs for them 阿谀奉承者；势利小人；马屁精

4. sufferance [ˈsʌf(ə)r(ə)ns] n. **on sufferance:** if you do sth on sufferance, sb allows you to do it although they do not really want you to 经勉强同意；由于（某人的）宽容

5. make up to sb to be pleasant to sb, praise them, etc. especially in order to get an advantage for yourself 献媚；奉承；讨好

6. scrape [skreɪp] n. a difficult situation that you have caused yourself 自己造成的困境

7. rope sb in to persuade sb to join in an activity or to help to do sth, even when they do not want to 劝说某人加入；说服某人帮忙

8. board [bɔːd] n. the meals that are provided when you stay in a hotel, guesthouse, etc.; what you pay for the meals （旅馆、招待所等提供的）伙食，膳食；膳食费用

9. fit sb/sth out to supply sb/sth with all the equipment,

		clothes, food, etc. they need 向……提供所需的东西（如装备、设备、衣服、粮食等）
10. row [rəʊ]	n.	a noisy argument between two or more people 吵架；争吵
11. turn in		to go to bed 上床睡觉
12. sneaky [ˈsniːki]	adj.	behaving in a secret and sometimes dishonest or unpleasant way 悄悄的；偷偷摸摸的；鬼鬼祟祟的
13. underhand [ˈʌndəhænd]	adj.	secret and dishonest 秘密的；阴险的；卑鄙的
14. admonish [ədˈmɒnɪʃ]	v.	to strongly advise sb to do sth 力劝；忠告

第十一回

庆寿辰宁府排家宴　见熙凤贾瑞起淫心

Chia Ching's Birthday Is Celebrated in the Ning Mansion
Chia Jui Meets and Lusts After Hsi-feng (Yang)

*Ning-guo House celebrates the birthday of an absent member
And Jia Rui conceives an illicit passion for his attractive cousin* (Hawkes)

一、本回概述

宁府设宴，为贾敬庆寿。饭后，熙凤、宝玉去探望秦可卿。可卿病重，宝玉伤心哭泣，熙凤便打发他先去会芳园，自己劝慰了秦氏一番。从秦氏房中出来，熙凤边行边欣赏园中景致，忽遇贾瑞拦路，没想到贾瑞言语轻佻，眼神暧昧，熙凤假意应承，内心恼火。可卿病情日渐沉重，众人忧心，独瞒贾母，熙凤经常前去探望宽慰。一日，回到家中，听平儿说贾瑞几次三番登门求见，熙凤心内发狠，准备用计惩罚贾瑞。

二、篇章节选

原文

　　秦氏拉着凤姐儿的手,强笑道:[1]"这都是我没福。[2]这样人家,公公婆婆当自己的女孩儿似的待。婶娘的侄儿虽说年轻,却也是他敬我,我敬他,从来没有红过脸儿。[3]就是一家子的长辈同辈之中,除了婶子倒不用说了,别人也从无不疼我的,也无不和我好的。这如今得了这个病,把我那要强的心一分也没了。公婆跟前未得孝顺一天;就是婶娘这样疼我,我就有十分孝顺的心,如今也不能够了。我自想着,未必熬的过年去呢。[4]"

　　宝玉正眼瞅着那《海棠春睡图》并那秦太虚写的"嫩寒锁梦因春冷,芳气笼人是酒香"的对联,[5]不觉想起在这里睡晌觉梦到"太虚幻境"的事来。正自出神,听得秦氏说了这些话,如万箭攒心,那眼泪不知不觉就流下来了。[6]凤姐儿心中虽十分难过,但恐怕病人见了众人这个样儿反添心酸,倒不是来开导劝解的意思了。[7]见宝玉这个样子,因说道:"宝兄弟,你忒婆婆妈妈的了。[8]他病人不过是这么说,那里就到得这个田地了?况且能多大年纪的人,略病一病儿就这么想那么想的,这不是自己倒给自己添病了么?"贾蓉道:"他这病也不用别的,只是吃得些饮食就不怕了。"凤姐儿道:"宝兄弟,太太叫你快过去呢。你别在这里只管这么着,倒招的媳妇也心里不好。太太那里又惦着你。"[9]因向贾蓉说道:"你先同你宝叔叔过去罢,我还略坐一坐儿。"贾蓉听说,即同宝玉过会芳园来了。

　　这里凤姐儿又劝解了秦氏一番,又低低的说了许多衷肠话儿,[10]尤氏打发人请了两三遍,凤姐儿才向秦氏说道:"你好生养着罢,我再来看你。合该你这病要好,所以前日就有人荐了这个好大夫来,再也是不怕的了。"秦氏笑道:"任凭神仙也罢,治得病治不得命。婶子,我知道我这病不过是挨日子。"[11]凤姐儿说道:"你只管这么想着,病那里能好呢?总要想开了才是。况且听得大夫说,若是不治,怕的是春天不好呢。如今才九月半,还有四五个月的工夫,什么病治不好呢?咱们若是不能吃人参的人家,这也难说了;你公公婆婆听见治得好你,别说一日二钱人参,就是二斤也能够吃的起。

对话杨宪益、霍克斯 ——《红楼梦》英译赏析（第一至四十回）

好生养着罢，我过园子里去了。"秦氏又道："婶子，恕我不能跟过去了。[12] 闲了时候还求婶子常过来瞧瞧我，咱们娘儿们坐坐，多说几遭话儿。"凤姐儿听了，不觉得又眼圈儿一红，遂说道："我得了闲儿必常来看你。"

杨译

Holding Hsi-feng's hand, Ko-ching forced a smile.[1]

"Living in a family like this is more than I deserve,"[2] she said. "My father-in-law and mother-in-law treat me as their own daughter. And although your nephew's young, we have such a regard for each other that we've never quarrelled.[3] In fact the whole family, old and young, not to mention you, dear aunt—that goes without saying—have been goodness itself to me and shown me nothing but kindness. But now that I've fallen ill all my will power's gone, and I haven't been able to be a good daughter-in-law. I want so much to show how I appreciate your goodness, aunt, but it's no longer in my power now. I doubt if I shall last the year out.[4]"

Pao-yu was looking pensively at the picture *Sleeping Under a Crab Apple Tree in Spring* and Chin Kuan's couplet:[5]

Coolness wraps her dream, for spring is chill;

A fragrance assails men, the aroma of wine.

As he raptly recalled his dream here of the Illusory Land of Great Void, Ko-ching's remarks pierced his heart like ten thousand arrows and unknown to himself his tears flowed.[6] Hsi-feng, distressed as she was, did not want to upset the patient even more, knowing it would be better to distract and console her.[7]

"You're a regular old woman, Pao-yu,"[8] she scolded. "It's not as bad as your niece would have us believe." She turned to Ko-ching. "How can someone your age give way to such foolish fancies just because of a little illness? Do you want to make yourself worse?"

"She'd be all right if only she'd eat," put in Chia Jung.

"Her Ladyship told you not to be too long," Hsi-feng reminded Pao-yu. "Don't hang about here upsetting Ko-ching and making Her Ladyship worry."[9] She then turned to Chia Jung and said, "Take Uncle Pao to rejoin the others while I stay here a little longer."

So Chia Jung led Pao-yu to the Garden of Concentrated Fragrance while Hsi-feng soothed Ko-ching and whispered some well-meant advice into her ear.[10]

When Madam Yu sent a servant for the third time to fetch her she said to Ko-ching, "Take good care of yourself. I'll come back again to see you. The fact that this good doctor has been recommended to us is a sign that you're going to get better. Don't you worry."

"Even if he were an immortal, he could cure a disease but not avert my fate," retorted Ko-ching with a smile. "I know it's only a matter of time now, auntie."[11]

"How can you get better if you keep thinking like that? You must look on the bright side. In any case, I'm told the doctor said that even if you're not cured there's no danger until the spring. It's only the middle of the ninth month now. You've four or five months yet, quite long enough to recover from any illness. It would be another matter if our family couldn't afford ginseng; but your father and mother-in-law can easily give you two catties of ginseng a day, not to mention two drams. Mind you rest well. I'm off now to the garden."

"I'm sorry I can't go with you, dear aunt,"[12] said Ko-ching. "Do come back again when you've time and let's have a few more good talks."

Hsi-feng's eyes smarted again at this. "Of course I'll come whenever I'm free," she promised.

霍译

Qin-shi grasped Xi-feng's hand and forced a smile to her wan face.[1]

'It looks as though I wasn't *meant* to be happy, Auntie!'[2] she said. 'This is such a lovely family to have married into. Rong's parents treat me as if I were their own daughter. Rong may be young, but he respects me, and I respect him; there has never been a cross word between us.[3] You, it goes without saying—but not only you, *all* the older members of the family—have always been goodness itself to me. I did so want to be worthy of all this kindness. But now this wretched illness has come along and taken away the chance. Now I shall never be able to be a good daughter to Rong's parents; and however badly I want to, I shall never be able to repay any of the love *you* have shown me. I have a feeling inside me, Auntie: I don't think I am going to last the year out. [4],

Bao-yu had been studying the 'Spring Slumber' painting on Qin-shi's wall all this time and re-reading the couplet by Qin Guan on the scrolls at each side of it: [5]

The coldness of spring has imprisoned the soft buds in a wintry dream.

The fragrance of wine has intoxicated the beholder with imagined flower-scents.

As he did so, the memory returned of that earlier afternoon when he had slept in that very same room and dreamed about the Land of Illusion. He was musing on the contents of that dream when he suddenly became aware of the words that Qin-shi was saying. They pierced his heart like the points of a thousand arrows. Great tears welled up in his eyes and rolled down his cheeks. [6] Xi-feng, seeing him, was herself deeply affected; but fearing that the sight of his grief might make Qin-shi even more distressed, whereas the declared purpose of their visit had been to cheer her up, she rallied him lightly on his tears. [7]

'Don't be such a baby, Bao-yu! [8] It's not really that serious: sick people always say things like that. Besides, she's still young, and when you are young you can shake an illness off in no time at all. —You mustn't let yourself think such stupid things,' she said, turning to Qin-shi. 'You'll make yourself worse.'

'If only she could get a bit of food inside her.' said Jia Rong. 'That's her real trouble: she won't eat anything.'

'Bao,' said Xi-feng, 'your mother told you not to stay long. If you're going to be like this, you will only upset her, and in any case I expect your mother is beginning to wonder about you. [9] —You go on ahead with Uncle Bao,' she said to Jia Rong. 'I am going to sit a little longer with your wife.'

Jia Rong at once led Bao-yu away to join the others in the All-scents Garden, while Xi-feng addressed some words of encouragement to Qin-shi, [10] after which,

dropping her voice to a murmur, she engaged in a long and intimate conversation with her, ignoring two or three messages from You-shi urging her to join the party. At last she felt unable to stay any longer.

'Look after yourself!' she said. 'I shall come again. I feel sure that you are meant to get better. It can't have been an accident that they found that doctor the other day; and now that you've got him, there's really nothing to worry about.'

Qin-shi smiled.

'Even if he's a miracle-man, Auntie, "death's a sickness none can cure", and I know that it's just a question of time now.'[11]

'If you *will* go on talking like that, how can you possibly get better?' said Xi-feng. 'If only you would try to look on the bright side. Remember what the doctor said. He said that if you weren't being properly treated, next spring would be dangerous for you. If this were a household which couldn't afford things like ginseng for your treatment, you might have something to worry about. But now they know that you can be cured, there's nothing Rong's parents wouldn't do and nothing they couldn't afford to do for you. Never mind two drams of ginseng a day; if you needed two *pounds* a day, they would get it for you gladly. So do try and get better! I must go over to the garden now.'

'Forgive me for not being able to see you out, Auntie,'[12] said Qin-shi. 'Please come again when you are free. We'll have a nice talk together, just the two of us.'

There were tears in Xi-feng's eyes as she promised to come often, whenever she was free.

三、注释评点

【1】"秦氏拉着凤姐儿的手,强笑道"一句,主语"秦氏"发出了两个动作:"拉着"和"笑道"。杨译是"Holding Hsi-feng's hand, Ko-ching forced a smile." 句式上呈现偏正结构,译者用现在分词短语"Holding Hsi-feng's hand"作伴随状语来翻译第一个动词"拉手",第二个动词"笑道"处理为该句的谓

语"forced a smile",表示"Holding Hsi-feng's hand"和"forced a smile"这两个动作同时发生。霍译"Qin-shi grasped Xi-feng's hand and forced a smile to her wan face."为并列结构,用"and"将两个动作"grasped Xi-feng's hand"和"forced a smile"连接起来,并且增译了"to her wan face"。

【2】"这都是我没福。"一句,杨译是"Living in a family like this is more than I deserve";霍译是"It looks as though I wasn't *meant* to be happy, Auntie!"两位译者都没有直接翻译"我没福"这一极具中国文化特色的小句,而是采用了归化策略去处理。

【3】"婶娘的侄儿虽说年轻,却也是他敬我,我敬他,从来没有红过脸儿。"一句,杨译是"And although your nephew's young, we have such a regard for each other that we've never quarrelled."译者用"although"和"such a... that"将原文中的四个小句"虽说年轻""他敬我""我敬他"和"从来没有红过脸儿"连接了起来;句首的"And"的作用是承接前句,"although"是引出下句。霍译"Rong may be young, but he respects me, and I respect him; there has never been a cross word between us."通过"but""and"以及分号进行句内连接。另外,译者用"he respects me, and I respect him"将"他敬我,我敬他"翻译得很完整,句式结构也与原文一致。

【4】"我自想着,未必熬的过年去呢。"一句,杨译是"I doubt if I shall last the year out."霍译是"I have a feeling inside me, Auntie: I don't think I am going to last the year out."首先,两位译者都用了"last the year out"这一非常地道的英语表达来翻译"熬的过年去"。另外,杨译将"我自想着"译为"I doubt",而霍译将其处理为"I have a feeling inside me",相比之下,霍译更能体现出人之将亡时的直觉感。

【5】"宝玉正眼瞅着那《海棠春睡图》并那秦太虚写的'嫩寒锁梦因春冷,芳气笼人是酒香'的对联"一句,杨译是"Pao-yu was looking pensively at the picture *Sleeping Under a Crab Apple Tree in Spring* and Chin Kuan's couplet...";霍译是"Bao-yu had been studying the 'Spring Slumber' painting on Qin-shi's wall all this time and re-reading the couplet by Qin Guan on the scrolls at each side of it"。杨译将"《海棠春睡图》"译为"*Sleeping Under a Crab Apple*

Tree in Spring",信息十分全面,霍克斯则将它略译为"Spring Slumber"。霍译中使用了"re-reading"一词,这个词建立了该句译文与前文的关联:第五回曾写道宝玉在可卿房中休息,读到过这副对联。另外,霍译中还有一处增译:"on the scrolls at each side of it",指明了对联的位置是在画的两边。对中国读者来说,这是无须赘言的文化现象,但对外国读者来说,这是文化空缺,所以有必要以增译的方式将其解释清楚。

【6】"正自出神。听得秦氏说了这些话,如万箭攒心,那眼泪不觉就流下来了。"杨译是"As he raptly recalled his dream here of the Illusory Land of Great Void, Ko-ching's remarks pierced his heart like ten thousand arrows and unknown to himself his tears flowed.";霍译是"He was musing on the contents of that dream when he suddenly became aware of the words that Qin-shi was saying. They pierced his heart like the points of a thousand arrows. Great tears welled up in his eyes and rolled down his cheeks."。杨译用"As""and"进行句内连接,"unknown to himself"是过去分词短语作伴随状语。霍译由三个句子构成:第一句使用了句型"sb was doing sth when sb (else) did sth (else)",表示一个过去的动作正在进行的时候,突然发生了另一个动作。而且,这个句子是从句套从句的结构:"when"引导的时间状语从句中套了"that"引导的定语从句。第二句中,霍译将"万箭"做了创造性的处理,将其译为"the points of a thousand arrows(千箭)"。不论是"千箭"还是"万箭",都是虚指,强调"多"的意思。

【7】"凤姐儿心中虽十分难过,但恐怕病人见了众人这个样儿反添心酸,倒不是来开导劝解的意思了。"一句,主语"凤姐儿"发出了一连串的动作:"难过""恐怕""开导劝解"。杨译"Hsi-feng, distressed as she was, did not want to upset the patient even more, knowing it would be better to distract and console her."将汉语流水句处理成英语句式的偏正结构。主语是"Hsi-feng";谓语部分是"did not want to upset the patient even more";"distressed as she was"是连词"as"引导的让步状语从句,相当于"although she was very distressed";"knowing it would be better to distract and console her"是现在分词短语作伴随状语。因此,全句的结构是:主语+让步状语从句+谓语部分+伴随状语。霍译是"Xi-feng, seeing him, was herself deeply affected; but fearing that the sight of his grief might make Qin-shi even more distressed, whereas the declared purpose of their visit had been to cheer her up, she rallied him lightly on his tears."全句通过"but""whereas"进行句内连接。由于该句中一个主语发出多个动作,译者很自然地使用了动词的非限定形式——现在分词:"seeing him"和"fearing that the sight of his grief..."这两个现在分词短语都充当原因状语。同时,在"fearing"之后的宾语从句中,译者用"whereas"进行句内连接,将意思相对立的两个部分"the sight of his grief might make Qin-shi even more distressed"和"the declared purpose of their visit had been to cheer her up"连接起来。

【8】"宝兄弟,你忒婆婆妈妈的了。"一句,杨译"You're a regular old woman, Pao-yu"将"婆婆妈妈"直译为"old woman";霍译"Don't be such a baby, Bao-yu!"将其改译为"a baby",意为"幼稚"。

【9】"你别在这里只管这么着,倒招的媳妇也心里不好。太太那里又惦着你。"一句由三个小句构成,杨译"Don't hang about here upsetting Ko-ching and making Her Ladyship worry."将其译为一句话,译者使用句子化短语法将两个小句"倒招的媳妇也心里不好"和"太太那里又惦着你"译为两个现在分词短语"upsetting Ko-ching"和"making Her Ladyship worry",由"and"连接,在译文中充当结果状语。霍译"If you're going to be like this, you will only upset her, and in any case I expect your mother is beginning to wonder about you."基本是按照原文的顺序翻译的,通过使用"if""and"完成了句内连接。

【10】"贾蓉听说,即同宝玉过会芳园来了。这里凤姐儿又劝解了秦氏一番,又低低的说了许多衷肠话儿"一句,杨译是"So Chia Jung led Pao-yu to the Garden of Concentrated Fragrance while Hsi-feng soothed Ko-ching and whispered some well-meant advice into her ear."霍译是"Jia Rong at once led Bao-yu away to join the others in the All-scents Garden, while Xi-feng addressed some words of encouragement to Qin-shi..."两位译者都使用并列连词"while"进行句内连接,表示前后两个分句中的动作同时发生。

【11】"秦氏笑道:'任凭神仙也罢,治得病治不得命。婶子,我知道我这病不过是挨日子。'"杨译是"'Even if he were an immortal, he could cure a disease but not avert my fate,' retorted Ko-ching with a smile. 'I know it's only a matter of time now, auntie.'"译者用异化策略将"神仙"译为"immortal"。霍译是"'Even if he's a miracle-man, Auntie, "death's a sickness none can cure", and I know that it's just a question of time now.'"译者用归化策略将"神仙"译为"miracle-man"。"治得病治不得命"一句,相比于杨译的"he could cure a disease but not avert my fate",霍译进行了创造性处理,即"death's a sickness none can cure",让人称妙。另外,"挨日子"一词,两位译者都采用了归化的手段,将其译为"a matter of time"和"a question of time"。

【12】"婶子,恕我不能跟过去了。"一句,杨译是"I'm sorry I can't go with you, dear aunt";霍译是"Forgive me for not being able to see you out, Auntie."两位译者对"跟过去了"的理解不同:杨译为"go with you",霍译为"see you out"。根据原文的语境,"跟过去"的意思应该是"跟您一起去参加生日庆典",并非"送您出去",所以,此处杨译更为准确。

四、词汇表

1. pensive [ˈpensɪv]	adj.	thinking deeply about sth, especially because you are sad or worried 沉思的;忧伤的;忧戚的
	adv.	pensively
2. assail [əˈseɪl]	v.	to attack sb violently, either physically or with words 攻击;抨击;袭击
3. rapt [ræpt]	adj.	so interested in one particular thing that you are not aware of anything else 全神贯注的;专心致志的
	adv.	raptly
4. distract [dɪˈstrækt]	v.	to take sb's attention away from what they are trying to do 转移(注意力);分散(思想);使分心
5. console [kənˈsəʊl]	v.	to give comfort or sympathy to sb who is

		unhappy or disappointed 安慰；抚慰；慰藉
6. avert [əˈvɜːt]	v.	to prevent sth bad or dangerous from happening 防止，避免（危险、坏事）
7. ginseng [ˈdʒɪnseŋ]	n.	a medicine obtained from a plant root that some people believe helps you stay young and healthy 人参；西洋参
8. wan [wæn]	adj.	looking pale and weak 苍白无力的；憔悴的
9. wretched [ˈretʃɪd]	adj.	extremely bad or unpleasant 极坏的；恶劣的
10. slumber [ˈslʌmbə]	n.	sleep 睡眠
11. intoxicate [ɪnˈtɒksɪkeɪt]	v.	make sb drunk 使醉酒
12. muse [mjuːz]	v.	to think carefully about sth for a time, ignoring what is happening around you 沉思；冥想

第十二回

王熙凤毒设相思局　贾天祥正照风月鉴

Hsi-feng Sets a Vicious Trap for a Lover
Chia Jui Looks into the Wrong Side of the Precious Mirror of Love (Yang)

Wang Xi-feng sets a trap for her admirer
And Jia Rui looks into the wrong side of the mirror (Hawkes)

一、本回概述

贾瑞常去给熙凤请安，熙凤假意欢迎，约定当晚私会于穿堂。熙凤故意爽约，贾瑞被困穿堂，腊月天气，朔风凛凛，侵肌裂骨，差点冻死。但他邪心不死，过了两日，又去找熙凤，熙凤见他不知悔改，约他晚上幽会于空屋。贾瑞不知是计，欣然前往，却被贾蓉、贾蔷二人戏弄，各勒索五十两白银，又被泼了一桶尿粪。回家后，贾瑞相思未解，又添债务，更有两回冻恼奔波，即发重病。家人请医治疗，于事无补。一日，跛足道人突然现身化缘，赠"风月宝鉴"，嘱他只能照反面，贾瑞不听劝阻，照了正面，一命呜呼。

二、篇章节选

原文

　　盼到晚上，果然黑地里摸入荣府，趁掩门时，钻入穿堂。[1] 果见漆黑无一人，往贾母那边去的门户已锁，倒只有向东的门未关。贾瑞侧耳听着，半日不见人来，忽听咯噔一声，东边的门也倒关了。贾瑞急的也不敢则声，只得悄悄的出来，将门撼了撼，关的铁桶一般。[2] 此时要求出去亦不能够，南北皆是大房墙，要跳亦无攀援。[3] 这屋内又是过门风，空落落。现是腊月天气，夜又长，朔风凛凛，侵肌裂骨，[4] 一夜几乎不曾冻死。好容易盼到早晨，只见一个老婆子先将东门开了，进去叫西门。贾瑞瞅他背着脸，一溜烟抱着肩跑了出来，[5] 幸而天气尚早，人都未起，[6] 从后门一径跑回家去。

　　原来贾瑞父母早亡，只有他祖父代儒教养。[7] 那代儒素日教训最严，不许贾瑞多走一步，生怕他在外吃酒赌钱，有误学业。今忽见他一夜不归，只料定他在外非饮即赌，嫖娼宿妓，那里想到这段公案，因此气了一夜。[8] 贾瑞也捏着一把汗，少不得回来撒慌，只说："往舅舅家去了，天黑了，留我住了一夜。"[9] 代儒道："自来出门，非禀我不敢擅出，如何昨日私自去了？据此亦该打，何况是撒谎。"因此，发恨到底打了三四十板，不许吃饭，令他跪在院内读文章，定要补出十天的工课来方罢。[10] 贾瑞直冻了一夜，今又遭了苦打，且饿着肚子，跪着在风地里读文章，其苦万状。[11]

杨译

　　That night, sure enough, he groped his way to the Jung Mansion, slipping into the entrance hall just before the gates were bolted.[1] It was pitch dark and not a soul was about. Already the gate to the Lady Dowager's quarters was locked, only the one on the east remaining open.

　　He waited, listening intently, but no one came. Then with a sudden clatter the east gate was bolted too. Frantic as he was, he dared not make a sound. He crept out to try the gate and found it securely closed.[2] Escape was out of the question, for the

walls on either side were too high to climb.[3]

The entrance hall was bare and draughty. As it was the depth of winter the nights were long and an icy north wind chilled him to the bone.[4] He almost froze to death.

At last dawn came and a matron appeared to open the east gate. As she went over to knock on the west gate and was looking the other way, Chia Jui shot out like a streak of smoke, hugging his shoulders.[5] Luckily no one else was up at this early hour.[6] He was able to escape unseen through the postern door.

Chia Jui had been orphaned early and left in the charge of his grandfather Chia Tai-ju,[7] a strict disciplinarian who allowed him no freedom for fear he drink or gamble outside and neglect his studies. Now that he had stayed out all night his grandfather was furious and suspected him of drinking, gambling or whoring, little guessing the truth of the matter.[8]

In a cold sweat with fright, Chia Jui tried to lie his way out.

"I went to my uncle's house, and because it was late he kept me for the night."[9]

"You have never dared leave home before without permission," thundered his grandfather. "You deserve a beating for sneaking off like that. And a worse one for deceiving me."

He gave Chia Jui thirty or forty strokes with a bamboo, would not let him have any food, and made him kneel in the courtyard to study ten days' lessons.[10] This thrashing on an empty stomach and kneeling in the wind to read essays completed the wretched youth's misery after his freezing night.[11]

霍译

Having waited impatiently for nightfall, he groped his way into the Rong-guo mansion just before they closed the gates and slipped into the gallery,[1] now totally deserted—as Xi-feng had promised it would be—and black as pitch.

The gate at the end of the alley-way opening on to Grandmother Jia's quarters had already been barred on the outer side; only the gate at the east end remained open. For a long time Jia Rui listened intently, but no one came. Suddenly there was a loud slam and the gate at the east end, too, banged shut. Alarmed, but not daring to make a sound, Jia Rui stealthily crept out and tried it. It was locked—as tight as a bucket. [2] Now even if he wanted to get out he could not, for the walls on either side of the alleyway were too high to scale. [3] Moreover the gallery was bare and draughty and this was the midwinter season when the nights are long and the bitter north wind seems to pierce into the very marrow of the bones. [4] By the end of the night he was almost dead with cold.

When at last morning came, Jia Rui saw the gate at the east end open and an old woman pass through to the gate opposite and call for someone to open up. Still hugging himself against the cold, he sprinted out of the other gate while her back was towards him. [5] Fortunately no one was about at that early hour, [6] and he was able to slip out of the rear entrance of the mansion and run back home unseen.

Jia Rui had lost both of his parents in infancy and had been brought up under the sole guardianship of his grandfather Jia Dai-ru. [7] Obsessed by the fear that once outside the house his grandson might indulge in drinking and gambling to the detriment of his studies, Dai-ru had subjected him since early youth to an iron discipline from which not the slightest deviation was tolerated. Seeing him now suddenly absent himself a whole night from home, and being incapable, in his wildest imaginings, of guessing what had really happened, he took it as a foregone conclusion that he had been either drinking or gaming and had probably passed the night in some house of prostitution—a supposition which caused the old gentleman to spend the whole night in a state of extreme choler. [8]

The prospect of facing his grandfather on arrival made Jia Rui sweat. A lie of some sort was indispensable.

'I went to see Uncle yesterday,' he managed to say, 'and as it was getting dark, he asked me to stay the night.' [9]

'I have always told you that you are not to go out of that gate without first informing me,' said his grandfather. 'Why then did you presume to go off on your own yesterday without saying a word to anybody? That in itself would constitute sufficient grounds for chastisement. But in addition to that you are lying!'

Thereupon he forced him to the ground, and, with the utmost savagery, dealt him thirty or forty whacks with the bamboo, after which he forbade him to eat and made him kneel in the open courtyard with a book in his hand until he had prepared the equivalent of ten days' homework.[10]

The exquisite torments suffered by Jia Rui, as he knelt with an empty stomach in the draughty courtyard reciting his homework after having already been frozen all night long and then beaten, can be imagined.[11]

三、注释评点

【1】"盼到晚上，果然黑地里摸入荣府，趁掩门时，钻入穿堂。"一句中，主语"贾瑞"发出了四个动作："盼、摸、趁、钻"。杨译"That night, sure enough, he groped his way to the Jung Mansion, slipping into the entrance hall just before the gates were bolted."省略了动词"盼"和"趁"，将"摸"和"钻"处理为偏正结构：其中，"正"是谓语部分"groped his way"；"偏"是现在分词短语充当的伴随状语"slipping into the entrance hall"，表示和"groped"这个动作几乎同时发生，意思是"摸进荣府后就钻入穿堂"。霍译"Having waited impatiently for nightfall, he groped his way into the Rong-guo mansion just before they closed the gates and slipped into the gallery"省译了动词"趁"，将另外三个动词分别处理为"having waited" "groped"和"slipped"，其中，"groped"和"slipped"是并列谓语，"having waited"是现在分词短语的完成式，充当时间状语，表示该动作先于"groped"和"slipped"发生。

【2】"贾瑞急的也不敢则声，只得悄悄的出来，将门撼了撼，关的铁桶一般。"一句，杨译"Frantic as he was, he dared not make a sound. He crept out to try the gate and found it securely closed."使用了归化法，将"关的铁桶一般"译为"found it securely closed"。霍译"Alarmed, but not daring to make a sound, Jia

Rui stealthily crept out and tried it. It was locked—as tight as a bucket." 使用了异化法直译该比喻,即"It was locked—as tight as a bucket."。

【3】"此时要求出去亦不能够,南北皆是大房墙,要跳亦无攀援。"一句,杨译"Escape was out of the question, for the walls on either side were too high to climb." 和霍译"Now even if he wanted to get out he could not, for the walls on either side of the alley-way were too high to scale." 都使用了表示原因的关系连词"for"进行句内连接。汉语是意合语言,很少用关系连词,句与句之间的逻辑关系是隐含的,是通过句意体现的;英语是形合语言,句与句之间的逻辑关系是显性的,要借助关系连词建构句子。

【4】"现是腊月天气,夜又长,朔风凛凛,侵肌裂骨"一句,杨译是"As it was the depth of winter the nights were long and an icy north wind chilled him to the bone."。句首是"As"引导的原因状语从句,其后是主句部分,由两个分句"the nights were long"和"an icy north wind chilled him to the bone"构成,之间由"and"连接。在第二个分句中,杨译将"朔风凛凛"译为名词短语"an icy north wind",在句中充当主语,将"侵肌裂骨"译为"chilled him to the bone",在句中充当谓语,巧妙地将原文中的两个小句合译为一句。霍译是"... this was the midwinter season when the nights are long and the bitter north wind seems to pierce into the very marrow of the bones.",主句"this was the midwinter season"是"主+系+表"结构,表语"the midwinter season"之后紧跟"when"引导的定语从句"when the nights are long and the bitter north wind seems to pierce into the very marrow of the bones",用来解释腊月天气的特点:"夜又长""朔风凛凛""侵肌裂骨"。与杨译不同,霍克斯在翻译腊月天气的特点时,用的时态是一般现在时,表明这是事实性的陈述。

【5】"一溜烟抱着肩跑了出来"一句,主语"贾瑞"发出了两个动作:"抱"和"跑"。杨译"Chia Jui shot out like a streak of smoke, hugging his shoulders." 将"抱肩(hugging his shoulders)"后置作伴随状语。霍译"Still hugging himself against the cold, he sprinted out of the other gate while her back was towards him." 也将"抱肩"译为伴随状语"hugging himself against the cold",将其置于句首。在英语中,状语的位置是非常灵活的,可位于句首、句中、句

尾。此外，霍克斯的增译部分"against the cold"给外国读者明示出"抱肩"的目的是为了"御寒"，使译文的语义更加完整。

【6】"幸而天气尚早，人都未起"一句，杨译"Luckily no one else was up at this early hour."和霍译"Fortunately no one was about at that early hour"都使用了句子化短语法，将小句"天气尚早"译为介词短语"at this early hour"和"at that early hour"，在译文中作时间状语。

【7】"原来贾瑞父母早亡，只有他祖父代儒教养。"一句中，主语分别是"贾瑞父母"和"他（贾瑞）祖父代儒"。为了使译文更加符合英语的行文习惯，杨译"Chia Jui had been orphaned early and left in the charge of his grandfather Chia Tai-ju,"和霍译"Jia Rui had lost both of his parents in infancy and had been brought up under the sole guardianship of his grandfather Jia Dai-ru."都将主语换成了"Chia Jui / Jia Rui（贾瑞）"。

【8】"今忽见他一夜不归，只料定他在外非饮即赌，嫖娼宿妓，那里想到这段公案，因此气了一夜。"一句，"非饮即赌，嫖娼宿妓"包含四个动词："饮、赌、嫖、宿"，其中"嫖娼"与"宿妓"是同义重复，两词意思基本相同。因此，杨译"Now that he had stayed out all night his grandfather was furious and suspected him of drinking, gambling or whoring, little guessing the truth of the matter."使用三个动名词"drinking"，"gambling"和"whoring"来翻译原文的四个动词，做介词of的宾语。此外，"那里想到这段公案"被译为现在分词短语"little guessing the truth of the matter"，在译文中充当伴随状语。霍译是"Seeing him now suddenly absent himself a whole night from home, and being incapable, in his wildest imaginings, of guessing what had really happened, he took it as a foregone conclusion that he had been either drinking or gaming and had probably passed the night in some house of prostitution—a supposition which caused the old gentleman to spend the whole night in a state of extreme choler."句首是两个表示原因的现在分词短语"seeing him now suddenly..."和"being incapable... of guessing..."。"conclusion"之后是由"that"引导的同位语从句"that he had been either drinking or gaming and had probably passed the night in some house of prostitution—a supposition which caused the old gentleman to spend the whole night in a state of extreme choler", 用来解释说明 "conclusion" 的具体内容; 破折号之后的 "a supposition" 也是 "conclusion" 的同位语。与杨译一样, 该译文也使用三个动词翻译原文的"饮、赌、嫖、宿", 在这里充当同位语从句的谓语: "had been either drinking or gaming" 和 "had probably passed the night..."。

【9】"往舅舅家去了, 天黑了, 留我住了一夜。"一句, 杨译 "I went to my uncle's house, and because it was late he kept me for the night." 使用 "and" 和 "because" 将原文中的三个小句连接起来; 霍译 "'I went to see Uncle yesterday,' he managed to say, 'and as it was getting dark, he asked me to stay the night.'" 也使用表示并列的 "and" 和表示原因的 "as" 进行连句。可以看出, 意合语言(汉语)向形合语言(英语)转换时, 经常需要增加表示逻辑关系的连接词, 以表明上下文之间的逻辑关系。

【10】"因此, 发恨到底打了三四十板, 不许吃饭, 令他跪在院内读文章, 定要补出十天的工课来方罢。"一句, 主语"贾代儒"发出了四个动作: "发恨、打、不许、令"。杨译 "He gave Chia Jui thirty or forty strokes with a bamboo, would not let him have any food, and made him kneel in the courtyard to study ten days' lessons." 将其中的三个动作译为并列谓语 "gave Chia Jui...(打)"、"would not let him...(不许)" 和 "made him...(令)"。霍译是 "Thereupon he, forced him to the ground, and, with the utmost savagery, dealt him thirty or forty whacks with the bamboo, after which he forbade him to eat and made him kneel in the open courtyard with a book in his hand until he had prepared the equivalent of ten days' homework.", 霍译主要依据程高本, 程高本此句的表述是: "因此发狠, 按倒打了三四十板, 还不许他吃饭, 叫他跪在院内读文章, 定要补出十天工课方罢。", 译者用 "Thereupon" 承接前文, 用 "and"、"after which"、"and"、"until" 进行句内连接, 其中, 主句和 "after which" 引导的从句中各有一个 "and": "forced... and... dealt... after which... forbade... and made...", 这个结构完成了四个动词的翻译: "按倒、打了、不许、叫", 随后, 用 "until" 与后文连接。

【11】"贾瑞直冻了一夜, 今又遭了苦打, 且饿着肚子, 跪着在风地里读文章, 其苦万状。"一句, 主语"贾瑞"发出了一系列的动作: "冻、遭

打、饿、跪、读"。杨译是"This thrashing on an empty stomach and kneeling in the wind to read essays completed the wretched youth's misery after his freezing night.",译者使用了不同的手法翻译这些动词:将多个汉语动词("冻、遭打、跪")转换为英语中的现在分词"freezing"、动名词"thrashing"和"kneeling";将"饿着肚子"处理为介词短语"on an empty stomach";将"读文章"处理为不定式"to read essays";另外,译者将"其苦万状"处理为谓语部分"completed the wretched youth's misery"。霍译"The exquisite torments suffered by Jia Rui, as he knelt with an empty stomach in the draughty courtyard reciting his homework after having already been frozen all night long and then beaten, can be imagined."的逻辑关系十分清楚,译者将"其苦万状"处理为主句"The exquisite torments suffered by Jia Rui can be imagined.";在主句的主语"The exquisite torments suffered by Jia Rui"和谓语"can be imagined"之间插入由"as"引导的时间状语从句;在这个时间状语从句中,"he"是主语,"knelt"是谓语,"with an empty stomach"是方式状语,"in the draughty courtyard"是地点状语,"reciting his homework"是伴随状语,"after having already been frozen all night long and then beaten"是时间状语。此处用了表示时间的介词"after"以及完成式"having already been frozen all night long and then beaten",说明"冻(frozen)"和"遭打(beaten)"这两个动作发生在前,"下跪(knelt)"和"读(reciting)"这两个动作发生在后,其逻辑关系为:贾瑞先被冻了一夜,然后挨了打,再饿着肚子跪在那儿背书。

四、词汇表

1. frantic [ˈfræntɪk]	*adj.*	unable to control your emotions because you are extremely frightened or worried about sth(由于恐惧或担心)无法控制感情的;发狂似的
2. draughty [ˈdrɑːfti]	*adj.*	(of a room, etc.) uncomfortable because cold air is blowing through 有过堂风的;

		有冷风吹过的
3. orphan [ˈɔːfn]	v.	to make a child an orphan 使成为孤儿
4. disciplinarian [ˌdɪsəplɪˈneəriən]	n.	a person who believes in using rules and punishments for controlling people 严格纪律信奉者；严格执行纪律者
5. furious [ˈfjʊəriəs]	adj.	very angry 狂怒的；暴怒的
6. wretched [ˈretʃɪd]	adj.	making you feel sympathy or pity 可怜的；悲惨的
7. scale [skeɪl]	v.	to climb to the top of sth very high and steep 攀登；到达……顶点
8. sprint [sprɪnt]	v.	to run or swim a short distance very fast 短距离快速奔跑（或游泳）；冲刺
9. guardianship [ˈgɑːdiənʃɪp]	n.	the state or position of being responsible for sb/sth 监护；监护地位；监护人的身份
10. obsess [əbˈses]	v.	to completely fill your mind so that you cannot think of anything else, in a way that is not normal 使痴迷；困扰
11. to the detriment of sb/sth		resulting in harm or damage to sb/sth （结果）不利于，有害于，有损于
12. deviation [ˌdiːviˈeɪʃn]	n.	the act of moving away from what is normal or acceptable 背离；偏离；违背
13. a foregone conclusion		if you say that sth is a foregone conclusion, you mean that it is a result that is certain to happen 预料的必然结局
14. chastise [tʃæˈstaɪz]	v.	to criticize sb for doing sth wrong 批评；指责；责备
	n.	chastisement

15. savagery [ˈsævɪdʒri]　　　*n.*　　behaviour that is very cruel and violent 残暴行为

16. whack [wæk]　　　*n.*　　the act of hitting sb/sth hard 重击

秦可卿死封龙禁尉[1]　　王熙凤协理宁国府

Ko-ching Dies and a Captain of the Imperial Guard Is Appointed[1]
Hsi-feng Helps to Manage Affairs in the Ning Mansion (Yang)

Qin-shi posthumously acquires the status of a Noble Dame[1]
And Xi-feng takes on the management of a neighbouring establishment (Hawkes)

一、本回概述

可卿病故，托梦给熙凤，提醒她盛筵必散，居安思危，并告知贾府近日将有喜事。宝玉听闻秦氏去世，急火攻心而吐血，连夜赶去吊唁。贾珍悲痛异常，高价购买了原为义忠亲王准备的棺木。秦氏的丫鬟瑞珠也触柱而亡，贾珍以孙女之礼殓殡。贾珍又为贾蓉捐得龙禁尉一职，这样可卿的葬礼就可以办得更风光一些。尤氏旧疾发作，贾珍身体欠佳，无人主事，遂听宝玉推荐，请熙凤协理宁国府。

第十三回

二、篇章节选

原文

话说凤姐儿自贾琏送黛玉往扬州去后,[2]心中实在无趣,每到晚间,不过和平儿说笑一回,就胡乱睡了。

这日夜间,正和平儿灯下拥炉倦绣,早命浓薰绣被,二人睡下,屈指算行程该到何处,不知不觉已交三鼓。平儿已睡熟了。凤姐方觉星眼微朦,恍惚只见秦氏从外走来,[3]含笑说道:"婶子好睡!我今日回去,你也不送我一程。因娘儿们素日相好,我舍不得婶子,故来别你一别。还有一件心愿未了,非告诉婶子,别人未必中用。"

凤姐听了,恍惚问道:"有何心愿?你只管托我就是了。"秦氏道:"婶婶,你是个脂粉队里的英雄,连那些束带顶冠的男子也不能过你,你如何连两句俗语也不晓得?[4]常言'月满则亏,水满则溢';[5]又道是'登高必跌重'。如今我们家赫赫扬扬,已将百载,一日倘或乐极悲生,若应了那句'树倒猢狲散'[6]的俗语,岂不虚称了一世的诗书旧族了!"凤姐听了此话,心胸大快,十分敬畏,忙问道:"这话虑的极是,但有何法可以永保无虞?"秦氏冷笑道:"婶子好痴也。[7]否极泰来,[8]荣辱自古周而复始,[9]岂人力能可保常的?[10]但如今能于荣时筹画下将来衰时的世业,亦可谓常保永全了。即如今日诸事都妥,只有两件未妥,若把此事如此一行,则后日可保永全了。"

杨译

Hsi-feng found life excessively dull after her husband's departure with Tai-yu for Yangchow.[2] She passed the evenings as best she could chatting with Ping-erh before retiring listlessly to bed.

One evening, tired of embroidering, she sat nursing her hand-stove by the lamp and told the maid to warm her embroidered quilt early, after which they both went to bed. When the third watch sounded they were still reckoning on their fingers the stage

Chia Lien must have reached on his journey. Soon after that, Ping-erh fell fast asleep. And Hsi-feng's eyelids were drooping drowsily when to her astonishment in came Ko-ching.[3]

"How you love to sleep, aunt!" cried Ko-ching playfully. "I'm going home today, yet you won't even see me one stage of the way. But we've always been so close, I couldn't go without coming to say goodbye. Besides, there's something I'd like done which it's no use my entrusting to anyone else."

"Just leave it to me," replied Hsi-feng, rather puzzled.

"You're such an exceptional woman, aunt, that even men in official belts and caps are no match for you. Is it possible you don't know the sayings[4] that 'the moon waxes only to wane, water brims only to overflow,'[5] and 'the higher the climb the harder the fall'? Our house has prospered for nearly a hundred years. If one day it happens that at the height of good fortune the 'tree falls and the monkeys scatter'[6] as the old saying has it, then what will become of our cultured old family?"

Quick to comprehend, Hsi-feng was awe-struck. "Your fears are well-founded," she said. "But how can we prevent such a calamity?"

"Now you're being naive, aunt,"[7] Ko-ching laughed caustically. "Fortune follows calamity[8] as disgrace follows honour.[9] This has been so from time immemorial. How can men prevent it?[10] The only thing one can do is to make some provision for lean years in times of plenty. All's well at present except for two things. Take care of them and the future will be secure."

霍译

After Jia Lian's departure for Yangchow[2] Xi-feng felt bored and unhappy, particularly in the evenings when, apart from chatting with Patience, there seemed little to do but sleep. On the occasion of which we write she had sat beside the lamp with Patience until late into the evening; then, the bedding having been well warmed, the two women had gone to bed, where they lay until after midnight discussing the stages of Jia Lian's journey and attempting to calculate what point he was likely to

have reached in it. By this time Patience was fast asleep and Xi-feng herself was on the point of dropping off when she became dimly aware that Qin-shi had just walked into the room from outside.[3]

'So fond of sleep, Auntie?' said Qin-shi with a gentle smile. 'I shall have to begin my journey today without you to see me off. But never mind! Since you cannot come to me, I have come to you instead. We two have always been so close, I could not have borne to leave you without saying good-bye. Besides, I have a last wish that you alone must hear, because I cannot trust anyone else with it.'

'What is your wish?' Xi-feng heard herself asking. 'You can trust me to carry it out for you.'

'Tell me, Auntie,' said Qin-shi, 'how is it that you who are such a paragon among women that even strong men find more than their match in you can yet be ignorant of the simple truths expressed in homely proverbs?[4] Take this one:

The full moon smaller grows,

Full water overflows.[5]

Or this:

The higher the climb, the harder the fall.

Our house has now enjoyed nearly a century of dazzling success. Suppose one day "joy at its height engenders sorrow". And suppose that, in the words of another proverb, "when the tree falls, the monkeys scatter".[6] Will not our reputation as one of the great, cultured households of the age then turn into a hollow mockery?'

Qin-shi's question made Xi-feng feel uneasy, though at the same time inspiring a deep respect in her for her niece's foresight.

'You are quite right to show concern,' she said. 'Is there any means by which we can keep permanently out of danger?'

'Now you are being silly, Auntie!'[7] said Qin-shi somewhat scornfully. '"The extreme of adversity is the beginning of prosperity"—and the reverse of that saying is also true.[8] Honour and disgrace follow each other in an unending cycle.[9] No human power can arrest that cycle and hold it permanently in one position.[10] What you *can* do, however, is to plan while we are still prosperous for the kind of heritage that will stand up to the hard times when they come.

'At the moment everything seems well looked after; but in fact there are still two matters that have not been properly taken care of. If you will deal with them in the way that I shall presently suggest, you will be able to face the future without fear of calamity.'

三、注释评点

【1】"秦可卿死封龙禁尉"是本回回目的上句，杨译"Ko-ching Dies and a Captain of the Imperial Guard Is Appointed"语义表达得较为模糊，容易被误解为"可卿故去，被封龙禁尉"，而小说情节是贾蓉在妻子可卿死后被封"龙禁尉"，这样可卿的葬礼就可以办得体面一些。霍译"Qin-shi posthumously acquires the status of a Noble Dame"避免直接翻译"龙禁尉"，而是说"可卿在身后获得'贵妇'地位"，堪称妙译。

【2】"自贾琏送黛玉往扬州去后"一句中出现了两个动词："送""去"。杨译"... after her husband's departure with Tai-yu for Yangchow"和霍译"After Jia Lian's departure for Yangchow..."都使用了名词"departure"和介词"for"来翻译原文中的动词。两个译文都体现出英汉两种语言的差异：汉语是动态语言，多用动词；英语是静态语言，介词、名词用得较多。

【3】"凤姐方觉星眼微朦，恍惚只见秦氏从外走来"一句，杨译"And Hsi-feng's eyelids were drooping drowsily when to her astonishment in came Ko-ching."的时态结构是：过去进行时（主句）+一般过去时（"when"引导的从句），表示主句的动作正在发生时，从句的动作突然发生。霍译是"Xi-feng herself was on the point of dropping off when she became dimly aware that Qin-shi had just walked into the room from outside."，主句中的"was on the point of dropping off"相当于"was dropping off"，所以，霍译的句子结构与杨译相同。

【4】"婶婶，你是个脂粉队里的英雄，连那些束带顶冠的男子也不能过你，你如何连两句俗语也不晓得？"一句，杨译是"You're such an exceptional woman, aunt, that even men in official belts and caps are no match for you. Is it possible you don't know the sayings..."；霍译是"how is it that you who are such a paragon among women that even strong men find more than their match in you can yet be ignorant of the simple truths expressed in homely proverbs?"，两个译文都使用"such a(n)... that..."进行连句。另外，"束带顶冠的男子"一词，杨译"men in official belts and caps"指的是学而优则仕的官僚阶层；霍译"strong men"更侧重于"体格健壮"。依据原文来看，杨译更准确一些。另外，霍译的整体结构是反问句"how is it that..."："it"是形式主语，真正的主语是紧跟其后的"that"引导的从句，该从句的主语"you"又带了一个"who"引导的定语从句。

【5】"月满则亏，水满则溢"一句，杨译"the moon waxes only to wane, water brims only to overflow"翻译得非常准确，与原文契合度很高。霍译"The full moon smaller grows, Full water overflows."在形式上很特别，上下两句，分别起段；另外，"grows"和"overflows"押尾韵，所以，霍译的句式和韵脚都体现出诗体美感。

【6】"树倒猢狲散"是一句俗语，其中，"树倒"是原因，"猢狲散"是结果。杨译"tree falls and the monkeys scatter"和霍译"when the tree falls, the monkeys scatter"都体现出意合语言（汉语）向形合语言（英语）转化时的技巧：汉语通常不需要关系连词，英语则需要表示逻辑关系的连词来连接上下文。此处，杨译用了表示结果的连词"and"，霍译用了表示时间的连词"when"。

【7】"婶子好痴也。"一句，杨译"Now you're being naive, aunt"和霍译"Now you are being silly, Auntie!"使用的句型都是"You are being..."。需要注意的是："sb is being naive/silly"和"sb is naive/silly"的区别在于：前者指某人在某件事上是一时糊涂，后者则表示一个人的常性就是糊涂。

【8】"否极泰来"的翻译，杨译"Fortune follows calamity"的意思是"灾难之后就是好运"，简单明了；霍译"'The extreme of adversity is the beginning of prosperity'—and the reverse of that saying is also true."将成语"否极泰来"中隐含的信息翻译得很完整，细节处理得极其到位，把其中包含的文化信息完全展示给英语读者。"否极泰来"指事物发展到极致，就开始向它的对立面转

化。当然，这个成语反着说（"泰极否来"）也成立。霍译中的"extreme"一词，将"极"的意思表达了出来，同时增译了"beginning"一词，意思是"灾难发展到极致的时候，就是好运的开始"。霍克斯透彻掌握了中华文化，把握住了两个非常重要的词汇："extreme"和原文中没有的"beginning"。此外，霍克斯的增译"and the reverse of that saying is also true"则说明并非"否极泰来"之后就永远如此了，"泰"极"否"也会来，这是一个不断相互转化，不断循环往复的过程。

【9】"荣辱自古周而复始"承接上文的"否极泰来"，并对其作出进一步的阐释。霍克斯已经把"否极泰来"翻译得非常清楚全面，所以霍译"Honour and disgrace follow each other in an unending cycle."承接前文，意思也非常明了。杨译"as disgrace follows honour"无法充分体现出"周而复始"的含义，只是通过"as"做句内连接让读者感受到"周而复始"的意味。

【10】"岂人力能可保常的？"一句，杨译"How can men prevent it?"是反问句；霍译"No human power can arrest that cycle and hold it permanently in one position."将原文的隐含信息深刻、细致地表达了出来，意思是：人力无法抓住那个循环，让它永远停留在"泰"或"荣"的一端。虽然霍译未点明"保常"什么，他只说"hold it permanently in one position"，但读者可以毫不费力地知道其中隐含的意思：人们知道"否极泰来"和"荣辱自古周而复始"的道理，但还是只想要"泰"和"荣"，不想要"否"和"辱"；"人力保常"保的就是"泰"和"荣"，所以霍译将"保常"的隐含之义翻译了出来，表明人力无法阻止这个循环，无法让这个循环停留在一端。

四、词汇表

1. embroider [ɪmˈbrɔɪdə(r)]　　v.　　to decorate cloth with pattern of stitches usually using coloured thread 刺绣

2. droop [druːp]　　v.　　to bend, hang or move downwards, especially because of being weak or tired

（尤指因衰弱或疲劳）低垂，垂落，垂下

3. playful [ˈpleɪfl]   *adj.*   (of a remark, an action, etc.) made or done in fun; not serious 打趣的；闹着玩的；嬉戏的

   adv.   playfully

4. entrust [ɪnˈtrʌst]   *v.*   to make sb responsible for doing sth or taking care of sb 委托；交托；托付

5. calamity [kəˈlæməti]   *n.*   an event that causes great damage to people's lives, property, etc. 灾难；灾祸

6. caustic [ˈkɔːstɪk]   *adj.*   critical in a bitter or sarcastic way 尖酸刻薄的；挖苦的；讥讽的

   adv.   caustically

7. provision [prəˈvɪʒn]   *n.*   preparations that you make for sth that might or will happen in the future（为将来做的）准备

8. paragon [ˈpærəgən]   *n.*   a person who is perfect or who is a perfect example of a particular good quality 完人；典范

9. engender [ɪnˈdʒendə(r)]   *v.*   to make a feeling or situation exist 产生；引起（某种感觉或情况）

10. mockery [ˈmɒkəri]   *n.*   comments or actions that are intended to make sb/sth seem ridiculous 嘲笑；愚弄

11. reverse [rɪˈvɜːs]   *n.*   the opposite of what has just been mentioned 相反的情况（或事物）

林如海捐馆扬州城　贾宝玉路谒北静王[1]

Lin Ju-hai Dies in Yangchow
Pao-yu Meets the Prince of Peiching on the Road [1] (Yang)

林如海灵返苏州郡　贾宝玉路谒北静王[1]

Lin Ru-hai is conveyed to his last resting-place in Soochow
And Jia Bao-yu is presented to the Prince of Bei-jing at a roadside halt [1] (Hawkes)

一、本回概述

　　熙凤操办丧事、整顿内务，赏罚分明，将宁国府治理得井井有条。昭儿返回贾府通报如海去世的消息，贾琏、黛玉送如海灵返苏州，赶年底能回到贾府。秦可卿出殡当日，场面浩大，许多名门贵族前来送殡，其中包括北静王水溶。贾政等人连忙上前，以国礼相见，北静王提出想见一下衔玉而生的宝玉，贾政忙回去，命宝玉脱去孝服，领他前去相见。

二、篇章节选

原文

　　话说宁国府中都总管来升闻得里面委请了凤姐,因传齐同事人等[2]说道:"如今请了西府里琏二奶奶管理内事,倘或他来支取东西,或是说话,我们须要比往日小心些。每日大家早来晚散,宁可辛苦这一个月,过后再歇着,[3]不要把老脸丢了。[4]那是个有名的烈货,脸酸心硬,一时恼了,不认人的。"[5]众人都道:"有理。"又有一个笑道:"论理,我们里面也须得他来整治整治,都忒不像了。"正说着,只见来旺媳妇拿了对牌来领取呈文京榜纸札,票上批着数目。众人连忙让坐倒茶,一面命人按数取纸来抱着,同来旺媳妇一路来至仪门口,方交与来旺媳妇自己抱进去了。

　　凤姐即命彩明钉造簿册。即时传来升媳妇,兼要家口花名册来查看,又限于明日一早传齐家人媳妇进来听差等语。大概点了一点数目单册,问了来升媳妇几句话,便坐车回家。[6]一宿无话。

　　至次日,卯正二刻便过来了。那宁国府中婆娘媳妇闻得到齐,只见凤姐正与来升媳妇分派,众人不敢擅入,只在窗外听觑。只听凤姐与来升媳妇道:"既托了我,我就说不得要讨你们嫌了。[7]我可比不得你们奶奶好性儿,由着你们去。[8]再不要说你们'这府里原是这样'的话。如今可要依着我行,错我半点儿,管不得谁是有脸的,谁是没脸的,一例现清白处治。"[9]

杨译

　　When the news that Hsi-feng was to take charge reached Lai Sheng, chief steward of the Ning Mansion, he summoned all his colleagues.[2]

　　"Madam Chia Lien of the West Mansion is coming to supervise our household," he told them. "When she asks for things or gives orders, we must be extra careful. Better turn up earlier and leave later every day, working hard this month and resting afterwards,[3] in order not to lose face.[4] You know what a terror she is, sour-faced, hard-hearted and no respecter of persons once she's angry."[5]

They agreed and one remarked with a laugh, "Actually we need her to get this place into shape. Things are too out of hand."

Along came Lai Wang's wife just then with a tally and a receipt for the amount required, to fetch sacrificial paper and paper for supplications and prayers. They made her take a seat and have some tea while someone went for the amount required and carried it for her to the inner gate, where he handed it over to her to take inside.

Then Hsi-feng ordered Tsai-ming to prepare a register and sent for Lai Sheng's wife to bring her a list of the staff. She announced that all the men-servants' wives were to come to her early the next morning for instructions. After checking quickly through the list and asking Lai Sheng's wife a couple of questions, she went home in her carriage.[6]

She was back at half past six the next morning to find all the old serving-women and stewards' wives assembled. They did not venture into the ante-chamber when they saw that she and Lai Sheng's wife were busy assigning tasks, but from outside the window they heard her tell the latter:

"Since I've been put in charge here I daresay I shall make myself unpopular.[7] I'm not as easy-going as your own mistress who lets you do as you please;[8] so don't tell me how things used to be managed here, but just do as I say. The least disobedience will be dealt with publicly, no matter how much face the offender may have."[9]

霍译

When Lai Sheng, the Chief Steward of the Ning-guo mansion, learned that Xi-feng had been invited to take on the management of the household, he called his cronies together[2] and addressed them in the following terms:

'Well lads, it seems that they've called in Mrs Lian from the other house to run things here for a bit; so if she should happen to come round asking for anything or have occasion to talk to you about anything, be sure to do what she says, won't you? During this coming month we shall all have to start work a bit earlier and knock off a bit later than usual. If you'll put up with a little extra hardship just for this month, we can make up for it by taking things easy when it's over.[3] Anyway, I'm relying on you not to let me down.[4] She's well known for a sour-faced, hard-hearted bitch is this one, and once she's got her back up, she'll give no quarter, no matter who you are.[5] So be careful!'

There was a chorus of agreement from the rest. One of them did observe, half-jokingly, that 'by rights they could do with someone like her to straighten things up a bit, considering the state they had got into'. But just at that moment Brightie's wife arrived on a mission from Xi-feng. She was to take receipt of some ledger-paper, buckram, and book-labels, and had a tally in her hand and a slip of paper specifying the quantities required. The men pressed round her offering her a place to sit and a cup of tea to drink while one of them hurried off with the list to fetch the needed items. Not only that, but, having fetched them, he carried them for her all the way to the inner gate of the mansion, only handing them to her then so that she could take them in to Xi-feng by herself. Xi-feng at once ordered Sunshine to make them up into stout workbooks for use in the office. At the same time she sent for Lai Sheng's wife and asked her for the register of the household staff. She also told her to get in touch with all the married females on the staff and arrange for them to assemble first thing next morning to be told their new duties. Then, after roughly checking through the numbers in the 'establishment' sheet and questioning Lai Sheng's wife on a few points, she got into her carriage and drove back home.[6]

At half past six next morning she was back at the Ning-guo mansion. By this time all the married women on the staff had been assembled. Not daring to go in, they hung about outside the window listening to Xi-feng discussing work-plans with Lai Sheng's wife inside the office. 'Now that I'm in charge here', they heard her telling the latter, 'I won't promise to make myself agreeable.[7] I haven't got a sweet temper like your mistress, you know. You won't find *me* letting you do everything just as it suits you.[8] So don't let me hear anyone saying "We don't do it that way here"! From now on, whatever it is, you do it the way I tell you to, and anyone who departs by as much as a hair's breadth from what I say is for it good and proper, no matter how senior or how important she thinks she is!' [9]

三、注释评点

【1】"林如海捐馆扬州城 贾宝玉路谒北静王"是本回回目，在程乙本中是"林如海灵返苏州郡 贾宝玉路谒北静王"。杨译"Lin Ju-hai Dies in Yangchow Pao-yu Meets the Prince of Peiching on the Road"用的是主动语态；霍译"Lin Ru-hai is conveyed to his last resting-place in Soochow And Jia Bao-yu is presented to the Prince of Bei-jing at a roadside halt"依据的是程乙本，用的是被动语态；霍译上下句对仗更加工整。

【2】"话说宁国府中都总管来升闻得里面委请了凤姐，因传齐同事人等"一句，杨译是"When the news that Hsi-feng was to take charge reached Lai Sheng, chief steward of the Ning Mansion, he summoned all his colleagues."霍译是"When Lai Sheng, the Chief Steward of the Ning-guo mansion, learned that Xi-feng had been invited to take on the management of the household, he called his cronies together."可以看出，在意合语言（汉语）向形合语言（英语）转化时，两位译者都用了"when"引导的时间状语从句。不同的是，在这个时间状语从句中，杨译用的是物化主语"the news"，之后是"that"引导的是同位语从句，说明"news"的内容；霍译用的是人格主语"Lai Sheng"。

【3】"宁可辛苦这一个月，过后再歇着"一句，杨译"working hard this month and resting afterwards"用"and"进行句内连接，体现了它连接的两个动作先后发生的逻辑关系。霍译是"If you'll put up with a little extra hardship just for this month, we can make up for it by taking things easy when it's over."，译者用"if"进行句内连接，而且增译了"make up for it"，意思是：如果大家现在能辛苦一个月，过后会得到补偿的。通过这种处理手法，译文句内的逻辑关系和语义表达得十分清楚饱满。

【4】"不要把老脸丢了"一句，根据原文可知，此处的"老脸"指的是大家的"老脸"。相比于杨译"... in order not to lose face"，霍克斯在这里进行了

改译："Anyway, I'm relying on you not to let me down.",强调的是"来升自己的老脸",和原文语义有出入。

【5】"那是个有名的烈货,脸酸心硬,一时恼了,不认人的。"杨译是"You know what a terror she is, sour-faced, hard-hearted and no respecter of persons once she's angry." "脸酸心硬"被译为"sour-faced"和"hard-hearted",这两个英语合成形容词都是由"形容词+名词+ed"构成的;另外,"脸酸心硬"和"一时恼了,不认人的"都是在说明熙凤是个烈货,杨译使用了并列结构"sour-faced, hard-hearted and no respecter of persons"补充说明前文的"what a terror she is"。霍译"She's well known for a sour-faced, hard-hearted bitch is this one, and once she's got her back up, she'll give no quarter, no matter who you are"传递出一种强调的语气。"and"之前的分句用不规范的句法及脏字"bitch",生动地刻画出都总管来升的语言特征及人物形象。"and"之后的分句"once she's got her back up, she'll give no quarter, no matter who you are"将"一时恼了,不认人的"翻译得非常自然,也符合原文的口语化语体。"get one's back up"意为"生气";"give no quarter"意为"不留情面";"give no quarter no matter who you are"将"不认人"翻译得十分到位。相较之下,杨译的"no respecter of persons"显得太书面化、太正式。

【6】"大概点了一点数目单册,问了来升媳妇几句话,便坐车回家。"句中,主语"熙凤"发出了四个动作:点、问、坐车、回家。杨译是"After checking quickly through the list and asking Lai Sheng's wife a couple of questions, she went home in her carriage."译者并列使用两个动名词短语"checking..."和"asking..."来翻译原文中的动作"点"和"问",同时还用表示时间关系的介词"after",说明"check"和"ask"这两个动作和谓语的动作"went"是先后发生;原文中的动作"坐车"被译为介词短语"in her carriage"。霍译是"Then, after roughly checking through the numbers in the 'establishment' sheet and questioning Lai Sheng's wife on a few points, she got into her carriage and drove back home."译者也并列使用两个动名词短语"checking..."和"questioning..."来翻译原文中的动作"点"和"问",介词"after"表明这两个动作和谓语的动作("got"和"drove")是先后发生。

【7】"我就说不得要讨你们嫌了。"一句，杨译是"I daresay I shall make myself unpopular."霍译是"I won't promise to make myself agreeable."两位译者一个用肯定句，一个用否定句，都生动准确地翻译出俗语"讨你们嫌了"的意思。

【8】"我可比不得你们奶奶好性儿，由着你们去。"一句，杨译是"I'm not as easy-going as your own mistress who lets you do as you please"译者用"who"进行句内连接，十分巧妙。霍译是"I haven't got a sweet temper like your mistress, you know. You won't find *me* letting you do everything just as it suits you."译者增译了"You won't find me..."，而且"me"用斜体表示强调，这些手法都体现出王熙凤威严霸气的性格特征。

【9】"错我半点儿，管不得谁是有脸的，谁是没脸的，一例现清白处治。"从原文可以看出：汉语句子经常省略主语。此处，"错我半点儿"的主语是"你们"，"管不得谁是有脸的，谁是没脸的，一例现清白处治"的主语是"我（王熙凤）"。杨译"The least disobedience will be dealt with publicly, no matter how much face the offender may have."使用了"no matter"进行句内连接，在主句部分，译者将原文的人格主语"你们"改为物化主语"disobedience"；将小句"错我半点儿"译为名词短语"the least disobedience"，在译文中充当主句的主语，整个句子的结构是：物化主语（the least disobedience）+谓语部分（will be dealt with publicly）+让步状语从句（no matter how much... may have）。霍译是"... anyone who departs by as much as a hair's breadth from what I say is for it good and proper, no matter how senior or how important she thinks she is!"该译文的结构是：人格主语（anyone）+定语从句（who departs... from what I say）+谓语部分（系表结构 is for it good and proper）+让步状语从句（no matter how... she is）。同时，霍译将"错我半点儿"创造性地译为"anyone who departs by as much as a hair's breadth from what I say"，意思是"哪怕错头发丝那么一点儿"。

四、词汇表

1. supervise [ˈsuːpəvaɪz]   v.   to be in charge of sb/sth and make sure that everything is done correctly, safely, etc. 监督；管理；指导；主管

2. tally [ˈtæli]   n.   a record of the number or amount of sth, especially one that you can keep adding to 记录；积分表；账

3. receipt [rɪˈsiːt]   n.   a piece of paper that shows that goods or services have been paid for 收据；收条

4. supplication [ˌsʌplɪˈkeɪʃn]   n.   the act of asking for sth with a very humble request or prayer 恳求；哀求；祈求

5. crony [ˈkrəʊni]   n.   a person that sb spends a lot of time with 好友；密友

6. chorus [ˈkɔːrəs]   n.   the sound of a lot of people expressing approval or disapproval at the same time 齐声；异口同声（表示同意或不同意）

7. ledger [ˈledʒə(r)]   n.   a book in which a bank, a business, etc. records the money it has paid and received 收支总账；分类账簿；分户账簿

8. buckram [ˈbʌkrəm]   n.   a type of stiff cloth made especially from cotton or linen, used in the past for covering books and for making clothes stiffer（旧时用作书皮或衣服衬里的）硬棉布；硬麻布；硬衬布

9. specify [ˈspesɪfaɪ]   v.   to state sth, especially by giving an exact measurement, time, exact instructions,

			etc. 具体说明；明确规定；详述；详列
10. stout [staʊt]		*adj.*	strong and thick 粗壮结实的；厚实牢固的

第十五回

王凤姐弄权铁槛寺　秦鲸卿得趣馒头庵

Hsi-feng Abuses Her Power at Iron Threshold Temple
Chin Chung Amuses Himself in Steamed-Bread Convent (Yang)

At Water-moon Priory Xi-feng finds how much profit may be procured by the abuse of power
And Qin Zhong discovers the pleasures that are to be had under the cover of darkness (Hawkes)

一、本回概述

　　北静王与宝玉相谈甚欢，临别时赠与宝玉一串念珠。宁府送殡途中，熙凤、宝玉、秦钟在田庄稍作休息。随后他们到了铁槛寺。贾府众人在此歇息，熙凤带着宝玉、秦钟去水月庵歇息。庵主静虚老尼告诉熙凤，长安府府太爷的小舅子李衙内看上了张财主家的小姐金哥，但金哥已许配给长安守备的公子。于是两家打起了官司，都要娶金哥。静虚求熙凤帮忙摆平此事，熙凤应了此事，开价三千两白银。庵中小尼智能与秦钟互相爱慕，情投意合。秦钟趁夜私会智能，两人正行好事，不想被宝玉抓了个正着。

二、篇章节选

原文

凤姐也略坐片时,便回至净室歇息,老尼相送。[1]此时众婆娘媳妇见无事,都陆续散了,自去歇息,跟前不过几个心腹常侍小婢,[2]老尼便趁机说道:"我正有一事,要到府里求太太,先请奶奶一个示下。"凤姐因问何事。

老尼道:"阿弥陀佛![3]只因当日我先在长安县内善才庵内出家的时节,那时有个施主姓张,是大财主。他有个女儿小名金哥,[4]那年都往我庙里来进香,不想遇见了长安府府太爷的小舅子李衙内。那李衙内一心看上,要娶金哥,打发人来求亲,不想金哥已受了原任长安守备的公子的聘定。[5]张家若退亲,又怕守备不依,因此说已有了人家。谁知李公子执意不依,定要娶他女儿,张家正无计策,两处为难。[6]不想守备家听了此信,也不管青红皂白,便来作践辱骂,[7]说一个女儿许几家,偏不许退定礼,就打官司告状起来。那张家急了,只得着人上京来寻门路,赌气偏要退定礼。[8]我想如今长安节度云老爷与府上最契,可以求太太与老爷说声,打发一封书去,求云老爷和那守备说一声,不怕那守备不依。若是肯行,张家连倾家孝顺也都情愿。"

凤姐听了笑道:"这事倒不大,只是太太再不管这样的事。"老尼道:"太太不管,奶奶也可以主张了。"凤姐听说笑道:"我也不等银子使,也不做这样的事。"[9]静虚听了,打去妄想,半晌叹道:"虽如此说,张家已知我来求府里,如今不管这事,张家不知道没工夫管这事,不希罕他的谢礼,倒像府里连这点子手段也没有的一般。"[10]

杨译

Hsi-feng retired presently, too, to the rest room accompanied by the abbess.[1] When the older maid-servants saw there was nothing to do they went off to bed themselves, leaving only a few trusted younger maids in attendance.[2]

The abbess seized this chance to say, "There's something I've been meaning to go and ask Her Ladyship, but I'd like to have your advice on it first, madam."

"What is it?" asked Hsi-feng.

"Amida Buddha!"[3] sighed the abbess. "When I became a nun in Shantsai Convent in the county of Changan, one of our benefactors was a very wealthy man called Chang, whose daughter Chin-ko often came to our temple to offer incense.[4] A young Mr. Li, who is brother-in-law to the prefect of Changan, met her there. He fell in love at first sight and sent to ask for her hand; but she was already engaged to the son of the former inspector of Changan.[5] The Changs would have liked to cancel the engagement but were afraid the inspector might object, so they explained to the Lis that she was betrothed. Still young Mr. Li insisted on having her, making things very difficult for the Changs.[6]

"When word of this reached the inspector's family, without even finding out the truth of the matter they came and stormed,[7] 'How many more men will you engage your daughter to?' They refused to take back the betrothal gifts and took the matter to court.

"The girl's family are desperate. They've sent to the capital to enlist help and are quite determined to return the gifts.[8]

"Well, I understand that General Yun the Military Governor of Changan is on friendly terms with your family. If Lady Wang would get His Lordship to write to General Yun, asking him to have a word with the inspector, I'm sure he'd drop the suit. And the Changs would gladly give anything—even their whole fortune—in return for this favour."

"There shouldn't be any great difficulty about this," rejoined Hsi-feng. "But Her Ladyship doesn't trouble herself with such matters."

"In that case, madam, could you attend to it?"

"I'm neither short of money nor do I meddle with affairs of this sort."[9]

The abbess' face fell. After a short pause she observed with a sigh, "Well, the Changs know that I'm appealing to your family. If you do nothing, they won't realize that you can't be troubled and don't want the money—it would look as if you can't even handle such a trifling business."[10]

> **霍译**

Xi-feng, too, soon left, and retired to her private room to rest, Euergesia accompanying her.[1] By this time the older servants, seeing that there was nothing further for them to do, had one by one drifted off to bed, leaving only a few personal maids, all of whom were in Xi-feng's confidence, in attendance.[2] The old nun deemed it safe to broach a private matter in their hearing.

'There is something I have been meaning to call at your house and ask Her Ladyship about, but I should like to have your opinion on it first before I see her.'

'What do you want to ask her?' said Xi-feng.

'Bless his Holy Name!'[3] the prioress began piously. 'When I was a nun at the Treasures in Heaven Convent in Chang-an, one of the convent's benefactors was a very wealthy man called Zhang, who had a daughter called Jin-ge.[4] A certain young Mr. Li, who is brother-in-law to the Governor of Chang-an, met her once when she was making an incense-offering in our temple and took a violent liking to her. He at once sent someone to the parents to ask for her hand in marriage, but unfortunately she was already betrothed to the son of a captain in the Chang-an garrison and the betrothal-presents had already been accepted.[5] The Zhangs would have liked to cancel the betrothal but were afraid that the captain would object, so they told Li's matchmaker that the girl was already engaged. But oh dear! young Mr. Li wouldn't take no for an answer, and the Zhangs were quite at their wit's end, being now in trouble with both parties.[6] You see, when the captain got to hear of these goings-on he was most unreasonable.[7] He came rushing along in a great rage and made a most terrible scene. 'Just how many young men is this girl betrothed to?" he said, and so on and so forth. He refused outright to take back the betrothal-gifts and straightway began an action for breach of promise. By now the Zhangs were really upset and sent to the capital for some moral support—for they are now quite determined to break off their daughter's engagement, seeing that the captain has been so unreasonable.[8]

'Well, it occurred to me that the Area Commander for Chang-an, General Yun, is on very good terms with your husband's family, and I thought I might try to find some way of persuading Her Ladyship to talk to Sir Zheng about this and get him to write a letter to General Yun and ask him to have a word with this captain. It is hardly likely that he would refuse to obey his commanding officer. The Zhangs would gladly pay *anything*—even if it meant bankrupting themselves—in return for this kindness.'

Xi-feng laughed.

'It doesn't sound very difficult. The only difficulty is that Lady Wang doesn't touch this kind of thing any more.'

'If Her Ladyship won't, what about you, Mrs Lian?'

Xi-feng laughed again.

'I'm not short of money; and besides, I don't touch that sort of thing either.'[9]

Euergesia's face assumed an expression of great benignity. After sitting for a while in silence she sighed.

'It's a pity I let the Zhangs know that I was going to talk to you about this,' she said. *'Now* if you don't do this favour for them, they will never believe that it is because you haven't the time or don't want the money; they will take it as a sign that you are not able.'[10]

三、注释评点

【1】"凤姐也略坐片时，便回至净室歇息，老尼相送。"一句有两个主语，分别是"凤姐"和"老尼"。杨译是"Hsi-feng retired presently, too, to the rest room accompanied by the abbess." 霍译是"Xi-feng, too, soon left, and retired to her private room to rest, Euergesia accompanying her." 两位译者都用"凤姐（Hsi-feng/Xi-feng）"作主语；对于"老尼相送"这一小句，杨译是过去分词短语"accompanied by the abbess"，充当伴随状语；霍译是独立主格结构"Euergesia accompanying her"，作伴随状语，和前文紧密相连，分别表述"凤姐"和"老尼"各自的动作。

【2】"此时众婆娘媳妇见无事，都陆续散了，自去歇息，跟前不过几个心腹常侍小婢"一句，杨译是"When the older maid-servants saw there was nothing to do they went off to bed themselves, leaving only a few trusted younger maids in attendance."该译文是一个复合句:"when"引导的时间状语从句+主句;在主句中,现在分词"leaving"引出结果状语。霍译是"By this time the older servants, seeing that there was nothing further for them to do, had one by one drifted off to bed, leaving only a few personal maids, all of whom were in Xi-feng's confidence, in attendance."该译文的句子结构是:主语"the older servants"+"seeing"引出的原因状语+谓语部分"had one by one drifted off to bed"+"leaving"引出的结果状语+"all of whom"引导的定语从句。

【3】"阿弥陀佛!"一词的翻译,杨译采用了异化策略,将其译为"Amida Buddha!";霍译"Bless his Holy Name!"使用了归化策略。

【4】"那时有个施主姓张,是大财主。他有个女儿小名金哥"一句,杨译"one of our benefactors was a very wealthy man called Chang, whose daughter Chin-ko often came to our temple to offer incense."用"whose"进行连句;霍译"one of the convent's benefactors was a very wealthy man called Zhang, who had a daughter called Jin-ge."用"who"进行连句。汉语句式较短,而英语多用长句,因此十分注重句内连接。

【5】"那李衙内一心看上,要娶金哥,打发人来求亲,不想金哥已受了原任长安守备的公子的聘定。"句中,"受了聘定"有两层意思:一是女方接受了男方的聘礼;二是男女双方确定了订婚关系。杨译是"He fell in love at first sight and sent to ask for her hand; but she was already engaged to the son of the former inspector of Changan."分号之后的分句"she was already engaged to the son of the former inspector of Changan"只是表明两人订婚了。霍译是"He at once sent someone to the parents to ask for her hand in marriage, but unfortunately she was already betrothed to the son of a captain in the Chang-an garrison and the betrothal-presents had already been accepted."该译文的信息更为全面完整,"but"之后的并列句"she was already betrothed to the son of a captain in the Chang-an garrison and the betrothal-presents had already been accepted",不仅说明女方已经收下了男方的聘礼,而且说明两人已经订婚的关系。

【6】"谁知李公子执意不依,定要娶他女儿,张家正无计策,两处为

难。""两处为难"指的是:张家想跟守备家退亲,守备不答应;想跟李家说女儿已经定亲,无法再承诺李家,李家也不答应。杨译"Still young Mr. Li insisted on having her, making things very difficult for the Changs."可回译为:李公子执意要娶,使张家十分为难。但原文是"张家两处为难",并非只是"李公子"一处使其为难。霍译是"But oh dear! young Mr. Li wouldn't take no for an answer, and the Zhangs were quite at their wit's end, being now in trouble with both parties."其中的"in trouble with both parties"非常准确地体现出张家进退两难的尴尬境地。

【7】"不想守备家听了此信,也不管青红皂白,便来作践辱骂"一句,杨译"When word of this reached the inspector's family, without even finding out the truth of the matter they came and stormed"和霍译"You see, when the captain got to hear of these goings-on he was most unreasonable."都增加了表示时间的关系连词"when",体现了意合语言(汉语)向形合语言(英语)转换时,会增加表示逻辑关系的连词。

【8】"那张家急了,只得着人上京来寻门路,赌气偏要退定礼"一句,杨译是"The girl's family are desperate. They've sent to the capital to enlist help and are quite determined to return the gifts."霍译是"By now the Zhangs were really upset and sent to the capital for some moral support—for they are now quite determined to break off their daughter's engagement, seeing that the captain has been so unreasonable."两位译者都使用了动词短语"sent to the capital"来翻译原文中的"着人上京","send"一词的常用搭配有:send sb to do sth, send sb for sth 等。需要注意的是:"send"是自己不去,而是打发别人完成的意思。此外,霍译中有一处增译"seeing that the captain has been so unreasonable",表达出张家退亲的原因是"觉得守备家不讲理",使得译文的信息更加完整。

【9】"我也不等银子使,也不做这样的事"一句,杨译"I'm neither short of money nor do I meddle with affairs of this sort."用词考究,书面气息浓厚;霍译"I'm not short of money; and besides, I don't touch that sort of thing either."则更为口语化,因此更符合原文中熙凤的语言风格。

【10】"如今不管这事,张家不知道没工夫管这事,不希罕他的谢礼,倒像府里连这点子手段也没有的一般。"杨译是"If you do nothing, they won't realize that you can't be troubled and don't want the money—it would look as if you can't even handle such a trifling business." 霍译是 "Now if you don't do this favour for them, they will never believe that it is because you haven't the time or don't want the money; they will take it as a sign that you are not able." 两位译者都使用了 "if" 进行连句，将原文中隐含的条件明示出来，体现了意合语言（汉语）向形合语言（英语）转换时，需要增加相应的关系连词。

四、词汇表

1. abbess [ˈæbes]	n.	a woman who is the head of a convent 女修院院长
2. benefactor [ˈbenɪfæktə(r)]	n.	a person who gives money or other help to a person or an organization such as a school or charity 施主；捐款人；赞助人
3. incense [ˈɪnsens]	n.	a substance that produces a pleasant smell when you burn it, used particularly in religious ceremonies 香（尤指宗教礼仪用的）
4. betrothed [bɪˈtrəʊðd]	adj.	having promised to marry sb 订了婚的
5. storm [stɔːm]	v.	to say in a loud angry way 怒吼；大发雷霆
6. betrothal [bɪˈtrəʊðl]	n.	an agreement to marry sb 婚约；订婚
7. trifling [ˈtraɪflɪŋ]	adj.	small and not important 琐碎的；微不足道的；无足轻重的
8. broach [brəʊtʃ]	v.	to begin talking about a subject that is difficult to discuss, especially because it is embarrassing or because people disagree about it 开始谈论，引入（尤指令人尴尬或有异议的话题）

9. pious [ˈpaɪəs]	*adj.*	having or showing a deep respect for God and religion 虔诚的；虔敬的	
	adv.	piously	
10. at one's wit's end		so worried by a problem that you do not know what to do next 智穷技尽；全然不知所措	
11. breach [briːtʃ]	*n.*	a failure to do sth that must be done by law （对法规等的）违背；违犯	

第十六回

贾元春才选凤藻宫　秦鲸卿夭逝黄泉路

Yuan-chun Is Selected as Imperial Consort in Phoenix Palace
Chin Chung Dying Before His Time Sets Off for the Nether Regions (Yang)

Jia Yuan-chun is selected for glorious promotion to the Imperial Bedchamber
And Qin Zhong is summoned for premature departure on the Journey into Night (Hawkes)

一、本回概述

秦钟途中感染风寒，加之与智能偷期缱绻，回家后便咳嗽伤风，卧床不起。熙凤得银三千两，出面帮助张家解决了纠纷，谁知金哥得知父母退了前夫之礼，自缢而亡，守备之子闻讯亦投河殉情，真是人财两空，唯有凤姐坐享其成，从此更加恣意妄为。适逢贾政生辰，宁荣二府齐聚庆贺，忽闻宫中有旨，全家惊惶不安。原来是贾元春封为凤藻宫尚书，加封贤德妃，贾府上下，顿时喜气洋洋，准备为元春修建省亲别院。秦钟病重将死，宝玉赶去相见。

第十六回

二、篇章节选

原文

　　且说贾琏自回家参见过众人，回至房中。[1]正值凤姐近日多事之时，无片刻闲暇之工，见贾琏远路归来，少不得拨冗接待，[2]因房内无外人，便笑道："国舅老爷大喜！国舅老爷一路风尘辛苦。小的听见昨日的头起报马来报，说今日大驾归府，略预备了一杯水酒掸尘，不知可赐光谬领否？"贾琏笑道："岂敢岂敢，多承多承。"[3]一面平儿与众丫鬟参拜毕，献茶。

　　贾琏遂问别后家中的诸事，又谢凤姐的操持劳碌。[4]凤姐道："我那里照管得这些事！见识又浅，口角又笨，心肠又直率，人家给个棒槌，我就认作'针'。[5]脸又软，搁不住人给两句好话，心里就慈悲了。[6]况且又没经历过大事，胆子又小，[7]太太略有些不自在，就吓的我连觉也睡不着了。[8]我苦辞了几回，太太又不容辞，倒反说我图受用，不肯习学了。[9]殊不知我是捻着一把汗儿呢。一句也不敢多说，一步也不敢多走。[10]你是知道的，咱们家所有的这些管家奶奶们，那一位是好缠的？错一点儿他们就笑话打趣，偏一点儿他们就指桑说槐的报怨。[11]'坐山观虎斗'，'借剑杀人'，'引风吹火'，'站干岸儿'，'推倒油瓶不扶'，[12]都是全挂子的武艺。况且我年纪轻，头等不压众，怨不得不放我在眼里。更可笑，那府里忽然蓉儿媳妇死了，珍大哥又再三再四的在太太跟前跪着讨情，只要请我帮他几日；我是再四推辞，太太断不依，只得从命。[13]依旧被我闹了个马仰人翻，更不成个体统，[14]至今珍大哥哥还抱怨后悔呢。你这一来了，明儿你见了他，好歹描补描补，就说我年纪小，原没见过世面，谁叫大爷错委他的。"[15]

杨译

　　But let us return to Chia Lien. After he had greeted the rest of the family he went to his own quarters;[1] and busy as Hsi-feng was, with not a moment to herself, she set everything aside to welcome her husband back from his long journey.[2]

　　Once they were alone she said jokingly, "Congratulations, Your Excellency, kinsman of the Imperial House! Your Excellency must have had a tiring journey. Your handmaid, hearing yesterday that your exalted carriage would return today, prepared some watery wine by way of welcome. Will the Imperial Kinsman deign to accept it?"

"You honour me too much," Chia Lien replied with a chuckle. "I am quite overwhelmed."[3]

When Ping-erh and the other maids had paid their respects and served tea, Chia Lien asked his wife what had happened during his absence and thanked her for looking after things so well.[4]

"I'm incapable of running things," she sighed. "I'm too ignorant, blunt and tactless, always getting hold of the wrong end of the stick.[5] And I'm so soft-hearted, anyone can get round me.[6] Besides, lack of experience makes me nervous.[7] When Her Ladyship is the least displeased I'm too frightened to sleep a wink.[8] Time and again I've begged to be relieved of such a responsibility, but instead of agreeing she accuses me of being lazy and unwilling to learn.[9] She doesn't realize what a cold sweat I'm in, terrified of saying one word out of turn or taking one false step.[10]

"And you know how difficult our old stewardesses are, laughing at the least mistake and 'accusing the elm while pointing at the mulberry tree' if one shows the least bias.[11] Talk about 'sitting on a hill to watch tigers fight,' 'murdering with a borrowed sword,' 'borrowing wind to fan the fire,' 'watching people drown from a dry bank' and 'not troubling to right an oil bottle that's been knocked over'[12] — they're all old hands at such tricks. On top of that, I'm too young to carry much weight; so naturally they pay no attention to me.

"As if that weren't bad enough, when Jung's wife suddenly died Cousin Chen repeatedly begged Her Ladyship on his knees to let me help them out for a few days. I declined over and over again, but as she insisted I had to have a try.[13] As usual I made a shocking mess of things—even worse than here.[14] I'm sure Cousin Chen is still regretting his rashness. When you see him tomorrow, do apologize for me. Tell him he should never have entrusted such a task to someone so young and inexperienced."[15]

霍译

But let us now turn to Jia Lian.

When he had finished seeing everyone in the family, Jia Lian returned at last to his own apartment.[1] Xi-feng, though still so busy that she had not a moment's leisure, had somehow contrived to find time to welcome back her wandering lord.[2]

'Congratulations, Imperial Kinsman!' she said with a smile when, except for the servants, they were at last alone together. 'You have had a tiring journey, Imperial Kinsman. Yesterday when the courier gave notice of your arrival, I prepared a humble entertainment to celebrate your homecoming. Will the Imperial Kinsman graciously condescend to take a cup of wine with his handmaid?'

Jia Lian replied in the same vein:

'Madam, you are too kind! I am your most *oble-e-eged* and humble servant, ma'am!'[3]

As they joked together, Patience and the other maids came forward to welcome their Master back, after which they served them both with tea. Jia Lian asked Xi-feng about the events that had occurred during his absence and thanked her for looking after things so well while he was away.[4]

'I am not much of a manager really,' said Xi-feng. 'I haven't got the knowledge, and I'm too poor at expressing myself and too simple-minded—always inclined to "take a ramrod for a needle", as they say.[5] Besides, I'm too soft-hearted for the job. Anyone who says a few kind words can get the better of me.[6] And my lack of experience makes me so nervous.[7] Aunt Wang only had to be the slightest bit displeased and I would get so upset that I couldn't sleep at night.[8] I begged her not to make me do all these things, but she insisted. She said I only refused out of laziness and unwillingness to learn.[9] I don't think she realizes even now the state I have been in—too scared to move or even to open my mouth for fear of saying or doing something wrong.[10] And you know what a difficult lot those old stewardesses are.

The tiniest mistake and they are all laughing at you and making fun; the tiniest hint of favouritism and they are grumbling and complaining. [11] *You* know their way of "cursing the oak-tree when they mean the ash". Those old women know just how to sit on the mountain-top and watch the tigers fight; how to murder with a borrowed knife, or help the wind to fan the fire. They will look on safely from the bank while you are drowning in the river. And the fallen oil-bottle can drain away: *they* are not going to pick it up. [12] On top of that, as I am so young, I haven't got much authority over them; so it was all I could do to prevent them from ignoring me altogether. And to crown it all, when Rong's wife died Cousin Zhen kept coming round to see Aunt Wang and begging her on his knees to let me help out for a day or two next door. I said again and again that I couldn't do it; but Aunt Wang agreed just to please him, so there was nothing for it but to do as I was told. [13] I'm afraid I made a terrible mess of it—even worse than I did here. [14] And now it seems Cousin Zhen is beginning to grumble and says he wishes he had never asked me. When you see him tomorrow, do please try to make it up with him. Tell him it's because I'm young and inexperienced. You might even hint that it's his own fault for having asked me in the first place!' [15]

三、注释评点

【1】"且说贾琏自回家参见过众人，回至房中。"一句，杨译是"But let us return to Chia Lien. After he had greeted the rest of the family he went to his own quarters"，第二句中使用"After"进行连句。霍译是"But let us now turn to Jia Lian. When he had finished seeing everyone in the family, Jia Lian returned at last to his own apartment"，第二句用"When"进行连句。两个译文都体现了意合语言（汉语）向形合语言（英语）转化时，要增加表示逻辑关系的连接词。此外，两个译文的第二句中运用的时态也是一致的：从句中使用过去完成时，主句中使用一般过去时，以表明动作发生的先后顺序。

【2】"正值凤姐近日多事之时，无片刻闲暇之工，见贾琏远路归来，少不得拨冗接待"一句，杨译是"... and busy as Hsi-feng was, with not a moment to herself, she set everything aside to welcome her husband back from his long journey",译者将小句"正值凤姐近日多事之时"和"无片刻闲暇之工"分别译为让步状语从句"busy as Hsi-feng was"和介词短语"with not a moment to herself"。霍译是"Xi-feng, though still so busy that she had not a moment's leisure, had somehow contrived to find time to welcome back her wandering lord",译者将小句"正值凤姐近日多事之时"译为"though"引导的让步状语从句的省略式"though still so busy";此外,霍译还使用"though"和"so… that"进行句内连接:"so… that"连接了"近日多事之时"和"无片刻闲暇之工"。

【3】"贾琏笑道:'岂敢岂敢,多承多承。'"一句,相比杨译"'You honour me too much,' Chia Lien replied with a chuckle. 'I am quite overwhelmed'",霍译"Jia Lian replied in the same vein: 'I am your most *oble-e-eged* and humble servant, ma'am!'"显得非常特别。原文中叠词的运用,如"岂敢岂敢"和"多承多承",既有久别重逢的客套,又有夫妻间打情骂俏的味道;霍克斯通过重复"*oble-e-eged*"中的字母"e",以期达到同样的语用效果。此外,霍译中用"Jia Lian replied in the same vein"也明示出他们夫妻二人在互相揶揄戏谑。

【4】"一面平儿与众丫鬟参拜毕,献茶。贾琏遂问别后家中的诸事,又谢凤姐的操持劳碌。"一句,杨译是"When Ping-erh and the other maids had paid their respects and served tea, Chia Lien asked his wife what had happened during his absence and thanked her for looking after things so well."句首是关系连词"When"引导的时间状语从句;在主句中,译者将原文中的两个动词"问"和"谢"译为并列谓语"asked… and thanked…"。霍译是"As they joked together, Patience and the other maids came forward to welcome their Master back, after which they served them both with tea. Jia Lian asked Xi-feng about the events that had occurred during his absence and thanked her for looking after things so well while he was away."句首增加了承上启下的时间状语从句"As they joked together"。此外,原文中的"参拜毕"和"献茶"是并列结构,杨译也将其译为并列结构"had paid their respects and served tea";霍译则使用"after which"将其译为偏正结构。

【5】"凤姐道:'我那里照管得这些事!见识又浅,口角又笨,心肠又直率,人家给个棒槌,我就认作"针"。'"一句,杨译是"'I'm incapable of running things,' she sighed. 'I'm too ignorant, blunt and tactless, always getting hold of the wrong end of the stick.'"译者主要用了三个形容词"ignorant""blunt"和"tactless"来翻译原文中的三个小句"见识又浅""口角又笨"和"心肠又直率";另外,译者用归化的手法将"给个棒槌认作'针'"译为"getting hold of the wrong end of the stick"。霍译是"'I am not much of a manager really,' said Xi-feng. 'I haven't got the knowledge, and I'm too poor at expressing myself and too simple-minded—always inclined to "take a ramrod for a needle", as they say.'"译者也使用形容词"poor"和"simple-minded"来翻译小句"口角又笨"和"心肠又直率";另外,译者使用异化的翻译手法将"给个棒槌认作'针'"译为"take a ramrod for a needle",生动地再现了源语文化。

【6】"脸又软,搁不住人给两句好话,心里就慈悲了。"一句,杨译"And I'm so soft-hearted, anyone can get round me"和霍译"Besides, I'm too soft-hearted for the job. Anyone who says a few kind words can get the better of me"都将"脸又软"翻译为"soft-hearted",即"心软"。"soft-hearted"是合成形容词,由形容词+名词+ed构成。

【7】"况且又没经历过大事,胆子又小"一句中,两个小句之间是并列关系,而两位译者都用"makes"一词将上下文译为因果关系。杨译是"Besides, lack of experience makes me nervous.",霍译是"And my lack of experience makes me so nervous."。两位译者都将小句"没经历过大事"译为名词短语"lack of experience",在译文中充当主语,将"胆子又小"译为"makes me (so) nervous",在译文中充当谓语部分。

【8】"太太略有些不自在,就吓的我连觉也睡不着了。"杨译"When Her Ladyship is the least displeased I'm too frightened to sleep a wink."用"When"进行连句,体现出意合语言向形合语言转化时,要增加表示逻辑关系的连词;主句中用"too... to"进行句内连接。同样,霍译"Aunt Wang only had to be the slightest bit displeased and I would get so upset that I couldn't sleep at night."使用"and"和"so... that"进行句内连接,"and"在此处表示结果,相当于"as a result"。

【9】"我苦辞了几回,太太又不容辞,倒反说我图受用,不肯习学了。"一句,杨译是"Time and again I've begged to be relieved of such a responsibility, but instead of agreeing she accuses me of being lazy and unwilling to learn.";霍译是"I begged her not to make me do all these things, but she insisted. She said I only refused out of laziness and unwillingness to learn.",两位译者将原文中含有动词的小句"图受用"和"不肯习学"分别译为动名词短语"being lazy and unwilling to learn"和名词短语"laziness and unwillingness to learn"。

【10】"殊不知我是捏着一把汗儿呢。一句也不敢多说,一步也不敢多走。"杨译"She doesn't realize what a cold sweat I'm in, terrified of saying one word out of turn or taking one false step."使用了句子化短语法将"一句也不敢多说,一步也不敢多走"译为形容词短语"terrified of…",做what引导的宾语从句中的主语"I"的补足语。霍译"I don't think she realizes even now the state I have been in—too scared to move or even to open my mouth for fear of saying or doing something wrong."并未翻译"捏着一把汗儿",译者使用了破折号,破折号后面的内容是在解释说明"the state"。

【11】"你是知道的,咱们家所有的这些管家奶奶们,那一位是好缠的?错一点儿他们就笑话打趣,偏一点儿他们就指桑说槐的报怨。"一句,杨译是"And you know how difficult our old stewardesses are, laughing at the least mistake and 'accusing the elm while pointing at the mulberry tree' if one shows the least bias.",其中的"laughing at…"和"accusing…"都是现在分词短语作伴随状语,用来解释"how difficult our old stewardesses are",具体说明管家奶奶们有多么难缠。在翻译"偏一点儿,他们就指桑说槐的报怨"时,译者增加了表示条件关系的连词"if"。霍译是"And you know what a difficult lot those old stewardesses are. The tiniest mistake <u>and</u> they are all laughing at you and making fun; the tiniest hint of favouritism <u>and</u> they are grumbling and complaining.",译文的第二句是由两个含有"tiniest"的分句"The tiniest mistake…"和"the tiniest hint of…"构成,整齐对称,和原文风格一致,生动地再现出原文中的两个"一点儿"的内涵;其次,两个加下画线的"and"都有表示结果之意。

【12】"'坐山观虎斗','借剑杀人','引风吹火','站干岸儿','推倒油瓶不扶'"一句，杨译是"Talk about 'sitting on a hill to watch tigers fight,' 'murdering with a borrowed sword,' 'borrowing wind to fan the fire,' 'watching people drown from a dry bank' and 'not troubling to right an oil bottle that's been knocked over'…"；霍译是"Those old women know just how to sit on the mountain-top and watch the tigers fight; how to murder with a borrowed knife, or help the wind to fan the fire. They will look on safely from the bank while you are drowning in the river. And the fallen oil-bottle can drain away: *they* are not going to pick it up."，两个译文基本上都使用了异化的翻译策略。

【13】"我是再四推辞，太太断不依，只得从命。"一句，杨译"I declined over and over again, but as she insisted I had to have a try."增加了表示逻辑关系的连接词"but"和"as"："but"的作用是承接上文，"as"的作用是开启下文。霍译"I said again and again that I couldn't do it; but Aunt Wang agreed just to please him, so there was nothing for it but to do as I was told."也增加了表示逻辑关系的连词"but"和"so"："but"用来承接上文，"so"用来引出下文。

【14】"依旧被我闹了个马仰人翻，更不成个体统"一句，杨译"As usual I made a shocking mess of things—even worse than here."和霍译"I'm afraid I made a terrible mess of it—even worse than I did here."都将"马仰人翻"作了归化处理，译为"a shocking mess of things"和"a terrible mess of it"。霍译将"更不成个体统"译为"even worse than I did here"，相比杨译只多了两个单词"I did"，但表述更加准确，语义更加饱满。

【15】"就说我年纪小，原没见过世面，谁叫大爷错委他的。"一句，杨译是"Tell him he should never have entrusted such a task to someone so young and inexperienced."，译者用句子化词法将"我年纪小"和"原没见过世面"这两个小句分别译为形容词"young"和"inexperienced"；霍译"Tell him it's because I'm young and inexperienced. You might even hint that it's his own fault for having asked me in the first place!"此处也作了类似的处理。第三个小句"谁叫大爷错委他的"暗示出"错也在他不识人，也不全是我的错"的意思，霍译用了

"it's his own fault"和"in the first place",将该句的言外之意表达了出来:是他的错,而且是他错在先。

四、词汇表

1. excellency [ˈeksələnsi]	n.	a title used when talking to or about sb who has a very important official position, especially an ambassador(对身居要职的人,尤其是大使的尊称)阁下
2. kinsman [ˈkɪnzmən]	n.	a relative 亲属;亲戚
3. deign [deɪn]	v.	to do sth in a way that shows you think you are too important to do it 屈尊,俯就,降低身份(做某事)
4. blunt [blʌnt]	adj.	(of a person or remark) very direct; saying exactly what you think without trying to be polite 嘴直的;直言的
5. tactless [ˈtæktləs]	adj.	saying or doing things that are likely to annoy or to upset other people 言行不得体的;得罪人的;不圆通的;没策略的
6. mulberry [ˈmʌlbəri]	n.	a tree with broad dark green leaves and berries that can be eaten 桑树
7. contrive [kənˈtraɪv]	v.	to manage to do sth despite difficulties(不顾困难而)设法做到
8. courier [ˈkʊriə(r)]	n.	a person or company whose job is to take packages or important papers somewhere(递送包裹或重要文件的)信使,通讯员,专递公司
9. condescend [ˌkɒndɪˈsend]	v.	to do sth that you think it is below your social or professional position to do 屈

		尊；俯就
10. vein [veɪn]	*n.*	a particular style or manner 风格；方式
11. ramrod [ˈræmrɒd]	*n.*	a long straight piece of iron used in the past to push explosive into a gun（旧时用以将火药推进枪支的）推弹杆，通条

大观园试才题对额　荣国府归省庆元宵

Literary Talent Is Tested by Composing Inscriptions in Grand View Garden
Those Losing Their Way at Happy Red Court Explore a Secluded Retreat (Yang)

*The inspection of the new garden becomes a test of talent
And Rong-guo House makes itself ready for an important visitor* (Hawkes)

一、本回概述

秦钟离世，宝玉十分悲痛。为迎接元春省亲，修建大观园，园内亭台池榭，富丽堂皇，贾政带领门客、宝玉巡视园内各处，协商匾额对联，宝玉引用古人诗句，题得几个巧妙之名，众人皆拍手称赞；宝玉大展才情，贾政心下欢喜，众小厮争要打赏，不由分说将宝玉身上所佩之物尽行解去。黛玉听闻此事，以为自己送给宝玉的荷包也被抢去，不免生气，后知宝玉十分珍视荷包，一直贴身携带，未被夺去，两人遂和好如初。

二、篇章节选

> 原文

　　说着，进入石洞来。只见佳木茏葱，奇花烁灼，[1]一带清流，从花木深处曲折泻于石隙之下。[2]再进数步，渐向北边，平坦宽豁，两边飞楼插空，雕甍绣槛，皆隐于山坳树杪之间。俯而视之，则清溪泻雪，石磴穿云，白石为栏，环抱池沿，石桥三港，兽面衔吐。[3]桥上有亭。贾政与诸人上了亭子，倚栏坐了，[4]因问："诸公以何题此？"诸人都道："当日欧阳公《醉翁亭记》有云：'有亭翼然'，就名'翼然'。"[5]贾政笑道："'翼然'虽佳，但此亭压水而成，还须偏于水题方称。[6]依我拙裁，欧阳公之'泻出于两峰之间'，竟用他这一个'泻'字。"有一客道："是极，是极。竟是'泻玉'二字妙。"[7]贾政拈髯寻思，因抬头见宝玉侍侧，便笑命他也拟一个来。[8]

　　宝玉听说，连忙回道："老爷方才所议已是。但是如今追究了去，似乎当日欧阳公题酿泉用一'泻'字则妥，今日此泉若亦用'泻'字，则觉不妥。况此处虽云省亲驻跸别墅，亦当入于应制之例，用此等字眼，亦觉粗陋不雅。[9]求再拟较此蕴藉含蓄者。"贾政笑道："诸公听此论若何？方才众人编新，你又说不如述古；如今我们述古，你又说粗陋不妥。你且说你的来我听。"宝玉道："有用'泻玉'二字，则莫若'沁芳'二字，岂不新雅？"[10]贾政拈髯点头不语。众人都忙迎合，赞宝玉才情不凡。[11]贾政道："匾上二字容易，再作一副七言对联来。"[12]宝玉听说，立于亭上，四顾一望，便机上心来，乃念道：

　　绕堤柳借三篙翠，隔岸花分一脉香。

　　贾政听了，点头微笑。众人先称赞不已。[13]

> 杨译

　　They walked on through a tunnel into a ravine green with magnificent trees and ablaze with rare flowers. [1] A clear stream welling up where the trees were thickest wound its way through clefts in the rocks. [2]

Some paces further north, on both sides of a level clearing, rose towering pavilions whose carved rafters and splendid balustrades were half hidden by the trees on the slopes. Looking downwards, they saw a crystal stream cascading as white as snow and stone steps going down through the mist to a pool. This was enclosed by marble balustrades and spanned by a stone bridge ornamented with the heads of beasts with gaping jaws.[3] On the bridge was a little pavilion in which the whole party sat down.[4]

"What would you call this, gentlemen?" asked Chia Cheng.

One volunteered, "Ouyang Hsiu's *Pavilion of the Old Drunkard* has the line, 'A winged pavilion hovers above.' Why not call this Winged Pavilion?"[5]

"A delightful name," rejoined Chia Cheng. "But as this pavilion is built over the pool there should be some allusion to the water.[6] Ouyang Hsiu also speaks of a fountain 'spilling between two peaks.' Could we not use that word 'spilling'?"

"Capital!" cried one gentleman. "'Spilling Jade' would be an excellent name."[7]

Chia Cheng tugging thoughtfully at his beard turned with a smile to ask Pao-yu for his suggestion.[8]

"I agree with what you just said, sir," replied his son. "But if we go into this a little deeper, although 'spilling' was an apt epithet for Ouyang Hsiu's fountain, which was called the Brewer's Spring, it would be unsuitable here. Then again, as this is designed as a residence for the Imperial Consort we should use more courtly language instead of coarse, inelegant expressions like this.[9] Could you not think of something more subtle?"

"Do you hear that, gentlemen?" Chia Cheng chuckled. "When we suggest something original he is all in favour of an old quotation; but now that we are using an old quotation he finds it too coarse. Well, what do *you* propose?"

"Wouldn't 'Seeping Fragrance' be more original and tasteful than 'Spilling Jade'?"[10]

Chia Cheng stroked his beard again and nodded in silence while the others, eager to please him, hastened to commend Pao-yu's remarkable talent.[11]

"The selection of two words for the tablet is easy," said his father. "Go on and make a seven-character couplet."[12]

Pao-yu rose to his feet and glanced round for inspiration. Then he declaimed:

"Willows on the dyke lend their verdancy to three punts;

Flowers on the further shore spare a breath of fragrance."

His father nodded with a faint smile amid another chorus of approval.[13]

霍译

As he spoke, they passed through a tunnel of rock in the mountain's shoulder into an artificial ravine ablaze with the vari-coloured flowers and foliage of many varieties of tree and shrub which grew there in great profusion.[1] Down below, where the trees were thickest, a clear stream gushed between the rocks.[2] After they had advanced a few paces in a somewhat northerly direction, the ravine broadened into a little flat-bottomed valley and the stream widened out to form a pool. Gaily painted and carved pavilions rose from the slopes on either side, their lower halves concealed amidst the trees, their tops reaching into the blue. In the midst of the prospect below them was a handsome bridge:

In a green ravine

A jade stream sped.

A stair of stone

Plunged to the brink.

where the water widened

To a placid pool,

A marble baluster

Ran round about.

A marble bridge crossed it

With triple span,

And a marble lion's maw

Crowned each of the arches.[3]

Over the centre of the bridge there was a little pavilion, which Jia Zheng and the others entered and sat down in. [4]

'Well, gentlemen!' said Jia Zheng. 'What are we going to call it?'

'Ou-yang Xiu in his *Pavilion of the Old Drunkard* speaks of "a pavilion poised above the water",' said one of them. 'what about "Poised Pavilion"?'.[5]

'"Poised Pavilion" is good,' said Jia Zheng, 'but *this* pavilion was put here in order to dominate the water it stands over, and I think there ought to be some reference to water in its name. [6] I seem to recollect that in that same essay you mention Ou-yang Xiu speaks of the water "gushing between twin peaks". Could we not use the word "gushing" in some way?'

'Yes, yes!' said one of the literary gentlemen. '"Gushing Jade" would do splendidly.' [7]

Jia Zheng fondled his beard meditatively, then turned to Bao-yu and asked him for *his* suggestion. [8]

'I agreed with what you said just now, Father,' said Bao-yu, 'but on second thoughts it seems to me that though it may have been all right for Ou-yang Xiu to use the word "gushing" in describing the source of the river Rang, it doesn't really suit the water round this pavilion. Then again, as this is a Separate Residence specially designed for the reception of a royal personage, it seems to me that something rather formal is called for, and that an expression taken from the *Drunkard's Pavilion* might seem a bit improper. [9] I think we should try to find a rather more imaginative, less obvious sort of name.'

'I hope you gentlemen are all taking this in!' said Jia Zheng sarcastically, 'You will observe that when we suggest something original we are recommended to prefer the old to the new, but that when we *do* make use of an old text we are "improper" and "unimaginative"!—Well, carry on then! Let's have your suggestion!'

'I think "Drenched Blossoms" would be more original and more tasteful than "Gushing Jade".' [10]

Jia Zheng stroked his beard and nodded silently. The literary gentlemen could see that he was pleased and hastened to commend Bao-yu's remarkable ability. [11]

'That's the two words for the framed board on top,' said Jia Zheng. '*Not* a very difficult task. But what about the seven-word lines for the sides?'[12]

Bao-yu glanced quickly round, seeking inspiration from the scene, and presently came up with the following couplet:

'Three pole-thrust lengths of bankside willows green,

One fragrant breath of bankside flowers sweet.'

Jia Zheng nodded and a barely perceptible smile played over his features. The literary gentlemen redoubled their praises.[13]

三、注释评点

【1】"说着，进入石洞来。只见佳木茏葱，奇花烔灼"一句，杨译"They walked on through a tunnel into a ravine green with magnificent trees and ablaze with rare flowers."将小句"佳木茏葱"和"奇花烔灼"译为两个并列的形容词短语"green with magnificent trees"和"ablaze with rare flowers"，在句中充当定语，修饰前面的名词"ravine"。霍译是"As he spoke, they passed through a tunnel of rock in the mountain's shoulder into an artificial ravine ablaze with the vari-coloured flowers and foliage of many varieties of tree and shrub which grew there in great profusion."译者用了一个较长的形容词短语"ablaze with the vari-coloured flowers and foliage of many varieties of tree and shrub which grew there in great profusion"作定语修饰"ravine"，其中，"which"引导的定语从句修饰"tree and shrub"，说明各种树木和灌木丛长得非常茂盛。

【2】"一带清流，从花木深处曲折泻于石隙之下。"一句，杨译"A clear stream welling up where the trees were thickest wound its way through clefts in the rocks."将"曲折泻于"译为"wound its way through"，译文更强调"曲折"。霍译"Down below, where the trees were thickest, a clear stream gushed between the rocks."用"Down below"与前文紧密衔接，描述的画面感更加完整一体；主句的谓语动词是"gushed"，说明译者更强调"泻"字。两位译者都使用了"where"引导的地点状语从句。

【3】"俯而视之，则清溪泻雪，石磴穿云，白石为栏，环抱池沿，石桥三港，兽面衔吐。"一句，均是用四字构成的小句来描写大观园的景象。霍克斯将其创造性地译为三至五字一小句的诗体，可以看出，译者想尽量保留原文的语言风格。

【4】"桥上有亭。贾政与诸人上了亭子，倚栏坐了"一句，杨译"On the bridge was a little pavilion in which the whole party sat down."用"in which"进行句内连接；而且，译文的主语"a little pavilion"因为带了定语从句"in which..."而显得较长，为了避免句式上的头重脚轻，译者采用了倒装语序。霍译"Over the centre of the bridge there was a little pavilion, which Jia Zheng and the others entered and sat down in."用"which"进行句内连接；此外，译者采用了"there be"句型，同时将状语"Over the centre of the bridge"置于句首。

【5】"就名'翼然'。"一句，杨译"Why not call this Winged Pavilion?"将"翼然"译为"Winged"；霍译"what about 'Poised Pavilion'?"将其译为"Poised"。相比之下，"Winged"一词更加生动，让人联想到鸟儿展翅欲飞的样子，用来描述我国古代建筑檐角上翘的样子，十分贴切。

【6】"但此亭压水而成，还须偏于水题方称。"一句，杨译是"But as this pavilion is built over the pool there should be some allusion to the water."，其中，"But"用来承接上文，"as"用来关联下文。霍译是"but this pavilion was put here in order to dominate the water it stands over, and I think there ought to be some reference to water in its name."，译者不仅用"it stands over"来翻译"压水"的字面含义，而且用"in order to dominate the water"来解释中国人素有在水上建亭阁、建雕像的风俗习惯，以期水面风平浪静，不起祸患。

【7】"竟是'泻玉'二字妙。"一句，杨译"'Spilling Jade' would be an excellent name."将"泻玉"译为"Spilling Jade"；霍译"'Gushing Jade' would do splendidly."将其译为"Gushing Jade"。从"泻"字的中文意思来看，霍译更为准确。

【8】"贾政拈髯寻思，因抬头见宝玉侍侧，便笑命他也拟一个来"一句中，主语"贾政"发出了一连串动作："拈、寻思、抬头、见、笑、命"。杨译是"Chia Cheng tugging thoughtfully at his beard turned with a smile to ask Pao-yu for his suggestion."译者将"拈"译为现在分词"tugging"，做伴随状语；

将"寻思"译为副词"thoughtfully";将"抬头"译为谓语动词"turned";将"笑"译为介词短语"with a smile",做方式状语;将"命"译为动词不定式"to ask"。霍译是"Jia Zheng fondled his beard meditatively, then turned to Bao-yu and asked him for his suggestion.",译者用三个并列的谓语动词"fondled""turned"和"asked"来翻译原文中的"抬、抬头、命";将"寻思"译为副词"meditatively",做方式状语。另外,两位译者都将含有动词"拟"的语句"也拟一个来"译为介词短语"for his suggestion"。

【9】"亦当入于应制之例,用此等字眼,亦觉粗陋不雅"一句中,作者并未解释为什么"用此等字眼就粗陋不雅"。相比于杨译"Then again, as this is designed as a residence for the Imperial Consort we should use more courtly language instead of coarse, inelegant expressions like this",霍译"Then again, as this is a Separate Residence specially designed for the reception of a royal personage, it seems to me that something rather formal is called for, and that an expression taken from the *Drunkard's Pavilion* might seem a bit improper"采用了增译手法,用"an expression taken from the *Drunkard's Pavilion* might seem a bit improper"一句为读者解释了"粗陋不雅"的原因,填补了语义沟,逻辑上更加通顺。

【10】"则莫若'沁芳'二字,岂不新雅?"一句,杨译"Wouldn't 'Seeping Fragrance' be more original and tasteful than 'Spilling Jade'?"将"沁芳"译为"Seeping Fragrance","seep"的发音是/si:p/,长音/i:/有缓慢渗入的感觉,而且使用了现在分词形式,表示动作正在进行;霍译"I think 'Drenched Blossoms' would be more original and more tasteful than 'Gushing Jade'."将"沁芳"译为"Drenched Blossoms",过去分词"drenched"在这里既表示动作已经完成也表示被动,意为"湿透的"。无论从措辞还是语义上看,杨译都更胜一筹。

【11】"贾政抬髯点头不语。众人都忙迎合,赞宝玉才情不凡。"一句,杨译是"Chia Cheng stroked his beard again and nodded in silence while the others, eager to please him, hastened to commend Pao-yu's remarkable talent.",整个句子用"while"进行句内连接,前后两个分句分别描述"贾政"和"众人"的动作。"贾政"发出了三个动作:"抬、点头、不语";在译文中,"stroked"(抬)和"nodded"(点头)作并列谓语,"不语"被译为介

词短语"in silence",修饰"nodded"。"众人"发出了两个动作:"忙迎合"和"赞";其中,"忙迎合"被译为形容词短语"eager to please him",充当原因状语。霍译是"Jia Zheng stroked his beard and nodded silently. The literary gentlemen could see that he was pleased and hastened to commend Bao-yu's remarkable ability.",其中,动词"不语"被译为副词"silently",修饰谓语动词"stroked(抚)"和"nodded(点)"。

【12】"贾政道:'匾上二字容易,再作一副七言对联来。'"一句,杨译是"'The selection of two words for the tablet is easy,' said his father. 'Go on and make a seven-character couplet.'",译者将"said his father"插在直接引语之间,这和汉语引语的行文习惯不同:汉语中的"某人说"经常位于句首;英语中的"said sb / sb said"位置灵活,可位于句首、句中或句末。霍译是"'That's the two words for the framed board on top,' said Jia Zheng. 'Not a very difficult task. But what about the seven-word lines for the sides?'",译者用"That's the two words"承接前文关于"沁芳"两个字的讨论,同时增译了"for the framed board on top"和"for the sides",阐明匾额和对联的位置关系,为译语读者补充了文化缺省的信息。

【13】"贾政听了,点头微笑。众人先称赞不已。"一句,杨译是"His father nodded with a faint smile amid another chorus of approval.",译者将原文中的并列词组"点头微笑"译为偏正结构"nodded with a faint smile",同时用句子化短语法将小句"众人先称赞不已"译为介词短语"amid another chorus of approval"。霍译是"Jia Zheng nodded and a barely perceptible smile played over his features. The literary gentlemen redoubled their praises.",译文的第一句使用"and"进行句内连接,其中的"play over"是"掠过"之意。

四、词汇表

1. tunnel [ˈtʌnl]　　　　　n.　　a passage built underground, for example to allow a road or railway/railroad to go through a hill, under a river, etc. 地下通

			道；地道；隧道
2. ravine [rəˈviːn]		n.	a deep and narrow valley with steep sides 沟壑；溪谷
3. ablaze [əˈbleɪz]		adj.	full of bright colours or light 闪耀；发光；明亮；色彩鲜艳
4. rafter [ˈrɑːftə(r)]		n.	one of the sloping pieces of wood that support a roof 椽子
5. balustrade [ˌbæləˈstreɪd]		n.	a row of posts, joined together at the top, built along the edge of a balcony, bridge, etc. to prevent people from falling off, or as a decoration 栏杆
6. cascade [kæˈskeɪd]		v.	to flow downwards in large amounts 倾泻；流注
7. rejoin [ˌriːˈdʒɔɪn]		v.	to say sth as an answer, especially sth quick, critical or amusing 回答；反驳
8. tug [tʌg]		v.	to pull sth hard, often several times（常为几次用力）拉，拖，拽
9. epithet [ˈepɪθet]		n.	an offensive word or phrase that is used about a person or group of people 别称；绰号；诨名
10. dyke [daɪk]		n.	a channel that carries water away from the land 渠；沟；壕沟
11. verdant [ˈvɜːd(ə)nt]		adj.	(of grass, plants, fields, etc.) fresh and green 嫩绿的；碧绿的；青翠的
		n.	verdancy
12. profusion [prəˈfjuːʒn]		n.	a very large quantity of sth 大量；众多
13. gush [gʌʃ]		v.	to flow or pour suddenly and quickly out of a hole in large amounts（从……中）喷出，涌出，冒出

14. gaily [ˈgeɪli]	*adv.*	in a bright and attractive way 花哨地；艳丽地；华丽地
15. placid [ˈplæsɪd]	*adj.*	calm and peaceful, with very little movement 平静的；宁静的；安静的
16. poise [pɔɪz]	*v.*	to be or hold sth steady in a particular position, especially above sth else 保持（某种姿势）；抓紧；使稳定
17. perceptible [pəˈseptəbl]	*adj.*	great enough for you to notice 可察觉到的；看得出的

第十八回

大观园试才题对额　荣国府归省庆元宵[1]

庆元宵贾元春归省　助情人林黛玉传诗[1]
Yuan-chun Visits Her Parents on the Feast of Lanterns
Tai-yu Helps Her True Love by Passing Him a Poem[1] (Yang)

皇恩重元妃省父母　天伦乐宝玉呈才藻[1]
A brief family reunion is permitted by the magnanimity of a gracious Emperor
And an Imperial Concubine takes pleasure in the literary progress of a younger brother[1] (Hawkes)

一、本回概述

元宵佳节，元妃省亲，仪仗阵容豪华，真是说不尽的富贵风流。元妃与贾母等一众家眷相见，悲喜交集，满心里的话说不出，只有呜咽对泣。随后元妃亲自为大观园各处赐名，并让众姊妹展示才情，各题一匾一诗。宝玉苦苦构思，宝钗便上前提示，黛玉帮作一首"杏帘在望"。之后，贾蔷带领戏班为元妃献唱，元妃心内欢喜，封赏众人。丑时三刻，元妃回宫，众人洒泪作别。

第十八回

二、篇章节选

原文

　　茶已三献，贾妃降座，乐止。退入侧殿更衣，[2] 方备省亲车驾出园。至贾母正室，欲行家礼，[3] 贾母等俱跪止不迭。贾妃满眼垂泪，方彼此上前厮见，一手搀贾母，一手搀王夫人，三个人满心里皆有许多话，只是俱说不出，只管呜咽对泣。[4] 邢夫人、李纨、王熙凤、迎、探、惜三姊妹等，俱在旁围绕，垂泪无言。[5]

　　半日，贾妃方忍悲强笑，安慰贾母、王夫人道："当日既送我到那不得见人的去处，好容易今日回家娘儿们一会，不说说笑笑，反倒哭起来。一会子我去了，又不知多早晚才来！"说到这句，不禁又哽咽起来。[6] 邢夫人等忙上来解劝。贾母等让贾妃归座，又逐次一一见过，又不免哭泣一番。然后东西两府掌家执事人丁在厅外行礼，及两府掌家执事媳妇领丫鬟等行礼毕。贾妃因问："薛姨妈、宝钗、黛玉因何不见？"王夫人启曰："外眷无职，未敢擅入。"[7] 贾妃听了，忙命快请。一时，薛姨妈等进来，欲行国礼，亦命免过，上前各叙阔别寒温。[8] 又有贾妃原带进宫去的丫鬟抱琴等上来叩见，贾母等连忙扶起，命人别室款待。执事太监及彩嫔、昭容各侍从人等，宁国府及贾赦那宅两处自有人款待，只留三四个小太监答应。[9] 母女姊妹深叙些离别情景，及家务私情。

杨译

　　After tea had been served three times, Yuan-chun descended from the throne and the music ceased while she went into a side chamber to change her clothes.[2] Meanwhile a carriage had been prepared to drive her out of the Garden to visit her parents.

　　First she went to the Lady Dowager's reception room to pay her respects as a grand-daughter of the house;[3] but before she could do so her grandmother and the others knelt to prevent her. The Imperial Consort's eyes were full of tears as her family drew near to greet her. As she clasped the hands of her grandmother and mother, the hearts of all three were too full to speak—they could do nothing but sob. [4] Lady Hsing, Li Wan, Hsi-feng, Yuan-chun's half sister Tan-chun and her cousins Ying-chun and Hsi-chun also stood beside them weeping silently. [5] But at last the Imperial Consort mastered her grief and forced a smile as she tried to comfort them.

"Since you sent me away to that forbidden place, it hasn't been easy getting this chance today to come home and see you all again," she said. "But instead of chatting and laughing, here we are crying! Soon I shall have to leave you, and there is no knowing when I can come back again." At this she broke down afresh. [6]

Lady Hsing and the others did their best to console her and the Lady Dowager asked her to take a seat, after which she exchanged courtesies with each in turn and more tears were shed. Next the stewards and attendants of both mansions paid their respects outside the door, and so did their wives and the maids.

This ceremony at an end, Yuan-chun asked why Aunt Hsueh, Pao-chai and Tai-yu were missing.

Lady Wang explained that they were afraid to presume, not being members of the Chia family and having no official status. [7]

The Imperial Consort asked them to be invited in at once, and they were about to pay homage according to Palace etiquette when she exempted them too and chatted with them. [8]

Next Pao-chin and the other maids whom Yuan-chun had taken with her to the Palace kowtowed to the Lady Dowager, who hastily stopped them and sent them off to have some refreshments in another room. The senior eunuchs and ladies-in-waiting were also entertained by members of the staff of both mansions, leaving only three or four young eunuchs in attendance. [9]

When the ladies of the family had spoken with feeling about their separation and all that had happened since, …

第十八回

霍译

After tea had been offered three times as etiquette prescribed, the Imperial Concubine descended from her throne, the music stopped, and she withdrew into a side room to 'change her clothes'.[2] A less formal carriage than the imperial palanquin had been prepared which carried her from the garden to her family's own quarters.

Inside Grandmother Jia's apartment Yuan-chun became a grandchild once more and knelt down to make her kotow.[3] But Grandmother Jia and the rest knelt down too and prevented her from prostrating herself. She ended up, clinging to Grandmother Jia by one hand and Lady Wang by the other, while the tears streamed down her face, too overcome to say anything.[4] All three of them, in fact, though there was so much they wanted to say, seemed quite incapable of speech and stood there holding each other and sobbing, apparently unable to stop. The others present— Lady Xing, Li Wan, Wang Xi-feng, Ying-chun, Tan-chun and Xi-chun—stood round them weeping silently.[5] No one spoke a word.

Yuan-chun at last restrained her sobs and forced a smile to her tear-stained face:

'It hasn't been easy, winning this chance of coming back among you after all those years since I was first walled up in That Place. Now that we are seeing each other at last, we ought to talk and be cheerful, not waste all the time crying! I shall be leaving again in no time at all, and Heaven only knows when I shall have another chance of seeing you!'

At this point she broke down once more[6] and had to be comforted by Lady Xing. When she had composed herself, Grandmother Jia made her sit down while the members of the family came forward one at a time to greet her and say a few words. This was an occasion for further tears. Then the senior menservants of both the Rong-guo and Ning-guo mansions assembled in the courtyard outside and paid their respects. They were followed by the women servants and maids, who were allowed to come inside the room to make their kotow.

Yuan-chun asked why her Aunt Xue and her cousins Bao-chai and Lin Dai-yu were missing.

'Relations outside the Jia family are not allowed to see you without a special invitation,[7] dear,' Lady Wang told her.

Yuan-chun asked them to be invited in immediately, and Aunt Xue and the two girls arrived after a few moments. They would have kotowed to her in accordance with court etiquette had not Yuan-chun hurriedly excused them from doing so.[8] The three of them went up to her, and niece and aunt exchanged news of the years that had elapsed since they last met.

Next Lutany and the other maids who had accompanied Yuan-chun into the Palace came forward to make their kotows to Grandmother Jia. The old lady at once motioned to them to rise and gave instructions to her own servants to entertain them in another room.

The senior eunuchs and the ladies-in-waiting were now led off by members of the staffs of Jia She's household and the Ning-guo mansion to be entertained elsewhere, leaving only three or four very junior eunuchs in attendance.[9] Yuan-chun was at last free to chat informally with her mother and the other female members of her family and learned for the first time about many personal and domestic events that had occurred in the household since she left it.

三、注释评点

【1】本回回目有多个版本，人民文学出版社的本子根据底本，还是把第十七、十八回的内容放在一回里，回目是"大观园试才题对额　荣国府归省庆元宵"。蒙府、戚序本第十七回回目是"大观园试才题对额　怡红院迷路探曲折"；第十八回回目是"庆元宵贾元春归省　助情人林黛玉传诗"。这也是杨译翻译本回回目所依据的底本。程本在分回后，第十七回回目仍用的是原来的回目，第十八回回目是"皇恩重元妃省父母　天伦乐宝玉呈才藻"，可以看出，霍译对本回回目的翻译依据的是程本。

【2】"茶已三献，贾妃降座，乐止。退入侧殿更衣"一句，杨译是"After tea had been served three times, Yuan-chun descended from the throne and the music ceased while she went into a side chamber to change her clothes.", 译者用"After" "and"和"while"进行句内连接；霍译是"After tea had been offered three times as etiquette prescribed, the Imperial Concubine descended from her throne, the music stopped, and she withdrew into a side room to 'change her clothes'.", 译者用"After"和"and"进行句内连接。此外，霍译增加了"as etiquette prescribed"，说明"茶已三献"是礼节规定，为读者填补了文化空白。

【3】"欲行家礼"一句，杨译"… pay her respects as a grand-daughter of the house"和霍译"… became a grandchild once more and knelt down to make her kotow."都将"家礼"具体化处理，对它作了解释性翻译。

【4】"一手搀贾母，一手搀王夫人，三个人满心里皆有许多话，只是俱说不出，只管呜咽对泣"一句，杨译是"As she clasped the hands of her grandmother and mother, the hearts of all three were too full to speak—they could do nothing but sob."译者用"As..., too...to..., nothing but..."以及破折号把原文中的五个小句连接了起来；对于"（元春）一手……一手……"，译者将其笼统地译为"she clasped the hands of her grandmother and mother"（回译：她拉住祖母和母亲的手）。霍译"She ended up, clinging to Grandmother Jia by one hand and Lady Wang by the other, while the tears streamed down her face, too overcome to say anything."则将"一手……一手……"准确地译为"clinging to Grandmother Jia by one hand and Lady Wang by the other"；另外，句内用"while"进行连接，"while"前后的动作同时发生，表示元妃一边拉着贾母和王夫人，一边泪流满面。"too overcome to say anything"是主语"She"的补足语。

【5】"俱在旁围绕，垂泪无言"一句，"众人"发出了三个动作："围绕、垂泪、无言"。杨译"… stood beside them weeping silently."将"在旁围绕"译为谓语部分"stood beside them"，"垂泪"译为伴随状语"weeping"，"无言"译为副词"silently"。霍译"… stood round them weeping silently."也采取了相同的翻译手法。

【6】"说到这句，不禁又哽咽起来"一句，杨译"At this she broke down

afresh"和霍译"At this point she broke down once more…"都用了句子化短语法将小句"说到这句"译为介词短语"At this"和"At this point"。

【7】"外眷无职,未敢擅入"一句中,"外眷无职"是原因,"未敢擅入"是结果。杨译"they were afraid to presume, not being members of the Chia family and having no official status."先翻译结果"未敢擅入",即"they were afraid to presume",后解释原因"外眷无职",即"not being members of the Chia family and having no official status";原因有两点:一是外眷(not being members of the Chia family),二是无职(having no official status),两者之间用"and"连接。霍译"Relations outside the Jia family are not allowed to see you without a special invitation"可以回译为"外眷未受邀请,不能相见"。相比之下,杨译的语义更加完整。

【8】"贾妃听了,忙命快请。一时,薛姨妈等进来,欲行国礼,亦命免过,上前各叙阔别寒温。"杨译是"The Imperial Consort asked them to be invited in at once, and they were about to pay homage according to Palace etiquette when she exempted them too and chatted with them."译者用"and"和"when"进行句内连接;霍译是"Yuan-chun asked them to be invited in immediately, and Aunt Xue and the two girls arrived after a few moments. They would have kotowed to her in accordance with court etiquette had not Yuan-chun hurriedly excused them from doing so."译文的第二句使用了虚拟语气,在省略了连词if的非真实条件状语从句中,很自然地运用了倒装语序,即"had not Yuan-chun hurriedly excused them from doing so",其正常的语序是"if Yuan-chun had not hurriedly excused them from doing so"。

【9】"只留三四个小太监答应"一句,杨译"… leaving only three or four young eunuchs in attendance"和霍译"… leaving only three or four very junior eunuchs in attendance"的翻译手法相同,都使用句子化短语法将该小句译为现在分词短语,在译文中充当结果状语。对于"小太监"一词的翻译,杨译"young eunuchs"强调年龄小,霍译"very junior eunuchs"强调职位低。

四、词汇表

1. presume [prɪˈzjuːm]	v.	to behave in a way that shows a lack of respect by doing sth that you have no right to do 妄行；越权行事
2. homage [ˈhɒmɪdʒ]	n.	something that is said or done to show respect for sb 敬辞；表示敬意的举动
3. etiquette [ˈetɪkət]	n.	the formal rules of correct or polite behavior in society or among members of a particular profession （社会或行业中的）礼节，礼仪，规矩
4. exempt [ɪgˈzempt]	v.	to give or get sb's official permission not to do sth or not pay sth they would normally have to do or pay 免除；豁免
5. eunuch [ˈjuːnək]	n.	a man who has been castrated, especially one who guarded women in some Asian countries in the past 阉人；太监；宦官
6. prescribe [prɪˈskraɪb]	v.	(used about a person or an organization with authority) to say what should be done or how sth should be done 规定；命令；指示
7. palanquin [ˌpælənˈkiːn]	n.	a covered litter for one passenger, consisting of a large box carried on two horizontal poles by four or six bearers 轿子
8. prostrate [ˈprɒstreɪt]	v.	~ oneself: to lie on one's front with one's face looking downwards 拜倒；俯伏

9. compose [kəmˈpəʊz]　　　　v.　　to manage to control your feelings or expression 使镇静；使平静

10. elapse [ɪˈlæps]　　　　　　v.　　if a period of time elapses, it passes （时间）消逝，流逝

情切切良宵花解语　　意绵绵静日玉生香

An Eloquent Maid Offers Earnest Advice One Fine Night
A Sweet Girl Shows Deep Feeling One Quiet Day (Yang)

*A very earnest young woman offers counsel by night
And a very endearing one is found to be a source of fragrance by day* (Hawkes)

一、本回概述

　　元妃回宫，见驾谢恩，回奏归省之事，龙颜大悦，封赏贾府众人。袭人回家过年，宝玉与茗烟同去探望，袭人让家人见识了一下宝玉的通灵玉。当日晚些时候，宝玉命人接回袭人，袭人以赎身离开贾府之事试探宝玉，宝玉不依，袭人便要宝玉依从自己三件事。次日，袭人身体不适，在屋中休息。宝玉自去探视黛玉，两人说笑打闹，两情相悦，宝玉瞎编典故取笑黛玉，宝钗走了进来，笑话宝玉作诗忘典的事情。

二、篇章节选

原文

宝玉方住了手,笑问道:"你还说这些不说了?"黛玉笑道:"再不敢了。"一面理鬓笑道:[1]"我有奇香,你有'暖香'没有?"

宝玉见问,一时解不来,因问:"什么'暖香'?"黛玉点头叹笑道:"蠢才,蠢才!你有玉,人家就有金来配你;人家有'冷香',你就没有'暖香'去配?"[2]宝玉方听出来,笑道:"方才求饶,如今更说狠了。"[3]说着,又去伸手。[4]黛玉忙笑道:"好哥哥,我可不敢了。"宝玉笑道:"饶便饶你,只把袖子我闻一闻。"[5]说着,便拉了袖子笼在面上,闻个不住。黛玉夺了手道:"这可该去了。"宝玉笑道:"去,不能。咱们斯斯文文的躺着说话儿。"说着,复又倒下。黛玉也倒下,用手帕子盖上脸。宝玉有一搭没一搭的说些鬼话,黛玉只不理。[6]宝玉问他几岁上京,路上见何景致古迹,扬州有何遗迹故事,土俗民风。黛玉只不答。

宝玉只怕他睡出病来,便哄他道:[7]"嗳哟!你们扬州衙门里有一件大故事,你可知道?"[8]黛玉见他说的郑重,且又正言厉色,只当是真事,因问:"什么事?"[9]宝玉见问,便忍着笑顺口诌道:[10]

"扬州有一座黛山,山上有个林子洞。"

黛玉笑道:"就是扯谎,自来也没听见这山。"宝玉道:"天下山水多着呢,你那里知道这些不成。等我说完了,你再批评。"[11]

杨译

He desisted then, demanding with a smile, "Will you talk that way any more?"

"I dare not." Smoothing her hair she laughed.[1] "You say I've an unusual scent, have you a *warm* scent?"

"A warm scent?" He looked puzzled.

Tai-yu shook her head with a sigh. "How dense you are! You have jade, and someone else has gold to match it. So don't you have a warm scent to match her cold

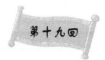

scent?"[2]

Pao-yu caught her meaning then and chuckled. "You were begging for mercy a minute ago, but now you're worse than ever."[3] He reached out again.[4]

"Dear cousin, I promise not to tease," she cried hastily.

"All right, I'll forgive you if you let me smell your sleeve."[5]

With that he covered his face with her sleeve and started sniffing as if he would never stop. She pulled away her arm.

"You ought to go now."

"Go I can't. Let's lie down in a civilized way and chat."

He stretched out again while Tai-yu lay down too, covering her face with her handkerchief and paying no attention to his rambling questions.[6] How old had she been when she came to the capital? What fine sights and monuments had she seen on the way? What places of historical interest were there in Yangchow? What were the local customs and traditions? Tai-yu made no reply and to keep her awake—for he feared sleep might give her indigestion—Pao-yu played a new trick.[7]

"Aiya!" he exclaimed. "Do you know the extraordinary thing that happened near your yamen in Yangchow?"[8]

Taken in by his straight face and earnest manner, Tai-yu asked to hear about it.[9] Then Pao-yu, suppressing a laugh, started romancing.[10]

"In Yangchow there's a hill called Mount Tai, in the side of which is a cavern called Lin Cavern."

"You're making this up," cried Tai-yu. "I've never heard of such a hill."

"Do you know all the hills and streams in the world? Let me finish my story before you pull it to pieces."[11]

霍译

'Will you say things like that any more?'

'No,' said Dai-yu, laughing weakly, 'I promise.'

She proceeded to pat her hair into place, smilingly complacently:[1]

'So I've got an unusual fragrance, have I? Have you got a *warm* fragrance?'

For the moment Bao-yu was puzzled:

'*Warm* fragrance?'

Dai-yu shook her head pityingly.

'Don't be so dense! You have your jade. *Somebody* has a gold thing to match. Somebody has Cold Fragrance, *ergo* you must have Warm Fragrance to go with it!' [2]

'I've only just let you off,' said Bao-yu, 'and here you go again, worse than ever!' [3]

Once more he stretched out the threatening fingers and Dai-yu again began to shriek. [4]

'No! Bao-yu! *Please*! I promise!'

'All right, I forgive you. But you must let me smell your sleeve.' [5]

He wrapped the free end of that garment over his face and abandoned himself to long and prodigious sniffs.

Dai-yu jerked away her arm.

'I really think you ought to go.'

'Couldn't go if I wanted to. Let's lie down very quietly and genteelly and have a conversation.' And he stretched himself out again.

Dai-yu lay down too, and covered her face with a handkerchief.

He tried to arouse her interest with desultory chat—talking for the sake of talking. Dai-yu took no notice. [6] He tried asking questions. How old was she when she first came to the Capital? What had the scenery been like on the journey? What places of historical interest were there in Yangchow? What were its inhabitants like? What were its local customs? Dai-yu made no reply. Still concerned that she might fall asleep and injure her health, he tried a ruse. [7]

'Why, *yes*!' he said, as if suddenly remembering something. 'There's a famous story that took place near Yangchow. I wonder if you know about it.' [8]

This was delivered with so straight a face and in so serious a tone of voice that

Dai-yu was quite taken in. [9]

'Oh? What?'

Mastering a strong inclination to laugh, he began to extemporize with whatever came into his head. [10]

'Near the city of Yangchow there is a mountain called Mt Yu-dai, in the side of which is a cavern called the Cave of Lin.'

'That's false, for a start,' said Dai-yu. 'I've never heard of a mountain of that name.'

'There are a great many mountains in this world,' said Bao-yu. 'You could hardly be expected to know all of them. Leave your criticisms until I have finished my story.' [11]

三、注释评点

【1】"一面理鬓笑道"一句中,"理鬓"和"笑道"是并列的动作。杨译是"Smoothing her hair she laughed.";霍译是"She proceeded to pat her hair into place, smilingly complacently"。两位译者都使用了偏正结构来翻译原文中的并列动作:杨译将"理鬓"和"笑"分别译为充当伴随状语的现在分词短语"Smoothing her hair"和谓语动词"laughed",表示这两个动作同时发生,译者省译了动词"道"。霍译将"理鬓"译为"proceeded to pat her hair into place",在译文中充当谓语,将"笑道"译为"smilingly complacently",此处应是一个错误,正确的表述是"smiling complacently",这是现在分词短语充当伴随状语,修饰谓语部分。

【2】"你有玉,人家就有金来配你;人家有'冷香',你就没有'暖香'去配?"一句,原文中出现了两个"人家",虽未指明"人家"是谁,但大家都知道指的就是薛宝钗,这种措辞和语气生动地刻画出黛玉嫉妒吃醋的心理状态。杨译"You have jade, and someone else has gold to match it. So don't you have a warm scent to match her cold scent?"将两个"人家"分别译为"someone else"和"her",与原文的风格不符。霍译"You have your jade. *Somebody* has a gold thing to match. Somebody has Cold Fragrance, *ergo* you must have Warm Fragrance to go with it!"则用了两个"Somebody"来翻译两个"人家",与原文风格十分契合;同时,译者还通过斜体"*Somebody*"和"*ergo*",利用语气来表意,生动地再现了黛玉吃醋的口气。

【3】"方才求饶,如今更说狠了。"一句,省略了主语。杨译"You were begging for mercy a minute ago, but now you're worse than ever."和霍译"… here you go again, worse than ever!"都补充了主语"you",体现出汉语和英语的差别,即意合语言(汉语)通常省略主语,形合语言(英语)的句子要有完整的主语和谓语。

【4】"又去伸手。"一句,杨译"He reached out again."和霍译"Once more he stretched out the threatening fingers..."都增加了主语"He"。此外,霍译增译了"threatening"一词,用来修饰"fingers",使语言顿时变得有趣,生动地刻画出宝、黛二人嬉笑打闹的场面。

【5】"饶便饶你,只把袖子我闻一闻。"一句,杨译"All right, I'll forgive you if you let me smell your sleeve."和霍译"All right, I forgive you. But you must let me smell your sleeve."分别增加了连接词"if"和"But",体现出意合语言(汉语)向形合语言(英语)转化时,需要增加表示逻辑关系的连接词。

【6】"说着,复又倒下。黛玉也倒下,用手帕子盖上脸。宝玉有一搭没一搭的说些鬼话,黛玉只不理。"一句,杨译是"He stretched out again while Tai-yu lay down too, covering her face with her handkerchief and paying no attention to his rambling questions.",译者用"while"连接两个分句,表示两个人的动作同时发生;在第二个分句中,黛玉的动作"lay down"后面跟了两个现在分词短语做伴随状语,即"covering her face with her handkerchief"和"paying no attention to his rambling questions",用来描述黛玉躺下后的伴随动作。此外,杨译用句子化短语法将小句"宝玉有一搭没一搭的说些鬼话"译为名词短语"his rambling questions"。霍译是"He tried to arouse her interest with desultory chat—talking for the sake of talking. Dai-yu took no notice.",译者将"有一搭没一搭的说些鬼话"译为"desultory chat—talking for the sake of talking",虽然没有直译,但是已经充分达意,妙趣横生。

【7】"宝玉只怕他睡出病来,便哄他道"一句,杨译是"… and to keep

her awake—for he feared sleep might give her indigestion—Pao-yu played a new trick."其中，不定式"to keep her awake"做目的状语，"for he feared might give her indigestion"是"for"引导的原因状语从句。霍译是"Still concerned that she might fall asleep and injure her health, he tried a ruse."整个句子呈现偏正结构，"concerned"引导的形容词短语作原因状语，说明"he tried a ruse"的原因。

【8】"嗳哟！你们扬州衙门里有一件大故事，你可知道？"一句，相比杨译"'Aiya!' he exclaimed. 'Do you know the extraordinary thing that happened near your yamen in Yangchow?'"，霍译"'Why, *yes*!' he said, as if suddenly remembering something. 'There's a famous story that took place near Yangchow. I wonder if you know about it.'"增译了"as if suddenly remembering something"，使语言更加生动，语义更加丰满。此外，杨译用音译法翻译原文中的"衙门"一词，霍克斯则省译该词。

【9】"黛玉见他说的郑重，且又正言厉色，只当是真事，因问：'什么事？'"一句，杨译是"Taken in by his straight face and earnest manner, Tai-yu asked to hear about it."译者用句子化短语法将两个小句"他说的郑重"和"且又正言厉色"译为两个名词短语"earnest manner"和"straight face"，之间用"and"连接。霍译是"This was delivered with so straight a face and in so serious a tone of voice that Dai-yu was quite taken in."译者也使用同样的方法，把上述两个小句译为两个介词短语"in so serious a tone of voice"和"with so straight a face"，在译文中充当方式状语。另外，整个句子用"so... that..."进行句内连接。霍译选用物化主语"This"，用来承接上文，同时指代上文的一番话，而杨译则选用人格主语"Tai-yu"。

【10】"宝玉见问，便忍着笑顺口诌道"一句，杨译是"Then Pao-yu, suppressing a laugh, started romancing."霍译是"Mastering a strong inclination to laugh, he began to extemporize with whatever came into his head."两个译文都呈现偏正结构：杨译将原文中的"忍着笑"译为现在分词短语"suppressing a laugh"，修饰谓语"started romancing"；霍译则将其译为"Mastering a strong inclination to laugh"，修饰谓语"began to extemporize..."；两个现在分词短语

都是伴随状语，表示与谓语的动作同时发生。

【11】"等我说完了，你再批评"一句，杨译"Let me finish my story before you pull it to pieces"和霍译"Leave your criticisms until I have finished my story"分别用连词"before"和"until"进行句内连接，体现出意合语言（汉语）向形合语言（英语）转化时，需要增加表示逻辑关系的连接词。

四、词汇表

1. desist [dɪˈzɪst; dɪˈsɪst]	v.	to stop doing sth 停止；结束
2. dense [dens]	adj.	stupid 愚笨的；迟钝的；笨拙的
3. sniff [snɪf]	v.	to breathe air in through the nose in order to discover or enjoy the smell of sth（吸着气）嗅，闻
4. rambling [ˈræmblɪŋ]	adj.	(of a speech or piece of writing) very long and confused 冗长而含糊的；不切题的
5. romance [rəʊˈmæns]	v.	to tell stories that are not true or to describe sth in a way that makes it seem more exciting or interesting than it really is 虚构（故事）；渲染
6. cavern [ˈkævərn]	n.	a cave, especially a large one 大洞穴；大山洞
7. proceed [prəˈsiːd]	v.	to do sth next, after having done sth else first 接着做；继而做
8. complacent [kəmˈpleɪsnt]	adj.	too satisfied with yourself or with a situation, so that you do not feel that any change is necessary 自满的；自鸣得意的
	adv.	complacently
9. ergo [ˈɜːgəʊ]	adv.	therefore 因此；所以

10. prodigious [prəˈdɪdʒəs]	*adj.*	very large or powerful and causing surprise or admiration 巨大的；伟大的
11. desultory [ˈdesəltri]	*adj.*	going from one thing to another, without a definite plan and without enthusiasm 漫无目的的；无条理的；随意的
12. ruse [ruːz]	*n.*	a way of doing sth or of getting sth by cheating sb 诡计；骗术
13. extemporize [ɪkˈstempəraɪz]	*v.*	to speak or perform without preparing or practising 即席发言；即兴表演

第二十回

王熙凤正言弹妒意　　林黛玉俏语谑娇音

Hsi-feng Reproves a Jealous Woman
Tai-yu Mocks a Prattling Girl (Yang)

Wang Xi-feng castigates a jealous attitude with some forthright speaking
And Lin Dai-yu makes a not unattractive speech impediment the subject of a jest (Hawkes)

一、本回概述

　　宝、黛、钗三人正在房中互相取笑，听到打牌输了钱的李嬷嬷大骂病中的袭人，嫌她怠慢少礼，宝玉替袭人辩护了两句，李嬷嬷仍不依不饶，熙凤恰巧经过，知她迁怒袭人，连哄带劝将她拉走了。次日，宝玉去薛姨妈处闲逛，碰见贾环和莺儿玩棋，输了钱正在耍赖，将他教训了一通，贾环找赵姨娘诉苦，反被责骂，恰被熙凤听见，便隔窗训诫赵姨娘。湘云来到贾府，宝、钗同去相见，黛玉看到他二人在一起，心中不乐，赌气回房。宝玉追过去哄劝黛玉。

第二十回

二、篇章节选

原文

贾环听了，只得回来。

赵姨娘见他这般，[1]因问："又是那里垫了踹窝来了？"一问不答，再问时，贾环便说："同宝姐姐玩的，莺儿欺负我，赖我的钱，宝玉哥哥撵我来了。"赵姨娘啐道："谁叫你上高台盘去了？下流没脸的东西！那里顽不得？谁叫你跑了去讨没意思！"

正说着，可巧凤姐在窗外过，都听在耳内。便隔窗说道：[2]"大正月又怎么了？环兄弟小孩子家，一半点儿错了，你只教导他，[3]说这些淡话作什么！凭他怎么去，还有太太老爷管他呢，[4]就大口啐他！他现是主子，不好了，横竖有教导他的人，与你什么相干！坏兄弟，出来，跟我顽去。"

贾环素日怕凤姐比怕王夫人更甚，听见叫他，忙唯唯的出来。赵姨娘也不敢则声。凤姐向贾环道："你也是个没气性的！[5]时常说给你：要吃，要喝，要顽，要笑，只爱同那一个姐姐妹妹哥哥嫂子顽，就同那个顽。你不听我的话，反叫这些人教的歪心邪意，狐媚子霸道的。自己不尊重，要往下流走，安着坏心，还只管怨人家偏心。[6]输了几个钱？就这么个样儿！"贾环见问，只得诺诺的回说："输了一二百。"凤姐道："亏你还是爷，输了一二百钱就这样！"[7]回头叫丰儿："去取一吊钱来，姑娘们都在后头顽呢，把他送了顽去。[8]——你明儿再这么下流狐媚子，我先打了你，打发人告诉学里，皮不揭了你的！[9]为你这个不尊重，恨的你哥哥牙根痒痒，不是我拦着，窝心脚把你的肠子窝出来了。"喝命："去罢！"贾环诺诺的跟了丰儿，得了钱，自己和迎春等顽去。不在话下。

杨译

Chia Huan went back to his mother, the concubine Chao.

At sight of his dejected face [1] she asked, "Who's been treating you as a doormat this time?" When he did not answer, she repeated the question.

"I was playing with Cousin Pao-chai. Ying-erh was mean to me and cheated me. Then Brother Pao-yu turned me out."

His mother spat in disgust.

"Shameless little brat! Who told you to put yourself forward? Is there nowhere else for you to play? Why go looking for trouble?"

Hsi-feng, who was passing outside, overheard this exchange and called back through the window:[2]

"What's this rumpus in the middle of the first month? Huan's only a child. If he makes some small mistake you can set him right.[3] Why carry on at him like that? No matter where he goes, the master and Her Ladyship are there to keep him in order.[4] Imagine spitting at him! He's one of the young masters, and if he does misbehave there are people to correct him—what business is it of yours? Come on, Brother Huan, come out and play with me."

Chia Huan stood in even greater awe of Hsi-feng than of Lady Wang. He made haste, therefore, to obey and his mother dared raise no objection.

"You're too spineless,"[5] Hsi-feng scolded. "I've told you time and again that you're free to eat or drink whatever you like and to play with any of the girls or boys. But instead of doing as I say, you let other people warp your mind and teach you these sneaky ways. You've no self-respect but *will* lower yourself. You behave spitefully yourself and then complain that everybody else is unfair![6] How much did you lose to make you take on like this?"

"A couple of hundred cash," he told her meekly.

"All this fuss over a couple of hundred cash! And you one of the young masters!"[7] She turned to Feng-erh. "Go and fetch a string of cash. Then take him to the back where the girls are playing.[8] If you do anything so mean and sneaky again, Huan, first I'll give you a good spanking and then send someone to tell your teacher about it—he'll flay you alive for it.[9] Your total lack of self-respect has got Cousin Lien gnashing his teeth. He'd have ripped out your guts before now if I hadn't stopped him. Now be off with you!"

"Yes," said Chia Huan and trotted off with Feng-erh, taking the string of cash. He then joined Ying-chun and the others at their game. And there we can leave him.

> 霍译

In the face of such an argument, Jia Huan could not very well remain.

When he got back to his own apartment, his real mother, 'Aunt' Zhao (Lady Wang was his mother only in name) observed the dejected state he was in. [1]

'Who's been making a doormat of you this time?' she asked him, and, obtaining no immediate reply, asked again.

'I've just been playing at Bao-chai's. Oriole cheated me and Bao-yu turned me out.'

Aunt Zhao spat contemptuously:

'Nasty little brat! That's what comes of getting above yourself. Who asked you to go playing with that lot? You could have gone anywhere else to play. Asking for trouble!'

Just at that moment Xi-feng happened to be passing by outside, and hearing what she said, shouted back at her through the window: [2]

'What sort of language is that to be using in the middle of the New Year holiday? He's only a child. He hasn't done anything terrible. [3] What do you want to go carrying on at him like that for? No matter *where* he's been, Sir Zheng and Lady Wang are quite capable of looking after him themselves. [4] There's no cause *for you* to go biting his head off! After all, he *is* one of the masters. If he's misbehaved himself, you should leave the telling-off to those whose job it is. It's no business of yours. Huan! Come out here! Come and play with me!'

Jia Huan had always been afraid of Xi-feng—more even than he was of Lady Wang—and hearing her call him, came running out immediately. Aunt Zhao dared not say a word.

'You're a poor-spirited creature!' [5] Xi-feng said to him. 'How many times have I told you that you can eat and drink and play with any of the boys and girls you like?

But instead of doing as I say, you hang about with these other people and let them warp your mind for you and fill it up with mischief. You've no self-respect, that's your trouble. Can't keep away from the gutter. You insist on making yourself disagreeable and then you complain that people are prejudiced against you!^[6] Fancy making a fuss like that about losing a few coppers! How much *did* you lose?'

'One or two hundred,' Jia Huan muttered abjectly.

'All this fuss about one or two hundred cash! And you one of the masters!'^[7] She turned to Felicity. 'Go and get a string of cash for him, Felicity, and take him round to the back where Miss Ying and the girls are playing!^[8] And if I have any more of this nonsense from you in future, young man,' she went on to Jia Huan, 'I'll first give you a good hiding myself and then send someone to tell the school about you and see if *they* can knock a bit of sense into you!^[9] It sets your Cousin Lian's teeth on edge to see you so wanting in self-respect. He'd have disembowelled you by now I shouldn't wonder, if I hadn't kept his hands off you! Now be off with you!'

'Yes,' said Jia Huan meekly and went off with Felicity. When he had got his money, he took himself off to play with Ying-chun and the girls.

And there we must leave him.

三、注释评点

【1】"赵姨娘见他这般"一句，杨译"At sight of his dejected face..."和霍译"Aunt Zhao observed the dejected state he was in"都采用将隐性信息显化的手法，使用"dejected"一词将语义含糊的"这般"翻译得非常具体。

【2】"可巧凤姐在窗外过，都听在耳内。便隔窗说道"一句中，主语"凤姐"发出了三个动作："过、听、说道"。杨译"Hsi-feng, who was passing outside, overheard this exchange and called back through the window"用关系连词"who"进行句内连接，将"过"译为"who"引导的定语从句的谓语"was passing"，将"听"和"说道"译为主句的并列谓语"overheard"和"called"，之间用"and"连接。霍译"Just at that moment Xi-feng happened to be passing by outside, and hearing what she said, shouted back at her through the window"用"and"进行句内连接，将"过"和"说道"译为并列谓语"happened to be passing by outside"和"shouted back"，之间用"and"连接，将"听"译为现在分词短语"hearing what she said"，做时间状语。

【3】"一半点儿错了，你只教导他"一句，杨译"If he makes some small mistake you can set him right."增加了表示逻辑关系的连接词"If"。霍译使用了反译法，将原文译为否定句："He hasn't done anything terrible."意思是"他并没有犯很大的错"。

【4】"凭他怎么去，还有太太老爷管他呢"一句，"太太""老爷"两词虽然所指宽泛，但说者、听者都知道这两个词分别指王夫人和贾政。杨译是"No matter where he goes, the master and Her Ladyship are there to keep him in order."其中的"the master"和"Her Ladyship"准确地译出了"老爷"和"太太"的意思。霍译是"No matter where he's been, Sir Zheng and Lady Wang are quite capable of looking after him themselves."译者点明了"太太老爷"是"Lady Wang"和"Sir Zheng"，便于英语读者理解，这是一种归化的处理手法；但是，这样的翻译是不符合中国文化中要回避尊者名讳的习俗。

【5】"你也是个没气性的！"一句，杨译是"You're too spineless"，霍译是"You're a poor-spirited creature!"。对于"没气性"这个文化词汇，两位译者都采用了意译手法。

【6】"安着坏心，还只管怨人家偏心。"一句，杨译是"You behave spitefully yourself and then complain that everybody else is unfair!"霍译是"You insist on making yourself disagreeable and then you complain that people are prejudiced against you!"可以看出，两位译者都根据英语的语言习惯，增加了主语"You"和连接词"and"；霍译还增加了"against you"，使语义更加完整、准确。

【7】"亏你还是爷，输了一二百钱就这样！"一句，杨译"All this fuss over a couple of hundred cash! And you one of the young masters!"和霍译"All this fuss about one or two hundred cash! And you one of the masters!"都调整了句序：先译"输了一二百钱就这样（All this fuss over a couple of hundred cash! / All this fuss about one or two hundred cash！）", 再译 "亏你还是爷（And you one of the (young) masters！）"。这是因为：英语和汉语所强调的部分在句中位置有所不同，汉语句子的强调部分一般后置，英语句子的强调部分一般前置。此外，"输了一二百钱就这样"中的"这样"语义抽象、模糊，两位译者都采用了将隐性信息显化的处理手法，将其具象翻译为"All this fuss"。

【8】"回头叫丰儿：'去取一吊钱来，姑娘们都在后头顽呢，把他送了顽去。'"杨译是"She turned to Feng-erh. 'Go and fetch a string of cash. Then take him to the back where the girls are playing.'" 直接引语部分使用"Then"和"where"进行连接："Then"用于句际连接，"where"用于句内连接。霍译是"She turned to Felicity. 'Go and get a string of cash for him, Felicity, <u>and</u> take him round to the back where Miss Ying and the girls are playing!'"直接引语部分使用"<u>and</u>"和"where"进行句内连接。

【9】"你明儿再这么下流狐媚子，我先打了你，打发人告诉学里，皮不揭了你的！"一句，杨译是"If you do anything so mean and sneaky again, Huan, first I'll give you a good spanking and then send someone to tell your teacher about it—he'll flay you alive for it."译者将中国文化色彩浓厚的"揭皮"一词直译为"flay you alive（活活揭皮）"；霍译是"'And if I have anymore of this nonsense from you in future, young man,' she went on to Jia Huan, 'I'll first give you a good hiding myself and then send someone to tell the school about you and see if they can knock a bit of sense into you!'"译者将"揭皮"意译为"knock a bit of sense into you（让你长点记性）"。对于"下流狐媚子"一词，两位译者都做了归化处理。另外，两位译者在译文中都增加了表示逻辑关系的连接词，如"if"和"and"。

四、词汇表

1. dejected [dɪˈdʒektɪd]   *adj.*   unhappy and disappointed 沮丧的；情绪低落的

2. spit [spɪt]   *v.*   to force saliva out of your mouth, often as

			a sign of anger or lack of respect 啐唾沫（常表示愤怒或鄙视）
3. brat [bræt]		n.	a person, especially a child, who behaves badly 没有规矩的人；（尤指）顽童
4. rumpus [ˈrʌmpəs]		n.	a lot of noise that is made especially by people who are complaining about sth 喧闹；吵吵嚷嚷
5. haste [heɪst]		n.	speed in doing sth, especially because you do not have enough time 急速；匆忙；仓促
6. spineless [ˈspaɪnləs]		adj.	(of people) weak and easily frightened 没有骨气的；怯懦的
7. warp [wɔːp]		v.	to influence sb so that they begin to behave in an unacceptable or shocking way 使（行为等）不合情理；使乖戾
8. sneaky [ˈsniːki]		adj.	behaving in a secret and sometimes dishonest or unpleasant way 悄悄的；偷偷摸摸的；鬼鬼祟祟的
9. spiteful [ˈspaɪtfl]		adj.	behaving in an unkind way in order to hurt or upset sb 恶意的；居心不良的；故意使人苦恼的
		adv.	spitefully
10. meek [miːk]		adj.	quiet, and always ready to do what other people want without expressing your own opinion 温顺的；谦恭的；驯服的
		adv.	meekly
11. spanking [ˈspæŋkɪŋ]		n.	a series of hits on the bottom, given to sb, especially a child, as a punishment 打屁股（尤指打小孩）

12. flay [fleɪ]	v.	to hit or whip sb very hard so that some of their skin comes off 毒打，狠狠鞭打（直至皮开肉绽）
13. gnash one's teeth		to feel very angry and upset about sth, especially because you cannot get what you want （气得）咬牙切齿
14. gut [gʌt]	n.	the organs in and around the stomach, especially in an animal （尤指动物的）内脏
15. trot [trɒt]	v.	to walk or go somewhere 步行；走；到……去
16. contemptuous [kənˈtemptʃʊəs]	adj.	feeling or showing that you have no respect for sb/sth 蔑视的；鄙视的；表示轻蔑的
	adv.	contemptuously
17. mischief [ˈmɪstʃɪf]	n.	the wish or tendency to behave or play in a way that causes trouble 恶意；使坏的念头
18. abject [ˈæbdʒekt]	adj.	without any pride or respect for yourself 下贱的；卑躬屈膝的；自卑的
	adv.	abjectly
19. wanting [ˈwɒntɪŋ]	adj.	not having enough of sth 缺少；缺乏；不足
20. disembowel [ˌdɪsɪmˈbaʊəl]	v.	to take the stomach, bowels and other organs out of a person or animal 取出……的内脏；开……的膛

第二十一回

贤袭人娇嗔箴宝玉　俏平儿软语救贾琏[1]

Prudent Hsi-jen Gently Takes Pao-yu to Task
Pretty Ping-erh Quietly Comes to Chia Lien's Rescue [1] (Yang)

*Righteous Aroma discovers how to rebuke her master by saying nothing
And artful Patience is able to rescue hers by being somewhat less than truthful* [1] (Hawkes)

一、本回概述

袭人见宝玉整日在大观园与众姐妹嬉闹度日，毫不避讳，有意劝谏，便故作嗔怒，希望宝玉有所收敛。无聊之下，宝玉闲读《庄子》，自以为得其意趣，并提笔续写。大姐儿出痘疹（天花），全家供奉"痘疹娘娘"，夫妻必须分房而居，贾琏搬出，趁机与多姑娘发生风流韵事，平儿整理贾琏衣物时，发现女人青丝，帮贾琏瞒下凤姐。

二、篇章节选

原文

　　一时宝玉来了，宝钗方出去。宝玉便问袭人道："怎么宝姐姐和你说的这么热闹，见我进来就跑了？"问一声不答，再问时，袭人方道："你问我么？我那里知道你们的原故。"宝玉听了这话，见他脸上气色非往日可比，便笑道："怎么动了真气？"袭人冷笑道："我那里敢动气！[2]只是从今以后别进这屋子了。[3]横竖有人服侍你，再别来支使我。我仍旧还服侍老太太去。"[4]一面说，一面便在炕上合眼倒下。[5]宝玉见了这般景况，深为骇异，禁不住赶来劝慰。那袭人只管合了眼不理。宝玉无了主意，因见麝月进来，便问道："你姐姐怎么了？"麝月道："我知道么？问你自己便明白了。"宝玉听说，呆了一回，自觉无趣，便起身叹道：[6]"不理我罢，我也睡去。"[7]说着，便起身下炕，到自己床上歪下。

　　袭人听他半日无动静，微微的打鼾，料他睡着，便起身拿一领斗篷来，替他刚压上，只听"忽"的一声，宝玉便掀过去，也仍合目装睡。袭人明知其意，便点头冷笑道：[8]"你也不用生气，从此后我只当哑子，再不说你一声儿，如何？"宝玉禁不住起身问道："我又怎么了？你又劝我。你劝我也罢了，才刚又没见你劝我，一进来你就不理我，赌气睡了。我还摸不着是为什么，[9]这会子你又说我恼了。我何尝听见你劝我什么话了。"袭人道："你心里还不明白，还等我说呢！"

杨译

But soon Pao-yu returned, and then she took her leave.

"You two seemed to be having a good chat," said Pao-yu to Hsi-jen. "Why did Cousin Pao-chai leave when I came in?"

Hsi-jen did not answer till he repeated the question.

"Why ask *me*?" she retorted then, "Do I know what goes on between you?"

Pao-yu saw she was not her usual self. "What's made you so cross?" he asked

gently.

"Who am I to be cross?"[2] Hsi-jen smiled sarcastically. "But you'd better keep away from here.[3] There are others who'll look after you, so don't bother me. I shall go back to wait on the old lady."[4] She lay down on the *kang* and closed her eyes.[5]

In dismay Pao-yu hurried to her side to soothe her, but she kept her eyes shut and paid no attention to him. He was puzzling over this when in came Sheh-yueh.

"What's the matter with her?" he asked.

"How should I know? Better ask yourself."

This took Pao-yu so aback that he said nothing. Then, sitting up, he sighed,[6] "All right. If you're going to ignore me I'll go to sleep too."[7]

He left the *kang* and went over to his own bed. When he had been quiet for some time and his regular breathing made Hsi-jen sure he was sleeping, she got up to put a cape over him. The next moment she heard a soft thud. With closed eyes, still shamming sleep, he had thrown it off. Hsi-jen smiled knowingly and nodded.[8]

"You needn't lose your temper. From now on I'll play dumb and not say one word against you—how about that?"

This goaded Pao-yu into sitting up.

"What have I done now?" he demanded. "Why do you keep on at me? I don't mind your scolding, but you didn't scold just now. When I came in you ignored me and lay down in a huff—I've no idea why.[9] Now you accuse me of temper, but I haven't heard you say anything against me yet."

"You know perfectly well without my telling you."

霍译

Presently Bao-yu came in, whereupon Bao-chai got up and left. Bao-yu commented on her departure:

'Cousin Bao-chai seemed to be very thick with you just now. Why should she suddenly rush off when *I* come into the room?'

There was no reply, so he repeated his question.

'Are you asking *me*?' said Aroma. '*I* don't know what reasons you all have for your comings and goings.'

The expression on her face as she uttered these words was angrier than he had ever seen her look before.

He laughed.

'Oh dear! Are you in a rage again?'

Aroma laughed mirthlessly.

'It's not for the likes of me to get into rages. [2] But I wish that from now on you would stop coming into this room. [3] After all, you *have* got people to wait on you elsewhere. You don't really need my services. I shall go back to serving Her Old Ladyship, like I used to before.' [4]

With that she closed her eyes and lay back upon the kang. [5]

Bao-yu was alarmed to see her in such a state and impulsively rushed over to the kang to soothe her. But Aroma kept her eyes tightly shut and would take no notice. Bao-yu did not know what to do. Just then Musk chanced to enter and he turned to her for help:

'What's up with Aroma?'

'How should I know?' said Musk. 'You'd do better to ask yourself that question.'

Bao-yu was so taken aback that for a while he said nothing. Then, finding their combined hostility too much for him, he got up with a sigh from his suppliant position on the kang. [6]

'All right, ignore me then! I'm going off to sleep, too.' [7]

And he slid from the kang and went off to his own bed to lie down.

For a long time there was no sound from him except for a gentle snoring. Judging that he must be really asleep, Aroma rose from the kang and took a large travelling-cloak to cover him with. A moment later she heard a gentle thud. He had whipped it from him and thrown it to the floor as soon as her back was turned. But when she looked, his eyes were closed as before and he was still pretending to be asleep. The significance of the gesture did not escape her. She nodded slowly and regarded the

feigned sleeper sarcastically:[8]

'All right, then! There's no need for *you* to get angry. From now on I'll just pretend I'm dumb. I won't say another word of criticism. Will that satisfy you?'

This was too much for Bao-yu. He sat bolt upright on his bed.

'What am I supposed to have done this time? And what's all this "criticism" you're talking about? If you *had* been criticizing me it wouldn't be so bad; but when I came in just now, you didn't say *anything*: you simply ignored me. You went and lay down in a huff without my having the faintest idea what it was all about,[9] and now you accuse *me* of behaving unreasonably! I haven't heard a single peep out of you yet to explain what it is that you are angry about!'

'Your own conscience ought to tell you that,' said Aroma. 'You don't need me to tell you.'

三、注释评点

【1】本回回目是"贤袭人娇嗔箴宝玉 俏平儿软语救贾琏",上下句各出现了一个修饰性形容词:"贤"和"俏",杨译"Prudent Hsi-jen Gently Takes Pao-yu to Task Pretty Ping-erh Quietly Comes to Chia Lien's Rescue" 将它们分别译为"prudent"和"pretty"。"贤"是中国文化特有的词汇,"prudent"的意思是"sensible and careful when you make judgments and decisions, avoiding unnecessary risks",即"谨慎的、慎重的"。从英文释义可以看出,"prudent"非常符合原文中"贤"的意思:小说中的袭人做事谨慎得体,深受王夫人器重,也是王夫人暗许的未来宝玉姨娘的人选,所以她一心要替王夫人照看好宝玉,生怕出点不好的事。"pretty"是漂亮的意思,用它来翻译原文中的"俏",显得分量不足,因为这里的"俏"不仅仅指容貌美丽。霍译"Righteous Aroma discovers how to rebuke her master by saying nothing And artful Patience is able to rescue hers by being somewhat less than truthful"用归化法将"贤"译为"righteous","righteous"的意思是"morally right or good",即"正直的、公正的",这个词的宗教色彩非常浓厚。"俏"被译为

"artful",的确很有技巧,因为此处的"俏"不仅指平儿外表俏丽可人,更指她聪明乖巧,善解人意,"artful"一词表现出平儿在帮助贾琏隐瞒出轨一事时的技巧和分寸。另外,霍译创造性地将"软语"译为"being somewhat less than truthful",虽然没有译出"软语"的字面意思,但是非常契合本回故事的具体情节。

【2】"我那里敢动气!"一句,杨译是"Who am I to be cross?",霍译是"It's not for the likes of me to get into rages."原文是袭人的一句气话,杨译使用反问句"Who am I to do...",传达出一种自轻的语气,表达出"我怎么有资格……?"的意思,十分符合袭人当时生气的心情和说话的语气。霍译使用的是陈述句,语气稍显平淡。

【3】"只是从今以后别进这屋子了。"一句,杨译是"But you'd better keep away from here."霍译是"But I wish that from now on you would stop coming into this room."原文是袭人一时的气话,其本意并非如此,事实上宝玉也不可能从此不进这屋子。杨译使用的"You'd better..."句型,虽然可以表示劝告、建议或愿望,但一般不用于对上级或长辈说话。袭人虽然是在气头上,但在封建礼制社会中逾矩说话办事毕竟少见,对于袭人来说,这样的口气太过强硬,并不合适。霍译在动词 wish 的宾语从句中使用了虚拟语气,即"I wish that... you would...",表达出一种不太可能实现的愿望,十分符合袭人的身份以及她当时的心情。

【4】"我仍旧还服侍老太太去"一句,杨译是"I shall go back to wait on the old lady."霍译是"I shall go back to serving Her Old Ladyship, like I used to before."可以看出,霍译增译了"like I used to before",不但译出了"仍旧"之意,而且和前文产生关联,使读者忆起袭人之前就是服侍贾母的。

【5】"一面说,一面便在炕上合眼倒下"一句,杨译"She lay down on the *kang* and closed her eyes."用"and"连接两个谓语动词"lay"和"closed",省译了"一面说"。霍译是"With that she closed her eyes and lay back upon the kang."句首用"With that"承上启下;译者将"合眼倒下"译为并列谓语"closed her eyes and lay back";"一面说"被译为介词短语"With that",在译文中充当伴随状语。有趣的是,两位译者对"合眼"和"倒下"的翻译顺序

不同：杨译是先倒下再合眼（lay down... and closed...），霍译是先合眼再倒下（closed... and lay back...）。

【6】"宝玉听说，呆了一回，自觉无趣，便起身叹道"一句中，主语"宝玉"发出了一连串的动作："听说、呆、自觉、起身、叹道"。杨译是"This took Pao-yu so aback that he said nothing. Then, sitting up, he sighed"，译者用句子化词法将小句"宝玉听说"译为"This"，充当译文第一句的主语，同时在该句中用"so... that..."进行句内连接，"Then"作句际连接；"起身"和"叹道"是并列的两个动作，在译文的第二句中被处理成偏正结构："偏"是现在分词短语"sitting up（起身）"，充当伴随状语；"正"是谓语"sighed（叹道）"。霍译是"Bao-yu was so taken aback that for a while he said nothing. Then, finding their combined hostility too much for him, he got up with a sigh from his suppliant position on the kang."，可以看出，译者也是用"so...that..."和"Then"分别做句内连接和句际连接的；另外，在"起身叹道"的处理上，霍译选择了"got up（起身）"作谓语，"with a sigh"作伴随状语，也是偏正结构。另外，霍译有两处增译："finding their combined hostility too much for him"和"from his suppliant position on the kang"，生动地体现出此刻的宝玉被两个丫鬟联手孤立起来的可怜相。

【7】"不理我罢，我也睡去。"一句，这是宝玉在袭人、麝月处遭冷遇后的气话，句式简短，语气不悦而无奈。杨译是"If you're going to ignore me I'll go to sleep too."，句子较长，语气节奏慢，不太符合原文的语境；霍译是"All right, ignore me then! I'm going off to sleep, too."，句式较短，还用了感叹句，恰当地表现出宝玉郁闷的情态。

【8】"袭人明知其意，便点头冷笑道"一句，杨译是"Hsi-jen smiled knowingly and nodded."译者用副词"knowingly"一笔带过原文中的"明知其意"。霍译是"The significance of the gesture did not escape her. She nodded slowly and regarded the feigned sleeper sarcastically"；在翻译"袭人明知其意"时，译者在译文的第一句中用了正说反译法——用否定形式来表达原文的肯定语义。另外，该句的主语是"the significance of the gesture"，体现出英、汉两种语言在主语上的差异：汉语多用人称主语；英语除了人称主语外，物化主语

也用得很普遍。

【9】"一进来你就不理我，赌气睡了。我还摸不着是为什么"一句，杨译"When I came in you ignored me and lay down in a huff—I've no idea why." 使用"When"和"and"进行句内连接；霍译"but when I came in just now, you didn't say anything: you simply ignored me. You went and lay down in a huff without my having the faintest idea what it was all about."，译文的第一句使用"but"和"when"进行连句，"but"承接上文，"when"引出下文。译文的第二句用句子化短语法将小句"我还摸不着是为什么"译为介词短语"without my having the faintest idea what it was all about"，充当状语；同时，该介词短语中还用了形容词的最高级形式"the faintest"，有强调意味，更贴切地表现出宝玉对于袭人无端生气的困惑不解。

四、词汇表

1. wait on sb		to act as a servant to sb 服侍，侍候
2. dismay [dɪsˈmeɪ]	n.	a strong feeling of fear, worry, or sadness that is caused by sth unpleasant and unexpected 惊愕；焦虑；气馁
3. soothe [suːð]	v.	to make sb who is anxious, upset, etc. feel calmer 安慰；抚慰
4. take sb aback		to surprise sb greatly 使吃惊；使困惑
5. cape [keɪp]	n.	a short cloak 披肩；斗篷
6. thud [θʌd]	n.	a sound like the one which is made when a heavy object hits sth else 砰的一声；扑通一声
7. sham [ʃæm]	v.	to make a pretence of 假装
8. goad [gəʊd]	v.	to provoke by constant criticism 激励；驱使
9. huff [hʌf]	n.	a state of irritation or annoyance 怒气冲

冲；发怒

10. mirthless [ˈmɜːθləs]	*adj.*	showing no real enjoyment or amusement 不快乐的；忧郁的
	adv.	mirthlessly
11. impulsively [ɪmˈpʌlsɪvli]	*adv.*	in an impulsive or impetuous way; without taking cautions 易冲动地；草率地
12. chance [tʃɑːns]	*v.*	to happen or to do sth by chance 偶然发生；碰巧
13. suppliant [ˈsʌpliənt]	*adj.*	humbly entreating 恳求的；哀求的；谦卑的
14. whip [hwɪp; wɪp]	*v.*	to remove or pull sth quickly and suddenly 快速移开；快速拿走
15. feign [feɪn]	*v.*	to pretend that you have a particular feeling or that you are ill/sick, tired, etc. 假装，装作，佯装（有某种感觉或生病、疲倦等）
16. peep [piːp]	*n.*	something that sb says or a sound that sb makes 说话；出声音

第二十二回

听曲文宝玉悟禅机　制灯谜贾政悲谶语[1]

A Song Awakens Pao-yu to Esoteric Truths
Lantern-Riddles Grieve Chia Cheng with Their Ill Omens [1] (Yang)

Bao-yu finds Zen enlightenment in an operatic aria
And Jia Zheng sees portents of doom in lantern riddles [1] (Hawkes)

一、本回概述

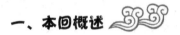

　　宝钗稳重平和，贾母深为喜爱，要为她举办生日宴。宴会上看戏时，宝钗为宝玉解读曲文，使他初悟禅机。湘云心直口快，说献唱的戏子长得像黛玉，惹得黛玉气恼不已。宝玉极力调解，反被双方奚落，自觉无趣，便做偈诗。钗、黛读诗，见宝玉空遁之意初现，黛玉便以禅机考问宝玉，宝玉竟不能答，大家遂劝其放弃参禅。上元佳节，元妃命人送来灯谜，贾母凑兴，举办灯谜会。贾政朝罢，承欢加入，却从众姑娘所作谜面上，读出谜底皆为不祥之物，不禁心下戚戚然。

二、篇章节选

原文

　　且说史湘云住了两日，因要回去。贾母因说："等过了你宝姐姐的生日，看了戏再回去。"[2] 史湘云听了，只得住下。又一面遣人回去，将自己旧日作的两色针线活计取来，为宝钗生辰之仪。

　　谁想贾母自见宝钗来了，喜他稳重和平，正值他才过第一个生辰，便自己蠲资二十两，唤了凤姐来，交与他置酒戏。[3] 凤姐凑趣笑道："一个老祖宗给孩子们作生日，不拘怎样，谁还敢争，又办什么酒戏。既高兴要热闹，就说不得自己花上几两。巴巴的找出这霉烂的二十两银子来作东道，这意思还叫我赔上。果然拿不出来也罢了，金的、银的、圆的、扁的，压塌了箱子底，只是勒掯我们。[4] 举眼看看，谁不是儿女？难道将来只有宝兄弟顶了你老人家上五台山不成？[5] 那些梯己只留与他，我们如今虽不配使，也别苦了我们。这个够酒的？够戏的？"说的满屋里都笑起来。贾母亦笑道："你们听听这嘴！我也算会说的，怎么说不过这猴儿。[6] 你婆婆也不敢强嘴，你和我哪哪的。"[7] 凤姐笑道："我婆婆也是一样的疼宝玉，[8] 我也没处去诉冤，倒说我强嘴。"说着，又引着贾母笑了一回，贾母十分喜悦。

　　到晚间，众人都在贾母前，定昏之馀，大家娘儿姊妹等说笑时，贾母因问宝钗爱听何戏，爱吃何物等语。宝钗深知贾母年老人，喜热闹戏文，爱吃甜烂之食，便总依贾母往日素喜者说了出来。贾母更加欢悦。[9] 次日便先送过衣服玩物礼去，王夫人、凤姐、黛玉等诸人皆有，随分不一，不须多记。

杨译

　　Let us return now to Hsiang-yun. After spending several days in the Jung Mansion it was time for her to go home, but the Lady Dowager urged her to wait until after Pao-chai's birthday and the performance of operas.[2] So Hsiang-yun, having to stay on, sent home for two pieces of her embroidery as a birthday-present for her cousin.

The fact was that the Lady Dowager had taken a fancy to Pao-chai since her arrival on account of her steady, amiable behaviour. And as this would be her first birthday in their house, the old lady summoned Hsi-feng and gave her twenty taels of silver from her own coffer for a feast and an opera. [3]

Hsi-feng teased, "When an Old Ancestress wants to celebrate some grandchild's birthday, no matter how grandly, who are we to protest? So there's to be a feast and opera too, is there? Well, if you want it to be lively you'll have to pay for it yourself instead of trying to play host with a mouldy twenty taels. I suppose you expect me to make up the rest? If you really couldn't afford it, all right. But your cases are bursting with gold and silver ingots of every shape and size—the bottoms of the chests are dropping out, they're so full. Yet you're still squeezing us. [4] Look, aren't all of us your children? Is Pao-yu the only one who'll carry you as an immortal on his head to Mount Wutai, that you keep everything for him? [5] Even if the rest of us aren't good enough, don't be so hard on us. Is this enough for a feast or theatricals?"

The whole company burst out laughing.

"Listen to that tongue of hers!" The old lady chuckled. "I'm not exactly tongue-tied myself but I'm no match for this monkey. [6] Not even your mother-in-law would think of arguing with me, but you give me tit for tat." [7]

"My mother-in-law dotes on Pao-yu just as much as you do," [8] retorted Hsi-feng with a smile. "So I've no one to take my side. Instead, you make me out a termagant."

That set the old lady crowing with laughter and put her in the highest of spirits.

That night, after the family had gathered to pay their evening respects to the Lady Dowager and then gone on to chat, she asked Pao-chai to name her favourite operas and dishes. Knowing the old lady's partiality for lively shows and sweet, pappy food, Pao-chai gave these as her own preferences, adding even more to the Lady Dowager's pleasure. [9]

The first thing next day she had presents of clothing and trinkets sent to the girl. Lady Wang, Hsi-feng, Tai-yu and the others also sent theirs according to the status of

each. But these need not be enumerated in detail.

霍译

It tells us instead that Shi Xiang-yun, having spent a considerable part of the New Year holiday with the Jias, was now on the point of returning home, but was urged by Grandmother Jia to wait for Bao-chai's birthday and not go back until she had seen the plays. [2] Xiang-yun agreed to stay and sent someone home with instructions to tell them that she would be returning a little later than planned and to fetch a couple of pieces of her own embroidery that she could give to Bao-chai as a birthday-present.

Ever since Bao-chai's first arrival, Grandmother Jia had been pleasurably impressed by her placid and dependable disposition, and now that she was about to spend her first 'big' birthday in the Jia household, the old lady resolved to make it a memorable one. Taking twenty taels of silver from her private store, she summoned Xi-feng and directed her to spend it on providing wine and plays for a celebration. [3] Xi-feng made this the occasion for a little raillery.

'If the old lady says she wants her grandchild's birthday celebrated,' she said, 'then celebrated it must be, and we must all jump to it without arguing! But if she's going to start asking for *plays* as well, all I can say to that is that if she's in the mood for a bit of fun, I'm afraid she's going to have to pay for it. She's going to have to cough up something out of those private savings of hers she's been hoarding all these years—not wait until the last minute and then fish out a measly little twenty taels to pay for the party: that's just another way of telling us we've got to pay for it ourselves. I mean, if you were really hard up, it would be another matter; but you've got boxes and boxes of boodle—the bottoms are dropping out of them, they're so full! It's pure meanness, that's what it is! [4] You forget, Grannie, when you go to heaven young Bao-yu won't be the only one who'll walk ahead of the hearse. [5] You've got other grandchildren too, don't forget! You don't have to leave *everything* to him. The rest of us may not be much use, but you mustn't be *too* hard on us. Twenty taels! Do you really think that's enough to pay for a party *and plays*?'

At this point the entire company burst into laughter, which Grandmother Jia joined in herself.

'Just listen to her!' she said. 'I thought *I* had a fairly sharp tongue, but I'm no match for *this* one: "Clack-clack, clack-clack"—it's worse than a pair of wooden clappers!'[6] Even your mother-in-law daren't argue with *me*, my dear! Don't pick on *me*!'[7]

'Mother-in-law is just as soppy about Bao-yu as you are,'[8] said Xi-feng. 'I've got no one to tell my troubles to. And you say I'm sharp-tongued!'

Xi-feng's mock-lugubriousness set the old lady off in another squall of laughter. She loved to be teased, and Xi-feng's bantering put her in great good humour.

That night, when the young folk had finished paying their evening duty and were standing round her laughing and talking a while before retiring to their own apartments, Grandmother Jia asked Bao-chai what sort of plays she liked best and what her favourite dishes were. Bao-chai was well aware that her grandmother, like most old women, enjoyed the livelier, more rackety sort of plays and liked sweet and pappy things to eat, so she framed her answers entirely in terms of these preferences. The old lady was delighted.[9]

Next day presents of clothing and various other objects, to which Lady Wang, Xi-feng, Dai-yu and the rest had all contributed, were sent round to Bao-chai's. Our narrative supplies no details.

三、注释评点

【1】本回回目为"听曲文宝玉悟禅机 制灯谜贾政悲谶语",杨译"A Song Awakens Pao-yu to Esoteric Truths Lantern-Riddles Grieve Chia Cheng with Their Ill Omens"使用了物化主语"A Song"和"Lantern-Riddles"。此处,物化主语表达出客观事物从外部强迫作用于人的认知的意味——宝玉、贾政皆是无意之中,感于外物刺激而心有所悟;另外,两个使动词"awaken"和"grieve"很好地体现出原文"悟"与"悲"的意思,与物化主语配合使用,

表达了宝玉忽然福至心灵、有所觉悟；贾政猝不及防，读到谜语的不祥信息，心中不胜悲戚。霍译"Bao-yu finds Zen enlightenment in an operatic aria And Jia Zheng sees portents of doom in lantern riddles"则使用了人称主语。

【2】"且说史湘云住了两日，因要回去。贾母因说：'等过了你宝姐姐的生日，看了戏再回去。'"一句，杨译是"Let us return now to Hsiang-yun. After spending several days in the Jung Mansion it was time for her to go home, but the Lady Dowager urged her to wait until after Pao-chai's birthday and the performance of operas."，译者使用"After，but，until after"进行译文第二句的句内连接；另外，译者用了句子化短语法将小句"且说史湘云住了两日"译为介词短语"After spending several days in the Jung Mansion"。霍译是"It tells us instead that Shi Xiang-yun, having spent a considerable part of the New Year holiday with the Jias, was now on the point of returning home, but was urged by Grandmother Jia to wait for Bao-chai's birthday and not go back until she had seen the plays."，译者使用"but，and，not... until..."进行句内连接；小句"且说史湘云住了两日"被译为现在分词短语"having spent a considerable part of the New Year holiday with the Jias"，在译文中充当时间状语。

【3】"谁想贾母自见宝钗来了，喜他稳重和平，正值他才过第一个生辰，便自己蠲资二十两，唤了凤姐来，交与他置酒戏。"一句中，作者使用了一连串的动词：见、来、喜、过、蠲、唤、交、置，是汉语中典型的连动句式。杨译是"The fact was that the Lady Dowager had taken a fancy to Pao-chai since her arrival on account of her steady, amiable behaviour. And as this would be her first birthday in their house, the old lady summoned Hsi-feng and gave her twenty taels of silver from her own coffer for a feast and an opera."，译文的第二句使用"And"和"as"进行连句："And"用于承接上一句，"as"用于引出后文；杨译还增译了"in their house"，点明这是宝钗在"贾府"过的第一个生日；此外，译者用句子化短语法将小句"自见宝钗来了"译为介词短语"since her arrival"。霍译是"Ever since Bao-chai's first arrival, Grandmother Jia had been pleasurably impressed by her placid and dependable disposition, and now that she was about to spend her first 'big' birthday in the Jia household, the old lady resolved to make it a memorable one. Taking twenty taels of silver from her private store, she summoned Xi-feng and directed her to spend it on providing wine and plays for a celebration.",译文的第一句主要使用"and"和"now that"进行句内连接:"and"承接上文,"now that"引出后文;译者增译了"the old lady resolved to make it a memorable one",进一步点明贾母费心为宝钗张罗生日宴会的原因;此外,译者将小句"自己蠲资二十两"译为现在分词短语"Taking twenty taels of silver from her private store",在译文的第二句中充当时间状语。

【4】"果然拿不出来也罢了,金的、银的、圆的、扁的,压塌了箱子底,只是勒掯我们。"一句,杨译是"If you really couldn't afford it, all right. But your cases are bursting with gold and silver ingots of every shape and size—the bottoms of the chests are dropping out, they're so full. Yet you're still squeezing us.",译者使用"If,But,Yet"进行连句:"If"用于第一句译文的句内连接,"But"和"Yet"用于句际连接。霍译是"I mean, if you were really hard up, it would be another matter: but you've got boxes and boxes of boodle—the bottoms are dropping out of them, they're so full! It's pure meanness, that's what it is!",译者在译文的第一句中使用"if"和"but"进行句内连接。"果然拿不出来也罢了"有与事实相反的意思,杨译"If you really couldn't afford it, all right."和霍译"if you were really hard up, it would be another matter"此处都使用了虚拟语气。"只是勒掯我们"中的"勒掯"一词是方言,意为"敲诈勒索",凤姐用这个词是玩笑话,杨译将它译为"squeeze",形象地表达出凤姐对贾母拿出区区二十两银子办生日宴会的调侃。

【5】"难道将来只有宝兄弟顶了你老人家上五台山不成?"一句中,"上五台山"是委婉语,意思是人去世后登仙成佛。杨译"Is Pao-yu the only one who'll carry you as an immortal on his head to Mount Wutai"采用了直译法,并增加了"as an immortal"作为文内补充信息;霍译"You forget, Grannie, when you go to heaven young Bao-yu won't be the only one who'll walk ahead of the hearse."舍弃了"上五台山"的字面义,采用意译手法,向英语读者介绍中国的丧葬习俗。

【6】"贾母亦笑道:'你们听听这嘴!我也算会说的,怎么说不过这猴

儿。'"一句，杨译是"'Listen to that tongue of hers!' The old lady chuckled. 'I'm not exactly tongue-tied myself but I'm no match for this monkey.'"；霍译是"'Just listen to her!' she said. 'I thought I had a fairly sharp tongue, but I'm no match for this one: "Clack-clack, clack-clack"—it's worse than a pair of wooden clappers!'"。关于引语的翻译，汉语和英语的行文习惯不同：汉语一般把"某人说"放在句首，而英语中的"sb says / says sb"可以出现在引文之前、之间和之后；霍译是出现在引文之后的例子。另外，杨译用了反译法，将"我也算会说的"译为否定句"I'm not exactly tongue-tied"。霍译没有直接翻译"猴儿"一词，而是巧妙地使用拟声词"clack-clack, clack-clack"，并用了比较级和借喻"worse than a pair of wooden clappers"来形容凤姐的口齿伶俐。

【7】"你婆婆也不敢强嘴，你和我哪哪的。"一句，杨译是"Not even your mother-in-law would think of arguing with me, but you give me tit for tat."，译者将"Not even"置于句首，有强调语气的作用。"哪哪"是河北丰润土语词汇，意思是"口齿伶俐，言语清楚，能言善辩"，译者采用意译手法将小句"你和我哪哪的"译为"you give me tit for tat"，即"你与我针锋相对"。霍译是"Even your mother-in-law daren't argue with me, my dear! Don't pick on me!"，译者将"Even"置于句首，也是起到强调的作用。另外，"哪哪"的含义已在上文中通过"clack-clack, clack-clack"和"worse than a pair of wooden clappers"充分体现出来，因此，译者在这里只说"Don't pick on me!"，即"不要针对我，不要欺负我"。

【8】"我婆婆也是一样的疼宝玉。"一句，杨译是"My mother-in-law dotes on Pao-yu just as much as you do"；霍译是"Mother-in-law is just as soppy about Bao-yu as you are"。"疼宝玉"中的"疼"是动词，意为"宠爱，宠溺"，杨译用了动词短语"dote on"，霍译则转换了词性，将其翻译为形容词"soppy"。

【9】"宝钗深知贾母年老人，喜热闹戏文，爱吃甜烂之食，便总依贾母往日素喜者说了出来。贾母更加欢悦。"一句，杨译是"Knowing the old lady's partiality for lively shows and sweet, pappy food, Pao-chai gave these as her own preferences, adding even more to the Lady Dowager's pleasure."，句式呈现出偏正

结构：主谓结构前、后分别使用现在分词短语"Knowing..."和"adding..."，前者在句中充当原因状语，后者充当结果状语。另外，杨译用句子化短语法将小句"喜热闹戏文，爱吃甜烂之食"译为名词短语"partiality for lively shows and sweet, pappy food"，原文中的动词"喜"和"爱"转化为译文中的名词"partiality"。霍译是"Bao-chai was well aware that her grandmother, like most old women, enjoyed the livelier, more rackety sort of plays and liked sweet and pappy things to eat, so she framed her answers entirely in terms of these preferences. The old lady was delighted."，译者主要使用"so"进行句内连接，表达一种因果关系。此外，"frame"一词用得十分生动，既可以从正面理解为：宝钗善解人意，孝敬老人，具有大家闺秀风范；也可以从反面理解为：宝钗富有心机，为了取悦贾母就按照贾母的喜好编出一套说辞。

四、词汇表

1. amiable [ˈeɪmiəbl]	adj.	pleasant; friendly and easy to like 友好的，易相处的；和蔼的，友善的
2. tael [teɪl]	n.	a unit of weight used in east Asia approximately equal to 1.3 ounces 两；银两
3. coffer [ˈkɒfə(r)]	n.	a large strong box, used in the past for storing money or valuable objects 保险柜，保险箱；金库
4. ingot [ˈɪŋgət]	n.	a solid piece of metal, especially gold or silver, usually shaped like a brick（常为砖形的）铸块，锭
5. theatricals [θɪˈætrɪklz]	n.	[pl.] performances of plays 戏剧演出
6. tit for tat		a situation in which you do sth bad to sb because they have done the same to you 针锋相对；以牙还牙

7. termagant [ˈtɜːməgənt]	n.	a woman who is very strict or who tries to tell people what to do, in an unpleasant way 苛刻的女人；专横的女人
8. pap [pæp]	n.	soft or almost liquid food eaten by babies or people who are ill 软食；流食
	adj.	pappy
9. trinket [ˈtrɪŋkɪt]	n.	a piece of jewelry or small decorative object that is not worth much money 小装饰品；小件饰物
10. enumerate [ɪˈnjuːməreɪt]	v.	to name things on a list one by one 列举；数
11. raillery [ˈreɪləri]	n.	friendly joking about a person 善意的嘲笑；逗弄
12. cough sth up		to give sth, especially money, unwillingly 勉强给（尤指钱）
13. measly [ˈmiːzli]	adj.	very small in size or quantity; not enough 少得可怜的；微不足道的
14. boodle [ˈbuːdl]	n.	a group 一群，一组
15. hearse [hɜːs]	n.	a long vehicle used for carrying the coffin at a funeral 柩车；灵车
16. soppy [ˈsɒpi]	adj.	full of unnecessary emotion 情意缠绵的；感情过于丰富的
17. lugubrious [ləˈguːbriəs]	adj.	sad and serious 阴郁的；悲伤的
	n.	lugubriousness
18. squall [skwɔːl]	n.	a sudden strong and violent wind, often during rain or snow storms 飑（常指暴风雨或暴风雪中突起的狂风）
19. banter [ˈbæntə(r)]	v.	to joke with sb （和某人）开玩笑；逗乐
20. rackety [ˈrækɪti]	adj.	uncontrollably noisy 喧扰的；喜欢吵闹的

第二十三回

西厢记妙词通戏语　牡丹亭艳曲警芳心[1]

Lines from "The Western Chamber" Are Quoted in Fun
A Song from "Peony Pavilion" Distresses a Tender Heart [1] (Yang)

Words from the 'Western Chamber' supply a joke that offends
And songs from the 'Soul's Return' move a tender heart to anguish [1] (Hawkes)

一、本回概述

　　元春省亲后，不舍大观园美景荒废，便命宝玉及众姐妹入住园中。众人入住后，每日探讨琴棋书画、猜谜游戏，十分快意。一日，黛玉在园中葬花，偶遇宝玉偷读《西厢记》，宝玉力荐黛玉同读，二人皆被戏曲的语言及情节吸引，借书中戏语，情窦初开的宝、黛二人互诉衷肠。葬花完毕，宝玉离开后，黛玉无意中听到梨香院女孩子的伤春唱词，联想到自己正值青春年华，却寄人篱下，内心无所依傍，不由悲痛落泪。

二、篇章节选

原文

宝玉听了喜不自禁，[2]笑道："待我放下书，帮你来收拾。"黛玉道："什么书？"宝玉见问，慌的藏之不迭，便说道："不过是《中庸》、《大学》。"黛玉笑道："你又在我跟前弄鬼。趁早儿给我瞧，好多着呢。"宝玉道："好妹妹，若论你，我是不怕的。你看了，好歹别告诉别人去。真真这是好书！你要看了，连饭也不想吃呢。"一面说，一面递了过去。林黛玉把花具且都放下，接书来瞧，从头看去，越看越爱看，不到一顿饭工夫，将十六出俱已看完，自觉词藻警人，馀香满口。[3]虽看完了书，却只管出神，心内还默默记诵。[4]

宝玉笑道："妹妹，你说好不好？"林黛玉笑道："果然有趣。"宝玉笑道："我就是个'多愁多病身'，你就是那'倾国倾城貌'。"[5]林黛玉听了，不觉带腮连耳通红，登时直竖起两道似蹙非蹙的眉，瞪了两只似睁非睁的眼，微腮带怒，薄面含嗔，指宝玉道：[6]"你这该死的胡说！好好的把这淫词艳曲弄了来，还学了这些混话来欺负我。我告诉舅舅舅母去！"说到"欺负"两个字上，早又把眼睛圈儿红了，转身就走。宝玉着了急，向前拦住说道："好妹妹，千万饶我这一遭，原是我说错了。若有心欺负你，明儿我掉在池子里，教个癞头鼋吞了去，变个大忘八，等你明儿做了'一品夫人'病老归西的时候，我往你坟上替你驮一辈子的碑去。"[7]说的林黛玉嗤的一声笑了，一面揉着眼睛，一面笑道："一般也唬的这个调儿，还只管胡说。'呸，原来是苗而不秀，是个银样镴枪头。'"宝玉听了，笑道："你这个呢？我也告诉去。"林黛玉笑道："你说你会过目成诵，难道我就不能一目十行么？"[8]

宝玉一面收书，一面笑道：[9]"正经快把花埋了罢，别提那个了。"

杨译

Pao-yu was delighted by this idea.[2]

"Just let me put this book somewhere and I'll help," he offered.

"What book's that?"

He hastily tucked it out of sight.

"Just the *Doctrine of the Mean* and *The Great Learning*."

"You're trying to fool me again. You'd have done better to show me in the first place."

"I don't mind showing *you,* dear cousin, but you mustn't tell anyone else. It's a real masterpiece. You won't be able to give a thought to eating once you start reading it." He passed her the book.

Tai-yu laid down her gardening tools to read, and the more she read the more enthralled she was. In less time than it takes for a meal she had read all the sixteen scenes. The sheer beauty of the language left a sweet taste in her mouth.[3] After finishing reading she sat there entranced, recalling some of the lines.[4]

"Well, don't you think it's wonderful?" he asked.

She smiled.

"It's certainly fascinating."

"I'm the one 'sick with longing,'" he joked. "And yours is the beauty which caused 'cities and kingdoms to fall.'"[5]

Tai-yu flushed to the tips of her ears. Knitting her sulky brows, her eyes flashing with anger beneath half-drooping lids, she pointed a finger at Pao-yu in accusal.[6]

"You really are the limit! Bringing such licentious songs in here and, what's more, insulting me with nasty quotations from them." Her eyes brimmed with tears. "I'm going to tell uncle and aunt."

She turned to go.

In dismay Pao-yu barred her way.

"Forgive me this once, dear cousin! I shouldn't have said that. But if I meant to insult you, I'll fall into the pond tomorrow and let the scabby-headed tortoise swallow me, so that I change into a big turtle myself. Then when you become a lady of the first rank and go at last to your paradise in the west, I shall bear the stone tablet at your grave on my back for ever."[7]

Tai-yu burst out laughing at this and wiped her eyes.

"You're so easy to scare, yet still you indulge in talking such nonsense," she teased. "Why, you're nothing but 'a flowerless sprout,' 'a lead spearhead that looks like silver.'"

It was Pao-yu's turn to laugh.

"Now listen to *you*! I'll tell on you too."

"You boast that you can 'memorize a passage with one reading.' Why can't I 'learn ten lines at a glance'?" [8]

Laughing he put the book away. [9]

"Never mind that. Let's get on with burying the flowers."

霍译

Bao-yu was full of admiration for this idea. [2]

'Just let me put this book somewhere and I'll give you a hand.'

'What book?' said Dai-yu.

'Oh... The *Doctrine of the Mean* and *The Greater Learning*,' he said, hastily concealing it.

'Don't try to fool *me*!' said Dai-yu. 'You would have done much better to let me look at it in the first place, instead of hiding it so guiltily.'

'In your case, coz, I have nothing to be afraid of,' said Bao-yu; 'but if I do let you look, you must promise not to tell anyone. It's marvelous stuff. Once you start reading it, you'll even stop wanting to eat!'

He handed the book to her, and Dai-yu put down her things and looked. The more she read, the more she liked it, and before very long she had read several acts. She felt the power of the words and their lingering fragrance. [3] Long after she had finished reading, when she had laid down the book and was sitting there rapt and silent, the lines continued to ring on in her head. [4]

'Well,' said Bao-yu, 'is it good?'

Dai-yu smiled and nodded.

Bao-yu laughed:

'How can I, full of sickness and of woe,

Withstand that face which kingdoms could o'erthrow?' [5]

Dai-yu reddened to the tips of her ears. The eyebrows that seemed to frown yet somehow didn't were raised now in anger and the lovely eyes flashed. There was rage in her crimson cheeks and resentment in all her looks.

'You're *hateful*!'—she pointed a finger at him in angry accusal [6] —'deliberately using that horrid play to take advantage of me. I'm going straight off to tell Uncle and Aunt!'

At the words 'take advantage of me' her eyes filled with tears, and as she finished speaking she turned from him and began to go. Bao-yu rushed after her and held her back:

'Please, *please* forgive me! Dearest coz! If I had the slightest intention of taking advantage of you, may I fall into the water and be eaten up by an old bald-headed turtle! When you have become a great lady and gone at last to your final resting-place, I shall become the stone turtle that stands in front of your grave and spend the rest of eternity carrying your tombstone on my back as a punishment!' [7]

His ridiculous declamation provoked a sudden explosion of mirth. She laughed and simultaneously wiped the tears away with her knuckles:

'Look at you—the same as ever! Scared as anything, but you still have to go on talking nonsense. Well, I know you now for what you are:

"Of silver spear the leaden counterfeit"!'

'Well! *You* can talk!' said Bao-yu laughing. 'Listen to *you*! Now *I'm* going off to tell on *you*!'

'You needn't imagine you're the only one with a good memory,' said Dai-yu haughtily. 'I suppose I'm allowed to remember lines too if I like.' [8]

Bao-yu took back the book from her with a good-natured laugh: [9]

'Never mind about all that now! Let's get on with this flower-burying!'

三、注释评点

【1】本回回目为"西厢记妙词通戏语　牡丹亭艳曲警芳心",杨译是"Lines from 'The Western Chamber' Are Quoted in Fun　A Song from 'Peony Pavilion' Distresses a Tender Heart",上下句分别使用了被动语态和主动语态,削弱了对称性。霍译是"Words from the 'Western Chamber' supply a joke that offends　And songs from the 'Soul's Return' move a tender heart to anguish",句式结构较为工整,上下句均为主谓宾结构。另外,霍克斯并未直译"牡丹亭",而是将它意译为"Soul's Return",使没有读过《牡丹亭》的外国读者也能猜出这本书的大概主题是"人鬼情未了"之类的内容。

【2】"宝玉听了喜不自禁"是宝玉对前文黛玉提出一起葬花的反应,杨译"Pao-yu was delighted by this idea"和霍译"Bao-yu was full of admiration for this idea"均将汉语"听了"这一动作暗含在英语名词"idea"中,显示了英语语言的静态特征。另外,两位译者均进行了句序的调整,将"喜不自禁(was delighted by 或 was full of admiration)"前置,"听了(by this idea 或 for this idea)"后置。

【3】"自觉词藻警人,馀香满口"一句的主语是前文的"林黛玉",杨译"The sheer beauty of the language left a sweet taste in her mouth."使用了物化主语"the sheer beauty of the language";霍译"She felt the power of the words and their lingering fragrance."使用了人称主语"she",而且巧妙地将两个四字短语"词藻警人"和"馀香满口"译为两个名词短语"the power of the words"和"their lingering fragrance",并由"and"连接,充当"felt"的并列宾语。

【4】"虽看完了书,却只管出神,心内还默默记诵。"包含了三个小句,杨译"After finishing reading she sat there entranced, recalling some of the lines."句式呈现偏正结构:主谓结构"she sat"前、后分别使用了介词短语"after finishing reading"和现在分词短语"recalling some of the lines",在译文中分别充当时间状语和伴随状语,过去分词"entranced"在译文中对应主语"she",充当补足语。霍译是"Long after she had finished reading, when she had laid down the book and was sitting there rapt and silent, the lines continued to ring on in her head.",译者通过"Long after, when, and"进行句内连接,译文中的动词呈现出不同的时态,包括过去完成时(had finished 和 had laid down)、过去进行时(was sitting)和一般过去时(continued),用以点明各动作发生的时间先后顺序。

【5】"我就是个'多愁多病身',你就是那'倾国倾城貌'。"一句,杨译"I'm the one 'sick with longing,'… And yours is the beauty which caused 'cities and kingdoms to fall.'"采用了直译手法。霍译"How can I, full of sickness and of woe, Withstand that face which kingdoms could o'erthrow?"通过增加"withstand"一词,揭示出了原文中两个小句之间的逻辑关系——宝玉借戏词表白,说自己多愁多病的身配不上黛玉倾国倾城的貌。其中,which 引导的定语从句的正常语序是:which could o'erthrow kingdoms。为了与原文戏词风格相符,霍译将"kingdoms"置于"could o'erthrow"之前,句尾实现了"woe"和"o'erthrow"的押韵,读起来十分上口。

【6】"登时直竖起两道似蹙非蹙的眉,瞪了两只似睁非睁的眼,微腮带怒,薄面含嗔,指宝玉道"一句中,主语"黛玉"发出了一连串的动作。杨译是"Knitting her sulky brows, her eyes flashing with anger beneath half-drooping lids, she pointed a finger at Pao-yu in accusal.",句式呈现偏正结构,在主谓宾结构"she pointed a finger"之前,译者使用了现在分词短语"Knitting her sulky brows"和独立主格结构"her eyes flashing with anger beneath half-drooping lids"来翻译原文的两个小句"竖起两道似蹙非蹙的眉"和"瞪了两只似睁非睁的眼";另外,译者省译了"微腮带怒,薄面含嗔",只是通过介词短语"with anger"和"in accusal"略为表述原意。霍译是"The eyebrows that seemed to frown yet somehow didn't were raised now in anger and the lovely eyes flashed. There was rage in her crimson cheeks and resentment in all her looks. 'You're hateful!'—she pointed a finger at him in angry accusal.",译者完整地翻译了原文的所有信息。译文的第一句通过"and"进行连句;第二句用"and"连接两个近义词"rage"和"resentment",对应的是原文中的两个近义词"怒"和"嗔"。霍译依据的程高本对"微腮带怒"的表述是"桃腮带怒",所以,霍译中有"crimson

cheeks"这样的表述。

【7】"若有心欺负你,明儿我掉在池子里,教个癞头鼋吞了去,变个大忘八,等你明儿做了'一品夫人'病老归西的时候,我往你坟上替你驮一辈子的碑去。"一句,杨译是"But if I meant to insult you, I'll fall into the pond tomorrow and let the scabby-headed tortoise swallow me, so that I change into a big turtle myself. Then when you become a lady of the first rank and go at last to your paradise in the west, I shall bear the stone tablet at your grave on my back for ever.",该译文由两个句子构成。译者通过"But"和"Then"进行句际连接;在第一句和第二句中分别使用"if, and, so that"和"when, and"进行句内连接。可以看出,译者完全根据原文信息翻译,但是这样会有一个逻辑问题:译者将"变个大忘八"直译为"I change into a big turtle myself",可能会让外国读者感到困惑——如果让癞头鼋吞了去,只会变成癞头鼋的排泄物,怎么会变成大忘八?霍译是"If I had the slightest intention of taking advantage of you, may I fall into the water and be eaten up by an old bald-headed turtle! When you have become a great lady and gone at last to your final resting-place, I shall become the stone turtle that stands in front of your grave and spend the rest of eternity carrying your tombstone on my back as a punishment!",译者对原文进行了创造性翻译,为西方读者把这个文化鸿沟给填平了:他在译完"教个癞头鼋吞了去"之后没有直接翻译下一句"变个大忘八",而是把这句译文后置到"驮一辈子的碑去"处,告诉西方读者,自己死后会化为石龟去驮碑,而且增译"as a punishment",使读者明白这是一种惩罚。另外,两位译者在翻译"若有心欺负你"时,都使用了虚拟语气(if I meant to insult you 和 If I had the slightest intention of taking advantage of you),霍译甚至使用了形容词的最高级形式"slightest",生动地表达出宝玉没有丝毫想伤害黛玉的心。

【8】"你说你会过目成诵,难道我就不能一目十行么?"一句,杨译"You boast that you can 'memorize a passage with one reading.' Why can't I 'learn ten lines at a glance'?"采用了直译手法翻译"一目十行",即"learn ten lines at a glance";霍译"'You needn't imagine you're the only one with a good memory,' said Dai-yu haughtily. 'I suppose I'm allowed to remember lines too if I like.'"则采

用了意译手法，将其译为"remember lines"。

【9】"宝玉一面收书，一面笑道"一句，杨译"Laughing he put the book away."呈现出偏正结构："Laughing"和"put the book away"分别充当译文的伴随状语和谓语。霍译"Bao-yu took back the book from her with a good-natured laugh"也呈现偏正结构：译者用句子化短语法将小句"一面笑道"译为介词短语"with a good-natured laugh"，在译文中充当伴随状语，修饰该句的谓语部分"took back the book"。另外，"good-natured"是合成形容词，构词方式是形容词+名词+ed。

四、词汇表

1. tuck [tʌk]	v.	to put sth into a small space, especially to hide it or keep it safe or comfortable 把……塞入；把……藏入
2. doctrine [ˈdɒktrɪn]	n.	a set of principles or beliefs, especially religious ones 信条；主义；学说；（尤指）宗教教义
3. entrance [ɪnˈtrɑːns]	v.	to make sb feel great pleasure and admiration so that they give sb/sth all their attention 使狂喜；使入迷
4. sulky [ˈsʌlki]	adj.	bad-tempered or not speaking because you are angry about sth 面有愠色的；闷闷不乐的
5. accusal [əˈkjuːzəl]	n.	a formal charge of wrongdoing brought against a person; the act of imputing blame or guilt 谴责；控告；罪名
6. indulge [ɪnˈdʌldʒ]	v.	to allow yourself to have or do sth that you like, especially sth that is considered bad for you 沉湎；沉迷

7. rapt [ræpt]	*adj.*	so interested in one particular thing that you are not aware of anything else 全神贯注的；入迷的
8. crimson [ˈkrɪmzn]	*adj.*	deep red in color 深红色的
9. resentment [rɪˈzentmənt]	*n.*	a feeling of anger or unhappiness about sth that you think is unfair 愤恨，怨恨
10. mirth [mɜːθ]	*n.*	happiness, fun and the sound of people laughing 欢乐；欢笑
11. simultaneous [ˌsɪmlˈteɪniəs]	*adj.*	happening or done at the same time as sth else 同时发生（或进行）的；同步的
	adv.	simultaneously
12. knuckle [ˈnʌkl]	*n.*	any of the joints in the fingers, especially those connecting the fingers to the rest of the hand 指关节
13. spear [spɪə(r)]	*n.*	a weapon consisting of a long pole with a sharp metal point attached to the end 矛；枪
14. counterfeit [ˈkaʊntəfɪt]	*n.*	sth likely to be mistaken for sth of higher value 仿制品；伪造物

第二十四回

醉金刚轻财尚义侠　痴女儿遗帕惹相思

The Drunken Diamond Proves Himself Generous and Gallant
An Ambitious Girl Loses Her Handkerchief as an Enticement (Yang)

The Drunken Diamond shows nobility of character in handling his money
And the Quiet-voiced Girl provides material for fantasy by losing her handkerchief (Hawkes)

一、本回概述

贾芸自幼丧父，和母亲相依为命，生活贫困。贾芸一心想在贾府谋份差事，却苦于无本钱打点。舅舅卜世仁经营香料铺，贾芸想赊些上好香料，用于讨好熙凤，却被舅舅无情拒绝，还被教训一番，贾芸赌气离开舅舅家，碰巧撞上平素无甚来往的邻居——高利贷债主泼皮倪二。倪二同情贾芸遭遇，仗义借他银两，且执意不收利钱，令贾芸刮目相看。随后，贾芸采办香料，送与熙凤，顺利谋得在大观园植树的差事。入园见宝玉时，无意邂逅怡红院丫头小红，二人互生情愫。

第二十四回

二、篇章节选

原文

　　凤姐正是要办端阳的节礼，采买香料药饵的时节，忽见贾芸如此一来，听这一篇话，心下又是得意又是欢喜，便命丰儿："接过芸哥儿的来，送了家去，交给平儿。"因又说道："看着你这样倒很知好歹，[1]怪道你叔叔常提你，说你说话儿也明白，心里有见识。"[2]贾芸听这话入了港，[3]便打进一步来，故意问道："原来叔叔也曾提我的？"凤姐见问，才要告诉他与他管事情的那话，便忙又止住，心下想道："我如今要告诉他那话，倒叫他看着我见不得东西似的，[4]为得了这点子香，就混许他管事了。今儿先别提起这事。"想毕，便把派他监种花木工程的事都隐瞒的一字不提，随口说了两句淡话，便往贾母那里去了。[5]

　　……

　　（贾芸）正是烦闷，只听门前娇声嫩语的叫了一声"哥哥"。[6]贾芸往外瞧时，看是一个十六七岁的丫头，生的倒也细巧干净。那丫头见了贾芸，便抽身躲了过去。恰值焙茗走来，见那丫头在门前，便说道："好，好，正抓不着个信儿。"贾芸见了焙茗，也就赶了出来，问怎么样。焙茗道："等了这一日，也没个人儿过来。这就是宝二爷房里的。好姑娘，你进去带个信儿，就说廊上的二爷来了。"

　　那丫头听说，方知是本家的爷们，便不似先前那等回避，下死眼把贾芸钉了两眼。[7]听那贾芸说道："什么是廊上廊下的，你只说是芸儿就是了。"

杨译

　　Hsi-feng, as it so happened, needed some festival gifts and had been thinking of buying some spices and aromatic herbs. Gratified and delighted by this unexpected gift and Chia Yun's little speech, she told Feng-erh:

　　"Take my nephew's present home and give it to Ping-erh."

　　Then to Chia Yun she said, "I see you have good sense.[1] No wonder your uncle is always telling me how sensibly you talk and what tact you have."[2]

Chia Yun, hearing this, felt he was getting somewhere.[3] He stepped closer.

"Has uncle been talking to you about me then?" he asked significantly.

Hsi-feng was tempted to tell him about the job of supervising tree-planting which they had in mind for him, but was afraid he might take it the wrong way[4] and imagine she was offering it in return for a few aromatics. So she refrained, saying not a word about it. And after a few casual remarks she went on to see the Lady Dowager.[5]

…

He was feeling put out and bored when a sweet voice just outside the door called: "Brother!"[6]

Looking out he discovered a maid of sixteen or seventeen, a slender, neat, clever-looking girl. She was shrinking back at sight of Chia Yun when Pei-ming returned.

"Good," he said. "I was looking for a messenger."

Chia Yun walked out to question the page, who told him:

"I waited for a long time, but nobody came out. This is one of the girls from Happy Red Court." He turned to her. "Be a good girl and tell him, will you, that the Second Master from the back lane has called."

On learning that Chia Yun belonged to her masters' clan, the maid did not avoid him as she had before but shot him one or two penetrating glances.[7]

"Never mind about the back lane," he joked. "Just tell him Yun has come."

霍译

Now Xi-feng *was* just beginning to think about the problem of purchasing aromatics for the Double Fifth festival, and it pleased her very much to be relieved of the trouble of doing so—especially when it was in so agreeable a manner. She smiled at him graciously before turning to her maid:

'Felicity, take my nephew's present and give it to Patience to take care of!'

The smile was directed once more on Jia Yun:

'You are very thoughtful.[1] I'm not surprised your Uncle speaks so highly of

you. He's often told me what a well-spoken, sensible young man you are.' [2]

They seemed to be sailing into harbour. [3] Jia Yun took a step closer:

'Has Uncle been talking to you about me then?'—The tone in which he asked the question was deliberately meaningful.

Xi-feng was on the point of telling him that he would get the tree-planting job when she reflected that by doing so she would be cheapening herself in his estimation. [4] He would almost certainly suppose that she was promising it in return for the perfume. In replying to his question she therefore confined herself to a few insipid civilities, avoiding all mention of jobs and trees, and presently continued on her way to Grandmother Jia's. [5]

...

Dejectedly he went back once more to wait.

'Tealeaf!' [6]

A soft and thrilling voice was calling from outside. Craning out to look he saw a fifteen- or sixteen-year-old maid standing near the entrance to the study. She was a neat, pleasant-looking girl with a pair of limpid, intelligent eyes. Seeing a strange man in the room, she quickly shrank back out of his line of vision. At that very moment Tealeaf walked back into the courtyard.

'Ah, good!' he said, catching sight of the maid. 'I was beginning to wonder how I'd ever get a message to him.'

Jia Yun ran out to question him:

'Well?'

'Waited for ages,' said Tealeaf, 'but no one came by. *She's* from his room, though'—he indicated the soft-voiced maid—'Listen, dear,' he said addressing her. 'Can you take a message for us? Tell him that Mr Jia from West Lane is here.'

On learning that the visitor was a member of the clan, the maid became less concerned about concealment and engaged the limpid eyes in bolder scrutiny of his features. [7] The object of her scrutiny now addressed her:

'Don't bother about the "West Lane" stuff! Just say that "Yun" has called!'

三、注释评点

【1】"看着你这样倒很知好歹"一句，杨译"I see you have good sense"和霍译"You are very thoughtful"都没有直译"知好歹"，而是采用了意译的手法。相比之下，"have good sense"语义太宽泛，"thoughtful"更加贴近原文，因为熙凤正要采办香料，贾芸就恭恭敬敬把香料送到手中，真是太"thoughtful"了。

【2】"怪道你叔叔常提你，说你说话儿也明白，心里有见识。"一句，杨译是"No wonder your uncle is always telling me how sensibly you talk and what tact you have."该译文用"No wonder"开句，句中含有两个直接宾语从句："how sensibly you talk"和"what tact you have"，分别对应原文中的两个小句"说话儿也明白"和"心里有见识"。"心里有见识"本是褒义，但"what tact you have"给人有贬义之感，而且用词稍显做作、不够自然。霍译是"I'm not surprised your Uncle speaks so highly of you. He's often told me what a well-spoken, sensible young man you are."译者用了两个形容词"well-spoken"和"sensible"就表达出原文两个小句"说话儿也明白"和"心里有见识"的内容。"well-spoken"是合成形容词，它的构词法是：副词+动词的过去分词。

【3】"贾芸听这话入了港"一句，杨译"Chia Yun, hearing this, felt he was getting somewhere."用意译的手法翻译"入了港"，即"he was getting somewhere"；霍译"They seemed to be sailing into harbour."则采用了直译手法，将其译为"to be sailing into harbour"。

【4】"倒叫他看着我见不得东西似的"一句，杨译"but was afraid he might take it the wrong way..."将"见不得东西似的"译得很笼统；霍译"... by doing so she would be cheapening herself in his estimation."则准确地体现出原文之意：熙凤是怕自己刚收下礼物，就告诉贾芸已把监种花木工程的事分派给他，会让贾芸看轻了自己。

【5】"想毕，便把派他监种花木工程的事都隐瞒的一字不提，随口说了两句淡话，便往贾母那里去了。"杨译是"So she refrained, saying not a word about it. And after a few casual remarks she went on to see the Lady Dowager."译者使用"So"和"And"来连句;另外,译者使用句子化短语法将原文的小句"隐瞒的一字不提"和"随口说了两句淡话"分别译为现在分词短语"saying not a word about it"和介词短语"after a few casual remarks"。霍译是"In replying to his question she therefore confined herself to a few insipid civilities, avoiding all mention of jobs and trees, <u>and</u> presently continued on her way to Grandmother Jia's."译者使用"therefore"和"<u>and</u>"来连句;另外,译者也用了句子化短语法,将原文的小句"把派他监种花木工程的事都隐瞒的一字不提"译为现在分词短语"avoiding all mention of jobs and trees"。

【6】"(贾芸)正是烦闷,只听门前娇声嫩语的叫了一声'哥哥'。"一句,杨译是"He was feeling put out and bored when a sweet voice just outside the door called: 'Brother!'"其中的句型"sb was doing sth when sb else did sth else"表示当过去的一个动作正在进行时,另一个过去的动作突然发生。后文"She was shrinking back at sight of Chia Yun when Pei-ming returned"一句也使用了这种句式。霍译"Dejectedly he went back once more to wait. 'Tealeaf!' A soft and thrilling voice was calling from outside."其中,"dejectedly"一词放在句首做状语,修饰谓语"went back",强调了贾芸此时烦闷的心理状态。

【7】"那丫头听说,方知是本家的爷们,便不似先前那等回避,下死眼把贾芸钉了两眼。"一句,杨译是"On learning that Chia Yun belonged to her masters' clan, the maid did not avoid him as she had before but shot him one or two penetrating glances."原文中的小句"那丫头听说,方知是本家的爷们"被译为介词短语"On learning that Chia Yun belonged to her masters' clan",在译文中充当时间状语;同时,译者使用"not... but..."进行句内连接。霍译是"On learning that the visitor was a member of the clan, the maid became less concerned about concealment and engaged the limpid eyes in bolder scrutiny of his features."译者也将小句"那丫头听说,方知是本家的爷们"译为介词短语"On learning that the visitor was a member of the clan",在译文中充当时间状语;同时,译者通过"and"实现句内连接。

四、词汇表

1. aromatic [ˌærəˈmætɪk]   adj.   having a pleasant noticeable smell 芳香的；有香味的

2. herb [hɜːb]   n.   a plant whose leaves, flowers or seeds are used to flavour food, in medicines or for their pleasant smell 药草；香草

3. gratify [ˈɡrætɪfaɪ]   v.   to please or satisfy sb 使高兴；使满意

4. shrink [ʃrɪŋk]   v.   to move back or away from sth because you are frightened or shocked 退缩；畏缩

5. lane [leɪn]   n.   a narrow road in the country（乡间）小路

6. clan [klæn]   n.   a very large family, or a group of people who are connected because of a particular thing 庞大的家族；宗派；帮派

7. penetrating [ˈpenɪtreɪtɪŋ]   adj.   (of sb's eyes or the way they look at you) making you feel uncomfortable because the person seems to know what you are thinking 锐利的；犀利的

8. gracious [ˈɡreɪʃəs]   adj.   (of people or behaviour) kind, polite and generous, especially to sb of a lower social position（尤指对社会地位较低者）和蔼的；有礼貌的

                           adv.   graciously

9. harbour [ˈhɑːbə(r)]   n.   an area of water on the coast, protected from the open sea by strong walls, where ships can shelter（海）港；港口；港湾

10. cheapen [ˈtʃiːpən]   v.   to make sb lose respect for himself or herself 使丧失威信；使贬低

11. perfume [ˈpɜːfjuːm]	*n.*	the ingredient that has a sweet and pleasant smell 香料，香精
12. confine [kənˈfaɪn]	*v.*	**~ sb/sth to sth:** to keep sb/sth inside the limits of a particular activity, subject, area, etc. 限制；限定
13. insipid [ɪnˈsɪpɪd]	*adj.*	not interesting or exciting 没有趣味的；枯燥乏味的
14. thrilling [ˈθrɪlɪŋ]	*adj.*	exciting and enjoyable 惊险的；紧张的；扣人心弦的
15. crane [kreɪn]	*v.*	to lean or stretch over sth in order to see sth better; to stretch your neck （为看得更清楚而）探着身子；伸长（脖子）
16. limpid [ˈlɪmpɪd]	*adj.*	(of liquids, etc.) clear 清澈的；清晰的；透明的
17. conceal [kənˈsiːl]	*v.*	to hide 隐藏；隐瞒；掩盖
	n.	concealment
18. scrutiny [ˈskruːtəni]	*n.*	careful observation or examination 仔细观察；仔细检查

第二十五回

魇魔法姊弟逢五鬼　红楼梦通灵遇双真

Five Devils Invoked by Sorcery Take Possession of Pao-yu and Hsi-feng
Two Sages See the Jade of Spiritual Understanding in the Dream of Red Mansions (Yang)

Two cousins are subjected by witchcraft to the assaults of demons
And the Magic Jade meets an old acquaintance while rather the worse for wear (Hawkes)

一、本回概述

贾环素日嫉恨宝玉，又见宝玉和他喜欢的彩霞笑闹，更加气愤，便佯装失手，欲要用滚烫的蜡油烫瞎宝玉的眼睛，结果宝玉左脸烫了一溜泡。王夫人、熙凤气急败坏，大骂赵姨娘及贾环，赵姨娘怀恨在心，趁马道婆到访贾府之际，与其合谋，令施邪法，加害宝玉、熙凤。宝玉、熙凤中魇魔法后，失智发疯，高烧糊涂，不省人事，三日后，竟奄奄一息，命在旦夕。贾府上下乱作一团，贾母、王夫人哭得肝肠寸断。绝望之际，癞头和尚与跛足道人忽然出现，持诵通灵宝玉，二人逐日好转。

第二十五回

二、篇章节选

原文

此时贾赦、贾政又恐哭坏了贾母，日夜熬油费火，闹的人口不安，也都没了主意。[1]贾赦还各处去寻僧觅道。贾政见不灵效，着实懊恼，因阻贾赦道："儿女之数，皆由天命，非人力可强者。他二人之病出于不意，百般医治不效，想天意该如此，也只好由他们去罢。"[2]贾赦也不理此话，仍是百般忙乱，那里见些效验。看看三日光阴，那凤姐和宝玉躺在床上，益发连气都将没了。[3]合家人口无不惊慌，都说没了指望，忙着将他二人的后世的衣履都治备下了。贾母、王夫人、贾琏、平儿、袭人这几个人更比诸人哭的忘餐废寝，觅死寻活。赵姨娘、贾环等自是称愿。

到了第四日早晨，贾母等正围着宝玉哭时，只见宝玉睁开眼说道："从今以后，我可不在你家了！快收拾了，打发我走罢。"贾母听了这话，如同摘心去肝一般。[4]赵姨娘在旁劝道："老太太也不必过于悲痛。哥儿已是不中用了，不如把哥儿的衣服穿好，让他早些回去，也免些苦。只管舍不得他，这口气不断，他在那世里也受罪不安生。"[5]这些话没说完，被贾母照脸啐了一口唾沫，骂道："烂了舌头的混帐老婆，谁叫你来多嘴多舌的！你怎么知道他在那世里受罪不安生？怎么见得不中用了？你愿他死了，有什么好处？你别做梦！他死了，我只和你们要命。[6]素日都不是你们调唆着逼他写字念书，把胆子唬破了，见了他老子不像个避猫鼠儿？[7]都不是你们这起淫妇调唆的！这会子逼死了，你们遂了心，我饶那一个！"一面骂，一面哭。

贾政在旁听见这些话，心里越发难过，便喝退赵姨娘，自己上来委婉解劝。[8]一时又有人来回说："两口棺椁都做齐了，请老爷出去看。"贾母听了，如火上浇油一般，便骂："是谁做了棺椁？"一叠声只叫把做棺材的拉来打死。

杨译

Afraid that their mother might fall ill of grief, Chia Sheh and Chia Cheng bestirred themselves so frantically day and night that no one, high or low, had any rest or could offer any advice.[1] Chia Sheh kept summoning more bonzes and Taoists, but because these could do no good Chia Cheng lost patience and tried to dissuade him.

"Their fate rests with Heaven," he said. "Human beings are powerless. Since their disorder is quite unforeseen and no drugs can cure it, it must be the will of Heaven. We shall just have to leave them to their fate."[2]

His counsel fell on deaf ears. Chia Sheh would not relax his exertions. But still there was no improvement.

By the third day the patients were lying at death's door[3] and the whole household despaired. Then, as all hope was relinquished, preparations were started for the funeral. The Lady Dowager, Lady Wang, Chia Lien, Ping-erh and Hsi-jen wept even more bitterly than the rest, unable to take food or sleep. Only the concubine Chao and Chia Huan were secretly exulting.

On the morning of the fourth day Pao-yu opened his eyes.

"I am going to leave you now," he told his weeping grandmother. "You must make haste and get me ready to go."

These words made her feel as if he had wrenched out her heart.[4]

"Don't take it too hard, madam," urged the concubine. "The boy's as good as gone. Better lay him out and let him make an end of his misery. If you insist on holding him back, he'll not be able to breathe his last and will only suffer for it in the next world...."[5]

Before she could finish the old lady spat in her face.

"May your tongue rot, you bitch!" she swore. "Who asked for your opinion? How do you know he'll suffer in the next world? Why say he's as good as gone? What good will it do *you* if he dies? You're dreaming! If he does die, I'll make you pay for it.[6] You're the ones to blame for this, forcing the child to study and breaking his spirit so that the sight of his father made him as scared as a mouse chased by a cat. [7] It's you bitches who have hounded him to his death. But don't gloat too soon—

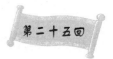

you've still me to reckon with."

Quite beside himself to hear her curses and sobs, Chia Cheng hastily ordered his concubine away and tried to calm his mother.[8] But just then a servant came in to announce that the two coffins were ready for his inspection. This added fuel to the fire of the old lady's anger.

"Who ordered coffins?" she screamed. "Fetch the coffin-makers here! Have them beaten to death!"

霍译

Jia She and Jia Zheng, afraid that their mother's health would suffer, displayed their concern by keeping themselves and everyone else up throughout most of the night. There were lights burning everywhere and hardly anyone slept at all.[1]

Jia She continued to hunt everywhere for monks and exorcists reputed able to cure diseases of the mind. Finally, Jia Zheng, who saw that their methods were all useless, lost patience with him and tried to make him stop:

'Young people will die if they must. Nothing can alter fate. And that they are fated to die would appear from the fact that all efforts to cure them have been unavailing. I think we should allow them to die in peace.'[2]

But Jia She took no notice, and the commotion continued as before.

By the third day the patients were so weakened that they lay on their beds motionless and their breathing was scarcely perceptible.[3] The whole family had by now abandoned hope and were already making preparations for their laying-out. Grandmother Jia, Lady Wang, Jia Lian, Patience and Aroma had cried themselves into a state bordering on prostration. Only Aunt Zhao was cheerful—though she did her best to look miserable.

Early on the fourth day Bao-yu suddenly opened his eyes wide and spoke to Grandmother Jia:

'From now on I can no longer stay in this family. You must get my things ready and let me go.'

To the old lady the words were a tearing of heart from body;[4] but Aunt Zhao, who also heard them, had the temerity to urge their acceptance:

'Your Ladyship shouldn't take it so hard. It's already all up with the boy. We should be getting his grave clothes ready so that he can go in peace. It will be better that way. If we won't let him go now, when he's ready, it will only make more suffering for him in the world to come…'[5]

She would have gone on, but Grandmother Jia spat in her face. No empty gesture: it was a full gob of spittle.

'Evil woman! May your tongue rot! How do you *know* it's all up with him? You *want* him to die, don't you? But if you think you will gain by his death, you must be dreaming; because if he does die, I shall hold you responsible.[6] It's your spiteful meddling that has forced him to do all this studying. You have reduced the poor child to such a state that the mere sight of his father makes him more scared than a mouse with the cat after it.[7] *You* have done this, you and the others of your kind. And now I suppose, if you succeed in murdering him, you will be satisfied. But don't imagine you will escape me—*any* of you!'

She railed and wept. Jia Zheng was close at hand while she was saying all this and was deeply distressed by it. Peremptorily dismissing the concubine, he tried to calm his mother and reasoned against the injustice of her charges.[8]

It was unfortunate that just at that moment a servant should have come in to announce that 'the two coffins that had been ordered were now ready'. The words were as oil upon fire. The old lady blazed.

'Who gave orders for those coffins to be made? Where is the man who made them? Go and get the man who made those coffins! Flog him to death!'

三、注释评点

【1】"此时贾赦、贾政又恐哭坏了贾母，日夜熬油费火，闹的人口不安，也都没了主意。"杨译是"Afraid that their mother might fall ill of grief, Chia Sheh

and Chia Cheng bestirred themselves so frantically day and night that no one, high or low, had any rest or could offer any advice."译者用"so... that"实现了句内连接,并使用句子化短语法将小句"又恐哭坏了贾母"译为形容词短语"Afraid that their mother might fall ill of grief",在译文中充当原因状语。霍译是"Jia She and Jia Zheng, afraid that their mother's health would suffer, displayed their concern by keeping themselves and everyone else up throughout most of the night. There were lights burning everywhere and hardly anyone slept at all."译者同样也用了句子化短语法将小句"又恐哭坏了贾母"译为形容词短语"afraid that their mother's health would suffer",在译文中也是充当原因状语。不同的是,两位译者分别将该状语放在了句首和句中。英语中状语的位置十分灵活:可位于句首、句中或句末。

【2】"他二人之病出于不意,百般医治不效,想天意该如此,也只好由他们去罢。"杨译是"Since their disorder is quite unforeseen and no drugs can cure it, it must be the will of Heaven. We shall just have to leave them to their fate."译文的第一句使用"since"和"and"进行句内连接。"也只好由他们去罢"是委婉语,杨译"We shall just have to leave them to their fate"意为"由命运说了算",表达出一种无可奈何的语气,比较符合原文的语言风格。霍译是"And that they are fated to die would appear from the fact that all efforts to cure them have been unavailing. I think we should allow them to die in peace."译文的第一句包含两个"that"引导的从句:主语从句"that they are fated to die"和同位语从句"that all efforts to cure them have been unavailing"。第二句"I think we should allow them to die in peace."语意过于直接,不太符合原句无可奈何的语气,也丧失了原句的委婉语风格。

【3】"看看三日光阴,那凤姐和宝玉躺在床上,益发连气都将没了。"杨译"By the third day the patients were lying at death's door"把原文的小句整合成了一句,译者使用句子化短语法将"益发连气都将没了"译为介词短语"at death's door"。霍译是"By the third day the patients were so weakened that they lay on their beds motionless and their breathing was scarcely perceptible."译者通过"so... that"和"and"进行句内连接。

【4】"贾母听了这话,如同摘心去肝一般。"杨译是"These words made her feel as if he had wrenched out her heart."霍译是"To the old lady the words were a tearing of heart from body;"两位译者都使用了句子化词法,将原文中的小句"贾母听了这话"译为名词短语"These words"和"the words",在译文中充当主语。在翻译小句"如同摘心去肝一般"时,两位译者都使用了直译手法。

【5】"赵姨娘在旁劝道:'只管舍不得他,这口气不断,他在那世里也受罪不安生。'"杨译是"If you insist on holding him back, he'll not be able to breathe his last and will only suffer for it in the next world..."译者使用"If"和"and"进行句内连接。霍译是"If we won't let him go now, when he's ready, it will only make more suffering for him in the world to come..."译者使用的连接手段是"If"和"when"。另外,在翻译"这口气不断"时,霍译使用了反译法,用肯定句"when he's ready"表达出"他已经准备咽气了"的意思。相比之下,杨译"If you insist on holding him back, he'll not be able to breathe his last..."更清楚地表达出原文两个小句"只管舍不得他"和"这口气不断"之间蕴含的因果关系。

【6】"你愿他死了,有什么好处?你别做梦!他死了,我只和你们要命。"一句,杨译是"What good will it do *you* if he dies? You're dreaming! If he does die, I'll make you pay for it.";霍译是"But if you think you will gain by his death, you must be dreaming; because if he does die, I shall hold you responsible."。可以看出,从意合语言(汉语)向形合语言(英语)转化时,译者需要增加表示逻辑关系的连接词。杨译由三个句子构成,第一句和第三句分别使用"if"进行句内连接。霍译由两个分句构成,中间用分号隔开;译者用"But"承接上文,用"because"完成两个分句的句际连接;在两个分句中都使用"if"进行句内连接。

【7】"素日都不是你们调唆着逼他写字念书,把胆子唬破了,见了他老子不像个避猫鼠儿?"杨译是"You're the ones to blame for this, forcing the child to study and breaking his spirit so that the sight of his father made him as scared as a mouse chased by a cat."译者用句子化短语法将原文的两个小句

"逼他写字念书"和"把胆子唬破了"分别译为两个现在分词短语"forcing the child to study"和"breaking his spirit",用"and"连接,在译文中充当原因状语,其后跟"so that"引导的结果状语从句。霍译是"It's your spiteful meddling that has forced him to do all this studying. You have reduced the poor child to such a state that the mere sight of his father makes him more scared than a mouse with the cat after it."译文的第一句使用了强调句型,被强调的部分是"your spiteful meddling";第二句通过"such a... that"实现句内连接。另外,在翻译"见了他老子"时,两位译者均使用了词性转换法,将动词"见"译为名词"sight",在结果状语从句中充当主语。

【8】"贾政在旁听见这些话,心里越发难过,便喝退赵姨娘,自己上来委婉解劝。"杨译是"Quite beside himself to hear her curses and sobs, Chia Cheng hastily ordered his concubine away and tried to calm his mother."译者使用句子化短语法将原文的小句"贾政在旁听见这些话,心里越发难过"译为介词短语"beside himself to hear her curses and sobs",在译文中充当原因状语;在句子的主干部分通过"and"实现句内连接。霍译是"Jia Zheng was close at hand while she was saying all this and was deeply distressed by it. Peremptorily dismissing the concubine, he tried to calm his mother and reasoned against the injustice of her charges."译文由两个句子构成,第一句通过"while"和"and"实现句内连接,第二句使用"and"进行句内连接。同时,霍译也使用句子化短语法,将小句"便喝退赵姨娘"译为现在分词短语"dismissing the concubine",在译文中充当时间状语。

四、词汇表

1. bestir [bɪˈstɜː(r)]	v.	to start doing things after a period during which you have been doing nothing 发奋;振作起来
2. summon [ˈsʌmən]	v.	to order sb to come to you 召唤
3. dissuade [dɪˈsweɪd]	v.	to persuade sb not to do sth 劝(某人)勿

做（某事）；劝阻

4. exertion [ɪgˈzɜːʃn]	n.	physical or mental effort; the act of making an effort 努力；尽力；费力
5. relinquish [rɪˈlɪŋkwɪʃ]	v.	to stop having sth, especially when this happens unwillingly（尤指不情愿地）放弃
6. exult [ɪgˈzʌlt]	v.	to feel and show that you are very excited and happy because of sth that has happened 欢欣鼓舞；兴高采烈；喜形于色
7. wrench [rentʃ]	v.	to pull or twist suddenly and violently 猛拉；猛扭；猛拧
8. hound [haʊnd]	v.	to keep following sb and not leave them alone, especially in order to get sth from them or ask them questions 追踪；追逐；纠缠
9. gloat [gləʊt]	v.	to show that you are happy about your own success or sb else's failure, in an unpleasant way 扬扬得意；沾沾自喜；幸灾乐祸
10. coffin [ˈkɒfɪn]	n.	a box in which a dead body is buried or cremated 棺材；棺椁
11. exorcist [ˈeksɔːsɪst]	n.	a person who makes evil spirits leave a place or a person's body by prayers or magic（用祈祷或法术）驱邪的法师；驱魔者
12. commotion [kəˈməʊʃn]	n.	sudden noisy confusion or excitement（突然发生的）喧闹，骚乱，骚动
13. prostration [prɒˈstreɪʃn]	n.	extreme physical weakness 筋疲力尽；极

度虚弱；虚脱

14. temerity [təˈmerəti]	n.	extremely confident behaviour that people are likely to consider rude 鲁莽；冒失；蛮勇
15. gob [gɒb]	n.	a large amount of sth 大量
16. spittle [ˈspɪtl]	n.	the liquid that forms in the mouth 唾沫；口水
17. spiteful [ˈspaɪtfl]	adj.	behaving in an unkind way in order to hurt or upset sb 恶意的；居心不良的；故意使人苦恼的
18. rail [reɪl]	v.	to complain about sth/sb in a very angry way 怒斥；责骂；抱怨
19. distress [dɪˈstres]	v.	to make sb feel very worried or unhappy 使忧虑；使悲伤；使苦恼
20. peremptorily [pəˈremptrəli]	adv.	in a way that allows no discussion or refusal 专横地；霸道地；不容商量地
21. blaze [bleɪz]	v.	if sb's eyes blaze, they look extremely angry 怒视；（怒火）燃烧
22. flog [flɒg]	v.	to punish sb by hitting them many times with a whip or stick 鞭笞；棒打（作为惩罚）

蜂腰桥设言传心事　潇湘馆春困发幽情[1]

On Wasp-Waist Bridge, Hsiao-hung Hints at Her Feelings
In Bamboo Lodge, Drowsy in Spring, Tai-yu Bares Her Heart[1] (Yang)

A conversation on Wasp Waist Bridge is a cover for communication of a different kind
And a soliloquy overheard in the Naiad's House reveals unsuspected
depths of feeling[1] (Hawkes)

一、本回概述

　　宝玉身体复原，贾芸前来请安。贾芸得知自己捡到的手帕果然是小红的，托坠儿带回。宝玉去看黛玉，闻黛玉吟诵"每日家情思睡昏昏"，宝玉用《西厢记》词句调笑，惹恼了黛玉，说要去告诉贾政，宝玉正要劝解，薛蟠谎称贾政要见宝玉，把宝玉骗出去与冯紫英等人喝酒。夜间，黛玉来找宝玉，晴雯因宝钗来访，迟迟不归而有气，又未听出黛玉的声音，竟不开门。黛玉深感寄人篱下之苦，又听得宝玉和宝钗说笑声音，误以为宝玉恼她，故意不见，不禁又悲又气，呜咽不止，附近宿鸟皆不忍闻听，纷纷远避。

二、篇章节选

原文

　　林黛玉素知丫头们的情性,他们彼此顽耍惯了,恐怕院内的丫头没听真是他的声音,只当是别的丫头们来了,所以不开门,因而又高声说道:[2]"是我,还不开么?"晴雯偏生还没听出来,便使性子说道:"凭你是谁,二爷吩咐的,一概不许放人进来呢!"

　　林黛玉听了,不觉气怔在门外,待要高声问他,逗起气来,自己又回思一番:"虽说是舅母家如同自己家一样,到底是客边。[3]如今父母双亡,无依无靠,现在他家依栖。如今认真淘气,也觉没趣。"一面想,一面又滚下泪珠来。[4]正是回去不是,站着不是。正没主意,只听里面一阵笑语之声,细听一听,竟是宝玉、宝钗二人,林黛玉心中益发动了气,[5]左思右想,忽然想起了早起的事来:"必竟是宝玉恼我要告他的原故。但只我何尝告你了,你也打听打听,就恼我到这步田地。[6]你今儿不叫我进来,难道明儿就不见面了!"越想越伤感起来,也不顾苍苔露冷,花径风寒,独立墙角边花阴之下,悲悲戚戚呜咽起来。[7]

　　原来这林黛玉秉绝代姿容,具希世俊美,不期这一哭,那附近柳枝花朵上的宿鸟栖鸦一闻此声,俱忒楞楞飞起远避,不忍再听。

杨译

　　Tai-yu knew the maids' ways and the tricks they played on each other. Assuming that the girl in the courtyard had failed to recognize her voice and taken her for another maid, she called out again more loudly.[2]

　　"It's me. Open the gate!"

　　Still Ching-wen did not recognize her voice.

　　"I don't care who you are," she said crossly. "Master Pao's given orders that no one's to be admitted."

　　Rooted indignantly to the spot and tempted to let fly at her, Tai-yu reflected,

"Although my aunt's house is a second home to me, I'm after all an outsider here. [3] With both my parents dead, I've no one to turn to except this family. It would be foolish to start a real rumpus."

As she thought thus, tears ran down her cheeks. [4] She was wondering whether or not to go back when the sound of talk and laughter inside—she distinguished the voices of Pao-yu and Pao-chai—upset her even more. [5] She thought back then to the events of the morning.

"Pao-yu must be angry with me, thinking I told on him," she reflected. "But I never did! You ought to investigate before flying into a temper like this. [6] You can shut me out today, but shall we not see each other still tomorrow?"

The more she thought, the more distressed she felt. Oblivious of the cold dew on the green moss and the chill wind on the path, standing under the blossom by the corner of the wall she gave way to sobs. [7] And the sound of this beauty's weeping—for Tai-yu was the loveliest creature ever seen—made the birds fly away from their roosts on the willows and flowering trees, unable to bear her distress.

霍译

Dai-yu was aware that Bao-yu's maids often played tricks on one another, and it occurred to her that the girl in the courtyard, not recognizing her voice, might have mistaken her for another maid and be keeping her locked out for a joke. She therefore called out again, this time somewhat louder than before: [2]

'Come on! Open up, please! It's me.'

Unfortunately Skybright had still not recognized the voice.

'I don't care who you are,' she replied bad-temperedly. 'Master Bao's orders are that I'm not to let *anyone* in.'

Dumbfounded by her insolence, Dai-yu stood outside the gate in silence. She could not, however much she felt like it, give vent to her anger in noisy expostulation. 'Although they are always telling me to treat my Uncle's house as my own,' she reflected, 'I am still really an outsider. [3] And now that Mother and Father are both

dead and I am on my own, to make a fuss about a thing like this when I am living in someone else's house could only lead to further unpleasantness.'

A big tear coursed, unregarded, down her cheek. [4]

She was still standing there irresolute, unable to decide whether to go or stay, when a sudden volley of talk and laughter reached her from inside. It resolved itself, as she listened attentively, into the voices of Bao-yu and Bao-chai. An even bitterer sense of chagrin took possession of her. [5] Suddenly, as she hunted in her mind for some possible reason for her exclusion, she remembered the events of the morning and concluded that Bao-yu must think she had told on him to his parents and was punishing her for her betrayal.

'But I would never betray you!' she expostulated with him in her mind. 'Why couldn't you have asked first, before letting your resentment carry you to such lengths? [6] If you won't see me today, does that mean that from now on we are going to stop seeing each other altogether?'

The more she thought about it the more distressed she became.

  Chill was the green moss pearled with dew

  And chill was the wind in the avenue;

but Dai-yu, all unmindful of the unwholesome damp, had withdrawn into the shadow of a flowering fruit-tree by the corner of the wall, and grieving now in real earnest, began to cry as though her heart would break. [7] And as if Nature herself were affected by the grief of so beautiful a creature, the crows who had been roosting in the trees round about flew up with a great commotion and removed themselves to another part of the Garden, unable to endure the sorrow of her weeping.

三、注释评点

【1】本回回目为"蜂腰桥设言传心事 潇湘馆春困发幽情",杨译"On Wasp-Waist Bridge, Hsiao-hung Hints at Her Feelings In Bamboo Lodge, Drowsy in Spring, Tai-yu Bares Her Heart"增加了人格主语"Hsiao-hung(小红)"和

"Tai-yu（黛玉）"；霍译"A conversation on Wasp Waist Bridge is a cover for communication of a different kind　And a soliloquy overheard in the Naiad's House reveals unsuspected depths of feeling"使用的是物化主语"conversation"和"soliloquy"。

【2】"恐怕院内的丫头没听真是他的声音，只当是别的丫头们来了，所以不开门，因而又高声说道"一句，"院内的丫头"连续发出三个动作：没听真、只当是、不开门。请注意译者是如何处理这些动词的。杨译是"Assuming that the girl in the courtyard had failed to recognize her voice and taken her for another maid, she called out again more loudly."句式呈现出偏正结构："偏"体现在现在分词短语"Assuming that..."充当的原因状语上，"正"体现在主句"she called out..."上。"Assuming"后带的宾语从句中，动词是过去完成时，体现出"had failed... and taken"和"called out"发生的先后顺序。霍译是"... and it occurred to her that the girl in the courtyard, not recognizing her voice, might have mistaken her for another maid and be keeping her locked out for a joke. She therefore called out again, ..."，译文第一句中的真正主语，即that引导的主语从句的句式也呈现出偏正结构：现在分词短语"not recognizing her voice"做原因状语，后接并列谓语"might have mistaken... and be keeping her locked..."，"might"之后的动词分别使用了完成式"have mistaken"和进行式"be keeping"，体现出这两个动作发生的先后顺序。

【3】"虽说是舅母家如同自己家一样，到底是客边"一句，杨译是"Although my aunt's house is a second home to me, I'm after all an outsider here."Although引导的让步状语从句中用"my aunt's house"做主语，句意是"尽管贾府就是我的第二个家"；霍译"'Although they are always telling me to treat my Uncle's house as my own,' she reflected, 'I am still really an outsider.'"增译了"they are always telling me"，衔接上更加自然顺畅。

【4】"一面想，一面又滚下泪珠来"一句，是典型的并列句式。杨译"As she thought thus, tears ran down her cheeks."将其处理成偏正句式，使用了"As"引导的时间状语从句；霍译"A big tear coursed, unregarded, down her cheek."只译出了后半句，省译了"一面想"。

【5】"正是回去不是,站着不是。正没主意,只听里面一阵笑语之声,细听一听,竟是宝玉、宝钗二人,林黛玉心中益发动了气"一句,杨译是"She was wondering whether or not to go back when the sound of talk and laughter inside—she distinguished the voices of Pao-yu and Pao-chai—upset her even more." 霍译是"She was still standing there irresolute, unable to decide whether to go or stay, when a sudden volley of talk and laughter reached her from inside. It resolved itself, as she listened attentively, into the voices of Bao-yu and Bao-chai. An even bitterer sense of chagrin took possession of her." 杨译和霍译的第一句使用了相同的句式结构,即:sb was doing sth when sb else did sth else / sth else happened,表示:主句动作正在发生时,从句动作突然同时发生。

【6】"你也打听打听,就恼我到这步田地"一句,杨译"You ought to investigate before flying into a temper like this"和霍译"Why couldn't you have asked first, before letting your resentment carry you to such lengths?"都使用了介词"before"进行句内连接。

【7】"也不顾苍苔露冷,花径风寒,独立墙角边花阴之下,悲悲戚戚呜咽起来。"句中,"黛玉"发出了三个动作:不顾、独立、呜咽。杨译是"Oblivious of the cold dew on the green moss and the chill wind on the path, standing under the blossom by the corner of the wall she gave way to sobs." 译者选择了原文中的第三个动词"呜咽"作谓语,将前面两个各自带动词的小句分别译为形容词短语"Oblivious of the cold dew..."和现在分词短语"standing...",都充当伴随状语,整个句子呈现出偏正结构。霍译是

Chill was the green moss pearled with dew

And chill was the wind in the avenue;

but Dai-yu, all unmindful of the unwholesome damp, had withdrawn into the shadow of a flowering fruit-tree by the corner of the wall, and grieving now in real earnest, began to cry as though her heart would break." 译者先是创造性地用两句诗行单独翻译"苍苔露冷,花径风寒",接着用"but"和前文相连,表达转折之义,再用"and"串连后文,"and"连接两个并列谓语"had withdrawn"和"began"。"but"之后的句式结构为:主语+形容词短语充当的伴随状语+谓语+地点状语+and+现在分词短语充当的原因状语+谓语+方式状语从句。

四、词汇表

1. indignant [ɪnˈdɪgnənt]	adj.	feeling or showing anger and surprise because you think that you have been treated unfairly 愤慨的；愤怒的；义愤的
	adv.	indignantly
2. let fly at sb		to attack sb by hitting them or speaking angrily to them （用……）打；（向某人）大发雷霆
3. rumpus [ˈrʌmpəs]	n.	a lot of noise that is made especially by people who are complaining about sth 喧闹；吵吵嚷嚷
4. tell on sb		to tell a person in authority about sth bad that sb has done 告发；打……的小报告；告……的狀
5. fly into a rage, temper, etc.		to become suddenly very angry 勃然大怒
6. oblivious [əˈblɪviəs]	adj.	not aware of sth 不知道；未注意；未察觉
7. dumbfounded [dʌmˈfaʊndɪd]	adj.	unable to speak because of surprise 惊呆了的
8. give (full) vent		to express a feeling, especially anger, strongly （充分）表达；（淋漓尽致地）发泄
9. expostulate [ɪkˈspɒstʃʊleɪt]	v.	to argue, disagree or protest about sth 争论；争执；抗议
	n.	expostulation
10. irresolute [ɪˈrezəljuːt]	adj.	not able to decide what to do 踌躇的；犹

豫不决的

11. volley [ˈvɒli]	n.	a lot of questions, comments, insults, etc. that are directed at sb quickly one after the other（质问、评论、辱骂等的）接连发出
12. chagrin [ˈʃæɡrɪn]	n.	a feeling of being disappointed or annoyed 失望；恼怒
13. unmindful [ʌnˈmaɪndfʊl]	adj.	not giving thought or attention to sb/sth 不注意的；不留心的；漫不经心的
14. unwholesome [ʌnˈhəʊlsəm]	adj.	harmful to health; not looking healthy 有损健康的；不健康的；不卫生的

第二十七回

滴翠亭杨妃戏彩蝶　埋香冢飞燕泣残红[1]

Pao-chai Chases a Butterfly to Dripping Emerald Pavilion
Tai-yu Weeps over Fallen Blossom by the Tomb of Flowers[1] (Yang)

Beauty Perspiring sports with butterflies by the Raindrop Pavilion
And Beauty Suspiring weeps for fallen blossoms by the Flowers' Grave[1] (Hawkes)

一、本回概述

宝钗挥扇扑蝶，一路追到滴翠亭，无意中听到小红、坠儿对话，原来贾芸、小红通过坠儿暗通款曲，互赠私物，宝钗心内吃惊，避嫌不及，只得用"金蝉脱壳"之法脱身。小红伶牙俐齿，办事得力，得到熙凤赏识，欲收为干女儿。宝玉不知昨夜晴雯拒给黛玉开门之事，去找黛玉，黛玉冷脸而去。宝玉见黛玉躲着自己，又见落花满地，便决定先收拾落花，到花冢葬花时，却听得黛玉呜咽吟唱《葬花吟》。

第二十七回

二、篇章节选

原文

　　宝钗在外面听见这话，心中吃惊，想道："怪道从古至今那些奸淫狗盗的人，心机都不错。这一开了，见我在这里，他们岂不臊了。[2] 况才说话的语音，大似宝玉房里的红儿的言语。他素昔眼空心大，[3] 是个头等刁钻古怪东西。今儿我听了他的短儿，一时人急造反，狗急跳墙，[4] 不但生事，而且我还没趣。如今便赶着躲了，料也躲不及，少不得要使个'金蝉脱壳'的法子。"[5] 犹未想完，只听"咯吱"一声，宝钗便故意放重了脚步，[6] 笑着叫道："颦儿，我看你往那里藏！"一面说，一面故意往前赶。

　　那亭内的红玉坠儿刚一推窗，只听宝钗如此说着往前赶，两个人都唬怔了。[7a] 宝钗反向他二人笑道：[7b] "你们把林姑娘藏在那里了？"坠儿道："何曾见林姑娘了？"宝钗道："我才在河那边看着林姑娘在这里蹲着弄水儿的。我要悄悄的唬他一跳，还没有走到跟前，他倒看见我了，朝东一绕就不见了。别是藏在这里头了。"一面说，一面故意进去寻了一寻，抽身就走，口内说道："一定是又钻在山子洞里去了。遇见蛇，咬一口也罢了。"一面说一面走，心中又好笑：这件事算遮过去了。不知他二人是怎样。[8]

　　谁知红玉听了宝钗的话，便信以为真，让宝钗去远，便拉坠儿道：[9] "了不得了！林姑娘蹲在这里，一定听了话去了！"坠儿听说，也半日不言语。红玉又道："这可怎么样呢？"坠儿道："便是听了，管谁筋疼，各人干各人的就完了。" 红玉道："若是宝姑娘听见，还倒罢了。林姑娘嘴里又爱刻薄人，心里又细，[10] 他一听见了，倘或走露了风声，怎么样呢？"

杨译

　　Pao-chai could hardly believe her ears.

　　"No wonder they say wicked people have always been cunning!" she thought. "How they're going to blush when they open the window and see me! [2] One of them sounded like that sly, conceited Hsiao-hung who works for Pao-yu. [3] She's a strange crafty creature if ever I saw one. 'Desperation drives men to rebel and a dog to jump over a wall.' [4] If she thinks I know her secret there may be trouble, and that would be awkward for me. Well, it's too late to hide now. I must try to avoid suspicion by throwing them off the scent...." [5]

That same instant she heard the thud of a window opening. At once she ran forward as noisily as she could, [6] calling out laughingly:

"Where are you hiding, Tai-yu?"

Hsiao-hung and Chui-erh, who had just opened the window, were staggered to see her before them. [7a]

"Where have you hidden Miss Lin?" Pao-chai asked them merrily.

"Miss Lin? We haven't seen her," Chui-erh answered.

"Just now, from the other bank, I saw her crouching here dabbling in the water. I meant to take her by surprise but she spotted me coming and dashed off to the east. And now she's disappeared. Are you sure she's not hiding in there?"

She deliberately went in and made a search before going on.

"She must have popped into some cave in the rocks," she muttered. "If a snake bites her, serve her right."

With that she went off, laughing up her sleeve at the way she had foxed them and wondering what they were thinking. [8]

Hsiao-hung, in fact, had been quite taken in. As soon as Pao-chai was safely out of earshot she caught Chui-erh by the arm. [9]

"Heaven help us!" she whispered. "If Miss Lin was here she must have overheard us."

Chui-erh said nothing, and a long pause followed.

"What shall we do?" asked Hsiao-hung.

"What if she *did* hear? This is none of her business."

"It wouldn't have been so bad Miss Hsueh overhearing. But Miss Lin's narrow-minded and likes to make cutting remarks. [10] If she heard, and gives us away, what shall we do?"

霍译

Bao-chai, listening outside, gave a start.

'No wonder they say "venery and thievery sharpen the wits",' she thought. 'If they open those windows and see me here, they are going to feel terribly embarrassed. [2] And one of those voices sounds like that proud, peculiar girl Crimson who works in Bao-yu's room. [3] If a girl like that knows that I have overheard her doing something she shouldn't be doing, it will be a case of "the desperate dog will jump a wall, the desperate man will hazard all": [4] there'll be a great deal of trouble and I shall be involved in it. There isn't time to hide. I shall have to do as the cicada does when he jumps out of his skin: give them something to put them off the scent—' [5]

There was a loud creak as the casement yielded. Bao-chai advanced with deliberately noisy tread. [6]

'Frowner!' she called out gaily. 'I know where you're hiding.'

Inside the pavilion Crimson and Trinket, who heard her say this and saw her advancing towards them just as they were opening the casement, were speechless with amazement; but Bao-chai ignored their confusion and addressed them genially: [7b]

'Have you two got Miss Lin hidden away in there?'

'I haven't *seen* Miss Lin,' said Trinket.

'I saw her just now from the river-bank,' said Bao-chai. 'She was squatting down over here playing with something in the water. I was going to creep up and surprise her, but she spotted me before I could get up to her and disappeared round this corner. Are you *sure* she's not hiding in there?'

She made a point of going inside the pavilion and searching; then, coming out again, she said in a voice loud enough for them to hear:

'If she's not in the pavilion, she must have crept into that grotto. Oh well, if she's not afraid of being bitten by a snake—!'

As she walked away she laughed inwardly at the ease with which she had extricated herself from a difficult situation.

'I think I'm fairly safely out of *that* one,' she thought. 'I wonder what those two will make of it.'[8]

What indeed! Crimson believed every word that Bao-chai had said, and as soon as the latter was at a distance, she seized hold of Trinket in alarm:[9]

'Oh, how terrible! If Miss Lin was squatting there, she must have heard what we said before she went away.'

Her companion was silent.

'Oh dear! What do you think she'll do?' said Crimson.

'Well, suppose she *did* hear,' said Trinket, 'it's not *her* backache. If we mind our business and she minds hers, there's no reason why anything should come of it.'

'If it were Miss Bao that had heard us, I don't suppose anything *would*,' said Crimson; 'but Miss Lin is so critical and so intolerant.[10] If *she* heard it and it gets about—oh dear!'

三、注释评点

【1】本回回目"滴翠亭杨妃戏彩蝶 埋香冢飞燕泣残红"出现了两个历史人物:"杨妃"和"飞燕",分别指代"宝钗"和"黛玉"。杨译是"Pao-chai Chases a Butterfly to Dripping Emerald Pavilion Tai-yu Weeps over Fallen Blossom by the Tomb of Flowers",译者直接使用"Pao-chai"和"Tai-yu"翻译原文中的"杨妃"和"飞燕"。霍译是"Beauty Perspiring sports with butterflies by the Raindrop Pavilion And Beauty Suspiring weeps for fallen blossoms by the Flowers' Grave",译者没有使用人名,而是用"Beauty Perspiring"和"Beauty Suspiring"分别指代"宝钗"和"黛玉",暗示宝钗体态丰满,稍微运动就会出汗,黛玉多愁善感,稍微感怀就会垂泪不已。霍译用词委婉,可能缘于与原文风格保持一致的考虑:原文既用"杨妃"和"飞燕"暗指钗、黛,霍译也就不明指二人,而是用她们的体态特征、性格特征来暗指。

【2】"这一开了,见我在这里,他们岂不臊了"一句,杨译"How they're going to blush when they open the window and see me!"使用了感叹句;同时,译者为将意合的汉语转化为形合的英语,增加了表示逻辑关系的连接

词"when"。此外，杨译将"How they're going to blush"放在句首，与原文的句序有所不同。汉语句子重心偏后，英语句子重心偏前：本句的强调部分是"他们岂不臊了"，位于原文句尾，按照英语行文习惯，"How they're going to blush"位于句首，有强调之意。霍译"If they open those windows and see me here, they are going to feel terribly embarrassed."使用了陈述句，句序和原文一致，也增加了表示逻辑关系的连接词"if"；另外，"他们岂不臊了"被译为主句"they are going to feel terribly embarrassed"，也有强调该部分之意。

【3】"他素昔眼空心大"一句，杨译"One of them sounded like that sly, conceited Hsiao-hung..."和霍译"And one of those voices sounds like that proud, peculiar girl Crimson..."都使用了句子化短语法，将这句话分别译为名词短语"sly, conceited Hsiao-hung"和"proud, peculiar girl Crimson"。

【4】"一时人急造反，狗急跳墙"一句，杨译"Desperation drives men to rebel and a dog to jump over a wall."采用直译法，忠实于原文。霍译"the desperate dog will jump a wall, the desperate man will hazard all"没有直接译出"造反"，但创造性的翻译不仅传达出原文的意涵，而且具有押韵的效果，十分巧妙。另外，原文出现两个"急"字，霍译也连用两个"desperate"，形式上与原文更加吻合。

【5】"少不得要使个'金蝉脱壳'的法子"一句，杨译"I must try to avoid suspicion by throwing them off the scent"采用意译手法，使用了短语"throw (one) off the scent"，意为"to misdirect one away from their pursuit; to steer one's investigation or suspicion in the wrong direction（转移追踪方向）"，解释了原文意涵，但失去了原文喻体"the cicada（金蝉）"。霍译"I shall have to do as the cicada does when he jumps out of his skin: give them something to put them off the scent"使用的短语"put (one) off the scent"也具有同样的意思。另外，霍译还保留了原文的喻体，既译出了"金蝉脱壳"的字面意思，也传达了该词在中国文化中的实际意涵，属于直译加意译的手法。

【6】"宝钗便故意放重了脚步"一句，杨译"At once she ran forward as noisily as she could"用"noisily"修饰"ran"，表示"跑的声音很大"；霍译"Bao-chai advanced with deliberately noisy tread."用词非常准确，"deliberately

（故意地）"和 "noisy tread（沉重的脚步）"贴切生动地表达了原文内涵。

【7a】"那亭内的红玉坠儿刚一推窗，只听宝钗如此说着往前赶，两个人都唬怔了。"一句，杨译"Hsiao-hung and Chui-erh, who had just opened the window, were staggered to see her before them."是主从结构句式，通过"who"进行句内连接；而且从句的动词和主句的动词分别使用了过去完成时（had opened）和一般过去时（were staggered），表达出这两个动作发生的先后顺序。

【7b】"那亭内的红玉坠儿刚一推窗，只听宝钗如此说着往前赶，两个人都唬怔了。宝钗反向他二人笑道……"，霍译是"Inside the pavilion Crimson and Trinket, who heard her say this and saw her advancing towards them just as they were opening the casement, were speechless with amazement; but Bao-chai ignored their confusion and addressed them genially…"，译者使用"who"和"just as"进行句内连接，并增译了"but Bao-chai ignored their confusion and…"一句，使得译文语言更有张力，上下文衔接得更加自然。

【8】"一面说一面走，心中又好笑：这件事算遮过去了。不知他二人是怎样。"这句话中省略的主语"宝钗"发出了三个几乎同时发生的动作：说、走、好笑。杨译是"With that she went off, laughing up her sleeve at the way she had foxed them and wondering what they were thinking."译者将动词"走"处理为谓语"went off"，将"一面说"处理为介词短语"With that"，在译文中作伴随状语；将"好笑"处理为现在分词短语"laughing up…"，在译文中作伴随状语，整个句式呈现偏正结构。霍译是"As she walked away she laughed inwardly at the ease with which she had extricated herself from a difficult situation. 'I think I'm fairly safely out of *that* one,' she thought. 'I wonder what those two will make of it.'"译文的第一句中通过"as"和"with which"进行句内连接。此外，霍译保留了原文直接引语的语体风格。

【9】"让宝钗去远，便拉坠儿说道"一句，杨译"As soon as Pao-chai was safely out of earshot she caught Chui-erh by the arm."是主从结构的句式，用"as soon as"连接句子，短语"out of earshot"十分生动，意为"不在听力所及范围"。霍译"… and as soon as the latter was at a distance, she seized hold of Trinket in alarm..."用"and"和"as soon as"连句:"and"用来承接上文,"as soon as"用来引出下文。

【10】"林姑娘嘴里又爱刻薄人,心里又细"一句的翻译,两位译者都使用了句子化词法:杨译"But Miss Lin's narrow-minded and likes to make cutting remarks"将小句"心里又细"译为形容词"narrow-minded";霍译"but Miss Lin is so critical and so intolerant"主要使用了两个形容词"critical"和"intolerant"来翻译原文中的两个小句"嘴里又爱刻薄人"和"心里又细"。

四、词汇表

1. conceited [kənˈsi:tɪd]	adj.	having too much pride in yourself and what you do 自负的;骄傲自大的
2. dabble [ˈdæbl]	v.	to move your hands, feet, etc. around in water 玩水;嬉水
3. pop [pɒp]	v.	to go somewhere quickly, suddenly or for a short time (突然或匆匆)去
4. venery [ˈven(ə)ri]	n.	the pursuit of sexual gratification 好色
5. thievery [ˈθi:vəri]	n.	the act of taking something from someone unlawfully 偷窃
6. hazard [ˈhæzəd]	v.	to risk sth or put it in danger 冒……的风险;使处于危险
7. cicada [sɪˈkɑ:də]	n.	a large insect with transparent wings, common in hot countries, that makes a continuous high sound by rubbing its legs together 蝉
8. casement [ˈkeɪsmənt]	n.	a window that opens on hinges like a door 竖铰链窗;门式窗
9. gaily [ˈgeɪli]	adv.	in a cheerful way 快乐地;欢乐地;喜气洋洋地

10. genial [ˈdʒi:njəl]	*adj.*		friendly and cheerful 友好的；亲切的；欢快的
	adv.		genially
11. creep up (on sb)			to move slowly nearer to sb, usually from behind, without being seen or heard （通常从后面）缓慢地悄悄靠近
12. grotto [ˈgrɒtəʊ]	*n.*		a small cave, especially one that has been made artificially, for example in a garden 洞穴；（尤指园林中的）人工洞室
13. extricate [ˈekstrɪkeɪt]	*v.*		to escape or enable sb to escape from a difficult situation （使）摆脱，脱离，脱出

第二十八回

蒋玉菡情赠茜香罗　　薛宝钗羞笼红麝串[1]

Chiang Yu-han Gives a New Friend a Scarlet Perfumed Sash
Pao-chai Bashfully Shows Her Red Bracelet Scented with Musk[1] (Yang)

A crimson cummerbund becomes a pledge of friendship
And a chaplet of medicine-beads becomes a source of embarrassment[1] (Hawkes)

一、本回概述

黛玉葬花伤己，吟唱《葬花吟》，宝玉听见，悲伤难禁，失声恸哭，惊动了黛玉，黛玉见是宝玉，转身离开。宝玉追上后，诉说衷肠，两人冰释前嫌，和好如初。冯紫英请宝玉饮酒唱曲，期间宝玉结识琪官，两人惺惺相惜，互赠汗巾。元妃赏赐众人，唯有宝玉和宝钗的赏品一样，黛玉心中不悦。宝玉要看宝钗的红麝串，不想看到宝钗雪白的胳膊，动了羡慕之心，不禁呆住了，这一幕恰巧被黛玉瞧见，不免醋意大发。

二、篇章节选

原文

　　这里宝玉悲恸了一回，忽然抬头不见了黛玉，便知黛玉看见他躲开了，[2] 自己也觉无味，抖抖土起来，下山寻归旧路，往怡红院来。[3] 可巧看见林黛玉在前头走，连忙赶上去，说道："你且站住。我知你不理我，我只说一句话，[4] 从今后撂开手。"林黛玉回头看见是宝玉，待要不理他，听他说"只说一句话，从此撂开手"，这话里有文章，少不得站住说道："有一句话，请说来。"宝玉笑道："两句话，说了你听不听？"黛玉听说，回头就走。宝玉在身后面叹道："既有今日，何必当初！"[5] 林黛玉听见这话，由不得站住，[6] 回头道："当初怎么样？今日怎么样？"宝玉叹道："当初姑娘来了，那不是我陪着玩笑？[7] 凭我心爱的，姑娘要，就拿去；我爱吃的，听见姑娘也爱吃，连忙干干净净收着等姑娘吃。[8] 一桌子吃饭，一床上睡觉。[9] 丫头们想不到的，我怕姑娘生气，我替丫头们想到了。我心里想着：姊妹们从小儿长大，亲也罢，热也罢，和气到了儿，才见得比人好。如今谁承望姑娘人大心大，不把我放在眼里，倒把外四路的什么宝姐姐凤姐姐的放在心坎儿上，倒把我三日不理四日不见的。我又没个亲兄弟亲姊妹。——虽然有两个，你难道不知道是和我隔母的？[10] 我也和你似的独出，只怕同我的心一样。谁知我是白操了这个心，弄的有冤无处诉！"说着不觉滴下眼泪来。

杨译

　　When Pao-yu recovered sufficiently to look up she had gone, obviously to avoid him.[2] Getting up rather sheepishly, he dusted off his clothes and walked down the hill to make his way back again to Happy Red Court.[3] Catching sight of Tai-yu ahead, he overtook her.

　　"Do stop!" he begged. "I know you won't look at me, but let me just say *one* word.[4] After that we can part company for good."

　　Tai-yu glanced round and would have ignored him, but was curious to hear this

"*one* word," thinking there must be something in it. She came to a halt.

"Out with it."

Pao-yu smiled.

"Would you listen if I said two words?" he asked.

At once she walked away.

Pao-yu, close behind her, sighed.

"Why are things so different now from in the past?"[5]

Against her will she stopped once more and turned her head.[6]

"What do you mean by 'now' and 'the past'?"

Pao-yu heaved another sigh.

"Wasn't I your playmate when you first came?" he demanded.[7] "Anything that pleased me was yours, cousin, for the asking. If I knew you fancied a favourite dish of mine, I put it away in a clean place till you came.[8] We ate at the same table and slept on the same bed.[9] I took care that the maids did nothing to upset you; for I thought cousins growing up together as such good friends should be kinder to each other than anyone else. I never expected you to grow so proud that now you have no use for me while you're so fond of outsiders like Pao-chai and Hsi-feng. You ignore me or cut me for three or four days at a time. I've no brothers or sisters of my own— only two by a different mother, as well you know.[10] So I'm an only child like you, and I thought that would make for an affinity between us. But apparently it was no use my hoping for that. There's nobody I can tell how unhappy I am." With that, he broke down again.

霍译

By the time Bao-yu's weeping was over, Dai-yu was no longer there. He realized that she must have seen him and have gone away in order to avoid him.[2] Feeling suddenly rather foolish, he rose to his feet and brushed the earth from his clothes. Then he descended from the rockery and began to retrace his steps in the direction of Green Delights.[3] Quite by coincidence Dai-yu was walking along the same path a little way ahead.

'Stop a minute!' he cried, hurrying forward to catch up with her. 'I know you are not taking any notice of me, but I only want to ask you one simple question,[4] and then you need never have anything more to do with me.'

Dai-yu had turned back to see who it was. When she saw that it was Bao-yu still, she was going to ignore him again; but hearing him say that he only wanted to ask her one question, she told him that he might do so.

Bao-yu could not resist teasing her a little.

'How about *two* questions? Would you wait for two?'

Dai-yu set her face forwards and began walking on again.

Bao-yu sighed.

'If it has to be like this now,' he said, as if to himself, 'it's a pity it was ever like it was in the beginning.'[5]

Dai-yu's curiosity got the better of her.[6] She stopped walking and turned once more towards him.

'Like *what* in the beginning?' she asked. 'And like what now?'

'Oh, the *beginning*!' said Bao-yu. 'In the *beginning*, when you first came here,[7] I was your faithful companion in all your games. Anything I had, even the thing most dear to me, was yours for the asking. If there was something to eat that I specially liked, I had only to hear that you were fond of it too and I would religiously hoard it away to share with you when you got back, not daring even to touch it until you came.[8] We ate at the same table. We slept in the same bed.[9] I used to think that because we were so close then, there would be something special about our relationship when we grew up—that even if we weren't particularly affectionate, we should at least have more understanding and forbearance for each other than the rest. But how wrong I was! Now that you *have* grown up, you seem only to have grown more touchy. You don't seem to care about *me* any more at all. You spend all your time brooding about outsiders like Feng and Chai. I haven't got any *real* brothers and sisters left here now. There are Huan and Tan, of course; but as you know, they're only my half-brother and

half-sister: they aren't my mother's children. [10] I'm on my own, like you. I should have thought we had so much in common—But what's the use? I try and try, but it gets me nowhere; and nobody knows or cares.'

At this point—in spite of himself—he burst into tears.

三、注释评点

【1】"蒋玉菡情赠茜香罗 薛宝钗羞笼红麝串"是本回回目，杨译"Chiang Yu-han Gives a New Friend a Scarlet Perfumed Sash Pao-chai Bashfully Shows Her Red Bracelet Scented with Musk"和原文一致，使用了人格主语"Chiang Yu-han"和"Pao-chai"；霍译"A crimson cummerbund becomes a pledge of friendship And a chaplet of medicine-beads becomes a source of embarrassment"使用了物化主语"A crimson cummerbund"和"a chaplet of medicine-beads"。此外，霍译上下两句对仗非常工整。

【2】"这里宝玉悲恸了一回，忽然抬头不见了黛玉，便知黛玉看见他躲开了"一句，杨译是"When Pao-yu recovered sufficiently to look up she had gone, obviously to avoid him."译者用"When"进行句内连接，整个句子的结构是："When"引导的时间状语从句+主句+不定式结构充当的目的状语。霍译是"By the time Bao-yu's weeping was over, Dai-yu was no longer there. He realized that she must have seen him and have gone away in order to avoid him."译文的第一句使用"By the time"进行句内连接；译文第二句：在that引导的宾语从句中，动词不定式结构"in order to avoid him"做目的状语。

【3】"自己也觉无味，抖抖土起来，下山寻归旧路，往怡红院来"一句，主语"宝玉"发出了一连串的动作：觉、抖抖、起来、下山、寻归、往……来，这是汉语中典型的连动句式。杨译是"Getting up rather sheepishly, he dusted off his clothes and walked down the hill to make his way back again to Happy Red Court."，句首是现在分词短语"Getting up rather sheepishly"作时间状语，表示该动作与后文中的谓语动词的动作先后发生；然后是并列谓语"dusted off"和"walked down"；接着使用了不定式短语"to make his way back again to

Happy Red Court",在译文中充当目的状语。霍译是"Feeling suddenly rather foolish, he rose to his feet and brushed the earth from his clothes. Then he descended from the rockery and began to retrace his steps in the direction of Green Delights."该译文由两个句子构成,用"then"进行句际连接。第一句的句首使用现在分词短语"Feeling suddenly rather foolish"作原因状语,接着是并列谓语"rose to his feet"和"brushed the earth";第二句中也使用了并列谓语"descended"和"began"。

【4】"我只说一句话"一句,杨译"...say one word"和霍译"...ask you one simple question"均未按照原文的字面意思来翻译,都作了改译处理。

【5】"既有今日,何必当初!"一句是感叹语气,杨译"Why are things so different now from in the past?"采用了问句形式,其中的"different"一词所表达的意思是"为什么今日与当初不同了?";而原文更强调"早知今日,当初就不应该开始"的意思,所以,译文与原文的意思有所不同。霍译"'If it has to be like this now,' he said, as if to himself, 'it's a pity it was ever like it was in the beginning.'"使用了陈述句的形式,并用"pity"一词将"既有今日,何必当初"中所包含的遗憾和无奈之情充分地翻译了出来。

【6】"由不得站住"一句,杨译"Against her will she stopped once more..."中的"Against her will"是"不情愿"的意思,与原文中"由不得"的意思有所不同。霍译"Dai-yu's curiosity got the better of her."中的"got the better of her"充分体现出"由不得"的意思。

【7】"回头道:'当初怎么样?今日怎么样?'宝玉叹道:'当初姑娘来了,那不是我陪着玩笑?……如今谁承望姑娘人大心大"一句中,黛玉用了"当初"和"今日"这两个词,宝玉回答时用了"当初"和"如今",可以看出,上下文的语义衔接十分紧密。杨译是"What do you mean by 'now' and 'the past'? Pao-yu heaved another sigh. 'Wasn't I your playmate when you first came?' he demanded... I never expected you to grow so proud that now you have no use for me",此处,杨译在上文中使用了"the past",下文中使用了"when you first came",这两个时间状语的对应度较弱。霍译是"'Like what in the beginning?' she asked. 'And like what now?'""'Oh, the beginning!' said Bao-yu. 'In the beginning, when you first came here... Now that you have grown up, you seem only to have grown more touchy." 可以看出，译者通过重复 "beginning" 一词，使上下文的过渡十分自然，衔接也十分紧密。

【8】"我爱吃的，听见姑娘也爱吃，连忙干干净净收着等姑娘吃"一句，杨译是 "If I knew you fancied a favourite dish of mine, I put it away in a clean place till you came." 译者使用 "if" 和 "till" 进行句内连接；霍译是 "If there was something to eat that I specially liked, I had only to hear that you were fond of it too and I would religiously hoard it away to share with you when you got back, not daring even to touch it until you came." 译者使用 "If"，"when" 和 "until" 进行连句，体现了意合语言（汉语）向形合语言（英语）转换时，要增加表示逻辑关系的连接词。

【9】"一桌子吃饭，一床上睡觉。"包含两个并列的小句。杨译 "We ate at the same table and slept on the same bed." 使用了并列谓语的结构，将两句合译为一句；霍译 "We ate at the same table. We slept in the same bed." 由两个句子构成，主语都是 "we"，强调的语气非常明显，增加了修辞效果。

【10】"我又没个亲兄弟亲姊妹。——虽然有两个，你难道不知道是和我隔母的？"一句，根据小说可以知道，宝玉本是有亲哥哥贾珠和亲姐姐贾元春的，但前者早年已故，后者进宫当了贵妃，均不在宝玉身边。杨译 "I've no brothers or sisters of my own—only two by a different mother, as well you know." 依照字面意思去翻译，与小说实际内容不符。霍译 "I haven't got any real brothers and sisters left here now. There are Huan and Tan, of course; but as you know, they're only my half-brother and half-sister: they aren't my mother's children." 的第一句只是增加了三个单词（"left here now"），就解决了这个问题，指出目前宝玉身边没有亲兄弟姐妹。

四、词汇表

1. sheepish [ˈʃiːpɪʃ]   adj.   looking or feeling embarrassed because you have done sth silly or wrong 窘迫的；

			难为情的；不好意思的
		adv.	sheepishly
2. halt [hɔːlt]		*n.*	an act of stopping the movement or progress of sb/sth 停止；阻止；暂停
3. heave [hiːv]		*v.*	to make a sound slowly and often with effort（常指吃力地）缓慢发出（声音）
4. affinity [əˈfɪnəti]		*n.*	a close relationship between two people 密切的关系
5. rockery [ˈrɒkəri]		*n.*	a garden or part of a garden consisting of an arrangement of large stones with plants growing among them 假山花园；假山
6. hoard [hɔːd]		*v.*	to collect and keep large amounts of food, money, etc., especially secretly 贮藏；囤积；（尤指）秘藏
7. forbearance [fɔːˈbeərəns]		*n.*	the quality of being patient and sympathetic towards other people, especially when they have done sth wrong 宽容
8. touchy [ˈtʌtʃi]		*adj.*	(of a person) easily upset or offended 易烦恼的；易生气的
9. brood [bruːd]		*adj.*	to think a lot about sth that makes you annoyed, anxious or upset 焦虑；忧思

第二十九回

享福人福深还祷福　痴情女情重愈斟情[1]

Favourites of Fortune Pray for Better Fortune
An Absurd, Loving Girl Falls Deeper in Love [1] (Yang)

*In which the greatly blessed pray for yet greater blessings
And the highly strung rise to new heights of passion* [1] (Hawkes)

一、本回概述

　　清虚观打醮，贾府众人前去听戏。寒暄时，张道士提出要给宝玉做媒说亲，后请宝玉解下通灵宝玉，让众道士开眼，众人也将传道的法器作为敬贺之礼回赠宝玉。宝、黛二人因说亲之事而心生嫌隙，起了口角，宝玉心中不爽，摔玉出气，黛玉也伤心痛哭。贾母听闻此事，忙来探望相劝，想着次日薛蟠生日，两人相见，就会和好，谁知两人都推辞不去，老太太又气又怨，忍不住哭起来。

二、篇章节选

原文

　　那宝玉又听见他说"好姻缘"三个字，越发逆了己意，心里干噎，口里说不出话来，[2] 便赌气向颈上抓下通灵宝玉，咬牙恨命往地下一摔，[3] 道："什么捞什骨子，我砸了你完事！"偏生那玉坚硬非常，摔了一下，竟文风没动。[4] 宝玉见没摔碎，便回身找东西来砸。林黛玉见他如此，早已哭起来，说道："何苦来，你摔砸那哑吧物件。有砸他的，不如来砸我。"二人闹着，紫鹃雪雁等忙来解劝。[5] 后来见宝玉下死砸玉，忙上来夺，又夺不下来，见比往日闹的大了，少不得去叫袭人。袭人忙赶了来，才夺了下来。[6] 宝玉冷笑道："我砸我的东西，与你们什么相干！"

　　袭人见他脸都气黄了，眼眉都变了，从来没气的这样，[7] 便拉着他的手，笑道："你同妹妹拌嘴，不犯着砸他；倘或砸坏了，叫他心里脸上怎么过的去？"[8] 林黛玉一行哭着，一行听了这话说到自己心坎儿上来，[9] 可见宝玉连袭人不如，越发伤心大哭起来。心里一烦恼，方才吃的香薷饮解暑汤便承受不住，"哇"的一声都吐了出来。[10] 紫鹃忙上来用手帕子接住，登时一口一口的把一块手帕子吐湿。[11] 雪雁忙上来捶。紫鹃道："虽然生气，姑娘到底也该保重着些。才吃了药好些，这会子因和宝二爷拌嘴，又吐出来。倘或犯了病，宝二爷怎么过的去呢？"宝玉听了这话说到自己心坎儿上来，可见黛玉不如一紫鹃。

　　又见林黛玉脸红头胀，一行啼哭，一行气凑，一行是泪，一行是汗，不胜怯弱。[12] 宝玉见了这般，又自己后悔方才不该同他较证，[13] 这会子他这样光景，我又替不了他。心里想着，也由不的滴下泪来了。

杨译

　　Those words "the match of your choice" infuriated Pao-yu. Too choked with rage to speak, [2] he tore the jade from his neck and dashed it to the floor. [3]

　　"You rubbishy thing!" he cried, gnashing his teeth. "I'll smash you to pieces and

have done with it."

The jade was so hard, however, that no damage was done.[4] So he looked around for something with which to smash it.

Tai-yu was already weeping.

"Why destroy that dumb object?" she sobbed. "Better destroy me instead."

Tzu-chuan and Hsueh-yen dashed in to stop this quarrel.[5] Seeing Pao-yu hammering at the jade they tried to snatch it away from him but failed. And since this was more serious than usual they had to send for Hsi-jen, who hurried in and managed to rescue the stone.[6]

Pao-yu smiled bitterly.

"I can smash what's mine, can't I? What business is it of yours?"

Hsi-jen had never before seen him so livid with rage, his whole face contorted.[7]

"Because you have words with your cousin is no reason to smash this up," she said coaxingly, taking his hand. "Suppose you broke it, think how bad she'd feel."[8]

This touched Tai-yu's heart,[9] yet it only made her more wretched to think that Pao-yu had less consideration for her than Hsi-jen. She sobbed even more bitterly, so distraught that she threw up the herbal medicine she had just taken.[10] Tzu-chuan hastily brought her a handkerchief which soon was completely soaked through.[11] Hsueh-yen meanwhile massaged her back.

"No matter how angry you are, miss, do think of your health!" Tzu-chuan urged. "You were feeling a little better after the medicine; it's this tiff with Master Pao that's made you retch. If you fall ill, how upset Master Pao will be."

This touched Pao-yu's heart, yet also struck him as proof that Tai-yu had less consideration for him than Tzu-chuan. But now Tai-yu's cheeks were flushed and swollen. Weeping and choking, her face streaked with tears and sweat, she looked most fearfully frail.[12] The sight filled him with compunction.[13]

"I should never have argued with her and got her into this state," he scolded himself. "I can't even suffer instead of her." He, too, shed tears.

> 霍译

When Dai-yu, far from saying something nice to him, once more made reference to the 'gold and jade', Bao-yu became so choked with rage that for a moment he was quite literally bereft of speech.[2] Frenziedly snatching the 'Magic Jade' from his neck and holding it by the end of its silken cord he gritted his teeth and dashed it against the floor with all the strength in his body.[3]

'*Beastly* thing!' he shouted. 'I'll smash you to pieces and put an end to this once and for all.'

But the jade, being exceptionally hard and resistant, was not the tiniest bit damaged.[4] Seeing that he had not broken it, Bao-yu began to look around for something to smash it with. Dai-yu, still crying, saw what he was going to do.

'Why smash a dumb, lifeless object?' she said. 'If you want to smash something, let it be me.'

The sound of their quarrelling brought Nightingale and Snowgoose hurrying in to keep the peace.[5] They found Bao-yu apparently bent on destroying his jade and tried to wrest it from him. Failing to do so, and sensing that the quarrel was of more than usual dimensions, they went off to fetch Aroma. Aroma came back with them as fast as she could run and eventually succeeded in prising the jade from his hand.[6] He glared at her scornfully.

'It's my own thing I'm smashing,' he said. 'What business is it of yours to interfere?'

Aroma saw that his face was white with anger and his eyes wild and dangerous. Never had she seen him in so terrible a rage.[7] She took him gently by the hand:

'You shouldn't smash the jade just because of a disagreement with your cousin,' she said. 'What do you think she would feel like and what sort of position would it put her in if you really *were* to break it?'[8]

Dai-yu heard these words through her sobs. They struck a responsive chord in her breast,[9] and she wept all the harder to think that even Aroma seemed to understand her better than Bao-yu did. So much emotion was too much for her weak stomach.

Suddenly there was a horrible retching noise and up came the tisane of elsholtzia leaves she had taken only a short while before.[10] Nightingale quickly held out her handkerchief to receive it and, while Snowgoose rubbed and pounded her back, Dai-yu continued to retch up wave upon wave of watery vomit, until the whole handkerchief was soaked with it.[11]

'However cross you may be, Miss, you ought to have more regard for your health,' said Nightingale. 'You'd only just taken that medicine and you were beginning to feel a little bit better for it, and now because of your argument with Master Bao you've gone and brought it all up again. Suppose you were to be *really* ill as a consequence. How do you think Master Bao would feel?'

When Bao-yu heard these words they struck a responsive chord in *his* breast, and he reflected bitterly that even Nightingale seemed to understand him better than Dai-yu. But then he looked again at Dai-yu, who was sobbing and panting by turns, and whose red and swollen face was wet with perspiration and tears,[12] and seeing how pitiably frail and ill she looked, his heart misgave him.[13]

'I shouldn't have taken her up on that "gold and jade" business,' he thought. 'I've got her into this state and now there's no way in which I can relieve her by sharing what she suffers.' As he thought this, he, too, began to cry.

三、注释评点

【1】本回回目是"享福人福深还祷福 痴情女情重愈斟情",可以看出,上句中"福"字重复了三次,下句中"情"字重复了三次。杨译和霍译在翻译该回目时,也想尽量保留原文中的重复现象:杨译是"Favourites of Fortune Pray for Better Fortune An Absurd Loving Girl Falls Deeper in Love",上句中重复"Fortune",下句中"Loving"和"Love"重复;霍译是"In which the greatly blessed pray for yet greater blessings And the highly strung rise to new heights of passion",上句中"greatly blessed"和"greater blessings"重复,下句中"highly"和"heights"重复。"In which"是英语中的一种旧用法,用于

引出下文，介绍下文。

【2】"那宝玉又听见他说'好姻缘'三个字，越发逆了己意，心里干噎，口里说不出话来"一句，杨译是"Those words 'the match of your choice' infuriated Pao-yu. Too choked with rage to speak…"，译文的第一句用句子化短语法将小句"那宝玉又听见他说'好姻缘'三个字"译为名词短语"Those words 'the match of your choice'"，在该句中充当主语；第二句句首的"Too choked with rage to speak"做原因状语。霍译是"When Dai-yu, far from saying something nice to him, once more made reference to the 'gold and jade', Bao-yu became so choked with rage that for a moment he was quite literally bereft of speech."，译者在主句中使用"so... that..."进行连句，"that"引导结果状语从句；"choked with rage"中的介词"with"表示原因。

【3】"便赌气向颈上抓下通灵宝玉，咬牙恨命往地下一摔"一句，描述了宝玉发疯失智的状态。杨译是"… he tore the jade from his neck and dashed it to the floor."霍译是"Frenziedly snatching the 'Magic Jade' from his neck and holding it by the end of its silken cord he gritted his teeth and dashed it against the floor with all the strength in his body."相比杨译，霍译中的几处用词——"Frenziedly""snatching""gritted his teeth""dashed""with all the strength in his body"——更加生动地刻画出宝玉气急败坏的情态。

【4】"偏生那玉坚硬非常，摔了一下，竟文风没动"一句，杨译"The jade was so hard, however, that no damage was done."是通过"so... that"进行连句的。霍译"But the jade, being exceptionally hard and resistant, was not the tiniest bit damaged."使用了现在分词短语"being exceptionally hard and resistant"作原因状语；此外，"not the tiniest bit damaged"将"文风没动"表达得十分准确。

【5】"紫鹃雪雁等忙来解劝"一句，杨译"Tzu-chuan and Hsueh-yen dashed in to stop this quarrel."使用了人格主语"Tzu-chuan and Hsueh-yen"；霍译"The sound of their quarrelling brought Nightingale and Snowgoose hurrying in to keep the peace."使用了物化主语"The sound of their quarrelling"。

【6】"见比往日闹的大了，少不得去叫袭人。袭人忙赶了来，才夺了下来"一句，杨译"And since this was more serious than usual they had to send for

Hsi-jen, who hurried in and managed to rescue the stone."使用"And""since"和"who"进行连句:"And"承接上文,"since"引出下文,引导原因状语从句。霍译是"(Failing to do so,) and sensing that the quarrel was of more than usual dimensions, they went off to fetch Aroma. Aroma came back with them as fast as she could run and eventually succeeded in prising the jade from his hand."第一句中并列的两个现在分词短语"Failing to do so"和"sensing that the quarrel was of more than usual dimensions"在句中充当原因状语。

【7】"袭人见他脸都气黄了,眼眉都变了,从来没气的这样"一句,杨译是"Hsi-jen had never before seen him so livid with rage, his whole face contorted.""livid with rage"中的介词"with"表原因;"his whole face contorted"是独立主格结构。霍译是"Aroma saw that his face was white with anger and his eyes wild and dangerous. Never had she seen him in so terrible a rage."第一句中的"his eyes"之后省略了系动词"were",在表述上避免和前文重复;第二句中,否定副词"Never"置于句首表示强调,该句自然就采用了倒装式。

【8】"倘或砸坏了,叫他心里脸上怎么过的去?"一句中,"叫他心里脸上怎么过的去"很难直译。杨译"Suppose you broke it, think how bad she'd feel."使用了"bad"一词进行概括翻译,显得分量不足。霍译"What do you think she would feel like and what sort of position would it put her in if you really were to break it?"保留了原文的反问句形式;此外,通过增加"what sort of position would it put her in",译者尽量全面准确地传达出原文的意思。

【9】"林黛玉一行哭着,一行听了这话说到自己心坎儿上来"是并列句,杨译"This touched Tai-yu's heart"使用物化主语"This"指代原文中的"这话",将两个并列句"一行……,一行……"合译为一句。霍译是"Dai-yu heard these words through her sobs. They struck a responsive chord in her breast",译者将"一行哭着,一行听了"译为"Dai-yu heard these words through her sobs";将"说到自己心坎上"译为"struck a responsive chord in her breast",语言十分生动,可读性强。

【10】"'哇'的一声都吐了出来。"一句中,"哇"是拟声词,在英

语中很难找到对应词。杨译是"she threw up the herbal medicine she had just taken",霍译是"Suddenly there was a horrible retching noise and up came the tisane of elsholtzia leaves she had taken only a short while before."比较两个译文可以看出,霍译增加了一些细节内容,如"a horrible retching noise"和"the tisane of elsholtzia leaves",为读者最大程度地展示了"哇"的内涵。

【11】"登时一口一口的把一块手帕子吐湿"一句,杨译"...which soon was completely soaked through."并未将"一口一口的"翻译出来。霍译"Dai-yu continued to retch up wave upon wave of watery vomit, until the whole handkerchief was soaked with it."则将"一口一口的"翻译为"wave upon wave of watery vomit",再使用"until"与后文连接,生动传神地再现了原文内容。

【12】"一行啼哭,一行气凑,一行是泪,一行是汗,不胜怯弱"一句,杨译是"Weeping and choking, her face streaked with tears and sweat, she looked most fearfully frail."译者将"一行啼哭,一行气凑"译为并列的现在分词短语"Weeping and choking",将"一行是泪,一行是汗"译为独立主格结构"her face streaked with tears and sweat",二者在译文中都充当伴随状语;将"不胜怯弱"译为句子的主干部分"she looked most fearfully frail"。霍译是"(But then he looked again at Dai-yu,) who was sobbing and panting by turns, and whose red and swollen face was wet with perspiration and tears...",译者将"一行啼哭,一行气凑"和"一行是泪,一行是汗"译为两个定语从句,分别由"who"和"whose"来引导,中间用"and"连接。

【13】"宝玉见了这般,又自己后悔方才不该同他较证"一句中的主语是"宝玉",杨译"The sight filled him with compunction."使用了物化主语"The sight",将原文中的两句合译为一句;霍译是"... and seeing how pitiably frail and ill she looked, his heart misgave him."句式呈现偏正结构:"偏"是现在分词短语"seeing how pitiably frail and ill she looked"充当的原因状语,"正"是主句"his heart misgave him"。

四、词汇表

1. infuriate [ɪnˈfjʊərieɪt]	v.	to make sb extremely angry 使极为生气；使大怒；激怒
2. rubbishy [ˈrʌbɪʃi]	adj.	of very poor quality 质量低劣的；非常差劲的
3. hammer [ˈhæmə(r)]	v.	to hit sth with a tool, like a hammer 锤打
4. livid [ˈlɪvɪd]	adj.	extremely angry 暴怒的；狂怒的
5. contort [kənˈtɔːt]	v.	to become twisted or make sth twisted out of its natural or normal shape（使）扭曲，走样
	adj.	contorted
6. distraught [dɪˈstrɔːt]	adj.	extremely upset and anxious so that you cannot think clearly 心烦意乱的；心急如焚的；发狂的
7. massage [ˈmæsɑːʒ]	v.	to rub and press a person's body with the hands to reduce pain in the muscles and joints 按摩；推拿
8. tiff [tɪf]	n.	a slight argument between close friends or lovers（朋友或情人之间的）争执，拌嘴，口角
9. retch [retʃ]	v.	to make sounds and movements as if you are vomiting although you do not actually do so 干呕；干哕
10. frail [freɪl]	adj.	(especially of an old person) physically weak and thin 瘦弱的
11. compunction [kəmˈpʌŋkʃn]	n.	a guilty feeling about doing sth 内疚；愧疚
12. bereft [bɪˈreft]	adj.	~ of sth: completely lacking sth; having

		lost sth 完全没有，丧失，失去（某物）
13. grit one's teeth		to bite one's teeth tightly together 咬紧牙关
14. wrest [rest]	v.	to take sth from sb that they do not want to give, suddenly or violently 抢，夺（物品）
15. prise [praɪz]	v.	to use force to separate sth from sth else 强行使分开；撬开
16. strike a chord		to say or do sth that makes people feel sympathy or enthusiasm 引起同情（或共鸣）
17. perspiration [ˌpɜːspəˈreɪʃn]	n.	drops of liquid that form on your skin when you are hot 汗；汗珠

第三十回

宝钗借扇机带双敲　龄官划蔷痴及局外[1]

Pao-chai Uses a Fan to Make an Insinuation
Ling-kuan Writes on the Ground and a Foolish Young Man Is Touched[1] (Yang)

Bao-chai speaks of a fan and castigates her deriders
Charmante scratches a 'qiang' and mystifies a beholder[1] (Hawkes)

一、本回概述

　　宝、黛二人口角后，心生悔意，彼此惺惺相惜，和好如初。熙凤见二人和好，便带他们去见贾母，宝钗亦在场。宝玉当众将宝钗比作杨妃，宝钗心中不快，便以典故"负荆请罪"讽刺宝、黛，二人羞愧不已。宝玉去见王夫人时，与丫鬟金钏打闹嬉笑，王夫人震怒，将金钏逐出贾府。宝玉见状，无趣地溜入大观园，蔷薇架下，听到哽噎之声，原来是龄官在用簪画"蔷"，画完一个又一个，局外的宝玉不由得看痴了，顿生同情恻隐之心。

二、篇章节选

原文

宝玉心中想道:"难道这也是个痴丫头,又像颦儿来葬花不成?"因又自叹道:"若真也葬花,可谓'东施效颦',不但不为新特,且更可厌了。"[2] 想毕,便要叫那女子,说:"你不用跟着那林姑娘学了。"话未出口,幸而再看时,这女孩子面生,不是个侍儿,倒像是那十二个学戏的女孩子之内的,却辨不出他是生旦净丑那一个角色来。[3] 宝玉忙把舌头一伸,将口掩住,[4] 自己想道:"幸而不曾造次。上两次皆因造次了,颦儿也生气,宝儿也多心,如今再得罪了他们,越发没意思了。"

一面想,一面又恨认不得这个是谁。再留神细看,[5] 只见这女孩子眉蹙春山,眼颦秋水,面薄腰纤,袅袅婷婷,大有林黛玉之态。宝玉早又不忍弃他而去,只管痴看。[6] 只见他虽然用金簪划地,并不是掘土埋花,竟是向土上画字。宝玉用眼随着簪子的起落,一直一画一点一勾的看了去,数一数,十八笔。自己又在手心里用指头按着他方才下笔的规矩写了,猜是个什么字。写成一想,原来就是个蔷薇花的"蔷"字。

宝玉想道:"必定是他也要作诗填词。这会子见了这花,因有所感,[7] 或者偶成了两句,一时兴至恐忘,在地下画着推敲,也未可知。且看他底下再写什么。"一面想,一面又看,只见那女孩子还在那里画呢,画来画去,还是个"蔷"字。再看,还是个"蔷"字。里面的原是早已痴了,画完一个又画一个,[8] 已经画了有几千个"蔷"。外面的不觉也看痴了,两个眼睛珠儿只管随着簪子动,心里却想:"这女孩子一定有什么话说不出来的大心事,才这样个形景。外面既是这个形景,心里不知怎么熬煎。[9] 看他的模样儿这般单薄,心里那里还搁的住熬煎。可恨我不能替你分些过来。"[10]

杨译

"Can this be another absurd maid come to bury flowers like Tai-yu?" he wondered in some amusement. "If so, she's 'Tung Shih imitating Hsi Shih,' which

isn't original but rather tiresome."[2]

He was on the point of calling out to the girl, "It's no use your trying to copy Miss Lin!" when he realized she was not one of the maids but looked like one of the twelve actresses, although he could not remember which role she played.[3] He grimaced then hastily covered his mouth.[4]

"It's a good thing I held my tongue," he told himself. "I've already annoyed Tai-yu and hurt Pao-chai's feelings by my tactlessness. It would be still more senseless to offend any of these girls."

With these reflections, he felt put out at not being able to identify the girl and he studied her more closely.[5] With her finely arched eyebrows and limpid eyes, her delicate features, slender waist and graceful movements, she bore a striking resemblance to Tai-yu. He stood staring, unable to tear himself away.[6] And now he observed that instead of using her hairpin to bury flowers she was writing something with it on the ground.

Pao-yu followed the pin with his eyes as it moved up and down. He counted the strokes—vertical, horizontal, dotted and curved—there were seventeen in all. Then he traced them in the same order on his palm and discovered that this was the character *chiang* for "rose."

"She must be trying to write a poem," he thought, "and these flowers have suggested the idea for a couple of lines.[7] For fear of forgetting it, she's tracing the character while she thinks it out. Yes, that may be it. Let me see what else she writes."

He went on watching as the girl went on writing, but she merely repeated the same character.

Lost in thought, the girl by the trellis traced one *chiang* after another[8] until she had written several dozen, while Pao-yu watched raptly from the other side, following the movements of the pin with his eyes.

"She must have some secret anxiety preying on her mind to carry on like this,"[9] he reflected. "Yet she looks too delicate to stand much anxiety. I wish I could share her troubles."[10]

> 霍译

'Can this be some silly maid come here to bury flowers like Frowner?' he wondered.

He was reminded of Zhuang-zi's story of the beautiful Xi-shi's ugly neighbour, whose endeavours to imitate the little frown that made Xi-shi captivating produced an aspect so hideous that people ran from her in terror. The recollection of it made him smile.

'This is "imitating the Frowner" with a vengeance,' he thought, 'if that is really what she is doing. Not merely unoriginal, but downright disgusting!' [2]

'Don't imitate Miss Lin,' he was about to shout; but a glimpse of the girl's face revealed to him just in time that this was no maid, but one of the twelve little actresses from Pear-tree Court—though which of them, since he had seen them only in their make-up on the stage, he was unable to make out. [3] He stuck out his tongue in a grimace and clapped a hand to his mouth. [4]

'Good job I didn't speak too soon,' he thought. 'I've been in trouble twice already today for doing that, once with Frowner and once with Chai. It only needs me to go and upset these twelve actresses as well and I shall be well and truly in the cart!'

His efforts to identify the girl made him study her more closely. [5] It was curious that he should have thought her an imitator of Dai-yu, for she had much of Dai-yu's ethereal grace in her looks: the same delicate face and frail, slender body; the same

... brows like hills in spring,

And eyes like autumn's limpid pools;

—even the same little frown that had often made him compare Dai-yu with Xi-shi of the legend.

It was now quite impossible for him to tear himself away. He watched her fascinated. [6] As he watched, he began to see that what she was doing with the pin was not scratching a hole to bury flowers in, but writing. He followed the movements of her hand, and each vertical and horizontal stroke, each dot and hook that she made he copied with a finger on the palm of his hand. Altogether there were eighteen strokes. He thought for a moment. The character he had just written in his hand was QIANG. The name of the roses which covered the pergola contained the same character: 'Qiang-wei'.

'The sight of the roses has inspired her to write a poem,'[7] he thought. 'Probably she's just thought of a good couplet and wants to write it down before she forgets it; or perhaps she has already composed several lines and wants to work on them a bit. Let's see what she writes next.'

The girl went on writing, and he followed the movements of her hand as before. It was another QIANG. Again she wrote, and again he followed, and again it was a QIANG. It was as though she were under some sort of spell. As soon as she had finished writing one QIANG she began writing another.

QIANG QIANG QIANG QIANG QIANG QIANG QIANG...[8]

He must have watched her write several dozen QIANG's in succession. He seemed to be as much affected by the spell on his side of the pergola as the girl herself was on hers, for his eyeballs continued to follow her pin long after he had learned to anticipate its movements.

'This girl must have something on her mind that she cannot tell anyone about to make her behave in this way,' he thought. 'One can see from her outward behaviour how much she must be suffering inwardly.[9] And she looks so frail. Too frail for suffering. I wish I could bear some of it for you, my dear!'[10]

三、注释评点

【1】本回回目是"宝钗借扇机带双敲　龄官划蔷痴及局外"，杨译是"Pao-chai Uses a Fan to Make an Insinuation　Ling-kuan Writes on the Ground and a Foolish Young Man Is Touched"，上句是一个简单句，下句是由"and"连接的一个并列句，上下句句式不一，长短不一，对仗不够工整。霍译是"Bao-chai speaks of a fan and castigates her deriders　Charmante scratches a 'qiang' and mystifies a beholder"，上下句的结构都是"主语+并列谓语"，句式对仗十分工整。

【2】"可谓'东施效颦'，不但不为新特，且更可厌了。"杨译"If so, she's 'Tung Shih imitating Hsi Shih,' which isn't original but rather tiresome."使用了直译加注的手法，注解在本页页尾，属于文外加注。译者为读者在文外补充了有关西施和东施的解释："Hsi Shih was a famous beauty in the ancient kingdom of Yueh. Tung Shih was an ugly girl who tried to imitate her ways."霍译"'This is "imitating the Frowner" with a vengeance,' he thought, 'if that is really what she is doing. Not merely unoriginal, but downright disgusting!'"译者在前文增译了"He was reminded of Zhuang-zi's story of the beautiful Xi-shi's ugly neighbour, whose endeavours to imitate the little frown that made Xi-shi captivating produced an aspect so hideous that people ran from her in terror. The recollection of it made him smile."可以看出，译者用文内加注的手法向英语读者解释了"东施效颦"的故事。文内加注的好处是不打扰读者阅读的连贯性。

【3】"想毕，便要叫那女子，说：'你不用跟着那林姑娘学了。'话未出口，幸而再看时，这女孩子面生，不是个侍儿，倒像是那十二个学戏的女孩子之内的，却辨不出他是生旦净丑那一个角色来。"杨译"He was on the point of calling out to the girl, 'It's no use your trying to copy Miss Lin!' when he realized she was not one of the maids but looked like one of the twelve actresses, although he could not remember which role she played."译者通过"when""not… but..."和"although"进行句内连接。霍译"'Don't imitate Miss Lin,' he was about to shout; but a glimpse of the girl's face revealed to him just in time that this was no maid, but one of the twelve little actresses from Pear-tree Court—though which of them, since he had seen them only in their make-up on the stage, he was unable to make out."译者通过"but""no… but..."和"though"进行句内连接。另外，霍译中有一处增译"since he had seen them only in their make-up on the stage"，用来解释宝玉为何认不出龄官，使得上下文的逻辑更加严谨，语义更加丰满。

【4】"宝玉忙把舌头一伸，将口掩住"一句，杨译是"He grimaced then hastily covered his mouth."霍译是"He stuck out his tongue in a grimace and

clapped a hand to his mouth."相比杨译,霍译的语言更为生动形象,成功地再现了宝玉当时的神情和动作。

【5】"一面想,一面又恨认不得这个是谁。再留神细看"一句,杨译是"With these reflections, he felt put out at not being able to identify the girl and he studied her more closely."译者将汉语中的并列结构"一面……一面……"译为偏正结构:将"一面想"译为介词短语"With these reflections",原文中的动词"想"转变为译文中的名词"reflections";将"一面又恨认不得这个是谁"译为句子的主干部分(并列句的第一个分句"he felt put out at not being able to identify the girl"),译者使用了人称主语"he"。霍译是"His efforts to identify the girl made him study her more closely."译者省译了"一面想",将"一面又恨认不得这个是谁"和"再留神细看"两句译为一个句子;与杨译不同的是,译者使用了物化主语"His efforts to identify the girl"。

【6】"宝玉早又不忍弃他而去,只管痴看"一句,杨译"He stood staring, unable to tear himself away."用句子化短语法将含有动词的汉语小句"宝玉早又不忍弃他而去"译为形容词短语"unable to tear himself away",在译文中充当主语"He"的补足语。霍译是"It was now quite impossible for him to tear himself away. He watched her fascinated."译者将"痴"译为形容词"fascinated",在译文的第二句中充当主语"He"的补足语。

【7】"这会子见了这花,因有所感"一句,杨译是"... these flowers have suggested the idea for a couple of lines."霍译是"The sight of the roses has inspired her to write a poem..."两位译者使用同样的方法,将原文的两个小句合译为一句,即:用句子化短语法将小句"这会子见了这花"分别译为名词短语"these flowers"和"The sight of the roses",在各自的译文中充当主语。

【8】"画完一个又画一个"一句,杨译是"... the girl by the trellis traced one *chiang* after another",霍译是"As soon as she had finished writing one QIANG she began writing another. QIANG QIANG QIANG QIANG QIANG QIANG QIANG..."相比杨译,霍译使用了具有创造性的译写策略,增加了译文的生动性。

【9】"外面既是这个形景,心里不知怎么熬煎"一句,杨译是"She must

have some secret anxiety preying on her mind to carry on like this",霍译是"One can see from her outward behaviour how much she must be suffering inwardly." 相比杨译,霍译使用意思相反的"outward"和"inwardly",对应翻译原文中的"外面"和"心里",译文形式上更接近原文,语义表达得也更加完整。

【10】"看他的模样儿这般单薄,心里那里还搁的住熬煎。可恨我不能替你分些过来。"杨译是"Yet she looks too delicate to stand much anxiety. I wish I could share her troubles."译文的第一句使用"too... to..."进行句内连接。霍译是"And she looks so frail. Too frail for suffering. I wish I could bear some of it for you, my dear!'" 译文前两句都含有"frail"一词,使得句子在语义上衔接得更加紧密,表达出宝玉对龄官的同情恻隐之心;第三句中增译了"my dear",恰到好处地体现出宝玉怜香惜玉、柔情似水的性格特点。在翻译"可恨我不能替你分些过来"时,两位译者在动词wish之后的宾语从句中,都使用了虚拟语气:"I could share her troubles"和"I could bear some of it for you",说明这只是宝玉的主观愿望。

四、词汇表

1. grimace [grɪˈmeɪs]　　v.　　to make an ugly expression with your face to show pain, disgust, etc.（因痛苦、厌恶等）做鬼脸,做怪相

2. resemblance [rɪˈzembləns]　　n.　　the fact of being or looking similar to sb 相似；相像

3. stroke [strəʊk]　　n.　　a mark made by moving a pen, brush, etc. once across a surface 一笔；一画；笔画

4. trace [treɪs]　　v.　　to draw a line or lines on a surface 画（线）

5. trellis [ˈtrelɪs]　　n.　　a light frame made of long narrow pieces of wood that cross each other, used to

		support climbing plants（支撑攀援植物的）棚、架子
6. prey on one's mind		(of a thought, problem, etc.) to make one think and worry about it all the time（想法、问题等）萦绕心头；使耿耿于怀
7. captivating [ˈkæptɪveɪtɪŋ]	adj.	taking all your attention; very attractive and interesting 迷人的；有魅力的；有吸引力的
8. hideous [ˈhɪdiəs]	adj.	very ugly or unpleasant 十分丑陋的；令人厌恶的
9. with a vengeance		to a greater degree than is expected or usual 程度更深地；出乎意料地
10. downright [ˈdaʊnraɪt]	adv.	used as a way of emphasizing sth negative or unpleasant（强调负面的或令人不快的事物）彻头彻尾地；完全地
11. ethereal [ɪˈθɪəriəl]	adj.	extremely delicate and light; seeming to belong to another more spiritual world 优雅的；轻飘的；超凡的
12. pergola [ˈpɜːɡələ]	n.	an arch in a garden/yard with a frame for plants to grow over and through 花架；蔓藤架
13. couplet [ˈkʌplət]	n.	two lines of poetry of equal length one after another 对句（相连的两行长度相等的诗句）；对联

撕扇子作千金一笑　　因麒麟伏白首双星[1]

A Torn Fan Wins a Smile from a Maid
A Pair of Unicorns Suggest a Match [1] (Yang)

A torn fan is the price of silver laughter
And a lost kylin is the clue to a happy marriage [1] (Hawkes)

一、本回概述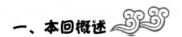

宝玉误踢袭人，心中不安。端阳宴会过于平淡，大家都无精打采，宝玉更觉闷闷不乐。晴雯失手跌折扇子，宝玉借机发泄郁闷，不料晴雯天性好胜，与宝玉针锋相对，对袭人冷嘲热讽，宝玉气愤不已。过后二人和解，上演了一出"晴雯撕扇"的好戏。湘云到贾府做客，与众姐妹重逢，好不欢喜。闲时，湘云与翠缕观赏池中荷花，一时兴起，从荷花扯到阴阳二气，并偶然捡到宝玉遗失的金麒麟。

第三十一回

二、篇章节选

原文

晴雯笑道:"我慌张的很,连扇子还跌折了,那里还配打发吃果子。倘或再打破了盘子,还更了不得呢。"宝玉笑道:"你爱打就打,这些东西原不过是借人所用,你爱这样,我爱那样,各自性情不同。[2]比如那扇子原是扇的,你要撕着玩也可以使得,只是不可生气时拿他出气。[3]就如杯盘,原是盛东西的,你喜欢听那一声响,就故意的碎了也可以使得,只是别在生气时拿他出气。这就是爱物了。"[4]晴雯听了,笑道:"既这么说,你就拿了扇子来我撕。我最喜欢撕的。"[5]宝玉听了,便笑着递与他。晴雯果然接过来,嗤的一声,撕了两半,接着嗤嗤又听几声。宝玉在旁笑着说:[6]"响的好,再撕响些!"

正说着,只见麝月走过来,笑道:"少作些孽罢。"宝玉赶上来,一把将他手里的扇子也夺了递与晴雯。晴雯接了,也撕了几半子,二人都大笑。[7]麝月道:"这是怎么说,拿我的东西开心儿?"宝玉笑道:"打开扇子匣子你拣去,什么好东西!"麝月道:"既这么说,就把匣子搬了出来,让他尽力的撕,岂不好?"宝玉笑道:"你就搬去。"麝月道:"我可不造这孽。他也没折了手,叫他自己搬去。"晴雯笑着,倚在床上[8]说道:"我也乏了,明儿再撕罢。"宝玉笑道:"古人云,'千金难买一笑',[9]几把扇子能值几何!"一面说着,一面叫袭人。袭人才换了衣服走出来,[10]小丫头佳蕙过来拾去破扇,大家乘凉,不消细说。

杨译

Ching-wen laughed.

"If I'm so careless that I even break fans, how can I fetch fruit? If I broke a plate too, I'd never hear the end of it."

"You can if you want. Such things are meant to be used. You may like one thing, I another. People's tastes differ.[2] For instance, fans are meant for fanning; but if I choose to break one for fun, what's wrong with that? But we shouldn't break things to work off a fit of temper.[3] It's the same with cups or plates which are for serving things in. If you smash them because you like the sound, all right. Just don't work off your temper on them. That's what's called caring for things."[4]

"If that's so, get me a fan to tear up. I love ripping things apart."[5]

With a smile he handed her his own. Sure enough, she ripped it in two, then tore it to pieces.

Pao-yu chuckled.[6]

"Well done! Try and make a bigger noise."

Just then along came Sheh-yueh.

"What a wicked waste!" she cried. "Stop it."

Pao-yu's answer was to snatch her fan from her and give it to Ching-wen, who promptly tore it up and joined in his loud laughter.[7]

"What's the idea?" demanded Sheh-yueh. "Spoiling my fan—is that your idea of fun?"

"Just pick another from the fan case," Pao-yu told her. "What's so wonderful about a fan?"

"You'd better bring the case out here then and let her tear the whole lot up."

"You bring it." Pao-yu chuckled.

"I won't do anything of the sort. She's not broken her wrist, let *her* fetch it."

"I'm tired." Ching-wen lay back laughing.[8] "I'll tear up some more tomorrow."

"You know the ancient saying," put in Pao-yu. "'A thousand pieces of gold can hardly purchase a smile.'[9] And what are a few fans worth?"

He called for Hsi-jen, who came out having just changed into clean clothes[10] and got little Chia-hui to clear away the broken fans. Then they sat outside for a while enjoying the cool.

霍译

Skybright smiled.

'You've already told me once today how clumsy I am. I can't even drop a fan

without treading on it. So I'm much too clumsy to get your fruit for you. Suppose I were to break a plate. That would be terrible!'

'If you *want* to break it, by all means break it,' said Bao-yu. 'These things are there for our use. What we use them *for* is a matter of individual taste.^[2] For example, fans are made for fanning with; but if you prefer to tear them up because it gives you pleasure, there's no reason why you shouldn't. What you *mustn't* do is to use them as objects to vent your anger on.^[3] It's the same with plates and cups. Plates and cups are made to put food and drink in. But if you want to smash them on purpose because you like the noise, it's perfectly all right to do so. As long as you don't get into a passion and start taking it out on *things*—that is the golden rule.'^[4]

'All right then,' said Skybright with a mischievous smile. 'Give me your fan to tear. I love the sound of a fan being torn.'^[5]

Bao-yu held it out to her. She took it eagerly and—chah! —promptly tore it in half. And again—chah! chah! chah! —she tore it several more times. Bao-yu, an appreciative onlooker, laughed and encouraged her.^[6]

'Well torn! Well torn! Now again—a really loud one!'

Just then Musk appeared. She stared at them indignantly.

'Don't do that!' she said. 'It's *wicked* to waste things like that.'

But Bao-yu leaped up to her, snatched the fan from her hand, and passed it to Skybright, who at once tore it into several pieces. The two of them, Bao-yu and Skybright, then burst into uproarious laughter.^[7]

'What do you think you're doing?' said Musk. 'That's *my fan* you've just ruined.'

'What's an old fan?' said Bao-yu. 'Open up the fan box and get yourself another.'

'If that's your attitude,' said Musk, 'we might as well carry out the whole boxful and let her tear away to her heart's content.'

'All right. Go and get it,' said Bao-yu.

'And be born a beggar in my next life?' said Musk. 'No thank you! She hasn't broken her arm. Let her go and get it herself.'

Skybright stretched back on the bed,^[8] smiling complacently. 'I'm rather tired just now. I think I shall tear some more tomorrow.'

Bao-yu laughed.

'The ancients used to say that for one smile of a beautiful woman a thousand taels are well spent. [9] For a few old fans it's cheap at the price!'

He called to Aroma, who had just finished changing into clean clothes, to come outside and join them. [10] Little Melilot came and cleared away the broken bits of fan, and everyone sat for a while and enjoyed the cool.

But our narrative supplies no further details of that evening.

三、注释评点

【1】"撕扇子作千金一笑　因麒麟伏白首双星"是本回回目，杨译是"A Torn Fan Wins a Smile from a Maid　A Pair of Unicorns Suggest a Match"，上下两句都是主谓宾结构；霍译是"A torn fan is the price of silver laughter　And a lost kylin is the clue to a happy marriage"，上下两句都是主系表结构，且句式对仗十分工整：主语都是名词短语："A torn fan"和"a lost kylin"，其中的两个过去分词"torn"和"lost"分别修饰两个名词"fan"和"kylin"；表语都是由名词+介词+名词短语构成的。

【2】"这些东西原不过是借人所用，你爱这样，我爱那样，各自性情不同"一句，意思是说"大家性情不同，使用东西的方式就不同：比如有人喜欢用扇子取凉，有人就喜欢撕扇取乐"。杨译是"Such things are meant to be used. You may like one thing, I another. People's tastes differ." 其中，"You may like one thing, I another." 的意思是"你喜欢这样东西，而我喜欢那样东西"，与原文意思有出入；霍译"These things are there for our use. What we use them *for* is a matter of individual taste." 紧扣原文，表达出"大家性情不同，对同一物件用法各异"的含义。

【3】"你要撕着玩也可以使得，只是不可生气时拿他出气"一句，杨译是"(For instance, fans are meant for fanning;) but if I choose to break one for fun, what's wrong with that? But we shouldn't break things to work off a fit of temper."

译文由两个句子构成，译者使用"but""if"和"But"进行连句：在第一句中，"but"和"if"用于句内连接，其中"but"与前文关联，"if"与后文关联；第二句句首的"But"是句际连接词。霍译是"For example, fans are made for fanning with; but if you prefer to tear them up because it gives you pleasure, there's no reason why you shouldn't. What you *mustn't* do is to use them as objects to vent your anger on."该译文也是由两个句子构成。译者使用了"but""if"和"because"进行句内连接。两个译文都体现出意合语言（汉语）向形合语言（英语）转化时，要增加表示逻辑关系的连词。"work off a fit of temper"和"vent one's anger on sth"都是"发怒、生气"的意思。

【4】"你喜欢听那一声响，就故意的碎了也可以使得，只是别在生气时拿他出气。这就是爱物了"一句，杨译是"If you smash them because you like the sound, all right. Just don't work off your temper on them. That's what's called caring for things."译文的第一句使用"If"和"because"进行句内连接。霍译是"But if you want to smash them on purpose because you like the noise, it's perfectly all right to do so. As long as you don't get into a passion and start taking it out on *things*—that is the golden rule."译文的第一句使用"But""if"和"because"进行连句："But"是和前文进行句际连接，"if"和"because"用于句内连接。同注【3】一样，这两个译文再次体现出意合语言（汉语）向形合语言（英语）转化时，要增加表示逻辑关系的连词。

【5】"我最喜欢撕的"一句，杨译"I love ripping things apart"是喜欢撕东西的意思；霍译"I love the sound of a fan being torn"的意思是晴雯喜欢撕扇子的声音。霍译依据的是程高本，此句在程高本中的表述是："我喜欢听撕的声儿。"

【6】"宝玉在旁笑着说"一句，杨译"Pao-yu chuckled."省译了"在旁"；霍译"Bao-yu, an appreciative onlooker, laughed and encouraged her."使用词性转化的翻译技巧，将动词"在旁"译为名词短语"an appreciative onlooker"，在译文中充当主语"Bao-yu"的同位语。

【7】"宝玉赶上来，一把将他手里的扇子也夺了递与晴雯。晴雯接了，也撕了几半子，二人都大笑。"此句包含多个动词：赶、夺、递、接、撕、大笑，

是汉语中典型的连动句。杨译是 "Pao-yu's answer was to snatch her fan from her and give it to Ching-wen, who promptly tore it up and joined in his loud laughter." 译者使用 "and" 和 "who" 进行句内连接，整个句式显得很平衡；宝玉的两个动作 "snatch（夺）her fan" 和 "give（递）it to Ching-wen" 并列充当主句的表语；晴雯的两个动作 "tore it up（撕）" 和 "joined in his loud laughter（大笑）" 并列充当 "who" 引导的定语从句的谓语。霍译是 "But Bao-yu leaped up to her, snatched the fan from her hand, and passed it to Skybright, who at once tore it into several pieces. The two of them, Bao-yu and Skybright, then burst into uproarious laughter." 该译文由两句构成，第一句中，译者使用 "But" "and" 和 "who" 进行连句："But" 用于句际连接，"and" 和 "who" 用于句内连接。另外，译者接连描述了宝玉的三个动作："leaped（赶）up to her" "snatched（夺）the fan from her hand" 和 "passed（递）it to Skybright"，其间用 "and" 连接，充分表达出宝玉迫不及待的心情。

【8】"倚在床上"一句，杨译是 "Ching-wen lay back laughing"，霍译是 "Skybright stretched back on the bed"。相比杨译中的动词 "lay"，霍译使用的 "stretched" 一词，更加生动贴切地表达出晴雯痛快淋漓地撕扇后舒畅的心情。

【9】"千金难买一笑"一句，杨译 "A thousand pieces of gold can hardly purchase a smile." 采用了直译手法；霍译 "... for one smile of a beautiful woman a thousand taels are well spent." 增译了 "of a beautiful woman"，译者用文内补偿的手法将 "千金一笑" 的典故部分翻译了出来。

【10】"一面叫袭人。袭人才换了衣服走出来"一句中，出现了两次"袭人"。杨译是 "He called for Hsi-jen, who came out having just changed into clean clothes"，霍译是 "He called to Aroma, who had just finished changing into clean clothes, to come outside and join them"，两个译文都使用了"who"引导的定语从句，一是化解了汉语中的重复现象（"袭人"一词），二是起到连句效果，将汉语的短句转化为英语的长句。

四、词汇表

1. work sth off		to get rid of sth, especially a strong feeling, by using physical effort（通过消耗体力）宣泄感情
2. rip [rɪp]	v.	to tear sth, often suddenly or violently（突然或猛烈地）撕破，裂开
3. wicked ['wɪkɪd]	adj.	morally bad 邪恶的；缺德的
4. snatch [snætʃ]	v.	to take sth quickly and often rudely or roughly 一把抓起；一把夺过
5. vent [vent]	v.	to express feelings, especially anger strongly 表达，发泄（感情，尤指愤怒）
6. mischievous ['mɪstʃɪvəs]	adj.	enjoying playing tricks and annoying people 顽皮的；捣蛋的
7. appreciative [ə'priːʃətɪv]	adj.	showing pleasure or enjoyment 欣赏的；赏识的
8. onlooker ['ɒnlʊkə(r)]	n.	a person who watches sth that is happening but is not involved in it 旁观者
9. uproarious [ʌp'rɔːriəs]	adj.	very noisy because a lot of people are laughing or shouting 喧闹的；人声鼎沸的
10. stretch [stretʃ]	v.	to put your arms or legs out straight and contract your muscles 伸展；舒展
11. complacent [kəm'pleɪsnt]	adj.	too satisfied with yourself or with a situation, so that you do not feel that any change is necessary 自满的；自鸣得意的
	adv.	complacently

第三十二回

诉肺腑心迷活宝玉　　含耻辱情烈死金钏

An Avowal Leaves Pao-yu Bemused
Disgrace Drives Chin-chuan to Suicide (Yang)

Bao-yu demonstrates confusion of mind by making his declaration to the wrong person
And Golden shows an unconquerable spirit by ending her humiliation in death
(Hawkes)

一、本回概述

　　湘云、袭人闲聊，宝钗贬黛，宝玉不满；又因湘云劝他学仕途经济，更加愤懑，竟在她们面前称赞黛玉，恰被黛玉听到，不禁又喜、又惊、又悲、又叹。宝玉向黛玉倾诉肺腑，表明心迹，劝黛玉"放心"，安心养病，他的真诚让黛玉动容。金钏被撵出后，不堪其辱，投井而死，在贾府上下一石激起千层浪，王夫人深感不安，宝钗不知内情，只一味劝慰王夫人，宝玉知晓此事，后悔伤心，并因此受到母亲的苛责。

二、篇章节选

原文

　　林黛玉听了这话,不觉又喜又惊,又悲又叹。[1]所喜者,[2]果然自己眼力不错,素日认他是个知己,果然是个知己。[3]所惊者,他在人前一片私心称扬于我,其亲热厚密,竟不避嫌疑。所叹者,你既为我之知己,自然我亦可为你之知己矣;既你我为知己,则又何必有金玉之论哉;既有金玉之论,亦该你我有之,则又何必来一宝钗哉![4]所悲者,父母早逝,虽有铭心刻骨之言,无人为我主张。况近日每觉神思恍惚,病已渐成,医者更云气弱血亏,恐致劳怯之症。[5]你我虽为知己,但恐自不能久待;你纵为我知己,奈我薄命何!想到此间,不禁滚下泪来。[6]待进去相见,自觉无味,便一面拭泪,一面抽身回去了。

　　……

　　宝玉瞅了半天,方说道"你放心"三个字。林黛玉听了,怔了半天,方说道:"我有什么不放心的?我不明白这话。你倒说说怎么放心不放心?"宝玉叹了一口气,问道:"你果不明白这话?难道我素日在你身上的心都用错了?连你的意思若体贴不着,就难怪你天天为我生气了。"林黛玉道:"果然我不明白放心不放心的话。"宝玉点头叹道:"好妹妹,你别哄我。果然不明白这话,不但我素日之意白用了,且连你素日待我之意也都辜负了。你皆因总是不放心的原故,才弄了一身病。[7]但凡宽慰些,这病也不得一日重似一日。"[8]

　　林黛玉听了这话,如轰雷掣电,细细思之,竟比自己肺腑中掏出来的还觉恳切,[9]竟有万句言语,满心要说,只是半个字也不能吐,却怔怔的望着他。此时宝玉心中也有万句言语,不知从那一句上说起,却也怔怔的望着黛玉。[10]两个人怔了半天,林黛玉只咳了一声,两眼不觉滚下泪来,回身便要走。宝玉忙上前拉住,说道:"好妹妹,且略站住,我说一句话再走。"林黛玉一面拭泪,一面将手推开,[11]说道:"有什么可说的。你的话我早知道了!"口里说着,却头也不回竟去了。

对话杨宪益、霍克斯——《红楼梦》英译赏析(第一至四十回)

宝玉站着,只管发起呆来。[12]

杨译

This surprised and delighted Tai-yu but also distressed and grieved her.[1] She was delighted to know[2] she had not misjudged him, for he had now proved just as understanding as she had always thought.[3] Surprised that he had been so indiscreet as to acknowledge his preference for her openly. Distressed because their mutual understanding ought to preclude all talk about gold matching jade, or she instead of Pao-chai should have the gold locket to match his jade amulet.[4] Grieved because her parents had died, and although his preference was so clear there was no one to propose the match for her. Besides, she had recently been suffering from dizzy spells which the doctor had warned might end in consumption, as she was so weak and frail.[5] Dear as she and Pao-yu were to each other, she might not have long to live. And what use was their affinity if she were fated to die? These thoughts sent tears coursing down her cheeks.[6] And therefore instead of entering she turned away, wiping her tears.

……

Pao-yu fixed his eyes on her.

After a while he said gently, "You mustn't worry."

Tai-yu gazed at him in silence.

"Worry?" she repeated at last. "I don't understand. What do you mean?"

"Don't you really understand?" He sighed. "Could it be that since I've known you all my feelings for you have been wrong? If I can't even enter into *your* feelings, then you're quite right to be angry with me all the time."

"I really don't understand what you mean by telling me not to worry."

"Dear cousin, don't tease." Pao-yu nodded and sighed. "If you really don't understand, all my devotion's been wasted and even your feeling for me has been thrown away. You ruin your health by worrying so much.[7] If you'd take things less to heart, your illness wouldn't be getting worse every day."[8]

These words struck Tai-yu like a thunderbolt. As she turned them over in her

mind, they seemed closer to her innermost thoughts than if wrung from her own heart. [9] There were a thousand things she longed to say, yet she could not utter a word. She just stared at him in silence. As Pao-yu was in similar case, he too stared at her without a word. [10] So they stood transfixed for some time. Then Tai-yu gave a choking cough and tears rolled down her cheeks. She was turning to go when Pao-yu caught hold of her.

"Dear cousin, wait. Just let me say one word."

She dried her tears with one hand, repulsing him with the other. [11]

"What more is there to say? I understand."

She hurried off without one look behind, while he just stood there like a man in a trance. [12]

霍译

Mingled emotions of happiness, alarm, sorrow and regret assailed her. [1]

Happiness: [2]

Because after all (she thought) I wasn't mistaken in my judgement of you. I always thought of you as a true friend, and I was right. [3]

Alarm:

Because if you praise me so unreservedly in front of other people, your warmth and affection are sure, sooner or later, to excite suspicion and be misunderstood.

Regret:

Because if you are my true friend, then I am yours and the two of us are a perfect match. But in that case why did there have to be all this talk of 'the gold and the jade'? Alternatively, if there had to be all this talk of gold and jade, why weren't we the two to have them? Why did there have to be a Bao-chai with her golden locket? [4]

Sorrow:

Because though there are things of burning importance to be said, without a father or a mother I have no one to say them for me. And besides, I feel so muzzy lately and I know that my illness is gradually gaining a hold on me. (The doctors say that the weakness and anaemia I suffer from may be the beginnings of a consumption.) [5] So even if I *am* your true love, I fear I may not be able to wait for you. And even though you are mine, you can do nothing to alter my fate.

At that point in her reflections she began to weep; [6] and feeling in no fit state to be seen, she turned away from the door and began to make her way back again.

……

For some moments he stood there motionless, staring at her. Then he said:

'*Don't worry*!'

Hearing this, Dai-yu herself was silent for some moments.

'Why *should* I worry?' she said eventually. 'I don't understand you. Would you mind telling me what you are talking about?'

Bao-yu sighed.

'Do you really not understand? Can I really have been all this time mistaken in my feelings towards you? If you don't even know your *own* mind, it's small wonder that you're always getting angry on *my* account.'

'I really don't understand what you mean about not worrying,' said Dai-yu.

Bao-yu sighed again and shook his head.

'My dear coz, don't think you can fool me. If you don't understand what I've just said, then not only have *my* feelings towards *you* been all along mistaken, but all that *you* have ever felt for *me* has been wasted, too. It's because you worry so much that you've made yourself ill. [7] If only you could take things a bit easier, your illness wouldn't go on getting more and more serious all the time.' [8]

Dai-yu was thunderstruck. He had read her mind—had seen inside her more clearly than if she had plucked out her entrails and held them out for his inspection. [9] And now there were a thousand things that she wanted to tell him; yet though she was dying to speak, she was unable to utter a single syllable and stood there like a simpleton, gazing at him in silence.

Bao-yu, too, had a thousand things to say, but he, too, stood mutely gazing at her, not knowing where to begin. [10]

After the two of them had stared at each other for some considerable time in silence, Dai-yu heaved a deep sigh. The tears gushed from her eyes and she turned and walked away. Bao-yu hurried after her and caught at her dress.

'Coz dear, stop a moment! Just let me say one word.'

As she wiped her eyes with one hand, Dai-yu pushed him away from her with the other.[11]

'There's nothing to say. I already know what you want to tell me.'

She said this without turning back her head, and having said it, passed swiftly on her way. Bao-yu remained where he was standing, gazing after her in silent stupefaction.[12]

三、注释评点

【1】"林黛玉听了这话，不觉又喜又惊，又悲又叹"一句，杨译是"This surprised and delighted Tai-yu but also distressed and grieved her."霍译是"Mingled emotions of happiness, alarm, sorrow and regret assailed her."两位译者都舍弃了原文的人格主语"黛玉"，选用了物化主语"This"和"Mingled emotions"；霍译中增译的"Mingled emotions"统领后面四种具体的情感。另外，关于"喜、惊、悲、叹"这四种感情，杨译使用了四个动词"surprised" "delighted" "distressed"和"grieved"；霍译使用了四个名词"happiness" "alarm" "sorrow"和"regret"，跟在"Mingled emotions of"后面，表达出黛玉这种复杂且交缠的情感。

【2】"所喜者……所惊者……所叹者……所悲者……"一段的翻译，杨译"She was delighted to know... Surprised that... Distressed because... Grieved because..."使用四个形容词"delighted" "Surprised" "Distressed"和"Grieved"，分别对应原文中的四种情感："喜""惊""叹"和"悲"；译者使用了主系表结构以及"for"和"because"引导的原因状语从句。霍译"Happiness:... Alarm:... Regret:... Sorrow:..."使用了四个名词来翻译原文中的四种情感；每个名词不仅独立成段，而且还各自统领独立的段落。

【3】"果然自己眼力不错，素日认他是个知己，果然是个知己"一句，杨译是"... she had not misjudged him, for he had now proved just as understanding as she had always thought." 译者使用归化策略，将"眼力不错"译为"she had not misjudged him"，其后跟"for"引导的原因状语从句，这里增加的连词"for"使汉语中隐性的因果关系在英语中显化了；此外，"proved"一词用得很恰当，表明黛玉经过一段时间的观察，证明宝玉是个知己；译者用形容词"understanding"对应原文的名词"知己"，旨在强调知己之间的心灵相通。霍译是"Because after all (she thought) I wasn't mistaken in my judgement of you. I always thought of you as a true friend, and I was right." 译者也用归化的策略，将"眼力不错"译为"I wasn't mistaken in my judgement of you"；对于"知己"一词，霍译是"a true friend"，意义显得太宽泛。

【4】"你既为我之知己，自然我亦可为你之知己矣；既你我为知己，则又何必有金玉之论哉；既有金玉之论，亦该你我有之，则又何必来一宝钗哉！"杨译是"… their mutual understanding ought to preclude all talk about gold matching jade, or she instead of Pao-chai should have the gold locket to match his jade amulet." 译者用句子化短语法将"你既为我之知己，自然我亦可为你之知己矣"译为名词短语"their mutual understanding"，在译文中充当主语。霍译是"Because if you are my true friend, then I am yours and the two of us are a perfect match. But in that case why did there have to be all this talk of 'the gold and the jade'? Alternatively, if there had to be all this talk of gold and jade, why weren't we the two to have them? Why did there have to be a Bao-chai with her golden locket?" 该译文一共包含四个句子，所以不可避免地使用了很多承上启下的词汇，如：第一句中的"Because""if""then"和"and"，第二句中的"But"和"in that case"，第三句中的"Alternatively"和"if"。可以看出，英语作为形合语言，特别注重句际和句内的逻辑连接。

【5】"况近日每觉神思恍惚，病已渐成，医者更云气弱血亏，恐致劳怯之症"一句，杨译是"Besides, she had recently been suffering from dizzy spells which the doctor had warned might end in consumption, as she was so weak and frail." 译者使用"Besides""which"和"as"进行连句；"医者更云气弱血

亏，恐致劳怯之症"被译为一个定语从句"which the doctor had warned might end in consumption as she was so weak and frail.",从句中包含了插入语"the doctor had warned",以及一个原因状语从句"as she was so weak and frail";"气弱血亏"被译为两个并列的形容词"weak"和"frail"。霍译是"And besides, I feel so muzzy lately and I know that my illness is gradually gaining a hold on me. (The doctors say that the weakness and anaemia I suffer from may be the beginnings of a consumption.)"该译文包含两个句子：第一句中，译者使用"And""besides"和"and"进行连句；第二句中，原文的"气弱血亏"被译为两个并列的名词"weakness"和"anaemia"。

【6】"想到此间，不禁滚下泪来"一句，杨译"These thoughts sent tears coursing down her cheeks."没有使用原文省略的人称主语"黛玉"，而是使用了物化主语"These thoughts"。霍译"At that point in her reflections she began to weep"将含有动词的小句"想到此间"译为介词短语"At that point in her reflections"，同时使用了人称主语"she"。

【7】"你皆因总是不放心的原故，才弄了一身病"一句，原因"皆因总是不放心的原故"在前，结果"弄了一身病"在后，体现出汉语句子的特点是前因后果。杨译"You ruin your health by worrying so much."将结果"you ruin your health"前置，原因"worrying so much"后置，这是英语与汉语表达习惯的不同之处。霍译"It's because you worry so much that you've made yourself ill"则使用了强调句型，强调"because you worry so much"这一原因，与原文的表述非常一致，表达出黛玉皆因不放心才导致一身病。

【8】"但凡宽慰些，这病也不得一日重似一日"一句，杨译"If you'd take things less to heart, your illness wouldn't be getting worse every day"和霍译"If only you could take things a bit easier, your illness wouldn't go on getting more and more serious all the time"都使用了虚拟语气，句式也相近：将"但凡宽慰些"分别译为"If you'd take things less to heart"和"If only you could take things a bit easier"，都很精妙。

【9】"细细思之，竟比自己肺腑中掏出来的还觉恳切"一句，杨译是"As she turned them over in her mind, they seemed closer to her innermost thoughts than if wrung from her own heart."译者首先使用了时间状语从句"as she turned them over in her mind",其中的连词"as"使汉语隐性的逻辑关系在英语这种形合语言中显化;而且译者用词精妙:将"细细思之"译为"she turned them over in her mind",即指黛玉在心中翻来覆去考量,将"自己肺腑中掏出来"译为"wrung from her own heart","wrung"意为"拧、绞出、费力得到",这些用词使得译文十分生动形象。霍译是"He had read her mind—had seen inside her more clearly than if she had plucked out her entrails and held them out for his inspection."虽然语言生动,却易遭人误解,例如,"she had plucked out her entrails and held them out for his inspection",意为"黛玉掏出肺腑,让宝玉查验",与原文意涵有出入:"肺腑中掏出来的"后面省略了"言语"二字,意即"肺腑之言",并非真的"掏出肺腑"的意思。

【10】"竟有万句言语,满心要说,只是半个字也不能吐,却怔怔的望着他。此时宝玉心中也有万句言语,不知从那一句上说起,却也怔怔的望着黛玉。"句中有两处重复的措辞:"万句言语"和"怔怔的望着",这两个语词在文中各出现了两次。杨译是"There were a thousand things she longed to say, yet she could not utter a word. She just stared at him in silence. As Pao-yu was in similar case, he too stared at her without a word."译者将两个"万句言语"分别译为"there were a thousand things she longed to say"和"Pao-yu was in similar case",其中"in similar case"指的就是"there were a thousand things Pao-yu longed to say",译者使用不同的措辞来避免英语中所忌讳的重复现象;两个"怔怔的望着"中的"怔怔的"分别被译为意思相近的"in silence"和"without a word",也避免了表述上的重复。霍译是"And now there were a thousand things that she wanted to tell him; yet though she was dying to speak, she was unable to utter a single syllable and stood there like a simpleton, gazing at him in silence. Bao-yu, too, had a thousand things to say, but he, too, stood mutely gazing at her, not knowing where to begin."译者在翻译"万句言语"时,为了保留原文的艺术风貌,刻意保留了重复现象,即"now there were a thousand things that she wanted to tell him"和"Bao-yu, too, had a thousand things to say"。有趣的是,此处杨译更多地考虑英语的表达习惯,而霍译更多地考虑汉语的表达习

惯。另外，对于"只是半个字也不能吐，却怔怔的望着他"和"不知从那一句上说起，却也怔怔的望着黛玉"两句，霍译都使用了英语中的偏正结构，将其分别译为"she was unable to utter a single syllable and stood there like a simpleton, gazing at him in silence"和"he, too, stood mutely gazing at her, not knowing where to begin"；其中，有些动作以谓语的形式出现，如"was unable to utter"和"stood"；有些动作以现在分词作伴随状语的形式出现，如"gazing"和"not knowing"；"like a simpleton"是增译。

【11】"林黛玉一面拭泪，一面将手推开"一句，两位译者都不约而同地将汉语中表示并列关系的"一面……一面……"处理为英语中的偏正结构。杨译"She dried her tears with one hand, repulsing him with the other."使用了现在分词短语作伴随状语，形成了"一正"（she dried her tears with one hand）"一偏"（repulsing him with the other）的结构。霍译"As she wiped her eyes with one hand, Dai-yu pushed him away from her with the other."使用了"As"引导的时间状语从句，也是"一正"（Dai-yu pushed him away from her with the other）和"一偏"（As she wiped her eyes with one hand）的结构。

【12】"口里说着，却头也不回竟去了。宝玉站着，只管发起呆来。"杨译"She hurried off without one look behind, while he just stood there like a man in a trance."用"while"进行句内连接，表示宝、黛二人的动作同时发生。霍译是"She said this without turning back her head, and having said it, passed swiftly on her way. Bao-yu remained where he was standing, gazing after her in silent stupefaction."译文由两个句子构成，其中有两个现在分词短语：第一句中的"having said it"充当时间状语，这个现在分词短语的完成式，清晰地表明它表述的动作"said"和谓语部分的动作"passed"是先后发生；第二句中的"gazing after her in silent stupefaction"做伴随状语，表示"gazing"这个动作和谓语部分的动作"remained where he was standing"是同时发生。

四、词汇表

1. indiscreet [ˌɪndɪˈskriːt]   adj.   not careful about what you say or do, especially when this embarrasses or offends sb 不慎重的；不审慎的；鲁莽的

2. preclude [prɪˈkluːd]   v.   to prevent sth from happening or sb from doing sth; to make sth impossible 使行不通；阻止；妨碍；排除

3. amulet [ˈæmjʊlət]   n.   a piece of jewelry that some people wear because they think it protects them from bad luck, illness, etc. 护身符，驱邪物（为驱邪防病等佩戴的珠宝）

4. consumption [kənˈsʌmpʃn]   n.   a serious infectious disease of the lungs 肺病；肺痨；肺结核

5. course [kɔːs]   v.   (of liquid) to move or flow quickly 快速地流动；奔流

6. wring [rɪŋ]   v.   **wring sth from/out of sb:** to obtain sth from sb with difficulty, especially by putting pressure on them 从……处费力弄到；从……压榨出

7. transfix [trænsˈfɪks]   v.   to make sb unable to move because they are afraid, surprised, etc.（因恐惧、惊愕等而）使动弹不得；使惊呆

8. repulse [rɪˈpʌls]   v.   to refuse to accept sb's help, attempts to be friendly, etc. 拒绝接受；回绝

9. trance [trɑːns]   n.   a state in which you are thinking so much about sth that you do not notice what is happening around you 出神；发呆

10. unreservedly [ˌʌnrɪˈzɜːvɪdli]	adv.		completely; without hesitating or having any doubts 完全地；坦诚地；无条件地；无保留地
11. alternatively [ɔːlˈtɜːnətɪvli]	adv.		used to introduce a suggestion that is a second choice or possibility（引出第二种选择或可能的建议）要不，或者
12. muzzy [ˈmʌzi]	adj.		unable to think in a clear way 头脑混乱的；迷糊的
13. anaemia [əˈniːmiə]	n.		a medical condition in which sb has too few red cells in their blood, making them look pale and feel weak 贫血（症）
14. thunderstruck [ˈθʌndəstrʌk]	adj		extremely surprised and shocked 大吃一惊
15. entrails [ˈentreɪlz]	n.		[pl.] the organs inside the body of a person or an animal, especially their intestines 内脏；（尤指）肠
16. mutely [ˈmjuːtli]	adv.		without speaking 无言地；一语不发地

手足耽耽小动唇舌　　不肖种种大承笞挞

A Jealous Younger Brother Tells Tales
A Worthless Son Receives a Fearful Flogging (Yang)

*An envious younger brother puts in a malicious word or two
And a scapegrace elder brother receives a terrible chastisement* (Hawkes)

一、本回概述

　　琪官私自外逃，忠顺王府找到宝玉，打探琪官下落。宝玉本想隐瞒，但琪官私赠的茜香罗暴露了两人的私交，宝玉只得说出琪官的藏身之处。金钏投井，身亡命殒，贾环不怀好意，在贾政面前添油加醋，说金钏之死乃宝玉所致。这两件事使贾政颜面扫地，大为光火，盛怒之下，命人暴打宝玉。可怜宝玉被打得皮开肉绽，几近晕厥。贾府上下大惊失措，贾母、王夫人伤心欲绝。最后，贾政在贾母的呵斥下，停止了对宝玉的索命笞挞。

第三十三回

二、篇章节选

原文

　　话未说完，把个贾政气的面如金纸，[1]大喝"快拿宝玉来！"一面说，一面便往里边书房里去，喝令"今日再有人劝我，我把这冠带家私一应交与他与宝玉过去！我免不得做个罪人，把这几根烦恼鬓毛剃去，寻个干净去处自了，也免得上辱先人下生逆子之罪。"[2]众门客仆从见贾政这个形景，便知又是为宝玉了，一个个都是咬指咬舌，连忙退出。那贾政喘吁吁直挺挺坐在椅子上，满面泪痕，一叠声"拿宝玉！拿大棍！拿索子捆上！把各门都关上！有人传信往里头去，立刻打死！"[3]众小厮们只得齐声答应，有几个来找宝玉。

　　那宝玉听见贾政吩咐他"不许动"，早知多凶少吉，那里承望贾环又添了许多的话。[4]正在厅上干转，怎得个人来往里头去捎信，[5]偏生没个人，连焙茗也不知在那里。正盼望时，只见一个老姆姆出来。宝玉如得了珍宝，便赶上来拉他，说道："快进去告诉：老爷要打我呢！快去，快去！要紧，要紧！"宝玉一则急了，说话不明白；二则老婆子偏生又聋，竟不曾听见是什么话，把"要紧"二字只听作"跳井"二字，[6]便笑道："跳井让他跳去，二爷怕什么？"宝玉见是个聋子，便着急道："你出去叫我的小厮来罢。"那婆子道："有什么不了的事？老早的完了。太太又赏了衣服，又赏了银子，怎么不了事的！"

　　宝玉急的跺脚，正没抓寻处，只见贾政的小厮走来，逼着他出去了。贾政一见，眼都红紫了，也不暇问他在外流荡优伶，表赠私物，在家荒疏学业，淫辱母婢等语，只喝令"堵起嘴来，着实打死！"小厮们不敢违拗，只得将宝玉按在凳上，举起大板打了十来下。贾政犹嫌打轻了，一脚踢开掌板的，自己夺过来，咬着牙狠命盖了三四十下。众门客见打的不祥了，忙上前夺劝。[7]贾政那里肯听，说道："你们问问他干的勾当可饶不可饶！素日皆是你们这些人把他酿坏了，到这步田地还来解劝。明日酿到他弑君杀父，你们才不劝不成！"

311

> 杨译

Before he had finished Chia Cheng was livid with fury.[1]

"Fetch Pao-yu! Quick!" he roared.

He strode to his study fuming, "If anybody tries to stop me *this* time, I'll make over to him my official insignia and property and let him serve Pao-yu! How can I escape blame? I'll shave off these few remaining hairs and retire to a monastery, there to atone for disgracing my ancestors by begetting such a monster."[2]

His secretaries and attendants bit their lips or fingers in dismay and hastily withdrew as they heard him raging at Pao-yu again. Then Chia Cheng, panting hard, his cheeks wet with tears, sat stiffly erect in his chair.

"Bring Pao-yu in!" he bellowed. "Fetch the heavy rod! Tie him up! Close all the doors. Anyone who sends word to the inner apartments will be killed on the spot."[3]

The servants had to obey. Some pages went to fetch Pao-yu.

Pao-yu knew he was in for trouble when ordered by his father to wait, but he had no idea of the tale Huan had since told.[4] He paced helplessly up and down the hall, wishing someone would carry the news to the inner apartments;[5] but it so happened that nobody was about—even Pei-ming had disappeared. As he was looking round anxiously, an old nanny finally appeared. He seized on her as if she were a treasure.

"Go in quick!" he cried. "Tell them the master's going to beat me. Do hurry! This is urgent!"

He was too terrified to speak distinctly and the old woman, being hard of hearing, mistook the word "urgent" for "drowning."[6]

"She chose drowning herself," she told him soothingly. "What does it matter to you?"

Her deafness made Pao-yu frantic.

"Go and get my page to come," he begged.

"It's over now. Over and done with. And the mistress has given them clothes and silver too. Don't fret."

Pao-yu was stamping his foot in desperation when his father's servants arrived

and he had perforce to go with them.

Chia Cheng's eyes blazed at the sight of him. He did not even ask his son what he meant by playing about outside and exchanging gifts with actors, or by neglecting his studies at home and attempting to rape his mother's maid.

"Gag him!" he roared. "Beat him to death!"

The attendants dared not disobey. They thrust Pao-yu down on a bench and gave him a dozen strokes with the heavy rod. His father, thinking these strokes too light, kicked aside the man with the rod and snatched it up himself. With clenched teeth he rained down dozens of vicious blows until his secretaries, foreseeing serious consequences, stepped forward to intervene.[7] But Chia Cheng refused to listen.

"Ask *him* if such conduct as his can be pardoned," he cried. "You're the ones who've been spoiling him. When it comes to this do you still intercede for him? Will you still persist when he commits regicide or parricide?"

霍译

Jia Zheng, whose face had now turned to a ghastly gold-leaf colour,[1] interrupted him with a dreadful cry.

'Fetch Bao-yu!'

He began to stride towards his study, shouting to all and sundry as he went.

'If anyone tries to stop me *this* time, I shall make over my house and property and my post at the Ministry and everything else I have to him and Bao-yu. I absolutely refuse to be responsible for the boy any longer. I shall cut off my few remaining hairs (those that worry and wretchedness have left me) and look for some clean and decent spot to end my days in. Perhaps in that way I shall escape the charge of having disgraced my ancestors by rearing this unnatural monster as my son.'[2]

When they saw the state he was in, the literary gentlemen and senior menservants who were waiting for him in the study, guessed that Bao-yu must be the cause of it and, looking at each other with various grimaces, biting their thumbs or sticking their tongues out, hastily retreated from the room. Jia Zheng entered it alone and sat down, stiffly upright, in a chair. He was breathing heavily and his face was bathed in tears. Presently, when he had regained his breath, he barked out a rapid series of commands:

'Bring Bao-yu here. Get a heavy bamboo. Get some rope to tie him with. Close the courtyard gates. If anyone tries to take word through inside, kill him!' [3]

'Sir! — Sir! — Sir!' the terrified pages chorused in unison at each of his commands, and some of them went off to look for Bao-yu.

Jia Zheng's ominous 'Stay where you are' as he went out with the chamberlain had warned Bao-yu that something dire was imminent—though just how much more dire as a result of Jia Huan's malicious intervention he could not have foreseen [4]—and as he stood where his father had left him, he twisted and turned himself about, anxiously looking for some passer-by who could take a message through to the womenfolk inside. [5] But no one came. Even the omnipresent Tealeaf was on this occasion nowhere to be seen. Then suddenly, in answer to his prayers, an old woman appeared—a darling, precious treasure of an old woman (or so she seemed at that moment)—and he dashed forward and clung to her beseechingly.

'Quickly!' he said. 'Go and tell them that Sir Zheng is going to beat me. Quickly! Quickly! Go and tell. GO AND TELL.'

Partly because agitation had made him incoherent and partly because, as ill luck would have it, the old woman was deaf, almost everything he said had escaped her—except for the 'Go and tell', which she misheard as 'in the well'. [6] She smiled at him reassuringly.

'Let her jump in the well then, young master. Don't you worry your pretty head about it!'

Realizing that she had deafness, too, to contend with, he now became quite frantic.

'GO AND TELL MY PAGES.'

'Her wages?' the old woman asked in some surprise. 'Bless you, of course they paid her wages! Her Ladyship gave a whole lot of money towards the funeral as well. And clothes. Paid her wages, indeed!'

Bao-yu stamped his feet in a frenzy of impatience. He was still wondering despairingly how to make her understand when Jia Zheng's pages arrived and forced him to go with them to the study.

Jia Zheng turned a pair of wild and bloodshot eyes on him as he entered. Forgetting the 'riotous and dissipated conduct abroad leading to the unseemly bestowal of impudicities on a theatrical performer' and the 'neglect of proper pursuits and studies at home culminating in the attempted violation of a parent's maidservant' and all the other high-sounding charges he had been preparing to hurl against him, he shouted two brief orders to the pages.

'Gag his mouth. Beat him to death.'

The pages were too frightened not to comply. Two held Bao-yu face downwards on a bench while a third lifted up the flattened bamboo sweep and began to strike him with it across the hams. After about a dozen blows Jia Zheng, not satisfied that his executioner was hitting hard enough, kicked him impatiently aside, wrested the bamboo from his grasp, and, gritting his teeth, brought it down with the utmost savagery on the places that had already been beaten.

At this point the literary gentlemen, sensing that Bao-yu was in serious danger of life and limb, came in again to remonstrate;[7] but Jia Zheng refused to hear them.

'Ask him what he has done and then tell me if you think I should spare him,' he said. 'It is the encouragement of people like you that has corrupted him; and now, when things have come to this pass, you intercede for him. I suppose you would like me to wait until he commits parricide, or worse. Would you still intercede for him then?'

三、注释评点

【1】"把个贾政气的面如金纸"一句，杨译"Chia Cheng was livid with fury."采用了意译法，译者并未翻译喻体"金纸"；霍译"Jia Zheng, whose face had now turned to a ghastly gold-leaf colour,…"采用了直译法，将"金纸"译为

"gold-leaf"。

【2】"把这几根烦恼鬓毛剃去，寻个干净去处自了，也免得上辱先人下生逆子之罪。"杨译是"I'll shave off these few remaining hairs and retire to a monastery, there to atone for disgracing my ancestors by begetting such a monster."霍译是"I shall cut off my few remaining hairs (those that worry and wretchedness have left me) and look for some clean and decent spot to end my days in. Perhaps in that way I shall escape the charge of having disgraced my ancestors by rearing this unnatural monster as my son."对于"这几根烦恼鬓毛"的翻译，杨译"these few remaining hairs"省译了"烦恼"二字；霍译"my few remaining hairs (those that worry and wretchedness have left me)"使用括号加注的方法解释了"烦恼"是导致自己只剩几根鬓毛的原因。另外，两位译者对于"上辱先人下生逆子"这个并列结构的处理方式一样，都使用了介词"by"（译文分别是"disgracing my ancestors by begetting such a monster"和"having disgraced my ancestors by rearing this unnatural monster as my son"），把原文中的并列结构转化为英语中的偏正结构，清晰地表达出隐含在汉语中的因果关系，即"因为生逆子所以辱先人"。

【3】"有人传信往里头去，立刻打死！"一句，杨译是"Anyone who sends word to the inner apartments will be killed on the spot."译者使用了定语从句"who sends word to the inner apartments"修饰主语"anyone"，语气过于正式，没有传达出原文"立刻打死"的严厉激烈。霍译是"If anyone tries to take word through inside, kill him!"译者用"If"引导条件状语从句，将汉语的意合结构转化为英语的形合结构；另外，祈使句"kill him"与"立刻打死"传递的命令口气也较为吻合。

【4】"那宝玉听见贾政吩咐他'不许动'，早知多凶少吉，那里承望贾环又添了许多的话。"杨译是"Pao-yu knew he was in for trouble when ordered by his father to wait, but he had no idea of the tale Huan had since told."霍译是"Jia Zheng's ominous 'Stay where you are' as he went out with the chamberlain had warned Bao-yu that something dire was imminent—though just how much more dire as a result of Jia Huan's malicious intervention he could not have foreseen"。两位译

者都采用了意译法来翻译"多凶少吉";霍译由于一些细节的处理,译文更加生动传神:"dire"和"imminent"的使用,生动地传达出祸事将至的紧迫感;对于"那里承望贾环又添了许多的话"这一小句,霍克斯增译了"malicious intervention",把原文中隐化的意义作了显化处理;另外,"though just how much more dire…"和前文"… something dire was imminent"衔接紧密,过渡自然。

【5】"怎得个人来往里头去捎信"一句,杨译"… wishing someone would carry the news to the inner apartments"将"里头"字面地译为"the inner apartments";霍译"… anxiously looking for some passer-by who could take a message through to the womenfolk inside"将"里头"译为"the womenfolk inside",确切地指出是给住在里间屋子的贾母、王夫人等人捎信。

【6】"竟不曾听见是什么话,把'要紧'二字只听作'跳井'二字"一句中,"要紧(yào jǐn)"和"跳井(tiào jǐng)"两词的汉语读音非常相似。在原文中,这位老妈妈患有耳疾,故而混淆了两词的读音。杨译是"… and the old woman, being hard of hearing, mistook the word 'urgent' for 'drowning'",译者采用直译手法,将"要紧"译为"urgent","跳井"译为"drowning",虽与原文意义相符,但"urgent"和"drowning"的读音差别很大,是听起来不容易混淆的两个词,故而直译也就失去了原文押韵的诙谐感。霍译是"the old woman was deaf, almost everything he said had escaped her—except for the 'Go and tell', which she misheard as 'in the well.'",译者采用译写策略,将"要紧"译为"go and tell","跳井"译为"in the well",其中的"tell"和"well"押尾韵,语音相似,听上去易混淆,符合原文中老妈妈因为耳疾而错听的语境。另外,后文中的"叫我的小厮来罢",老妈妈听成"有什么不了的事",霍译使用"my pages"和"her wages"作押韵处理,也是妙译。

【7】"贾政犹嫌打轻了,一脚踢开掌板的,自己夺过来,咬着牙狠命盖了三四十下。众门客见打的不祥了,忙上前夺劝。"这是典型的汉语连动句式——贾政发出了一连串的动作:犹嫌、踢开、夺过来、咬着牙、狠命盖了;众门客也发出了一连串的动作:见、上前、夺、劝。杨译是"His father, thinking these strokes too light, kicked aside the man with the rod and snatched it up himself. With clenched teeth he rained down dozens of vicious blows until his secretaries, foreseeing serious consequences, stepped forward to intervene."该译文由两个句子构成。在第一句中,译者用句子化短语法将小句"犹嫌打轻了"译为现在分词短语"thinking these strokes too light",在译文中充当原因状语;"kicked aside(踢开)"和"snatched it up(夺过来)"是并列谓语。在第二句中,译者使用"until"进行句内连接,"until"前后分别表述贾政和众门客的动作,其中的"with clenched teeth(咬着牙)"是介词短语做伴随状语,表示谓语部分的动作"rained down dozens of vicious blows(狠命盖了)"是贾政咬着牙做出来的;此外,译者再次使用句子化短语法将小句"见打的不祥了"译为现在分词短语"foreseeing serious consequences",在译文中充当原因状语。霍译是"Jia Zheng, not satisfied that his executioner was hitting hard enough, kicked him impatiently aside, wrested the bamboo from his grasp, and, gritting his teeth, brought it down with the utmost savagery on the places that had already been beaten. At this point the literary gentlemen, sensing that Bao-yu was in serious danger of life and limb, came in again to remonstrate."该译文也是由两个句子构成。在第一句中,译者使用句子化短语法将小句"犹嫌打轻了"译为形容词短语"not satisfied that his executioner was hitting hard enough",在译文中充当原因状语;接着,译者用"and"连接贾政发出的一连串动作,即三个并列的谓语"kicked(踢)""wrested(夺)"和"brought it down(盖)",并在第三个谓语"brought it down"之前使用现在分词短语"gritting his teeth"作伴随状语,表明"gritting his teeth(咬着牙)"和"brought it down with the utmost savagery(狠命盖了)"这两个动作是同时发生。在第二句中,译者也是用句子化短语法将小句"见打的不祥了"译为现在分词短语"sensing that Bao-yu was in serious danger of life and limb",在译文中充当原因状语。

四、词汇表

1. insignia [ɪnˈsɪɡniə]　　　　n.　　the symbol, badge or sign that shows sb's rank or that they are a member of a group

		or an organization （级别或成员的）标记，象征；徽章；证章
2. atone [əˈtəʊn]	v.	to act in a way that shows that you are sorry for doing sth wrong in the past 赎罪；弥补过错
3. bellow [ˈbeləʊ]	v.	to shout in a loud deep voice, especially because you are angry （对某人）大声吼叫，怒吼
4. fret [fret]	v.	to be worried or unhappy and not able to relax 苦恼；烦躁；焦虑不安
5. perforce [pəˈfɔːs]	adv.	because it is necessary or can't be avoided 必须；必定
6. gag [gæg]	v.	to put a piece of cloth in or over sb's mouth to prevent them from speaking or shouting 捂住，塞住（某人的嘴）
7. thrust [θrʌst]	v.	to push sth/sb suddenly or violently in a particular direction 猛推
8. intercede [ˌɪntəˈsiːd]	v.	to speak to sb in order to persuade them to show pity on sb else or to help settle an argument （为某人）说情；（向某人）求情
9. regicide [ˈredʒɪsaɪd]	n.	the crime of killing a king or queen 弑君罪
10. parricide [ˈpærɪsaɪd]	n.	the crime of killing your father, mother or a close relative 杀父（或母、近亲）罪
11. all and sundry		everyone, not just a few special people 所有人；各色人等
12. ominous [ˈɒmɪnəs]	adj.	suggesting that sth bad is going to happen in the future 预兆的；恶兆的；不吉利的

13. chamberlain [ˈtʃeɪmbəlɪn]	n.	an official who managed the home and servants of a king, queen or important family in past centuries（国王或女王的）内侍；（旧时贵族的）管家
14. dire [ˈdaɪə(r)]	adj.	very serious 极其严重的；危急的
15. imminent [ˈɪmɪnənt]	adj.	(especially of sth unpleasant) likely to happen very soon 即将发生的；临近的
16. omnipresent [ˌɒmnɪˈpreznt]	adj.	present everywhere 无所不在的；遍及各处的
17. beseeching [bɪˈsiːtʃɪŋ]	adj.	(of a look, tone of voice, etc.) showing that you want sth very much 恳求的；哀求的；乞求的
	adv.	beseechingly
18. riotous [ˈraɪətəs]	adj.	noisy, exciting and enjoyable in an uncontrolled way 狂欢的；纵情欢闹的
19. dissipated [ˈdɪsɪpeɪtɪd]	adj.	enjoying activities that are harmful such as drinking too much alcohol 放荡的；耽于享乐的
20. impudicity [ˌɪmpjʊˈdɪsɪti]	n.	shamelessness; immodesty 无耻；放肆
21. culminate [ˈkʌlmɪneɪt]	v.	to end with a particular result, or at a particular point（以某种结果）告终；（在某一点）结束
22. comply [kəmˈplaɪ]	v.	to obey a rule, an order, etc. 遵从；服从；顺从
23. ham [hæm]	n.	the back part of a person's leg above the knee（人的）大腿后部
24. remonstrate [ˈremənstreɪt]	v.	protest to sb about sth you do not approve of or agree with, and you try to get it changed or stopped 抗议；表示异议，反对

第三十四回

情中情因情感妹妹　错里错以错劝哥哥[1]

Moved by Affection, Pao-yu Moves His Cousin
A Wrong Report Makes Pao-chai Wrong Her Brother [1] (Yang)

*A wordless message meets with silent understanding
And a groundless imputation leads to undeserved rebukes* [1] (Hawkes)

一、本回概述

宝玉挨打，众人唏嘘不已。袭人、宝钗趁机劝诫宝玉听从贾政教诲。黛玉探望宝玉，心疼不已，哭肿双眼，宝玉软言安慰，两人惺惺相惜。宝玉送旧帕，黛玉题新诗，字字呕心沥血，两人心有灵犀。袭人向王夫人提议，让宝玉搬出大观园，以免是非纷扰，王夫人极为赞赏，认为袭人行事周全，不由得对她刮目相看。薛家兄妹因宝玉被打之事引发争执，薛蟠一时气急，说了重话，令宝钗委屈不已。

二、篇章节选

> **原文**
>
> 　　袭人道:"我也没什么别的说。我只想着讨太太一个示下,怎么变个法儿,以后竟还教二爷搬出园外来住就好了。"[2]王夫人听了,吃一大惊,忙拉了袭人的手问道:"宝玉难道和谁作怪了不成?"[3]袭人连忙回道:"太太别多心,[4]并没有这话。这不过是我的小见识。如今二爷也大了,里头姑娘们也大了,况且林姑娘宝姑娘又是两姨姑表姊妹,虽说是姊妹们,到底是男女之分,日夜一处起坐不方便,由不得叫人悬心,便是外人看着也不像。一家子的事,俗语说的'没事常思有事',世上多少无头脑的事,多半因为无心中做出,有心人看见,当做有心事,反说坏了。只是预先不防着,断然不好。二爷素日性格,太太是知道的。他又偏好在我们队里闹,倘或不防,前后错了一点半点,[5]不论真假,人多口杂,那起小人的嘴有什么避讳,心顺了,说的比菩萨还好,心不顺,就贬的连畜牲不如。[6]二爷将来倘或有人说好,不过大家直过没事;若要叫人说出一个不好字来,我们不用说,粉身碎骨,[7]罪有万重,都是平常小事,便后来二爷一生的声名品行岂不完了,二则太太也难见老爷。[8]俗语又说'君子防不然',不如这会子防避的为是。太太事情多,一时固然想不到。我们想不到则可,既想到了,若不回明太太,罪越重了。近来我为这事日夜悬心,[9]又不好说与人,惟有灯知道罢了。"
>
> 　　王夫人听了这话,如雷轰电掣的一般,正触了金钏儿之事,心内越发感爱袭人不尽,忙笑道:"我的儿,你竟有这个心胸,想的这样周全!我何曾又不想到这里,只是这几次有事就忘了。你今儿这一番话提醒了我。难为你成全我娘儿两个声名体面,真真我竟不知道你这样好。罢了,你且去罢,我自有道理。[10]只是还有一句话:你今既说了这样的话,我就把他交给你了,好歹留心,保全了他,就是保全了我。我自然不辜负你。"
>
> 　　袭人连连答应着去了。

> 杨译

"It's nothing else, only that I was hoping Your Ladyship might arrange for Master Pao to move out of the Garden."[2]

Lady Wang was shocked. She caught hold of Hsi-jen's hand.

"Has Pao-yu been up to anything improper?"[3]

"No, no, madam. Don't misunderstand me.[4] Nothing of that sort. But in my humble opinion, now that he and the young ladies are no longer children and, what's more, Miss Lin and Miss Pao aren't members of the family, cousins of different sexes should live apart. When they spend all their time together every day, it's not convenient for them and we can't help worrying. Besides, it doesn't look good to people outside. As the proverb has it: Best be prepared for the worst. A lot of foolishness is quite innocent, but suspicious people always think the worst. Better make sure in advance that there's no trouble.

"*You* know, madam, what Master Pao is like and how he enjoys amusing himself with us girls. If no precautions are taken and he does something the least bit foolish[5]—no matter whether it's true or not—there's bound to be talk. Low-class people *will* gossip. When they're well disposed, they laud you to the skies; when they're not, they talk as if you were worse than a beast.[6] If people speak well of him, that's as it should be. If a single slighting remark is passed, not only shall we deserve a thousand deaths[7]—that's not important—but his reputation will be ruined for life and how will you answer for it to His Lordship?[8] Another proverb says: A gentleman should show providence. Better guard against this now. You're naturally too busy, madam, to think of these things, and they might not occur to us either. But if they do and we fail to mention it, that would be very remiss. Lately this has been preying on my mind day and night,[9] but I couldn't mention it to anyone else. Only my lamp at night knew how I worried!"

Lady Wang felt thunderstruck on hearing this, borne out as it was by the case of Chin-chuan. The more she thought, the more grateful she felt to Hsi-jen.

"What a wise child you are to see so far!" she exclaimed. "Of course I've given some thought to this myself, but lately I've had too much else on my mind. Now you've reminded me. I'm glad you're so concerned for our reputation. I really had no idea what a good girl you are! All right, you may go now. Leave everything to me. [10] But I tell you this: after what you've said today, I mean to entrust Pao-yu to you. You must look after him and keep him safe. That way, you'll be safeguarding *me* as well, and I shan't forget our obligation to you."

Hsi-jen hastily assented and withdrew.

霍译

'All I really wanted to ask,' said Aroma, 'was if Your Ladyship could advise me how later on we can somehow or other contrive to get Master Bao moved back outside the Garden.' [2]

Lady Wang looked startled and clutched Aroma's hand in some alarm.

'I hope Bao-yu hasn't been doing something dreadful with one of the girls?' [3]

'Oh no, Your Ladyship, please don't suspect that!' said Aroma hurriedly. [4] 'That wasn't my meaning at all. It's just that—if you'll allow me to say so—Master Bao and the young ladies are beginning to grow up now, and though they are all cousins, there *is* the difference of sex between them, which makes it very awkward sometimes when they are all living together, especially in the case of Miss Lin and Miss Bao, who aren't even of the same clan. One can't help feeling uneasy. Even to outsiders it looks like a very strange sort of family. They say "where nothing happens, imagination is busiest", and I'm sure lots of unaccountable misfortunes begin when some innocent little thing we did unthinkingly gets misconstrued in someone else's imagination and reported as something terrible. We just have to be on our guard against that sort of thing happening—especially when Master Bao has such a peculiar character, as Your Ladyship knows, and spends all his time with girls. He only has to make the tiniest slip in an unguarded moment, [5] and whether he really did anything or not, with so many people about—and some of them no better than they should be—there is sure to be scandal. For you know what some of these people are like, Your Ladyship. If

they feel well-disposed towards you, they'll make you out to be a saint; but if they're not, then Heaven help you! [6] If Master Bao lives to be spoken well of, we can count ourselves lucky; but the way things are, it only needs someone to breathe a word of scandal and—I say nothing of what will happen to us servants—it's of no consequence if *we*'re all chopped up for mincemeat [7]—but what's more important, Master Bao's reputation will be destroyed for life and all the care and worry Your Ladyship and Sir Zheng have had on his account will have been wasted. [8] I know Your Ladyship is very busy and can't be expected to think of everything, and I probably shouldn't have thought of this myself, but once I *had* thought of it, it seemed to me that it would be wrong of me not to tell Your Ladyship, and it's been preying on my mind ever since. [9] The only reason I haven't mentioned it before is because I was afraid Your Ladyship might be angry with me.'

What Aroma had just been saying about misconstructions and scandals so exactly fitted what had in fact happened in the case of Golden that for a moment Lady Wang was quite taken aback. But on reflection she felt nothing but love and gratitude for this humble servant-girl who had shown so much solicitude on her behalf.

'It is very perceptive of you, my dear, to have thought it all out so carefully,' she said. 'I have, of course, thought about this matter myself but other things have put it from my mind, and what you have just said has reminded me. It is most thoughtful of you. You are a very, very good girl—Well, you may go now. I think I now know what to do. [10] There is just one thing before you go, though. Now that you have spoken to me like this, I am going to place Bao-yu entirely in your hands. Be very careful with him, won't you? Remember that anything you do for him you will be doing also for me. You will find that I am not ungrateful.'

Aroma stood for a moment with bowed head, weighing the import of these words. Then she said:

'I will do what Your Ladyship has asked me to the utmost of my ability.'

She left the apartment slowly and made her way back to Green Delights, pondering as she went.

三、注释评点

【1】本回回目为"情中情因情感妹妹 错里错以错劝哥哥",其中重复出现"情"和"错"二字。杨译"Moved by Affection, Pao-yu Moves His Cousin A Wrong Report Makes Pao-chai Wrong Her Brother"采用了直译法,译者尽量贴近原文风格,在译文中重复使用"move"和"wrong"两词。霍译"A wordless message meets with silent understanding And a groundless imputation leads to undeserved rebukes"跳出了原文的规范,在理解本回大意的基础上对回目进行了再创作:"无言之心意遇无声之理解;无据之流言致错误之劝诫";另外,霍译上下句的用词对仗十分工整:主语分别是两个名词短语"A wordless message"和"a groundless imputation",其中的两个形容词"wordless"和"groundless"都带有表示否定意义的后缀"-less";谓语部分的动词短语中都分别有一个介词"with"和"to";宾语都是由名词短语来充当。

【2】"我只想着讨太太一个示下,怎么变个法儿,以后竟还教二爷搬出园外来住就好了。"杨译是"It's nothing else, only that I was hoping Your Ladyship might arrange for Master Pao to move out of the Garden."霍译是"'All I really wanted to ask,' said Aroma, 'was if Your Ladyship could advise me how later on we can somehow or other contrive to get Master Bao moved back outside the Garden.'"两位译者分别将"变个法儿"译为"arrange for"和"contrive to","contrive to"有"谋划,设计"之意,显然较为贴近原文。另外,霍译将"讨太太一个示下"译为"All I really wanted to ask was if Your Ladyship could advise me…",语气委婉,体现出袭人作为婢女对王夫人的尊重。

【3】"宝玉难道和谁作怪了不成?"一句中,"作怪"是委婉语,暗指男女之事。杨译"Has Pao-yu been up to anything improper?"将"作怪"模糊地译为"be up to anything improper",译文的语义范围比原文宽泛。霍译是"I hope Bao-yu hasn't been doing something dreadful with one of the girls?"译者把"作怪"译为"do something dreadful with one of the girls",接近原文的语义,但是却失去了原文委婉的语言风格。

【4】"太太别多心"一句,杨译是"Don't misunderstand me",意为"请

您不要误会我（说这话的意思）"；霍译是"please don't suspect that"，意为"请您不要怀疑宝玉和姑娘们有不雅之事"，两位译者强调的侧重点不同。

【5】"倘或不防，前后错了一点半点"一句，杨译是"If no precautions are taken and he does something the least bit foolish…"；霍译是"He only has to make the tiniest slip in an unguarded moment…"。两位译者把"错了一点半点"分别译为"do something the least bit foolish"和"make the tiniest slip"，都使用了最高级形式"the least"和"the tiniest"，准确充分地传达了原文的语义。另外，原文的小句"倘或不防"没有主语，根据上下文可以看出，其主语可以是"我们（王夫人和袭人）"，也可以是"宝玉"，杨译"if no precautions are taken"使用被动语态，巧妙地回避了原文主语难以确定的问题。

【6】"心顺了，说的比菩萨还好，心不顺，就贬的连畜牲不如"一句，杨译是"When they're well disposed, they laud you to the skies; when they're not, they talk as if you were worse than a beast." 译者将"说的比菩萨还好"用归化法译为"they laud you to the skies"；将"就贬的连畜牲不如"用异化法译为"they talk as if you were worse than a beast"。霍译是"If they feel well-disposed towards you, they'll make you out to be a saint; but if they're not, then Heaven help you!" "说的比菩萨还好"被译为"they'll make you out to be a saint"，此处，译者用归化法将充满佛教色彩的"菩萨"转换成西方宗教中的"圣人（saint）"；至于"就贬的连畜牲不如"一句，霍译处理得诙谐幽默："then Heaven help you!"意为"他们会极尽贬低污蔑之能事，你只能求上帝保佑了！"

【7】"我们不用说，粉身碎骨"一句，杨译"… not only shall we deserve a thousand deaths…"将"粉身碎骨"译为"a thousand deaths"，即"死一千次"；霍译"I say nothing of what will happen to us servants—it's of no consequence if we're all chopped up for mincemeat…"则将"粉身碎骨"译为"we're all chopped up for mincemeat"，即"我们都被剁成了肉酱"。两位译者都使用了夸张的手法，生动准确地传达出"粉身碎骨"的含义。

【8】"二则太太也难见老爷"一句，霍译"all the care and worry Your Ladyship and Sir Zheng have had on his account will have been wasted"是按照程乙本"那时老爷太太也白疼了，白操了心了"翻译的。

【9】"近来我为这事日夜悬心"一句，杨译是"Lately this has been

preying on my mind day and night",霍译是"… it's been preying on my mind ever since."两个译文的翻译风格非常一致:都舍弃原文中的人称主语"我",使用物化主语"这件事(分别是"this"和"it")",而且都使用了动词短语"prey on my mind",意为"某个想法萦绕心头",用词生动准确。

【10】"我自有道理"一句,杨译是"Leave everything to me."意为"把所有的事都交给我处理";但从原文看,王夫人的意思是"此事我自有主张",故译文与原文意思有出入。霍译是"I think I now know what to do."意为"我知道如何去做了",语义更为贴近原文。

四、词汇表

1. disposed [dɪsˈpəʊzd]	*adj.*	having a good/bad opinion of a person or thing 对……有好感(或恶感)
2. laud [lɔːd]	*v.*	to praise sb/sth 赞扬;赞美;称赞
3. slight [slaɪt]	*v.*	to treat sb rudely or without respect 侮慢;冷落;轻视
	adj.	slighting
4. remiss [rɪˈmɪs]	*adj.*	not giving sth enough care and attention 疏忽;玩忽职守
5. clutch [klʌtʃ]	*v.*	to hold sb/sth tightly 紧握;抱紧;抓紧
6. unthinkingly [ʌnˈθɪŋkɪŋli]	*adv.*	not thinking about the effects of what you do or say; not thinking much about serious things 不计后果地;考虑不周地
7. misconstrue [ˌmɪskənˈstruː]	*v.*	to understand sb's words or actions wrongly 误解某人的言行
	n.	misconstruction
8. slip [slɪp]	*n.*	a small mistake, usually made by being careless or not paying attention 差错;疏漏;纰漏
9. solicitude [səˈlɪsɪtjuːd]	*n.*	anxious care for sb's comfort, health or

happiness 牵挂；关怀；关切

10. perceptive [pəˈseptɪv]   *adj.*   having or showing the ability to see or understand things quickly, especially things that are not obvious 理解力强的；有洞察力的；思维敏捷的

第三十五回

白玉钏亲尝莲叶羹　黄金莺巧结梅花络[1]

Yu-chuan Tastes Some Lotus-Leaf Broth
Ying-erh Skilfully Makes a Plum-Blossom Net [1] (Yang)

*Sulky Silver tastes some lotus-leaf soup
And Golden Oriole knots a flower-patterned fringe* [1] (Hawkes)

一、本回概述

　　黛玉远望怡红院人群往来，不禁落寞伤感，感叹他人家有父母的好处。宝玉要吃荷叶汤，贾母派玉钏送去。宝玉见到玉钏，想起金钏，又伤心又惭愧；玉钏本因金钏一事，余怒未消，满腔怨恨，但见宝玉百般讨好，温存和气，心中暗暗谅解。袭人请宝钗贴身丫鬟莺儿来怡红院打梅花络，莺儿不仅手巧，且对各种颜色和样式的搭配很有悟性，宝玉十分欣赏。袭人自上次与王夫人深谈之后，深受王夫人器重，今日竟蒙专门赠菜，袭人受宠若惊，宝玉对此不以为然，宝钗却深明其意。

二、篇章节选

原文

　　宝玉见莺儿来了，却倒十分欢喜；忽见了玉钏儿，便想到他姐姐金钏儿身上，又是伤心，又是惭愧，便把莺儿丢下，且和玉钏儿说话。[2]袭人见把莺儿不理，恐莺儿没好意思的，又见莺儿不肯坐，便拉了莺儿出来，到那边房里去吃茶说话儿去了。[3]

　　这里麝月等预备了碗箸来伺候吃饭。宝玉只是不吃，问玉钏儿道："你母亲身子好？"玉钏儿满脸怒色，正眼也不看宝玉，半日，方说了一个"好"字。宝玉便觉没趣，半日，只得又陪笑问道："谁叫你给我送来的？"[4]玉钏儿道："不过是奶奶太太们！"宝玉见他还是这样哭丧，便知他是为金钏儿的原故；待要虚心下气磨转他，又见人多，不好下气的，因而变尽方法，将人都支出去，然后又陪笑问长问短。[5]

　　那玉钏儿先虽不悦，只管见宝玉一些性子没有，凭他怎么丧谤，他还是温存和气，自己倒不好意思的了，脸上方有三分喜色。[6]宝玉便笑求他："好姐姐，你把那汤拿了来我尝尝。"玉钏儿道："我从不会喂人东西，等他们来了再吃。"宝玉笑道："我不是要你喂我。我因为走不动，你递给我吃了，你好赶早儿回去交代了，你好吃饭的。我只管耽误时候，你岂不饿坏了。你要懒待动，我少不了忍了疼下去取来。"说着便要下床来，扎挣起来，禁不住嗳哟之声。玉钏儿见他这般，忍不住起身说道："躺下罢！那世里造了来的业，这会子现世现报。[7]教我那一个眼睛看的上！"一面说，一面哧的一声又笑了，端过汤来。

　　宝玉笑道："好姐姐，你要生气只管在这里生罢，见了老太太、太太可放和气些，若还这样，你就又捱骂了。"玉钏儿道："吃罢，吃罢！不用和我甜嘴蜜舌的，我可不信这样话！"说着，催宝玉喝了两口汤。[8]宝玉故意说："不好吃，不吃了。"玉钏儿道："阿弥陀佛！[9]这还不好吃，什么好吃。"宝玉道："一点味儿也没有，你不信，尝一尝就知道了。"玉钏儿真就赌气尝了一尝。宝玉笑道："这可好吃了。"玉钏儿听说，方解过意来，原是宝玉哄他吃一口，便说道："你既说不好吃，这会子说好吃也不给你吃了。"宝玉只管央求陪笑要吃，玉钏儿又不给他，一面又叫人打发吃饭。

杨译

Pao-yu was delighted by Ying-erh's arrival but distressed and embarrassed by the sight of Yu-chuan, who reminded him of her elder sister Chin-chuan. For this reason he addressed himself exclusively to her. [2] This made Hsi-jen afraid that Ying-erh might feel slighted, and since she refused to be seated she took her to the outer room for some tea and a chat. [3]

Meanwhile Sheh-yueh and the others had fetched Pao-yu's bowl and chopsticks, but instead of starting his lunch he asked Yu-chuan:

"How is your mother?"

Scowling and refusing to look at him, for a long time she did not answer. Then she snapped out:

"All right."

Silence followed this snub. Then Pao-yu tried again.

"Who asked you to bring me my lunch?" [4]

"The madams and the ladies, naturally."

Well aware that Chin-chuan's death was behind Yu-chuan's displeasure, Pao-yu cast about for some means to placate her. Not wanting to humble himself in front of the others, he dismissed them on various pretexts and then put himself out to be pleasant. [5] And tempted though Yu-chuan was to cold-shoulder him, she could not but be mollified by the amiable way in which he put up with all her rudeness. It was her turn to feel embarrassed.

"Do pass me the broth to taste, dear sister," he begged when he saw her face begin to brighten. [6]

"I've never fed anyone. Wait till the others come back."

"I don't want you to feed me but I can't get out of bed," he said coaxingly. "If you'll just pass me the bowl, you can report back so much the sooner and have your

own meal. I mustn't keep you here starving. If you can't be bothered to move I'll have to fetch the bowl myself, however much it hurts."

He struggled to get out of bed and could not suppress a groan. At that Yu-chuan no longer had the heart to refuse.

"Lie down," she said, leaving her seat. "What a sight you are, suffering for the sins committed in your previous incarnations."[7]

With a giggle she passed him the bowl.

"If you must be angry, dear sister, be angry here," advised Pao-yu amiably. "Try to keep your temper in front of the old lady and the mistress. If you carry on like this with them, you'll get another scolding."

"Drink your soup, go on, I'm not taken in by that sweet talk."

She made him drink a couple of mouthfuls,[8] but Pao-yu pretended not to like the flavour and left the rest untouched.

"Gracious Buddha!"[9] she exclaimed. "You're hard to please."

"It's got no taste at all. If you don't believe me, try it."

Rising to his bait, Yu-chuan took a sip. At once he cried with a laugh:

"Now it must taste delicious!"

Realizing that she had been tricked she said, "First you don't like it, now you say it's delicious. Well, I shan't let you have any more."

Though he smiled and pleaded she was adamant. She called the others to come to serve him his meal.

霍译

Bao-yu was naturally very pleased to see Oriole; but the sight of Silver, reminding him, with a pang of mingled shame and sorrow, of her sister Golden, impelled him to ignore Oriole and concentrate his attention on the other girl.[2] Aroma noticed this neglect and was afraid that Oriole might be offended. Partly for this reason and partly because Oriole looked so uncomfortable standing up, but was evidently determined not to sit down in Bao-yu's presence, she took her by the hand

and drew her into the adjoining room for a cup of tea and a chat. [3]

Meanwhile in the inner room Musk and Ripple had laid out the bowls and chopsticks and were waiting in readiness to serve Bao-yu his lunch; but Bao-yu was still occupied with Silver and seemed in no hurry to begin.

'How is your mother?' he asked her.

The girl sat silent, with a sullen, angry look on her face. When, with a muttered 'all right', she did at last answer him, she averted her eyes and would not look at him. Bao-yu was very much put out, but did his best to be pleasant.

'Who told *you* to bring this for me?' [4]

'Her Ladyship and Mrs Lian. Who do you think?'

Bao-yu could see the misery in her face and knew that it was because of Golden that she looked like that. He wished he could humble himself before her, but the presence of the other maids inhibited him. He had to think of some way of getting rid of them. Having succeeded at last in doing so, he began, as soon as they were out of the room, to exercise all his charm upon Silver. [5] At first she tried to ignore the questions with which he plied her; but he was so patient and persistent, meeting her unyielding stiffness with such warmth and gentleness, that in the end her heart misgave her and a faintly pleased expression began to steal over her face. [6] Bao-yu judged the time ripe to entreat her smilingly for his lunch.

'Fetch me that soup will you, there's a dear. I'd like to try it now.'

'I can't feed other people,' said Silver. 'I never could. You'll have to wait till the others come back.'

'I'm not asking you to feed me,' said Bao-yu. 'I'm just asking you to get it for me because I can't walk. Once you've done that you can go back and tell them you've finished your errand and get on with your own lunch. I don't want to keep you from your food: you're probably starving. However, if you don't even feel up to passing me a bowl of soup, I'll just have to put up with the pain and get it myself.'

He tried to rise from his bed, but the effort cost him a cry of pain. Unable to hold out any longer when she saw the state he was in, Silver jumped to her feet.

'All right. Lie down, lie down!' she said. '"Past sin, present suffering."[7] You've got *your* retribution without having to wait for it, so you needn't expect me to feel sorry for you!'

She broke into a sudden peal of laughter and fetched him the soup.

'Silver dear,' said Bao-yu, 'if you still feel angry with me, get it over with now. Try to look pleasanter when you are with Their Ladyships. You mustn't look angry all the time when you are with *them*, or you'll be getting yourself into trouble.'

'Go on, get on with your soup!' said Silver. 'Keep the sugary stuff for other people. I know all about it!'

Bao-yu drank a couple of mouthfuls of the soup at her insistence,[8] but artfully pretended not to like it.

'It doesn't taste nice.'

'Doesn't *taste* nice?' said Silver with an expression of extreme disgust. 'Holy Name![9] if *that* doesn't taste nice, I'd like to know what does!'

'It's got no flavour,' said Bao-yu. 'Taste it yourself, if you don't believe me.'

Silver—to prove him wrong—indignantly raised the spoon to her lips and tasted. Bao-yu laughed.

'Ah, *now* it'll taste all right!'

Silver realized that he had deliberately tricked her into drinking from the same bowl.

'You wouldn't drink it a moment ago,' she said, 'so now you shan't have any even if you say you want it.'

And though Bao-yu laughingly begged and pleaded, she refused to let him have it back and called in the other maids to give him the rest of his meal.

三、注释评点

【1】"白玉钏亲尝莲叶羹 黄金莺巧结梅花络"为本回回目,其中人名的翻译,杨译使用了音译法,将"白玉钏"译为"Yu-chuan","黄金莺"译为

"Ying-erh"；霍译使用了意译法，将两者分别译为"Sulky Silver"和"Golden Oriole"。霍译在"Silver"前增加形容词"Sulky"，意为"面有愠色的、生闷气的"，一是符合玉钏当时的心境，二是达到与下句中"Golden Oriole"字数相同、句式对仗的目的。

【2】"宝玉见莺儿来了，却倒十分欢喜；忽见了玉钏儿，便想到他姐姐金钏儿身上，又是伤心，又是惭愧，便把莺儿丢下，且和玉钏儿说话。"杨译是"Pao-yu was delighted by Ying-erh's arrival but distressed and embarrassed by the sight of Yu-chuan, who reminded him of her elder sister Chin-chuan. For this reason he addressed himself exclusively to her."译文第一句中，译者使用"but"和"who"进行句内连接；同时用句子化短语法将小句"忽见了玉钏儿"译为介词短语"by the sight of Yu-chuan"，其后接"who"引导的定语从句，用来修饰"Yu-chuan"。霍译是"Bao-yu was naturally very pleased to see Oriole; but the sight of Silver, reminding him, with a pang of mingled shame and sorrow, of her sister Golden, impelled him to ignore Oriole and concentrate his attention on the other girl."译者使用"but"进行句内连接；同时也使用句子化短语法将"忽见了玉钏儿"译为名词短语"the sight of Silver"，在"but"之后的分句中充当主语；此外，"a pang of mingled shame and sorrow"翻译得非常生动："shame and sorrow"准确地表达出宝玉当时又惭愧又伤心的心情，增译的"pang"表示"心中突然感到一阵剧痛"，强调宝玉一看见玉钏，立刻勾起伤心往事，心中十分痛苦；原文中的小句"便想到他姐姐金钏儿身上"被译为现在分词短语"reminding him... of her sister Golden"，在句中充当原因状语。原文是由八个小句构成的连动式句子，霍译将其译为一个长句，充分体现出英语为形合语言，注重连接，句子偏长的特点。

【3】"袭人见把莺儿不理，恐莺儿没好意思的，又见莺儿不肯坐，便拉了莺儿出来，到那边房里去吃茶说话儿去了。"杨译是"This made Hsi-jen afraid that Ying-erh might feel slighted, and since she refused to be seated she took her to the outer room for some tea and a chat."译者使用"and"和"since"进行连句："and"用于连接前后两个分句，"since"用于引出第二个分句的原因状语；另外，译者用句子化词法将小句"袭人见把莺儿不理"译为"This"，用来指

代上文内容，在该译文的第一个分句中充当主语。霍译是"Aroma noticed this neglect and was afraid that Oriole might be offended. Partly for this reason and partly because Oriole looked so uncomfortable standing up, but was evidently determined not to sit down in Bao-yu's presence, she took her by the hand and drew her into the adjoining room for a cup of tea and a chat."译文由两个句子构成。第二句句首增译的"Partly for this reason and partly because Oriole looked so uncomfortable standing up"，使得译文信息更加完整，语意更加连贯。另外，译者在该译文中用了四个"and"和一个"but"进行连句；可以看出，英文十分注重句子的连接，连词"and"的使用频率很高。

【4】"玉钏儿满脸怒色，正眼也不看宝玉，半日，方说了一个'好'字。宝玉便觉没趣，半日，只得又陪笑问道：'谁叫你给我送来的？'"该句中出现了两个"半日"，两位译者的翻译各有不同：杨译分别是"for a long time"和"silence followed this snub"；霍译的第一个"半日"是"at last"，表现出玉钏故意拖延回答，不想搭理宝玉的情景，第二个"半日"作了省译的处理。

【5】"宝玉见他还是这样哭丧，便知他是为金钏儿的原故；待要虚心下气磨转他，又见人多，不好下气的，因而变尽方法，将人都支出去，然后又陪笑问长问短。"杨译是"Well aware that Chin-chuan's death was behind Yu-chuan's displeasure, Pao-yu cast about for some means to placate her. Not wanting to humble himself in front of the others, he dismissed them on various pretexts and then put himself out to be pleasant."译文包含两个句子，这两个句子的句首都是原因状语，分别由形容词短语"Well aware that..."和现在分词短语"Not wanting to..."来充当；译者用句子化词（组）法将小句"他还是这样哭丧"译为名词短语"Yu-chuan's displeasure"，将动词短语"变尽方法"译为介词短语"on various pretexts"。霍译是"Bao-yu could see the misery in her face and knew that it was because of Golden that she looked like that. He wished he could humble himself before her, but the presence of the other maids inhibited him. He had to think of some way of getting rid of them. Having succeeded at last in doing so, he began, as soon as they were out of the room, to exercise all his charm upon Silver."该译文由四个句子构成。第一句中，译者使用"misery"翻译"哭丧"一词，比杨译所用的

"displeasure"更具体,也更符合玉钏痛失姐姐的悲痛心情;"it was because of Golden that she looked like that"是强调句型,着重表达玉钏"looked like that(这样哭丧)"的原因是"because of Golden(为金钏儿的原故)"。第二句中,译者用句子化短语法将小句"又见人多"译为名词短语"the presence of the other maids",在"but"之后的分句中充当主语。第四句中,译者使用归化法,将"又陪笑问长问短"译为"exercise all his charm upon Silver",十分生动有趣。

【6】"那玉钏儿先虽不悦,只管见宝玉一些性子没有,凭他怎么丧谤,他还是温存和气,自己倒不好意思的了,脸上方有三分喜色。"杨译是"And tempted though Yu-chuan was to cold-shoulder him, she could not but be mollified by the amiable way in which he put up with all her rudeness. It was her turn to feel embarrassed. … he begged when he saw her face begin to brighten."该译文包含三个句子。第一句中,译者使用了倒装的让步状语从句"tempted though Yu-chuan was to cold-shoulder him",其正常语序是"though Yu-chuan was tempted to cold-shoulder him";译者还使用句子化短语法,将小句"凭他怎么丧谤,他还是温存和气"译为名词短语"the amiable way in which he put up with all her rudeness"。霍译是"At first she tried to ignore the questions with which he plied her; but he was so patient and persistent, meeting her unyielding stiffness with such warmth and gentleness, that in the end her heart misgave her and a faintly pleased expression began to steal over her face."该译文由两个分句构成,其间由分号和"but"进行连接。在第一个分句中,译者使用"with which"进行连句;在第二个分句中,译者使用"so... that..."和"and"进行句内连接。此外,译者将"脸上方有三分喜色"译为"a faintly pleased expression began to steal over her face",其中的"faintly"和"steal over"表达出玉钏淡淡的、不易觉察的喜色,准确地对应了原文的"三分喜色"。

【7】"那世里造了来的业,这会子现世现报"一句,杨译是"What a sight you are, suffering for the sins committed in your previous incarnations."原文中的"那世里"指的是过去的某一世,杨译中使用的是复数形式"in your previous incarnations";"incarnation"一词充满佛教色彩,原文中的"业"和"现世现报"都属于佛教词汇。霍译是"Past sin, present suffering",译者不再纠结

于"那世",而是采用了模糊的处理方法;译文中的"sin"一词充满基督教色彩,替换了原文中的佛教意象;整个句子用词精准,对仗工整。

【8】"催宝玉喝了两口汤"一句,杨译是"She made him drink a couple of mouthfuls";霍译是"Bao-yu drank a couple of mouthfuls of the soup at her insistence"。对于"催"字,杨译使用的是动词短语"made him...";霍译使用了介词短语"at her insistence";两个译文的主语也有所不同:杨译的主语是"she(Yu-chuan)",霍译的主语是"Bao-yu"。

【9】"阿弥陀佛"一词,杨译是"Gracious Buddha!",虽未译出"阿弥陀"三字,但保留了原文的佛教色彩;霍译使用了归化法,将其译为充满西方宗教色彩的"Holy Name!"。

四、词汇表

1. scowl [skaʊl]	v.	to look at sb/sth in an angry or annoyed way 怒视(某人或某物)
2. snub [snʌb]	n.	an action or a comment that is deliberately rude in order to show sb that you do not like or respect them 冷落;怠慢的言辞(或行为)
3. placate [pləˈkeɪt]	v.	to make sb feel less angry about sth 安抚;平息(怒气)
4. humble [ˈhʌmbl]	v.	to show that you are not too proud to ask for sth, admit that you have been wrong, etc. 低声下气;谦逊;虚心
5. pretext [ˈpriːtekst]	n.	a false reason that you give for doing sth, usually sth bad, in order to hide the real reason; an excuse 借口;托词
6. cold-shoulder [ˈkəʊldˈʃəʊldə]	v.	to treat sb in an unfriendly way 冷待;冷落;慢待
7. mollify [ˈmɒlɪfaɪ]	v.	to make sb feel less angry or upset 使平静;抚慰

8. broth [brɒθ]	n.	thick soup made by boiling meat or fish and vegetables in water（加入蔬菜的）肉汤，鱼汤
9. incarnation [ˌɪnkɑːˈneɪʃn]	n.	the state of living in the form of a particular person or animal 前世；今世；来世；轮回
10. adamant [ˈædəmənt]	adj.	determined not to change your mind or to be persuaded about sth 坚决的；坚定不移的
11. sullen [ˈsʌlən]	adj.	bad-tempered and not speaking, either on a particular occasion or because it is part of your character 面有愠色的；闷闷不乐的；郁郁寡欢的
12. avert [əˈvɜːt]	v.	to turn your eyes, etc. away from sth that you do not want to see 转移目光；背过脸
13. ply [plaɪ]	v.	to keep asking sb questions 不停地提问
14. unyielding [ʌnˈjiːldɪŋ]	adj.	if a person is unyielding, they are not easily influenced and they are unlikely to change their mind 坚定的；顽强不屈的；固执的
15. entreat [ɪnˈtriːt]	v.	to ask sb to do sth in a serious and often emotional way 恳求；乞求
16. peal [piːl]	n.	a loud sound or series of sounds 响亮的声音；轰轰的响声
17. sugary [ˈʃʊɡəri]	adj.	seeming too full of emotion in a way that is not sincere（态度等）甜腻腻的，媚人的，甜言蜜语的

绣鸳鸯梦兆绛芸轩　识分定情悟梨香院[1]

A Dream During the Embroidering of Mandarin Ducks in Red Rue Studio Foretells the Future
Pao-yu Learns in Pear Fragrance Court that Each Has His Share of Love [1] (Yang)

Bao-chai visits Green Delights and hears strange words from a sleeper
Bao-yu visits Pear-tree Court and learns hard facts from a performer [1] (Hawkes)

一、本回概述

　　宝玉身体渐渐好转，因有贾母之言，得以日日在园中闲消岁月，宝钗等人偶劝其立业扬名，却令之反感。王夫人授意熙凤，让袭人享受姨娘待遇，认定她为宝玉之妾。一日，宝钗找宝玉闲聊，逢其熟睡，帮袭人绣鸳鸯兜肚之际，偶然听宝玉睡梦中喊出"不要金玉姻缘，偏要木石姻缘"，不禁怔住。袭人将王夫人授意之事告知宝玉，宝玉大喜。二人闲谈，宝玉论及文武之死，并说死后愿用众女之泪葬己。宝玉去梨香院寻龄官唱《牡丹亭》，遭其冷落，无意中得知贾蔷与龄官相互怜惜，深悟人生情缘，各有分定。

对话杨宪益、霍克斯——《红楼梦》英译赏析（第一至四十回）

二、篇章节选

原文

宝玉此刻把听曲子的心都没了，且要看他和龄官是怎样。只见贾蔷进去笑道："你起来，瞧这个顽意儿。"龄官起身问是什么，贾蔷道："买了雀儿你顽，省得天天闷闷的无个开心。[2]我先顽个你看。"说着，便拿些谷子哄的那个雀儿在戏台上乱串，衔鬼脸旗帜。众女孩子都笑道"有趣"，独龄官冷笑了两声，赌气仍睡去了。贾蔷还只管陪笑，问他好不好。龄官道："你们家把好好的人弄了来，关在这牢坑里学这个劳什子还不算，你这会子又弄个雀儿来，也偏生干这个。你分明是弄了他来打趣形容我们，[3]还问我好不好。"贾蔷听了，不觉慌起来，连忙赌身立誓。[4]又道："今儿我那里的香脂油蒙了心！[5]费一二两银子买他来，原说解闷，就没有想到这上头。[6]罢，罢，放了生，免免你的灾病。"[7]说着，果然将雀儿放了，一顿把将笼子拆了。

龄官还说："那雀儿虽不如人，他也有个老雀儿在窝里，[8]你拿了他来弄这个劳什子也忍得！今儿我咳嗽出两口血来，太太叫大夫来瞧，不说替我细问问，你且弄这个来取笑。偏生我这没人管没人理的，又偏病。"说着又哭起来。贾蔷忙道："昨儿晚上我问了大夫，他说不相干。他说吃两剂药，后儿再瞧。谁知今儿又吐了。这会子请他去。"说着，便要请去。龄官又叫"站住，这会子大毒日头地下，你赌气自去请了来我也不瞧。"贾蔷听如此说，只得又站住。

宝玉见了这般景况，不觉痴了，这才领会了划"蔷"深意。自己站不住，便抽身走了。贾蔷一心都在龄官身上，也不顾送，倒是别的女孩子送了出来。[9]

杨译

By now Pao-yu no longer wanted to hear her sing but was curious to know her relationship to Chia Chiang, who had walked in gaily calling out:

"Get up and look at this!"

"What is it?" Ling-kuan raised herself on one elbow.

"I've brought you a bird to stop you feeling so bored.[2] Let me show you how to put it through its tricks."

Holding out a few seeds, he coaxed the bird to pick up a mask and flag and strut round the stage. All the other girls laughed, exclaiming "How amusing!", but Ling-kuan gave a couple of snorts and lay down again in disgust.

"Like it?" Chia Chiang asked with a smile.

"It's bad enough your family cooping *us* up here to learn that old trash," she retorted. "And now you get a *bird* to do the same. You've obviously bought it to make fun of us,[3] yet you ask whether I like it."

Chia Chiang was disconcerted and swore that he had never meant to hurt her.[4]

"What a fool I am!"[5] he cried. "I gave a couple of taels for this in the hope that it would amuse you, never dreaming that you'd feel this way about it.[6] All right, I'll set it free—to make you feel better."[7]

With that he let the bird out and smashed the cage.

"That bird may not be human," said Ling-kuan, "but it has a mother bird in its nest.[8] How heartless you are, bringing it here to play with. I coughed blood twice today, and Her Ladyship said that a doctor should be sent to examine me. But *you*—you bring this here to make fun of me. How unlucky I am, ill, with no one to care for me."

She started sobbing again.

"I spoke to the doctor last night," Chia Chiang replied hastily. "He said it was nothing serious and he'd come to examine you again after you'd taken a dose or two of the medicine prescribed. I'd no idea you'd coughed blood again. I'll go and get him at once."

He started off, but Ling-kuan called him back.

"The sun's scorching just now," she said. "If you go off in a huff to fetch him, I won't see him."

So the young man had to remain where he was.

Meanwhile Pao-yu was lost in wonder as the significance of all those *chiangs* written on the ground dawned on him. And feeling superfluous there he took his leave. Chia Chiang being too absorbed in Ling-kuan to notice, it was left to the other girls to see him out. [9]

霍译

He invited Bao-yu to be seated while he went into Charmante's room to show off his purchase; but Bao-yu, whose desire to hear Charmante sing was now quite forgotten in his eagerness to find out exactly how things lay between her and Jia Qiang, joined the girls as they clustered round the door-way to watch.

'Look! Look what I've brought for you,' said Jia Qiang, full of smiles.

'What is it?'

Charmante had been lying down again, but sat up when he entered.

'I've got a little bird to keep you company, to stop you getting so depressed. [2] You watch! I'll make him perform for you.'

He took a few grains from his pocket and coaxed the bird out on to the stage, where it picked up a diminutive mask and flag and hopped and pirouetted about like an actor playing the warrior's part in a play. The girls all laughed delightedly and said it was 'sweet'. All except Charmante. She merely gave a scornful 'huh!' or two and lay back on the bed again in disgust.

Jia Qiang smiled—almost beseechingly.

'How do you like it?'

'You and your family!' said Charmante bitterly. 'It isn't enough to take decent girls from their homes and shut them up in this prison to learn beastly opera all day. Now you have to bring a bird along to do it as well. I suppose it's to keep me reminded of my misery. [3] And you have the audacity to ask me "do I like it?"!'

Her words appeared to make Jia Qiang quite frantic, for he uttered a string of the most violent and passionate oaths in reply. [4]

'I'm a stupid fool and I should have known better,' [5] he said. 'I spent all that money on the thing because I thought it might cheer you up. It never occurred to me

that you might take it like this.[6] Well, let the thing go then! It's an "act of merit" to free living creatures, so at least you'll get some good from it. Either it will help you in the next life or free you from sickness in this one.'[7]

With that he released the bird, which promptly flew away, and stamped on the cage until it was smashed to pieces.

'Maybe birds aren't as important as human beings,' said Charmante, 'but they have mothers and fathers just the same.[8] Can't you see how cruel it is to take them away from their nests and make them perform for people's amusement? I coughed up two mouthfuls of blood today. Her Ladyship sent someone to look for you. She wanted you to get me a doctor so that we could find out what to do, but instead of a doctor you bring this thing back with you, to make a mock of me. It's just my luck to fall ill when I've got no one to care for me or take any notice.'

She began to cry.

'But I asked the doctor about you yesterday evening and he said it wasn't serious,' Jia Qiang protested. 'He said you were to take a couple of doses of that medicine and he'd come and look at you again in two days' time. I'd no idea that you'd been spitting blood. Well, I'd better go and get him straight away.'

He began to go, but Charmante called him back.

'Stay where you are! Don't go rushing off in this burning heat. You're only going to fetch him because you're in a temper, anyway. I wouldn't see him now if he came!'

Hearing her say this, Jia Qiang halted.

Bao-yu had been watching this scene with open-mouthed fascination. At last he understood the real meaning of all those QIANGS. There was obviously no place for him here, so he slipped away. Jia Qiang was so absorbed in his concern for Charmante that he did not even notice him go and it was left to the little actresses to see him out.[9]

三、注释评点

【1】本回回目是"绣鸳鸯梦兆绛芸轩　识分定情悟梨香院",杨译是"A

对话杨宪益、霍克斯——《红楼梦》英译赏析（第一至四十回）

Dream During the Embroidering of Mandarin Ducks in Red Rue Studio Foretells the Future　Pao-yu Learns in Pear Fragrance Court that Each Has His Share of Love",上下两句分别用了物化主语"A Dream"和人格主语"Pao-yu",上句是主谓宾结构,主语"A Dream"和谓语"Foretells"之间加入时间状语"During the Embroidering of Mandarin Ducks"和地点状语"in Red Rue Studio",宾语由名词短语"the Future"来充当;下句使用主语+谓语+宾语从句的结构,谓语"Learns"和宾语从句"that Each Has His Share of Love"之间加入地点状语"in Pear Fragrance Court"。霍译是"Bao-chai visits Green Delights and hears strange words from a sleeper　Bao-yu visits Pear-tree Court and learns hard facts from a performer",相比杨译,霍译的上下两句对应得更为工整：一是均使用了人格主语"Bao-chai"和"Bao-yu",二是均采用了"主语+谓语+宾语+and+谓语+宾语+状语"的结构,对应得十分整齐;此外,译者未完全按照本回目的字面意思翻译,而是在总结原文大意的基础上进行创造性译写。

【2】"买了雀儿你顽,省得天天闷闷的无个开心"一句,杨译是"I've brought you a bird to stop you feeling so bored.";霍译是"I've got a little bird to keep you company, to stop you getting so depressed."原文包含两个小句,从语义上来讲,后小句是前小句的目的。为了在英语这种形合语言中显化这一逻辑关系,两位译者都使用不定式结构充当目的状语,对应原文中的"省得天天闷闷的无个开心",译文分别是"to stop you feeling so bored"和"to stop you getting so depressed"。此外,霍译中增译的"to keep you company",也是不定式结构充当目的状语,表明贾蔷买鸟的目的是为了用它来陪伴龄官。

【3】"你分明是弄了他来打趣形容我们"一句,杨译是"You've obviously bought it to make fun of us","打趣形容我们"被译为"make fun of us",译者只译了"打趣",未译"形容"。其实,原文的意思是"make fun of us（打趣我们）by comparing us to the caged bird which sings to entertain people（形容我们）"。霍译是"I suppose it's to keep me reminded of my misery."译者虽未依照字面直译原文,却把原文隐含的意义表达了出来。

【4】"不觉慌起来,连忙赌身立誓"一句,杨译是"Chia Chiang was disconcerted and swore that he had never meant to hurt her.""赌身立誓"被译

为"swore","swore"之后增译了宾语从句"that he had never meant to hurt her"。霍译是"Her words appeared to make Jia Qiang quite frantic, for he uttered a string of the most violent and passionate oaths in reply."译者用连词"for"进行句内连接,点明了前后两部分之间的因果关系。

【5】"香脂油蒙了心!"是中国民间俗语,意思是糊涂不清,事理不明。杨译是"What a fool I am!",霍译是"'I'm a stupid fool and I should have known better",两位译者都使用了归化法。

【6】"费一二两银子买他来,原说解闷,就没有想到这上头。"杨译是"I gave a couple of taels for this in the hope that it would amuse you, never dreaming that you'd feel this way about it."译者使用句子化短语法将两个小句"原说解闷"和"就没有想到这上头"分别译为介词短语"in the hope that it would amuse you"和现在分词短语"never dreaming that you'd feel this way about it",在译文中分别充当目的状语和伴随状语。霍译是"I spent all that money on the thing because I thought it might cheer you up. It never occurred to me that you might take it like this."该译文由两个句子构成。在第一句中,译者使用"because"连句,点明上下文之间的因果关系;第二句中出现了一个很常用的结构"It (never) occurred to sb that…",其中,"It"是形式主语,真正的主语是"that"引导的从句"that you might take it like this"。对于"解闷"一词,杨译是"amuse you",霍译是"cheer you up"。根据原文可以看出,对于龄官这样一个因患病而情绪低落,担心爱情中途夭折的花季少女而言,"cheer sb up(意思是to make sb more cheerful or happy)"更符合"解闷"在此处的涵义。

【7】"放了生,免免你的灾病"一句,充满了佛教色彩,中国人认为放生是行善,能改变命运,免除灾难。杨译是"I'll set it free—to make you feel better",译者将"放生"译为"set it free",但对于"免免你的灾病"中包含的文化信息并未直接译出,而是将其改译为"to make you feel better"。霍译是"... let the thing go then! It's an 'act of merit' to free living creatures, so at least you'll get *some* good from it. Either it will help you in the next life or free you from sickness in this one."译者使用增译手法,将放生可免灾病的文化信息传达给西

方读者：先是用解释性的译文"It's an 'act of merit' to free living creatures, so at least you'll get some good from it."为读者说明放生是一种善行，可以使施行者得到善果；接着，进一步说明"Either it will help you in the next life or free you from sickness in this one."，即"放生要么在来世会对你有好处，要么在现世使你免除疾病"。译者使用文内增译的手法，在不干扰阅读连贯性的情况下，将空缺的文化信息为读者补全。

【8】"龄官还说：'那雀儿虽不如人，他也有个老雀儿在窝里……'"一句，杨译是"'That bird may not be human,' said Ling-kuan, 'but it has a mother bird in its nest.'"；霍译是"'Maybe birds aren't as important as human beings,' said Charmante, 'but they have mothers and fathers just the same.'"。汉语和英语中引文的句式结构有所不同：汉语中的"某人说"一般置于句首；英语中"said sb / sb said"可以置于句首、句中或句末，此处的两个译文就是"said Ling-kuan"和"said Charmante"置于句中的例子。关于"那雀儿"的翻译，杨译是"that bird"，特指笼中那只鸟；霍译用了复数形式"birds"，泛指一切鸟类。从上下文来看，作者应是特指那只笼中鸟。

【9】"贾蔷一心都在龄官身上，也不顾送，倒是别的女孩子送了出来。"杨译是"Chia Chiang being too absorbed in Ling-kuan to notice, it was left to the other girls to see him out."译文的前半部分是独立主格结构"Chia Chiang being too absorbed in Ling-kuan to notice"，充当原因状语，其中的"too... to..."将两个小句"贾蔷一心都在龄官身上（Chia Chiang being too absorbed in Ling-kuan）"和"也不顾送（to notice）"连接了起来；在译文的主干部分，"it"是形式主语，真正的主语是不定式短语"to see him out"。霍译是"Jia Qiang was so absorbed in his concern for Charmante that he did not even notice him go and it was left to the little actresses to see him out."译者通过"so... that..."和"and"完成句内连接。

四、词汇表

1. strut [strʌt]	v.	to walk proudly with your head up and chest out to show that you think you are important 趾高气扬地走；高视阔步
2. snort [snɔːt]	n.	a loud sound that you make by breathing air out noisily through your nose, especially to show that you are angry or amused （尤指表示气愤或被逗乐的）哼
3. coop [kuːp]	v.	~ sb/sth up: to keep a person or an animal inside a building or in a small space 把……关（或禁锢）起来；拘禁
4. disconcert [ˌdɪskənˈsɜːt]	v.	to make sb feel anxious, confused or embarrassed 使不安；使困惑；使尴尬
	adj.	disconcerted
5. scorching [ˈskɔːtʃɪŋ]	adj.	very hot 酷热的
6. superfluous [suːˈpɜːfluəs]	adj.	more than you need or want 过剩的；多余的
7. cluster [ˈklʌstə(r)]	v.	to come together in a small group or groups 群聚；聚集
8. diminutive [dɪˈmɪnjətɪv]	adj.	very small 极小的；微小的；特小的
9. pirouette [ˌpɪruˈet]	v.	(esp. a ballet dancer) to turn or spin fast on one foot （尤指芭蕾舞者）单脚尖旋转
10. beseechingly [bɪˈsiːtʃɪŋli]	adv.	showing that you want sth very much 恳求地；哀求地；乞求地
11. audacity [ɔːˈdæsəti]	n.	brave but rude or shocking behavior 鲁莽；大胆无礼

12. string [strɪŋ]	*n.*	a series of things or people that come closely one after another 一系列；一连串；一批
13. temper [ˈtempə(r)]	*n.*	a short period of feeling very angry 怒气；火气；阵怒

秋爽斋偶结海棠社　蘅芜苑夜拟菊花题[1]

Begonia Club Takes Form One Day in the Studio of Autumn Freshness
Themes for Poems on Chrysanthemums Are Prepared One Evening in Alpinia Park[1] (Yang)

*A happy inspiration prompts Tan-chun to found the Crab-flower Club
And an ingenious arrangement enables Bao-chai to settle the chrysanthemum poem titles*[1] (Hawkes)

一、本回概述

　　探春向宝玉倡议，在大观园内创建诗社，适值贾芸送来两盆海棠花，遂起名"海棠社"。李纨自荐掌坛，自称稻香老农，社中他人也各有别号，如黛玉叫潇湘妃子，宝钗称蘅芜君等。众人决定当日开社，定题为"咏白海棠"，限作七律，压"门"字韵。结果，宝钗以"含蓄浑厚"夺冠，黛玉以"风流别致"居次。其后，湘云受邀加入诗社，与宝钗共拟菊花题。

二、篇章节选

原文

　　这里宝钗又向湘云道："诗题也不要过于新巧了。你看古人诗中那些刁钻古怪的题目和那极险的韵了，若题过于新巧，韵过于险，再不得有好诗，终是小家气。[2]诗固然怕说熟话，更不可过于求生，只要头一件立意清新，自然措词就不俗了。究竟这也算不得什么，还是纺绩针黹是你我的本等。一时闲了，倒是于你我深有益的书看几章是正经。"

　　湘云只答应着，因笑道："我如今心里想着，昨日作了海棠诗，我如今要作个菊花诗如何？"[3]宝钗道："菊花倒也合景，只是前人太多了。"湘云道："我也是如此想着，恐怕落套。"宝钗想了一想，说道："有了，如今以菊花为宾，以人为主，竟拟出几个题目来，都是两个字：一个虚字，一个实字，实字便用'菊'字，虚字就用通用门的。如此又是咏菊，又是赋事，前人也没作过，也不能落套。赋景咏物两关着，又新鲜，又大方。"

　　湘云笑道："这却很好。只是不知用何等虚字才好？你先想一个我听听。"宝钗想了一想，笑道："《菊梦》就好。"湘云笑道："果然好。我也有一个，《菊影》可使得？"宝钗道："也罢了。只是也有人作过，若题目多，这个也算的上。我又有了一个。"湘云道："快说出来。"宝钗道："《问菊》如何？"湘云拍案叫妙，[4]因接说道："我也有了，《访菊》如何？"宝钗也赞有趣，因说道："越性拟出十个来，写上再来。"说着，二人研墨蘸笔，湘云便写，宝钗便念，[5]一时凑了十个。湘云看了一遍，又笑道："十个还不成幅，越性凑成十二个便全了，也如人家的字画册页一样。"

　　宝钗听说，又想了两个，一共凑成十二。又说道："既这样，越性编出他个次序先后来。"湘云道："如此更妙，竟弄成个菊谱了。"宝钗道："起首是《忆菊》；忆之不得，故访，[6]第二是《访菊》；访之既得，便种，第三是《种菊》；种既盛开，故相对而赏，第四是《对菊》；[7]相对而兴有馀，故折来供瓶为玩，第五是《供菊》；既供而不吟，亦觉菊无彩色，第六便是《咏菊》；[8]既入词章，不可不供笔墨，第七便是《画菊》；既为菊如是碌碌，究竟不知菊有何妙处，不禁有所问，第八便是《问菊》；菊如解语，使人狂喜

不禁,第九便是《簪菊》;如此人事虽尽,犹有菊之可咏者,《菊影》、《菊梦》二首续在第十第十一;末卷便以《残菊》总收前题之盛。[9] 这便是三秋的妙景妙事都有了。"[10]

杨译

Then Pao-chai advised Hsiang-yun, "The themes for verses shouldn't be too outlandish. You can see that the poets of old times didn't go in for far-fetched subjects or freakish rhymes. Such things don't make for good poems and seem rather low-class.[2] Of course, poetry shouldn't be stereotyped, but we mustn't overdo the emphasis on originality either. So long as our ideas are fresh, the language can't be vulgar. In any case, writing poetry isn't important. *Our* main jobs are spinning and sewing. If we've time to spare, the proper thing for us is to read a few chapters of some improving book."

Hsiang-yun, having agreed to this, suggested, "As we wrote poems on the begonia yesterday, I wonder if we could write about the chrysanthemum this time?"[3]

"Yes, the chrysanthemum is suitable for autumn. The only objection is that too many poems have been written about it in the past."

"That's what I feel. We could hardly avoid plagiarism."

Pao-chai thought this over.

"I know," she said presently. "We'll lay stress not on the chrysanthemum but on the people looking at it, and set themes about their *reactions* to the flower. In this way we shall have tributes to the chrysanthemum as well as descriptions of feeling. This hasn't been done before and can't be too stereotyped. In fact, this combination will have freshness and distinction."

"A good idea," agreed Hsiang-yun. "But how will you introduce the feeling? Give me an example."

After a moment's thought Pao-chai replied, "*A Dream of Chrysanthemums* for instance."

"Of course. I've got one too. How about *The Chrysanthemum's Shadow*?"

"Can do, although of course it's been used before. If we have a fair number of themes we can include it. I've thought of another."

"Go on!"

"*Questioning the Chrysanthemum.*"

"Splendid!" Hsiang-yun clapped one hand on the table.[4] "I know. How'd you like *Seeking Out the Chrysanthemum*?"

"Good. We may as well think of ten themes and write them out."

They ground ink and dipped in the brush. Hsiang-yun wrote the themes out at Pao-chai's dictation,[5] and in no time at all they had ten. After reading them through Hsiang-yun said:

"Ten doesn't make a set. Let's have twelve while we're about it, like those albums of calligraphy and painting."

So Pao-chai thought up two more, making twelve in all.

"In this case let's arrange them in the right order," she said.

"Better still!" cried Hsiang-yun. "We shall have a chrysanthemum album."

"We'll start with *Thinking of the Chrysanthemum*. After thinking of it we seek it out;[6] so number two will be *Visiting the Chrysanthemum*. After finding it we plant it; so the third will be *Planting the Chrysanthemum*. After it has been planted and flowers, we face it and enjoy it; so four is *Facing the Chrysanthemum*.[7] To enjoy it further we pick it to put in a vase; so five is *Displaying the Chrysanthemum*. But to bring out its splendour once it is displayed we must write poems about it; so six is *Writing about the Chrysanthemum*.[8] And as a verse must be accompanied by a painting, number seven is *Painting the Chrysanthemum*. Even though we've been to so much trouble over it, we shan't know all its rare qualities unless we ask questions; so eight is *Questioning the Chrysanthemum*. If the flower seems able to understand, we are so thrilled that we want to get closer to it; hence nine is *Wearing the Chrysanthemum*.

"This exhausts all that men can do but, as there still remain certain aspects of the flower which can be described, ten and eleven are *The Chrysanthemum's Shadow* and

A Dream of Chrysanthemum. And we end with *The Withered Chrysanthemum* to sum up all the emotions expressed before.[9] In this way we shall cover all the fine sights and occupations of autumn."[10]

霍译

Bao-chai resumed her conversation with Xiang-yun.

'About the theme for tomorrow's poems,' she said. 'We don't want anything too outlandish. If you look at the works of the great poets, you find that *they* didn't go in for the weird and wonderful titles and "daring" rhymes that people nowadays are so fond of. Outlandish themes and daring rhymes do not produce good poetry. They merely show up the poverty of the writer's ideas.[2] Certainly one wants to avoid clichés; but one can easily go too far in the pursuit of novelty. The important thing is to have fresh ideas. If one has fresh ideas, one does not need to worry about clichés: the words take care of themselves. But what am I saying all this for? Spinning and sewing is the proper occupation for girls like us. Any time we have left over from that should be spent in reading a few pages of some improving book—not on this sort of thing!'

'Yes,' said Xiang-yun, without much conviction; but presently smiled as a new idea occurred to her.

'I've just thought of something. Yesterday's theme was "White Crab-blossom". The flower I'd like to write about is the chrysanthemum. Couldn't we have "Chrysanthemums" as our theme for tomorrow?'[3]

'It is certainly a very seasonable one,' said Bao-chai. 'The trouble is that *so* many people have written about it before.'

'Yes,' said Xiang-yun, 'I suppose it *is* rather a hackneyed one.'

Bao-chai thought for a bit.

'Unless of course you somehow involved the *poet* in the theme,' she said. 'You could do that by making up verb-object or concrete-abstract titles in which "chrysanthemums" was the concrete noun or the object of the verb as the case might be. Then your poem would be both a celebration of chrysanthemums and at the same time a description of some action or situation. Such a treatment of the subject *has* been tried in the past, but it is a much less hackneyed one. The combining of narrative and lyrical elements in a single treatment makes for freshness and greater freedom.'

'It sounds a splendid idea,' said Xiang-yun. 'But what sort of verbs or abstract nouns had you in mind? Can you give me an example?'

Bao-chai thought for a bit.

'What about "The Dream of the Chrysanthemums"?'

'Yes, that's a good one,' said Xiang-yun. 'I've thought of one too. Couldn't we have "The Shadow of the Chrysanthemums"?'

'Ye-e-es,' said Bao-chai, doubtfully. 'The trouble is, it's been used before. Still, if we had a *lot* of titles we could probably slip it in. I've thought of another.'

'Well, come on then!' said Xiang-yun.

'What about "Questioning the Chrysanthemums"?'

Xiang-yun slapped the table appreciatively. [4]

'That's a lovely one!' Presently she added: 'I've thought of another. What do you think of "Seeking the Chrysanthemums"?'

'That should be interesting,' said Bao-chai. 'Let's start making a list. We'll write down up to ten titles and then see what we think of them.'

The two of them busied themselves for some minutes grinding ink and softening a brush. Xiang-yun then proceeded to write down the titles at Bao-chai's dictation. [5] Soon they had ten. Xiang-yun read them over.

'Ten doesn't make a set,' she said. 'We need two more to make a round dozen, then we shall have just the right number for a little album.'

Bao-chai supplied two more without too much difficulty.

'If we're thinking in terms of a *sequence* of poems,' she said, 'we may as well, while we're about it, arrange these titles in some sort of order.'

'That's it!' said Xiang-yun. 'Then they will be all ready for making our "Chrysanthemum Album" with afterwards.'

'"Remembering the Chrysanthemums" should come first,' said Bao-chai.

'Now, let's see. When you remember them, you realize you haven't got any, so you go and look for some.[6] So "Seeking the Chrysanthemums" will be the second title.

'Well, having found some, you will want to plant them; so "Planting the Chrysanthemums" will be the third title.

'After you've planted them and the flowers have come out, you'll want to stand and look at them; so the fourth title will be "Admiring the Chrysanthemums".[7]

'You won't be able to have enough of them by just standing and admiring them, so you'll naturally want to pick some and arrange them in a vase so that you can enjoy them indoors. That means "Arranging the Chrysanthemums" for Number Five.

'But however much you enjoy them, you will feel that they somehow lack their full lustre without words to grace them, and so you will want to celebrate them in verse. That means "Celebrating the Chrysanthemums" will be the sixth title.[8]

'Well now, let's suppose you've just finished writing some verses about them. You've got the ink ready-made and the brush is still in your hand and you feel like paying the chrysanthemums a further tribute. What should you do but paint them? That's Number Seven: "Painting the Chrysanthemums".

'Now in spite of these silent tributes, you still don't know the secret of the chrysanthemums' mysterious charm and you can't resist asking them. Which brings us to Number Eight: "Questioning the Chrysanthemums".

'And if the chrysanthemums could really reply, it would be so delightful that you would want to have them near you all the time—and how better than by "Wearing the Chrysanthemums"? That's Number Nine.

'That brings us to the end of the verb-object titles which involve the poet himself as the understood subject of the action. But there remain other kinds of treatment, in which we consider the flowers by themselves without postulating the presence of the poet. So we have "The Shadow of the Chrysanthemums" and "The Dream of the Chrysanthemums" as Numbers Ten and Eleven.

'And of course "The Death of the Chrysanthemums" at the end of the album to round off on a suitable note of melancholy.'[9]

'There you are! All three months of autumn condensed into a single sequence of a dozen poems!'[10]

三、注释评点

【1】本回回目是"秋爽斋偶结海棠社　蘅芜苑夜拟菊花题",杨译是"Begonia Club Takes Form One Day in the Studio of Autumn Freshness Themes for Poems on Chrysanthemums Are Prepared One Evening in Alpinia Park",该译文上下句对称度较弱,主要表现在使用的语态不同:上句是主动语态,下句是被动语态。霍译是"A happy inspiration prompts Tan-chun to found the Crab-flower Club　And an ingenious arrangement enables Bao-chai to settle the chrysanthemum poem titles",译者在上下句中分别使用了两个物化主语"A happy inspiration"和"an ingenious arrangement";原文中的"秋爽斋"和"蘅芜苑"这两个住所的名称,在译文中分别由其主人的名字"Tan-chun(探春)"和"Bao-chai(宝钗)"替代;另外,霍译上下句的句式结构对应得十分工整,均是"主语+谓语+宾语+宾补"的结构。

【2】"若题过于新巧,韵过于险,再不得有好诗,终是小家气"一句,杨译是"Such things don't make for good poems and seem rather low-class."句首的"Such things"指代前一句中的"far-fetched subjects or freakish rhymes(刁钻古怪的题目和极险的韵)",为了避免表述上的重复,译者使用了代称的翻译手法,用"Such things"来指代前文已经提及的内容。霍译是"Outlandish themes and daring rhymes do not produce good poetry. They merely show up the poverty of the writer's ideas."译文包括两个句子。第一句中,译者使用句子化词组法,将两个小句"题过于新巧"和"韵过于险"译为两个并列的名词短语"outlandish themes"和"daring rhymes",其间用"and"连接,在该句中充当主语。译文第二句,对于原文中的"终是小家气",译者没有直译其字面意思,而是用意

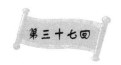

译的手法将其译为"merely show up the poverty of the writer's ideas",表达得又到位又有趣。

【3】"湘云只答应着,因笑道:'我如今心里想着,昨日作了海棠诗,我如今要作个菊花诗如何?'"一句,杨译是"Hsiang-yun, having agreed to this, suggested, 'As we wrote poems on the begonia yesterday, I wonder if we could write about the chrysanthemum this time?'"译者将原文中的并列结构"只答应着,因笑道"转化为译文中的偏正结构:"正"是谓语动词"suggested(道)","偏"是现在分词短语"having agreed to this(答应)"充当的时间状语;在直接引语中,译者使用连词"As",将原文中隐含的因果关系在译文中清晰地表达了出来。霍译是"'Yes,' said Xiang-yun, without much conviction; but presently smiled as a new idea occurred to her."译者增译了"without much conviction",表明湘云不太相信宝钗的一番话,只是应承而已。

【4】"湘云拍案叫妙"一句,杨译是"'Splendid!' Hsiang-yun clapped one hand on the table." 霍译是"Xiang-yun slapped the table appreciatively."对于原文中的"妙"字,杨译选择了形容词"Splendid",同时使用了直接引语的形式,整句译文十分生动;霍译则使用副词"appreciatively"来对应"妙"字,用来修饰谓语动词"slapped",体现出湘云因为宝钗灵感忽至,心中欣喜不已、拍案叫绝的情景。

【5】"湘云便写,宝钗便念"一句,是由主语不同的两个并列的小句构成。杨译"Hsiang-yun wrote the themes out at Pao-chai's dictation"将原文的两个小句巧妙地译为一句,此处有两个转化:一是原文中的动词"念"转化为英语中的名词"dictation";二是原文中的并列结构转化为英语中的偏正结构:"正"是"Hsiang-yun wrote the themes out(湘云便写)","偏"是"at Pao-chai's dictation(宝钗便念)"。霍译是"Xiang-yun then proceeded to write down the titles at Bao-chai's dictation.",其翻译手法与杨译一样。

【6】"忆之不得,故访"一句,杨译是"After thinking of it we seek it out",译者依据英语的行文习惯,增加了表达时间关系的介词"After"和充当主语的人称代词"we",译文简单明了。霍译是"Now, let's see. When you remember them, you realize you haven't got any, so you go and look for some." 译

者增译了较多内容，包括：表示宝钗边思考边叙说的"Now, let's see"，与上文"'Remembering the Chrysanthemums' should come first"对应的"When you remember them"，以及表达因果关系的连词"so"，这些增译的细节使得该译文的逻辑更严谨，行文更顺畅，语义更丰满。

【7】"种既盛开，故相对而赏，第四是《对菊》"一句中的"对菊"，杨译是"Facing the Chrysanthemum"，霍译是"Admiring the Chrysanthemums"；联系上下文可以看出，"admiring"一词更符合原文意思，有欣赏菊花盛开之意。

【8】"第六便是《咏菊》"一句中的"咏菊"，杨译是"Writing about the Chrysanthemum"，霍译是"Celebrating the Chrysanthemums"；"celebrating"有"赞美、歌颂"的意思，比"writing about"的意义更为丰满、贴切。

【9】"末卷便以《残菊》总收前题之盛"一句，杨译是"And we end with *The Withered Chrysanthemum* to sum up all the emotions expressed before."霍译是"And of course 'The Death of the Chrysanthemums' at the end of the album to round off on a suitable note of melancholy."对于"总收"一词，杨译使用了意为"总结"的"sum up"，即"用末卷《残菊》来总结前诗中表达的所有思想情感"，这在逻辑和语义上都讲不通，因为：一是《残菊》所表达的情感显然不同于前诗所表达的情感，二是《残菊》所表达的情感只是十二首菊花诗所表达的情感的一个构成部分。霍译使用了"round off"一词，有"以此圆满结束"之意，即"用末卷《残菊》来结尾，圆满完成'菊花诗'的撰写"；此外，霍译中增译的"on a suitable note of melancholy"，含有"前诗均写繁盛之景，现用有悲伤调子的《残菊》来收尾"的意思，其中"suitable"一词的使用显示出"用恰到好处的悲伤之调演绎菊花诗的完美落幕"。相比之下，霍译更符合原文的意思。

【10】"这便是三秋的妙景妙事都有了"一句，杨译将该句直译为"In this way we shall cover all the fine sights and occupations of autumn."霍译是"All three months of autumn condensed into a single sequence of a dozen poems!"意为"这三秋之景都浓缩在了这一系列的十二首诗中"，这种再创造的译文令人拍案叫绝。可以看出，霍译吃透了原文，然后用地道、准确的译文再现原文，且有出

自原文而高于原文之感。从总体结构上来看,霍译中每首诗的题目以及解析都单独成段,自成体系,段与段之间又前后相接,语义相连。虽然与原文十二个菊花题为一段的结构不同,但译文的层次更加分明,结构更加清晰。

四、词汇表

1. outlandish [aʊtˈlændɪʃ]	*adj.*	strange or extremely unusual 古怪的;奇特的
2. far-fetched [ˈfɑːˈfetʃt]	*adj.*	difficult to believe 难以置信的;牵强的
3. freakish [ˈfriːkɪʃ]	*adj.*	very strange, unusual or unexpected 怪异的;反常的;意外的
4. stereotyped [ˈsteriətaɪpt]	*adj.*	lacking originality, trite 老一套的,陈腐的
5. begonia [bɪˈɡəʊniə]	*n.*	a plant with large shiny flowers that may be pink, red, yellow or white, grown indoors or in a garden 秋海棠
6. chrysanthemum [krɪˈsænθəməm]	*n.*	a large, brightly colored garden flower that is shaped like a ball and made up of many long narrow petals 菊花
7. plagiarism [ˈpleɪdʒərɪzəm]	*n.*	the practice of copying another person's ideas, words or work and pretending that they are your own 剽窃;抄袭
8. presently [ˈprezntli]	*adv.*	used to show that sth happened after a short time 不久以后;不一会儿
9. tribute [ˈtrɪbjuːt]	*n.*	an act, a statement or a gift that is intended to show your respect or admiration, especially for a dead person (尤指对死者的)致敬,颂词;悼念;致哀;吊唁礼物

10. calligraphy [kəˈlɪgrəfi]	n.	beautiful handwriting that you do with a special pen or brush; the art of producing this 书法；书法艺术
11. exhaust [ɪgˈzɔːst]	v.	to use all of sth so that there is none left 用光；花光；耗尽
12. daring [ˈdeərɪŋ]	adj.	brave; willing to do dangerous or unusual things; involving danger or taking risks 勇敢的；敢于冒险的
13. cliché [ˈkliːʃeɪ; kliːˈʃeɪ]	n.	a phrase or an idea that has been used so often that it no longer has much meaning and is not interesting 陈词滥调；陈腐的套语
14. hackneyed [ˈhæknɪd]	adj.	used too often and therefore boring 陈腐的
15. lustre [ˈlʌstə]	n.	the shining quality of a surface 光泽；光辉
16. postulate [ˈpɒstjʊleɪt]	v.	to suggest or accept that sth is true so that it can be used as the basis for a theory, etc. 假定；假设
17. round off		to finish an activity or complete sth in a good or suitable way 圆满结束；圆满完成
18. condense [kənˈdens]	v.	to put sth such as a piece of writing into fewer words; to put a lot of information into a small space 简缩，压缩（文字、信息等）

第三十八回

林潇湘魁夺菊花诗　薛蘅芜讽和螃蟹咏

The Queen of Bamboos Wins First Place with Her Poems on Chrysanthemums
The Lady of the Alpinia Writes a Satire upon Crabs (Yang)

*River Queen triumphs in her treatment of chrysanthemum themes
And Lady Allspice is satirical on the subject of crabs* (Hawkes)

一、本回概述

　　湘云、宝钗请贾母、王夫人等人赏花食蟹，一时间，主仆上下嬉笑取乐，好不快活。茶余饭后，众人散尽，湘云将前日所拟"菊花题"公布于众，诗社各家尽兴创作。创作出的十二首菊花诗各具特色，评判官李纨以"题目新、诗也新、立意更新"为由，推黛玉为魁首。后宝玉提议："持螯赏桂，亦不可无诗"，大家就又做了几首螃蟹诗，宝钗写的螃蟹诗可谓绝唱，借螃蟹而讽世人，众姐妹赞叹不已。

二、篇章节选

原文

众人看一首,赞一首,彼此称扬不已。[1]李纨笑道:"等我从公评来。通篇看来,各人有各人的警句。今日公评:《咏菊》第一,《问菊》第二,《菊梦》第三,题目新,诗也新,立意更新,恼不得要推潇湘妃子为魁了;[2]然后《簪菊》、《对菊》、《供菊》、《画菊》、《忆菊》次之。"[3]宝玉听说,喜的拍手叫[4]"极是,极公道。"黛玉道:"我那首也不好,到底伤于纤巧些。"[5]李纨道:"巧的却好,不露堆砌生硬。"

黛玉道:"据我看来,头一句好的是'圃冷斜阳忆旧游',这句背面傅粉。'抛书人对一枝秋'已经妙绝,将供菊说完,没处再说,故翻回来想到未折未供之先,意思深透。"李纨笑道:"固如此说,你的'口齿噙香'句也敌的过了。"探春又道:"到底要算蘅芜君沉着,'秋无迹','梦有知',把个忆字竟烘染出来了。"宝钗笑道:"你的'短鬓冷沾','葛巾香染',也就把簪菊形容的一个缝儿也没了。"湘云道:"'偕谁隐','为底迟',真个把个菊花问的无言可对。"李纨笑道:"你的'科头坐','抱膝吟',竟一时也不能别开,菊花有知,也必腻烦了。"[6]说的大家都笑了。

宝玉笑道:"我又落第。难道'谁家种','何处秋','蜡屐远来','冷吟不尽',都不是访,'昨夜雨','今朝霜',都不是种不成?但恨敌不上[7]'口齿噙香对月吟'、'清冷香中抱膝吟'、'短鬓'、'葛巾'、'金淡泊'、'翠离披'、'秋无迹'、'梦有知'这几句罢了。"又道:"明儿闲了,我一个人作出十二首来。"李纨道:"你的也好,[8]只是不及这几句新巧就是了。"

杨译

As they read each poem they praised it, heaping compliments on each other. [1]

"Let me try to pass fair judgement now," said Li Wan with a smile. "On the whole each poem has striking lines but, speaking impartially, I rank *Writing about*

the Chrysanthemum first, Questioning the Chrysanthemum second, and A Dream of Chrysanthemums third; for all three show originality in the theme, ideas and style. The Queen of Bamboos will have to be given first place.[2] Next in order of merit come Wearing the Chrysanthemum, Facing the Chrysanthemum, Displaying the Chrysanthemum, Painting the Chrysanthemum and Thinking of the Chrysanthemum."[3]

Pao-yu clapped his hands in delight at this, exclaiming,[4] "Absolutely right. Very fair."

"Mine didn't amount to much," Tai-yu observed. "They're rather contrived."[5]

"But aptly so," rejoined Li Wan. "Not stiff and overloaded."

"To my mind," continued Tai-yu, "the best line of all is 'Sunset in chill garden recalls a former visit' which presents such a strong contrast. And 'Tossing my book aside I face a spray of autumn' is perfect, leaving nothing more to be said about displaying chrysanthemums, so that she had to revert to the time before the flower was plucked and put in the vase. Very penetrating, very subtle."

"Quite so. Still, your line about 'sweet melodies' is even better," countered Li Wan.

Tan-chun put in, "And what about the Lady of the Alpinia? 'No sign is there of autumn' and 'yet in dream I see' bring out the idea of nostalgia so vividly."

Pao-chai smiled and replied, "Your 'short hair wet with cold dew' and 'coarse cap stained with fragrance' do full justice to the subject too."

Hsiang-yun remarked gaily, "Questions like 'With what hermit are you taking refuge?' and 'What makes you bloom so late?' are bound to stump the flower."

Li Wan retorted, "I daresay your sitting bareheaded and hugging your knees while you chant, refusing to leave, would get on the flower's nerves too—if it had any."[6]

At that there was general laughter.

"I'm last again," said Pao-yu cheerfully. "But surely my 'Who has planted this flower?', 'Whence springs this autumn glory?', 'waxed sandals come from far away,' and 'chants endless poems' describe visiting the chrysanthemum all right? And don't 'rain last night' and 'this morning's frost' describe the planting? It's just that they're not up to such images as [7] 'facing the moon croon their sweet melodies,' 'In the cold clean scent I hug my knees and chant,' 'short hair,' 'coarse cap, 'pale gold,' 'the marred green leaves are withering,' 'no sign is there of autumn' and 'seen in dreams.'" He added, "Tomorrow when I've time, I mean to write on all twelve themes."

"Your verses aren't bad," [8] Li Wan told him. "They're not as distinctive as the others though."

霍译

Each poem was praised in turn, and the reading of the whole twelve concluded amidst cries of mutual admiration. [1]

'Now just a moment!' said Li Wan, interrupting their encomiums. 'Let me first try to give you an impartial judgement. I think there were good lines in *all* of the poems, but comparing one with another, it seems to be that one is bound to place "Celebrating the Chrysanthemums" first, with "Questioning the Chrysanthemums" second and "The Dream of the Chrysanthemums" third. The titles themselves were original, and—particularly in their treatment of the subject—these are three highly original poems. So I think that today the first place must undoubtedly go to River Queen. [2] After those first three I would place "Wearing the Chrysanthemums", "Admiring the Chrysanthemums", "Arranging the Chrysanthemums", "Painting the Chrysanthemums" and "Remembering the Chrysanthemums" in that order.' [3]

Bao-yu clapped his hands delightedly. [4]

'Absolutely right! A very fair judgement!'

'I'm afraid mine *aren't* really all that good,' said Dai-yu. 'They are a bit too contrived.' [5]

'There's nothing wrong with a bit of contrivance,' said Li Wan. 'One doesn't want the structure of a poem to stand out too ruggedly.'

'I very much like that couplet of Cloud Maiden's,' said Dai-yu:

'On frosty nights I'll dream you back again,

Brave in your garden bed at close of day.

It's a technique that painters call "white-backing". That marvellous couplet that comes before it:

> To hold the garden's fragrance in a vase,
>
> And see all autumn in a single spray

already sums up all there is to be said on the subject of flower arrangement. You feel that she's left herself nothing else to say. So what does she do? She goes back to the time before the flowers were arranged—before they were picked, even. That *going back* in her "frosty nights" couplet is a very subtle way of throwing the main theme into relief, just as the artist's white-backing sharpens the highlights on the other side of the painting.'

Li Wan smiled.

'That may be so; but your own "acrid-sweet" couplet is more than a match for it.'

'*I* think Lady Allspice dealt with her subject most effectively,' said Tan-chun. 'That couplet of hers:

> But autumn's guest, who last year graced this plot,
>
> Only as yet in dreams of night appears

seems to bring out the idea of *remembering* so vividly.'

'Well, your "head-cloth reeking of autumn's acrid perfume" and "chill dew of autumn pearling the hair" give a pretty vivid image of *wearing* chrysanthemums,' said Bao-chai with a laugh.

'And River Queen's "who shares your hiding place?" "why do you bloom so late?",' said Xiang-yun, smiling mischievously, 'make so thorough a job of *questioning* them, that one feels the poor things must have been quite tongue-tied!'

'For that matter,' said Li Wan, entering into the spirit of the thing, 'your persistent haunting of the chrysanthemums—"sitting bare-headed by their wintry bed" and "hugging your knees and singing to them"—makes one suspect that if the chrysanthemums *really* had consciousness, they might, in the end, have grown just a tiny bit tired of your company!'[6]

The others all laughed.

'I seem to be bottom again,' said Bao-yu ruefully. 'Though I must say I should have thought that

… to go on an excursion—

Some garden where… was planted

The glory of autumn being our destination

and so forth was a perfectly satisfactory exposition of "*seeking* the chrysanthemums"; and that

A shower last night the wilting leaves revived,

Opening the morning-buds all silver-hoar

dealt with the theme of *transplanting* chrysanthemums rather successfully. Heigh-ho! I suppose it's just that I couldn't produce anything quite as good as [7] River Queen's "acrid-sweet" line, or Cloud Maiden's "bare-headed by your wintry bed", or Plaintain lover's "reeking head-cloth" or "few poor, tattered leaves", or Lady Allspice's "autumn guest in dreams of night appears".

'Well, never mind,' he went on, after a moment's reflection. 'Perhaps tomorrow or the day after, if I've got the time, I'll try to do all twelve of them again on my own.'

'Your poems were perfectly all right,'[8] said Li Wan consolingly. 'It's simply — as you yourself have just said—that they didn't have anything *quite* as good as the lines you have mentioned.'

三、注释评点

【1】"众人看一首，赞一首，彼此称扬不已"一句，主语"众人"发出了三个动作：看、赞、称扬。杨译是"As they read each poem they praised it, heaping compliments on each other"，译者用连词"As"进行句内连接，将原文中并列的三个动词"看、赞、称扬"，分别译为"As"引导的时间状语从句的谓语"read（看）"、主句的谓语"praised（赞）"和充当伴随状语的现在分词短语"heaping compliments（称扬）on each other"，使译文呈现出"偏—正—偏"的结构。霍译是"Each poem was praised in turn, and the reading of the whole

twelve concluded amidst cries of mutual admiration." 译文由两个分句构成,中间用"and"连接;在两个分句中,译者都没有使用原文中的人格主语"众人",而是分别用了物化主语"each poem"和"reading"。另外,原文中的动词短语"看一首"被译为英语的名词短语"the reading of the whole twelve",充当第二个分句的主语。

【2】"恼不得要推潇湘妃子为魁了"一句,杨译"The Queen of Bamboos will have to be given first place." 使用了不定式的被动式,其中的"have to"让人体会到黛玉的诗写得无可争议的好,让大家觉得必须要推她为魁首;霍译"So I think that today the first place must undoubtedly go to River Queen." 使用了情态动词"must"和表示肯定语气的副词"undoubtedly",把李纨认为黛玉当之无愧为菊花诗魁首的意思表达得淋漓尽致,也体现出李纨作为裁判的权威感。

【3】"然后《簪菊》、《对菊》、《供菊》、《画菊》、《忆菊》次之"一句,杨译是"Next in order of merit come *Wearing the Chrysanthemum, Facing the Chrysanthemum, Displaying the Chrysanthemum, Painting the Chrysanthemum* and *Thinking of the Chrysanthemum*." 译文的主语很长(包含五个菊花题),为了避免句式上的头重脚轻,译者采用了倒装式。霍译是"After those first three I would place 'Wearing the Chrysanthemums', 'Admiring the Chrysanthemums', 'Arranging the Chrysanthemums', 'Painting the Chrysanthemums' and 'Remembering the Chrysanthemums' in that order." 译者增译了照应前文的介宾短语"After those first three",清楚地告诉读者,菊花诗的前三甲已花落别家,《簪菊》等五首诗只能排在三甲之后。

【4】"宝玉听说,喜的拍手叫"一句,主语"宝玉"发出了三个动作:听说、拍手、叫。杨译是"Pao-yu clapped his hands in delight at this, exclaiming…" 译者将原文中的三个动词分别译为介词短语"at this(听说)"、谓语"clapped his hands(拍手)"和现在分词"exclaiming(叫)",体现出英语句式的层次感。霍译是"Bao-yu clapped his hands delightedly." 译者只翻译了原文中的动词"拍手(clapped his hands)"。

【5】"我那首也不好,到底伤于纤巧些"一句,杨译是"'Mine didn't amount to much,' Tai-yu observed. 'They're rather contrived.'"霍译是"'I'm afraid mine *aren't* really all that good,' said Dai-yu. 'They are a bit too contrived.'"杨译中的"amount to much"是固定短语,意为"了不起"。对于原文中"纤巧"一词的翻译,两位译者都选择了"contrived",意为"不自然的、刻意的、矫揉造作的",因为黛玉在这里所说的"纤巧"明显带有贬义的色彩。

【6】"菊花有知,也必腻烦了"一句,杨译是"… would get on the flower's nerves too—if it had any."霍译是"… makes one suspect that if the chrysanthemums *really* had consciousness, they might, in the end, have grown just a tiny bit tired of your company!"两个译文中都使用了虚拟语气。

【7】"但恨敌不上"一句,杨译是"It's just that they're not up to such images as…",霍译是"… it's just that I couldn't produce anything quite as good as…"。两位译者都使用了句型"it's just that…",其中的"that"相当于"because",用来表示原因;霍译后文中再次用到这个句型"It's simply that…",意为"问题是……","只是……"。这个句型用于委婉地表达说话者不喜欢、不认同的事情。

【8】"你的也好"一句,杨译是"Your verses aren't bad",霍译是"Your poems were perfectly all right"。杨译使用了"反译(negation)"的技巧,而霍译则是完全地忠实于原文。

四、词汇表

1. heap [hi:p]	v.	to give a lot of sth such as praise or criticism to sb 对(某人)大加赞扬(或批评等)
2. contrived [kənˈtraɪvd]	adj.	planned in advance and not natural or genuine; written or arranged in a way that is not natural or realistic 预谋的;不自然的;人为的;矫揉造作的
3. aptly [ˈæptli]	adv.	suitably or appropriately in the circumstances 恰当地;适当地
4. toss [tɒs]	v.	to throw sth slightly or carelessly(轻轻

		或漫不经心地）扔，抛，掷
5. revert [rɪˈvɜːt]	v.	**~ to sth**: to return to an earlier topic or subject 重提，回到，恢复（先前的话题或主题）
6. penetrating [ˈpenɪtreɪtɪŋ]	adj.	showing that you have understood sth quickly and completely 深刻的；精辟的
7. nostalgia [nɒˈstældʒə]	n.	a feeling of sadness mixed with pleasure and affection when you think of happy times in the past 怀旧；念旧
8. stump [stʌmp]	v.	to ask sb a question that is too difficult for them to answer or give them a problem that they cannot solve 把……难住；难倒
9. croon [kruːn]	v.	to sing sth quietly and gently 低声哼唱
10. mar [mɑː(r)]	v.	to damage or spoil sth good 破坏；毁坏；损毁；损害
11. encomium [enˈkəʊmiəm]	n.	a speech or piece of writing that praises sb or sth highly 高度赞扬的话（或文章）；颂词
12. grace [ɡreɪs]	v.	to bring honor to sb/sth; to be kind enough to attend or take part in sth 使荣耀；使生辉；承蒙光临
13. reek [riːk]	v.	to smell very strongly of sth unpleasant 散发臭气；发出难闻的气味
14. acrid [ˈækrɪd]	adj.	having a strong, bitter smell or taste that is unpleasant（气、味）辛辣的；难闻的；刺激的
15. haunt [hɔːnt]	v.	to continue to cause problems for sb for a long time 长期不断地缠绕（某人）
16. rueful [ˈruːfl]	adj.	feeling or showing that you are sad or

		sorry 悲伤的；懊悔的；沮丧的
	adv.	ruefully
17. excursion [ɪkˈskɜːʃn]	*n.*	a short journey made for pleasure, especially one that has been organized for a group of people（尤指集体）远足，短途旅行
18. wilt [wɪlt]	*v.*	if a plant or flower wilts, or sth wilts it, it bends towards the ground because of the heat or a lack of water（使）枯萎，凋谢，蔫

村姥姥是信口开河　情哥哥偏寻根究底[1]

An Old Village Woman Tells Tall Stories
A Romantic Youth Insists on Following Them Up [1] (Yang)

An inventive old countrywoman tells a story of somewhat questionable veracity
And an impressionable young listener insists on getting to the bottom of the matter [1]
(Hawkes)

一、本回概述

袭人问平儿何故晚发月钱，意外得知熙凤用公款放贷的生财之道。刘姥姥再进大观园，信口开河，编造乡野故事，引得贾府上下很是稀奇。宝玉对"女孩雪地抽柴"的故事尤感兴趣，众人散后，又向刘姥姥寻根究底，引得她继续胡诌，宝玉却信以为真，派茗烟去寻找女孩的塑像，一无所获。

二、篇章节选

原文

一时散了，背地里宝玉足的拉了刘姥姥，细问那女孩儿是谁。[2] 刘姥姥只得编了告诉他道：[3]"那原是我们庄北沿地埂子上有一个小祠堂里供的，不是神佛，当先有个什么老爷。"说着又想名姓。[4] 宝玉道："不拘什么名姓，你不必想了，只说原故就是了。"刘姥姥道："这老爷没有儿子，只有一位小姐，名叫茗玉。小姐知书识字，老爷太太爱如珍宝。[5] 可惜这茗玉小姐生到十七岁，一病死了。"宝玉听了，跌足叹惜，又问后来怎么样。刘姥姥道："因为老爷太太思念不尽，便盖了这祠堂，塑了这茗玉小姐的像，派了人烧香拨火。[6] 如今日久年深的，人也没了，庙也烂了，那个像就成了精。"[7] 宝玉忙道："不是成精，规矩这样人是虽死不死的。"刘姥姥道："阿弥陀佛！[8] 原来如此。不是哥儿说，我们都当他成精。他时常变了人出来各村庄店道上闲逛。我才说这抽柴火的就是他了。我们村庄上的人还商议着要打了这塑像平了庙呢。"宝玉忙道："快别如此。若平了庙，罪过不小。"刘姥姥道："幸亏哥儿告诉我，我明儿回去告诉他们就是了。"

宝玉道："我们老太太、太太都是善人，合家大小也都好善喜舍，[9] 最爱修庙塑神的。[10] 我明儿做一个疏头，替你化些布施，[11] 你就做香头，攒了钱把这庙修盖，再装潢了泥像，每月给你香火钱烧香岂不好？"刘姥姥道："若这样，我托那小姐的福，也有几个钱使了。"宝玉又问他地名庄名，来往远近，坐落何方。刘姥姥便顺口胡诌了出来。

宝玉信以为真，回至房中，盘算了一夜。[12] 次日一早，便出来给了茗烟几百钱，按着刘姥姥说的方向地名，着茗烟去先踏看明白，回来再做主意。[13] 那茗烟去后，宝玉左等也不来，右等也不来，急的热锅上的蚂蚁一般。[14]

杨译

As soon as the party broke up, he quietly took Granny Liu aside to ask her who the girl in her story was.[2] This forced the old woman to improvise again.[3]

"In the fields just north of our village there stands a small shrine," she said. "It wasn't built for any god or Buddha, but there was once a gentleman..." She stopped to think of a name.[4]

"Never mind," said Pao-yu. "Names don't matter, just tell me the story."

"This gentleman had no son, only one daughter called Ming-yu," continued Granny Liu. "She could read and write and was her parents' most precious treasure,[5] but when she reached the age of seventeen the poor girl fell ill and died..."

Pao-yu stamped his foot and sighed.

"What happened afterwards?" he asked.

"Her parents were so heartbroken that they built this shrine, had an effigy made of the girl, and kept someone there to burn incense and keep the lamp burning.[6] That was many years ago. Those people are dead now, the temple is in ruins, and a spirit has taken possession of the effigy."[7]

"It's not that a spirit's taken possession of it," he retorted quickly. "The rule is that people of this kind are immortal."

"You don't say! Gracious Buddha![8] If you hadn't told me, I'd have sworn it was magic. She often takes human form to roam about through the villages, farmsteads and highways, and it was *she* who took that firewood. In our village they're talking of smashing up this image and razing the shrine to the ground."

"Don't let them do that!" urged Pao-yu hastily. "It would be a great sin to destroy that shrine."

"I'm glad you told me, sir," said Granny Liu. "When I go back tomorrow I'll stop them."

"My grandmother and my mother are both charitable people. In fact, our whole family, old and young, like to do good deeds and give alms;[9] and they take the greatest delight in building temples and having images made.[10] So tomorrow I'll draw up a subscription notice to collect donations for you.[11] When enough contributions have come in, you can take charge of repairing the shrine and restoring the image, and every month I'll give you money for incense. Wouldn't that be a good thing?"

"If you do that I'll have a few cash to spend too, all thanks to this young lady!"

Pao-yu then asked her the name of the district and village, how far it was there and back, and just where the shrine stood. She made up answers at random but he believed her, and on his return to his room he spent the whole night thinking the matter over. [12]

The next morning, as soon as it was light, he sent Ming-yen with several hundred cash to find the place described by Granny Liu and bring him back a clear report so that he could make further plans. [13]

Pao-yu waited hour after hour for Ming-yen's return, as frantic as an ant on a hot pan. [14]

霍译

After the company had dispersed, Bao-yu finally managed to get Grannie Liu into a corner and question her in detail about the mysterious snow maiden. [2] Grannie Liu's inventiveness was once more put to the test. [3]

'On the embankment that runs along the north side of our land,' she said, 'there is a little shrine. The image inside it is not a god or a Buddha, though. There used at one time to be a gentleman living in our parts—'

She broke off at this point and appeared to be trying to remember a name. [4]

'Never mind his name,' said Bao-yu. 'Don't try to remember it. Just tell me what happened.'

'This gentleman had no son, but he had an only daughter called—I think it was Ruo-yu. She could read books as well as any scholar, this Ruo-yu, and the gentleman loved her more than all the treasure in the world. [5] But sad to say, she took sick and died when she was only seventeen years old—'

Bao-yu groaned and stamped his foot.

'So what happened then?'

'Because the gentleman loved her so dearly, he had this shrine built for her out in the fields and had a likeness of her made out of wood and clay to put inside it; and he arranged for someone to burn incense there and always keep a spark of fire going inside the burner.[6] But as the years went by, both the gentleman and the people who used to tend the shrine for him all died, and now the shrine is falling into ruin and the statue has come to life and started haunting people.'[7]

'No, no,' Bao-yu interrupted hurriedly, 'that wouldn't be the statue coming to life. People like that are never really dead, even after they have died.'

'Holy Name!'[8] said Grannie Liu. 'Fancy that now! And me thinking all along it was the statue. Well, whatever it is, every so often it takes on human shape and goes wandering abroad troubling people. And that's what I saw when I looked out that time and saw someone taking our firewood. The people in our village are talking of breaking up the image and knocking the shrine down so as to put a stop to the haunting.'

'Good gracious! they mustn't do that!' said Bao-yu. 'That's a terrible sin, knocking a temple down!'

'Now I am glad you told me that,' said Grannie Liu gravely. 'When I get back, I shall do my best to stop them.'

'My grandmother and Lady Wang and in fact just about everyone in this family is terribly keen on good works,'[9] said Bao-yu. 'There's nothing they like better than repairing temples and restoring things.[10] Tomorrow I'll write out an appeal and collect some subscriptions for you.[11] *You* can be the fund's Treasurer, and when we've got enough money together, *you* can supervise the restoration. And I'll get them to send you some money every month for incense. How would that be?'

'Statue or spirit or whatever she is,' said Grannie Liu, 'I shall certainly be grateful to her for the money.'

Bao-yu pressed her for the names of the nearest farms and villages and the exact location of the shrine in relation to them as well as the distance to it and the general direction in which it lay. Answering all these questions with whatever came first into her head, Grannie Liu supplied a set of fictitious directions which Bao-yu, believing them to be genuine, carefully committed to memory and carried back to his room, where he lay awake half the night planning what he would do for the beautiful wood-thief in the days ahead.[12]

He went out of the Garden first thing next morning, and handing Tealeaf a few hundred cash, told him the directions for getting to the shrine as given him by Grannie Liu the night before, and instructed him to follow them, inspect the shrine, and report back on what he saw. He would await Tealeaf's report before deciding what to do next.[13]

But once Tealeaf had gone he found the waiting very tedious, and as the day wore on and Tealeaf still failed to return, he became as fidgety as a worm on hot earth.[14]

三、注释评点

【1】"村姥姥是信口开河 情哥哥偏寻根究底"是本回回目,杨译是"An Old Village Woman Tells Tall Stories A Romantic Youth Insists on Following Them Up";霍译是"An inventive old countrywoman tells a story of somewhat questionable veracity And an impressionable young listener insists on getting to the bottom of the matter",两个译文都与原文的意思非常贴合。此外,霍译增加了两个形容词:"inventive"和"impressionable",不仅没有画蛇添足之嫌,反有锦上添花之妙。

【2】"一时散了,背地里宝玉足的拉了刘姥姥,细问那女孩儿是谁"一句,杨译是"As soon as the party broke up, he quietly took Granny Liu aside to ask her who the girl in her story was."霍译是"After the company had dispersed, Bao-yu finally managed to get Grannie Liu into a corner and question her in detail about the mysterious snow maiden."两位译者都将小句"一时散了"译为时间状语从句,分别由表示时间关系的连词"as soon as"和"after"引导。对于原文中两个并列的动词"拉"和"问",杨译将其转化为偏正结构:"正"是主句中的谓语"took … aside(拉)","偏"是不定式短语充当的目的状语"to ask her……（问）"；霍译则保留了原文的并列结构，将其译为动词不定式短语"to get Grannie Liu into a corner（拉）"和"(to) question her in detail（问）"，中间用"and"连接。

【3】"刘姥姥只得编了告诉他道"一句，杨译是"This forced the old woman to improvise again."译者用物化主语"This"代替了原文中的人格主语"刘姥姥"；指示代词"This"有承上启下的作用，使得该句与前文衔接紧密。霍译是"Grannie Liu's inventiveness was once more put to the test."译文虽然与原文的字面形式略有不同，却语义诙谐，表意准确到位。

【4】"说着又想名姓"一句，杨译"She stopped to think of a name"是按照原文的字面意思翻译的；霍译是"She broke off at this point and appeared to be trying to remember a name."第二个谓语动词"appeared"和紧随其后的不定式的进行式"to be trying"，将刘姥姥装模作样编故事的神态栩栩如生地再现出来。

【5】"小姐知书识字，老爷太太爱如珍宝"一句，杨译是"She could read and write and was her parents' most precious treasure"；霍译是"She could read books as well as any scholar,… and the gentleman loved her more than all the treasure in the world"。原文中出现了两个主语："小姐"和"老爷太太"，杨译非常巧妙地只用"小姐（She）"做主语，把"老爷太太"译为定语"her parents"，跟在系动词"was"之后，做表语的一部分；霍译的结构与原文基本相同，使用了两个不同的主语"She（小姐）"和"the gentleman（老爷）"。

【6】"因为老爷太太思念不尽，便盖了这祠堂，塑了这茗玉小姐的像，派了人烧香拨火。"主语"老爷太太"发出了四个动作：思念、盖、塑、派。杨译是"Her parents were so heartbroken that they built this shrine, had an effigy made of the girl, and kept someone there to burn incense and keep the lamp burning."译者使用"so… that…"结构来连句，其中的形容词"heartbroken"对应的是原文的动词"思念（不尽）"，"that"引导的结果状语从句中的三个并列谓语"built"，"had an effigy made"和"kept"，对应翻译"老爷太太"发出的另外三个动作"盖""塑"和"派"。霍译是"Because the gentleman loved her so dearly, he had this shrine built for her out in the fields <u>and</u> had a likeness of her made out of wood and clay to put inside it; <u>and</u> he arranged for someone to burn incense there and always keep a spark of fire going inside the burner." 译文是由分号前后的两个分句构成，译者使用"Because"和两个"and"进行连句：第一个"and"连接第一个分句中主句部分的两个谓语，即两个使役用法"had this shrine built"和"had a likeness of her made"，第二个"and"连结前后两个分句；此外，动词"盖""塑"和"派"分别被译为"had this shrine built"，"had a likeness of her made"和"arranged for someone to burn"，这些短语表达的都是指派别人去做某事的意思。

【7】"如今日久年深的，人也没了，庙也烂了，那个像就成了精"一句，包含四个小句。杨译是"That was many years ago. Those people are dead now, the temple is in ruins, and a spirit has taken possession of the effigy." 译文由两个句子构成：第一句"That was many years ago"对应的是原文的第一个小句"如今日久年深的"；第二句是由"and"连接的三个分句构成，分别对应原文的三个小句："Those people are dead now（人也没了）"，"the temple is in ruins（庙也烂了）"和"a spirit has taken possession of the effigy（那个像就成了精）"。霍译是"But as the years went by, both the gentleman and the people who used to tend the shrine for him all died, and now the shrine is falling into ruin and the statue has come to life and started haunting people." 与杨译不同的是，该译文是一个主从复合句，译者使用"But""as"和两个"and"进行连句："But"用来承上；"as"用来启下，引导时间状语从句"as the years went by"，对应原文的第一个小句"如今日久年深的"；两个"and"连接主句中的三个分句，分别对应原文的三个小句："both the gentleman and the people… all died（人也没了）"，"now the shrine is falling into ruin（庙也烂了）"和"the statue has come to life and started haunting people（那个像就成了精）"。另外，对于"人也没了"中的"人"字，霍译翻译得十分细致具体：both the gentleman and the people who used to tend the shrine for him，特指"老爷及看护祠堂的人"，这些人都去世了，所以祠堂才破败了。当然，杨译也使用了限定词"Those"进行特指，但"Those people"仍显得太宽泛。

【8】关于"阿弥陀佛"的翻译，杨译"Gracious Buddha"用的是异化法；霍译"Holy Name"用的是归化法。

【9】"我们老太太、太太都是善人,合家大小也都好善喜舍"一句,杨译是"My grandmother and my mother are both charitable people. In fact, our whole family, old and young, like to do good deeds and give alms";霍译是"My grandmother and Lady Wang and in fact just about everyone in this family is terribly keen on good works"。原文中的"也都"一词含有递进、增强语气的意味,杨译使用词组"in fact"来表达这层意思;霍译除了用"in fact"之外,还使用了"just about everyone"来加强语气,表达出"也都"的含义。另外,杨译使用两个独立的句子对应翻译原文的两个小句,结构和原文比较一致;霍译则认为"都是善人"和"好善喜舍"是同义,故将这两个短句合译为一句"… is terribly keen on good works"。

【10】"最爱修庙塑神的"一句,杨译是"… and they take the greatest delight in building temples and having images made";霍译是"There's nothing they like better than repairing temples and restoring things"。对于"最爱"一词的翻译,杨译使用了短语"take delight in doing something",同时用最高级的形式"the greatest delight"来表达最高级的语义"最爱";霍译的结构是主从复合句,使用比较级的形式(nothing they like better than…)来表达最高级的语义"最爱"。对于"修庙塑神"一词,杨译是"building temples and having images made",用词十分准确;霍译是"repairing temples and restoring things",译者将"修"和"塑"二字理解为"修理"和"重塑"之意,恐和原文意思有出入。

【11】"我明儿做一个疏头,替你化些布施"一句,由两个并列的小句构成。杨译是"So tomorrow I'll draw up a subscription notice to collect donations for you."译者将原文中的并列结构译为偏正结构:"正"是谓语部分(I)'ll draw up a subscription notice(做一个疏头)","偏"是不定式短语充当的目的状语"to collect donations for you(替你化些布施)"。霍译是"Tomorrow I'll write out an appeal and collect some subscriptions for you."译者沿用了原文中的并列结构,用"and"连接两个谓语"(I)'ll write out an appeal"和"collect some subscriptions for you"。

【12】"刘姥姥便顺口胡诌了出来。宝玉信以为真,回至房中,盘算了一夜。"杨译是"She made up answers at random but he believed her, and on his return to his room he spent the whole night thinking the matter over." 译者使用"but"和"and"进行连句；同时使用词性转化法将原文中的动词"回"译为英语的名词"return"；汉译英时，汉语中的动词转化为英语中的名词是十分常用的一种技巧。霍译是"Answering all these questions with whatever came first into her head, Grannie Liu supplied a set of fictitious directions which Bao-yu, believing them to be genuine, carefully committed to memory and carried back to his room, where he lay awake half the night planning what he would do for the beautiful wood-thief in the days ahead." 该译文是一个结构十分复杂的复合句，主要是通过"whatever""which""where"和"what"这四个"wh-"词汇进行连句："Answering all these questions with whatever came first into her head"是现在分词短语充当的伴随状语，其中的"whatever came first into her head"是介词"with"的宾语从句；接下来的主句部分包含三个从句："which"引导的定语从句，修饰"directions"，其中套了一个"where"引导的定语从句，修饰"room"，这其中又套了一个"what"引导的名词性从句，充当"planning"的宾语；该译文非常典型地体现出英语复合句的"从句套从句"的结构。

【13】"次日一早，便出来给了茗烟几百钱，按着刘姥姥说的方向地名，着茗烟去先踏看明白，回来再做主意。"杨译是"The next morning, as soon as it was light, he sent Ming-yen with several hundred cash to find the place described by Granny Liu and bring him back a clear report so that he could make further plans." 该译文是一个主从复合句，其中包含两个从句："as soon as"引导的时间状语从句和"so that"引导的目的状语从句。霍译是"He went out of the Garden first thing next morning, and handing Tealeaf a few hundred cash, told him the directions for getting to the shrine as given him by Grannie Liu the night before, and instructed him to follow them, inspect the shrine, and report back on what he saw. He would await Tealeaf's report before deciding what to do next." 该译文由两个句子构成。第一句中，译者主要使用三个"and"进行句内连接：前两个"and"连接三个并列的谓语动词"went""told"和"instructed"；第三个"and"连接的是"instructed"的宾语"him"之后的三个并列的宾语补足语："to follow them""inspect the shrine"和"report back on…"。

【14】"急的热锅上的蚂蚁一般。"一句,杨译"as frantic as an ant on a hot pan"使用了直译法,表述十分生动;霍译"as fidgety as a worm on hot earth"对原文中的喻体"热锅上的蚂蚁"进行了再创造,将其变为"a worm on hot earth"。

四、词汇表

1. improvise [ˈɪmprəvaɪz]	v.	to invent music, the words in a play, a statement, etc. while you are playing or speaking, instead of planning it in advance 即兴创作(音乐、台词、演讲辞等)
2. effigy [ˈefɪdʒi]	n.	a statue of a famous person, a saint or a god(名人、圣人或神的)雕像,塑像
3. farmstead [ˈfɑːmsted]	n.	a farmhouse and the buildings near it 农舍及附近建筑物
4. smash sth up		to destroy sth deliberately(蓄意)捣毁,破坏
5. raze [reɪz]	v.	to completely destroy a building, town, etc. so that nothing is left 彻底摧毁;将……夷为平地
6. subscription [səbˈskrɪpʃn]	n.	the act of people paying money for sth to be done 集体资助;集体捐助
7. embankment [ɪmˈbæŋkmənt]	n.	a wall of stone or earth made to keep water back or to carry a road or railway/railroad over low ground 堤;堤岸;堤围;(公路和铁路)路堤
8. likeness [ˈlaɪknəs]	n.	a painting, drawing, etc. of a person, especially one that looks very like them(尤指画得像的)肖像,画像

9. fancy [ˈfænsi]	v.		used to show that you are surprised or shocked by sth（表示惊奇或震惊）真想不到，竟然
10. treasurer [ˈtreʒərə(r)]	n.		a person who is responsible for the money and accounts of a club or an organization（俱乐部或组织的）司库，会计，出纳，财务主管
11. fictitious [fɪkˈtɪʃəs]	adj.		invented by sb rather than true 虚构的；虚假的
12. tedious [ˈtiːdiəs]	adj.		lasting or taking too long and not interesting 冗长的；啰嗦的；单调乏味的
13. wear on			(of time) to pass, especially in a way that seems slow 慢慢地过去；（光阴）荏苒
14. fidgety [ˈfɪdʒɪti]	adj.		(of a person) unable to remain still or quiet, usually because of being bored or nervous 坐立不安的

第四十回

史太君两宴大观园　金鸳鸯三宣牙牌令

The Lady Dowager Feasts Again in Grand View Garden
Yuan-yang Presides over a Drinking Game (Yang)

Lady Jia holds two feasts in one day in the Prospect Garden
And Faithful makes four calls on three dominoes in the Painted Chamber (Hawkes)

一、本回概述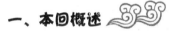

　　贾母、王夫人为湘云还席，贾府上下齐聚大观园；刘姥姥亦受邀赴宴。贾母、王夫人借机重游大观园，去了潇湘馆、蘅芜苑等地；随后，众人在秋爽斋开宴。在家宴中，凤姐、鸳鸯合伙捉弄刘姥姥，这个老实的乡下人配合她们，摆出各种憨态，引得所有人大笑不止。之后，在贾母的提议下，大家行酒令助兴，由鸳鸯主持，黛玉不慎引用《牡丹亭》《西厢记》，引起了宝钗的注意。刘姥姥入乡随俗，行出了庄家人本色的酒令，众人听了，由不得大笑起来。

二、篇章节选

原文

　　只见一个媳妇端了一个盒子站在当地,一个丫鬟上来揭去盒盖,里面盛着两碗菜。[1] 李纨端了一碗放在贾母桌上。凤姐儿偏拣了一碗鸽子蛋放在刘姥姥桌上。[2] 贾母这边说声"请",刘姥姥便站起身来,高声说道:"老刘,老刘,食量大似牛,吃一个老母猪不抬头。"[3] 自己却鼓着腮不语。

　　众人先是发怔,后来一听,上上下下都哈哈的大笑起来。[4] 史湘云撑不住,一口饭都喷了出来;林黛玉笑岔了气,伏着桌子叫"嗳哟";宝玉早滚到贾母怀里,贾母笑的搂着宝玉叫"心肝";王夫人笑的用手指着凤姐儿,只说不出话来;薛姨妈也撑不住,口里茶喷了探春一裙子;探春手里的饭碗都合在迎春身上;惜春离了坐位,拉着他奶母叫揉一揉肠子。[5] 地下的无一个不弯腰屈背,也有躲出去蹲着笑去的,也有忍着笑上来替他姊妹换衣裳的,独有凤姐鸳鸯二人撑着,还只管让刘姥姥。

　　刘姥姥拿起箸来,只觉不听使,又说道:"这里的鸡儿也俊,下的这蛋也小巧,怪俊的。我且肏攮一个。"众人方住了笑,听见这话又笑起来。贾母笑的眼泪出来,琥珀在后捶着。贾母笑道:"这定是凤丫头促狭鬼儿闹的,快别信他的话了。"那刘姥姥正夸鸡蛋小巧,要肏攮一个,凤姐儿笑道:"一两银子一个呢,你快尝尝罢,那冷了就不好吃了。"刘姥姥便伸箸子要夹,那里夹的起来,满碗里闹了一阵好的,好容易撮起一个来,才伸着脖子要吃,[6] 偏又滑下来滚在地下,[7] 忙放下箸子要亲自去捡,早有地下的人捡了出去了。[8] 刘姥姥叹道:"一两银子,也没听见个响声儿就没了。"[9]

　　众人已没心吃饭,都看着他笑。

杨译

　　As everyone laughed, a matron brought in a box and stood holding it while a maid removed the cover, revealing two bowls.[1] Li Wan put one on the Lady Dowager's table and Hsi-feng set the other, containing pigeon's eggs, before Granny

Liu.[2] The Lady Dowager urged her to make a start.

Granny Liu stood up then and declaimed at the top of her voice:

"Old woman Liu, I vow,

Eats more than any cow,

And down she settles now

To gobble an enormous sow."[3]

Then she dried up abruptly, puffing out her cheeks and staring down at her bowl.

The others had been staggered at first but now everyone, high and low, started roaring with laughter.[4] Hsiang-yun shook so uncontrollably that she sputtered out the rice she had in her mouth, while Tai-yu nearly choked and collapsed over the table gasping, "Mercy!" Pao-yu fell convulsively into his grandmother's arms and she chuckled as she hugged him to her crying, "My precious!" Lady Wang wagged one finger at Hsi-feng but was laughing too much to speak. Aunt Hsueh, too, exploded in such mirth that she sprayed tea all over Tan-chun's skirt, making her upset her bowl over Ying-chun, while Hsi-chun left her seat and begged her nurse to rub her stomach for her.[5]

As for the maids, some doubled up in hysterics, others sneaked outside to squat down in a fit of giggles, yet others controlled themselves sufficiently to fetch clean clothes for their young mistresses.

Hsi-feng and Yuan-yang, the only ones with straight faces, urged Granny Liu to eat. But when she picked up the chopsticks she still found them unwieldy.

"Even your hens here are refined," she remarked, "laying such tiny, dainty eggs as these. Well, let me fuck one of them."

This caused a fresh outburst of laughter. The Lady Dowager laughed so much that tears streamed from her eyes and Hu-po had to pat her on the back.

"That wretch Hsi-feng's up to her tricks again," she gasped. "Don't believe a word she says."

Granny Liu was still admiring the dainty eggs and saying she wanted to "fuck" one, when Hsi-feng told her merrily:

"They cost one tael of silver each. Better try one while they're hot."

The old woman reached out with her chopsticks but failed to secure an egg. After chasing them round the bowl for a time she finally succeeded in catching one; but as she craned forward to eat it, [6] the egg slipped and fell to the floor. [7] She hastily put down her chopsticks and stooped to retrieve it. However, a maid had already picked it up. [8]

"A tael of silver!" Granny Liu sighed. "And gone without a sound." [9]

The others had long since stopped eating to watch her antics.

霍译

A woman-servant now entered carrying one of the luncheonboxes and stood in the middle of the room holding it while a maid removed the lid. There were two dishes inside. [1] Li Wan took out one of them and set it down on Grandmother Jia's table. The second, a bowl of pigeon's eggs (deliberately chosen for their mirth-provoking possibilities) was taken out by Xi-feng and set down in front of Grannie Liu. [2]

'Please!' said Grandmother Jia, waving her chopsticks at the food as a polite indication that they should begin. At once Grannie Liu leaped to her feet and, in ringing tones, recited the following grace:

'My name it is Liu,

I'm a trencherman true;

I can eat a whole sow

With her little pigs too.' [3]

Having concluded, she puffed out both her cheeks and stared in front of her with an expression of great determination.

There was a moment of awestruck silence; then, as it dawned on them that they really had heard what they thought they had heard, the whole company, both masters and servants, burst out into roars of laughter. [4]

Shi Xiang-yun, unable to contain herself, spat out a whole mouthful of rice.

Lin Dai-yu, made breathless by laughter, collapsed on the table, uttering weak

'Aiyos'.

Bao-yu rolled over, convulsed, on to his grandmother's bosom.

Grandmother Jia, exclaiming helplessly 'Oh, my heart!' 'Oh, my child!', clung tightly to her heaving grandson.

Lady Wang pointed an accusing finger at Xi-feng, but laughter had deprived her of speech.

Aunt Xue exploded a mouthful of tea over Tan-chun's skirt.

Tan-chun planted a bowlful of rice on the person of Ying-chun.

Xi-chun got up from the table and going over to her nurse, took her by the hand and asked her to massage her stomach. [5]

The servants were all doubled up. Some had to go outside where they could squat down and laugh with abandon. Those who could control themselves sufficiently helped the casualties to mop up or change their clothes.

Only Xi-feng and Faithful remained straight-faced throughout this outburst, politely urging Grannie Liu to begin. Manipulating the unwieldy chopsticks with considerable difficulty, the old woman prepared to do so.

'Even your hens here are special,' she remarked. 'Such pretty little eggs they lay! I must see if I can't get one of these under me belt!'

Under the impact of these remarks the company's composure, which it had only just recovered, once more broke down. Grandmother Jia, abandoning any attempt at self-control, was now actually weeping with laughter. Amber, who feared a seizure, pounded her energetically on the back.

'That wicked devil Feng is behind this,' said Grandmother Jia. 'Don't believe a thing she tells you!'

'They cost a silver tael apiece,' said Xi-feng, as Grannie Liu continued to praise the diminutive 'hen's' eggs. 'You should eat them quickly, while they're still hot. They won't be so nice when they're cold.'

Grannie Liu obediently held out her chopsticks and tried to take hold of one, but the egg eluded her. After chasing it several times round the inside of the bowl, she did at last succeed in getting a grip on it. But as she craned forward with open mouth to reach it, [6] it slipped through the chopsticks and rolled on to the floor. [7] At once she laid down the chopsticks, and would have gone down on hands and knees to pick it up, but before she could do so one of the servants had retrieved it and carried it off for disposal. [8]

'That's a tael of silver gone,' Grannie Liu said regretfully, 'and we didn't even hear the clink!' [9]

The others had by now lost all interest in eating, absorbed by the entertaining antics of their guest.

三、注释评点

【1】"只见一个媳妇端了一个盒子站在当地，一个丫鬟上来揭去盒盖，里面盛着两碗菜。"杨译是"As everyone laughed, a matron brought in a box and stood holding it while a maid removed the cover, revealing two bowls."译者在主句部分使用"while"连接两个分句，"while"前后分别表述"a matron"和"a maid"发出的动作；第一个分句中，主语"a matron"后面紧跟两个并列的谓语"brought in"和"stood"，现在分词短语"holding it"是"stood"的伴随状语，表明这两个动作是同时发生；第二个分句中，现在分词短语"revealing two bowls"充当结果状语，表达的是谓语"removed the cover"的结果。霍译是"A woman-servant now entered carrying one of the luncheonboxes and stood in the middle of the room holding it while a maid removed the lid. There were two dishes inside."该译文由两个句子构成。第一句的结构与杨译的主句部分相似，也是用"while"连接两个分句；第一个分句中，"entered"和"stood"是并列的谓语，其间用"and"连接，现在分词短语"carrying one of the luncheonboxes"和"holding it"分别是两个谓语的伴随状语。

【2】"李纨端了一碗放在贾母桌上。凤姐儿偏拣了一碗鸽子蛋放在刘姥姥桌上。"杨译是"Li Wan put one on the Lady Dowager's table and Hsi-feng set the other, containing pigeon's eggs, before Granny Liu."译文是由"and"连接的

两个分句构成，分别对应原文的两个句子，两个分句的主语就是原文的两个人格主语"李纨（Li Wan）"和"凤姐儿（Hsi-feng）"，译文的结构与原文比较一致。霍译是"Li Wan took out one of them and set it down on Grandmother Jia's table. The second, a bowl of pigeon's eggs (deliberately chosen for their mirth-provoking possibilities) was taken out by Xi-feng and set down in front of Grannie Liu."该译文由两个句子构成，其中的第二句有两点特别之处：一是使用了被动语态，译者用"The second"做主语，有强调的作用，且与第一句中的"one of them"相呼应；主语"The second"的同位语"a bowl of pigeon's eggs"，也有强调"这碗鸽子蛋"的意思；二是括号中增译的"deliberately chosen for their mirth-provoking possibilities"，清晰地表达出凤姐居心不良，想利用鸽子蛋戏弄刘姥姥，为大家制造笑料的意图。这样的处理手法，增加了小说的趣味性和可读性。

【3】"老刘，老刘，食量大似牛，吃一个老母猪不抬头。"一句，

杨译：Old woman Liu, I vow,

Eats more than any cow,

And down she settles now

To gobble an enormous sow.

霍译：My name it is Liu,

I'm a trencherman true;

I can eat a whole sow

With her little pigs too.

两位译者都使用了诗歌的形式翻译原文：杨译的每一行末尾都押尾韵[aʊ]（vow, cow, now和sow），霍译的第2、4两行押尾韵[uː]（true和too）；另外，霍译对原文进行了创造性翻译，意思和原文语义有些出入。

【4】"众人先是发怔，后来一听，上上下下都哈哈的大笑起来。"杨译是"The others had been staggered at first but now everyone, high and low, started roaring with laughter."霍译是"There was a moment of awestruck silence; then, as it dawned on them that they really had heard what they thought they had heard, the whole company, both masters and servants, burst out into roars of laughter."原文中

"上上下下"一词的翻译,杨译用的是两个形容词,即"high and low",表达的是名词性的含义,即"上上下下的人";霍译用的是两个名词,即"both masters and servants",表达的是同样的意思。霍译中,"发怔"是"awestruck silence",非常生动;对于"后来一听"这一小句,霍译使用了增译:"then, as it dawned on them that they really had heard what they thought they had heard",译者把原文中暗含的"众人刚开始不敢相信自己的耳朵"这层意思充分地展示给读者,堪称绝妙。

【5】"史湘云撑不住……拉着他奶母叫揉一揉肠子"一段,描述了众人在听到刘姥姥说的话之后的反应。两位译者使用不同的结构来安排这段文字:杨译沿用原文的结构,将所有的内容放在一段中描述,通过使用诸多连词,如:"so… that""while""and""as""but"和"such… that"进行上下文的衔接,结构比较紧凑;霍译则将对每个人的描述独立成段,虽然与原文结构有所不同,但是层次非常清晰。

【6】"才伸着脖子要吃"一句,杨译是"… but as she craned forward to eat it…";霍译是"But as she craned forward with open mouth to reach it…"。两位译者都使用了动词"crane",用来描述人伸长脖子够某物的样子,让人联想到鹤的长颈,措词准确生动;另外,霍译中增译的"with open mouth",将刘姥姥的吃相描画得淋漓尽致。

【7】"偏又滑下来滚在地下"一句,杨译是"… the egg slipped and fell to the floor",译者严格地按照原文的字面意思进行翻译。霍译是"… it slipped through the chopsticks and rolled on to the floor",该译文中的动词"rolled"以及增译的"through the chopsticks",准确生动地再现了鸽子蛋滚落下去的情景,画面感很强。

【8】"忙放下筷子要亲自去捡,早有地下的人捡了出去了"一句,杨译是"She hastily put down her chopsticks and stooped to retrieve it. However, a maid had already picked it up."霍译是"At once she laid down the chopsticks, and would have gone down on hands and knees to pick it up, but before she could do so one of the servants had retrieved it and carried it off for disposal."可以看出,霍译有两处增译:一是介词短语"on hands and knees",生动地描绘出刘姥姥本来是要四

肢伏地去捡蛋的；二是介词短语"for disposal"，准确地表达出原文的"捡了出去"是"丢弃不要"的意思。

【9】"刘姥姥叹道：'一两银子，也没听见个响声儿就没了。'"杨译是"'A tael of silver!' Granny Liu sighed. 'And gone without a sound.'"霍译是"'That's a tael of silver gone,' Grannie Liu said regretfully, 'and we didn't even hear the clink!'"原文中的"一两银子"和"也没听见个响声儿就没了"之间有递进关系，两位译者都使用了连词"and"来体现这种逻辑关系。

四、词汇表

1. gobble [ˈgɒbl]	v.	to eat sth very fast, in a way that people consider rude or greedy 狼吞虎咽；贪婪地吃
2. sow [saʊ]	n.	a female pig 母猪
3. puff sth out		to make sth bigger and rounder, especially by filling it with air 吹胀；使鼓起来
4. stagger [ˈstægə(r)]	v.	to shock or surprise sb very much 使震惊；使大吃一惊
5. convulsive [kənˈvʌlsɪv]	adj.	(of movements or actions) sudden and impossible to control 突然而无法控制的；痉挛的；抽搐的
	adv.	convulsively
6. wag [wæg]	v.	to shake your finger or your head from side to side or up and down, often as a sign of disapproval 摆动，摇（头或手指，常表示不赞成）
7. double up		to bend or to make your body bend over quickly, for example because you are in pain （使）弯腰，弓身

8. unwieldy [ʌnˈwi:ldi]	adj.	(of an object) difficult to move or control because of its size, shape or weight 笨重的；笨拙的；不灵巧的
9. retrieve [rɪˈtri:v]	v.	to bring or get sth back, especially from a place where it should not be 取回；索回
10. antics [ˈæntɪks]	n.	behavior which is silly and funny in a way that people usually like 滑稽可笑的举止
11. awestruck [ˈɔ:strʌk]	adj.	feeling very impressed by sth 惊叹的
12. dawn on sb		if sth dawns on you, you begin to realize it for the first time 使开始明白；使渐渐领悟；使开始理解
13. manipulate [məˈnɪpjʊleɪt]	v.	to control or use sth in a skilful way （熟练地）操作，使用
14. composure [kəmˈpəʊʒə(r)]	n.	the state of being calm and in control of your feelings or behavior 沉着；镇静；镇定
15. elude [ɪˈlu:d]	v.	to manage to avoid or escape from sb/sth, especially in a clever way （尤指机敏地）避开，逃避，躲避
16. clink [klɪŋk]	n.	a sharp ringing sound like the sound made by glasses being hit against each other 叮当声

后 记

　　五年前,我们几位师友创建了一个微信群,名为"善书善友"。因为这个缘起,一些毕业多年的学生又和我们几位老师聚在了一起,这些学生中,有几位已是从教多年的资深英语教师。大家聚在这个群里,聊自己最近在读的书,讲自己的生活经历,分享学习资料、人生感悟和喜怒哀乐,群里的气氛和谐融洽,大家都能从中受益,因为有各位师友的相伴和畅聊,那段日子倒也过得十分快乐惬意。

　　后来我突发奇想,觉得我们应该在一起做些更有意义的事情,这样也不枉费大家又聚在一起的缘分。做什么事情比较有价值呢?思来想去,我想到了自己教授多年的一门课程:"《红楼梦》英译赏析"。我在西安外国语大学的英文学院、通识学院和研究生院都讲授过这门课程,学生还挺喜欢这门课。想到"善书善友"群里有好几位高校英语教师,想到我多年教授这门课程已经有些成熟的想法,就决定一起做件有意义的事情——带领大家编写这本教材,如此既不辜负相聚的缘分,或许也能使众多的英语学习者由此受益。大家一拍即合,于是,我们说干就干了。

　　第一次领众编书,又想做出一本既对得起自己,又对得起读者的书,投入的精力和时间是我始料未及的。我们编写的程序是:每位编者根据我们事先定好的选材原则,在自己负责的语料中选出合适的段落,独立完成"本回概述"和"词汇表"的编写,然后在主编的指导下逐条编写"注释评点"的内容。编写过程中一般要来回修改三次才能基本定稿,四十回的内容编写完毕,才完成了总工作量的一半。接着,我和锦萍老师分别刈全书进行了两次(共四次)地毯式的校对和修改。在这个过程中,我们主要把控内容增删和用语规范,努力做到语言表述清楚简洁,让四位编者的语言风格尽可能统一。经过一遍遍细致的校对,语言趋于规范统一。经过反复修改,我期望这本教材不会让读者感到由多位编者编写造成的割裂感,希望大家会感受到本书的编者为了全书编写风格

对话杨宪益、霍克斯——《红楼梦》英译赏析（第一至四十回）

和语言表述的一致而做出的努力。在校对过程中，当我和锦萍老师因为个别语法现象意见不一致时，我们会查张道真老师的语法书，会请教西安外国语大学的语法大咖王九萍老师和王满良老师，以及我的外国朋友、英籍教师Carole。衷心感谢他们的无私帮助，和他们讨论语法问题是一件非常快乐的事情。

在本书长达两年多的编写过程中，我们的编写思路和语言表述越来越清晰统一，两位主编和四位编者都从中受益匪浅。虽然后来"善书善友"群解散了，但是每当想到编书的缘起来自这个温暖的小群，我就会觉得这本书是"善书善友"开出的一朵芬芳四溢的花，是对那段师友畅聊快乐时光的纪念。

我们的编写分工如下：

张文锦、张锦萍：确定本书结构框架和编写内容；指导选材；指导"注释评点"的编写；校对全书。

杨浩楠：负责第一至十回、第二十六、二十七回的编写；

彭雪妮：负责第十一至二十回、第二十八、二十九回的编写；

薛雯：负责第二十一至二十五回的编写；

赵青：负责第三十至四十回的编写。

最后，我要特别感谢本书的责任编辑严悦老师，他花了不少精力，细致地校对全书，并提出了许多宝贵的修改意见。有时，我们会就某个细节反复、长时间地沟通直到定稿，他的敬业精神以及专业素养让我敬佩不已；还要感谢亦师亦友的李本现老师不辞辛苦，在百忙之中替我们审读全书，并给与各位参编者肯定与鼓励，这些温暖的力量将不断鞭策我们继续努力；还要感谢西北农林科技大学的周仕慧老师，她对本书最后确定书名提供了不少思路和专业的建议。另外，本书还得到了西安外国语大学的资助以及学校党委、英文学院党委的支持，承蒙北京大学出版社的厚爱，本书得以顺利立项并且出版，在此一并致谢。

一本书，从最初孕育思路到变成白纸黑字，中间凝结了太多人的心血与劳动、呵护与扶持、温暖与感动，在此衷心感谢帮助本书从立项，到成书，再到出版过程中的各位同事与友人，也衷心希望本书能得到广大读者的认可与喜爱。

主　编
2022年春于西安

参考文献

曹雪芹著，无名氏续：《红楼梦》，北京：人民文学出版社，2008年。

杨宪益、戴乃迭：*A Dream of Red Mansions*, Peking, Foreign Languages Press,1978.

David Hawkes: *The Story of the Stone*, vol. I II, England, Clays Ltd., 1973.

【英】霍恩比：《牛津高阶英汉双解词典》（第七版），北京：商务印书馆，2009年。

陈宏薇、李亚丹主编：《汉英翻译教程》，上海：上海外语教育出版社，2018年。

杨立民主编：《现代大学英语》，北京：外语教学与研究出版社，2010年。

马经义：《中国红学概论》（下册），成都：四川大学出版社，2008年。

李晶：《杨宪益、戴乃迭的〈红楼梦〉英译本底本研究初探》，《红楼梦学刊》，2012年第一辑。

郑铁生：《〈红楼梦〉回目程乙本优于程甲本和脂评本》，《文学与文化》，2021年第三期。

姜其煌：《〈好了歌〉的七种英译》，《中国翻译》，1996年第四期。